WOMEN AND THE WIND OF CHANGE

WOMEN AND THE WIND OF CHANGE

Dr. Vinita Kaul

GYAN PUBLISHING HOUSE

Women and The Wind of Change
(*Women*)
ISBN : 81-212-0656-1

Published in 2000 in India by
Gyan Publishing House
5, Ansari Road,
New Delhi 110 002
Laser Typeset at 'Fine Computers', New Delhi.
Printed at Mehra Offset Printers, New Delhi.

CONTENTS

	Preface	*7*
	Foreward	*9*
1.	Back to the Roots	11
2.	Emergence of Women's Organizations Practice and Prejudice	17
3.	Emulation and Emancipation	41
4.	The Winds of Change—The Fight for Freedom	59
5.	Education and Enlightenment	81
6.	Crime and Punishment	125
7.	An Economic Perspective	163
8.	The Economics of Entrepreneurs and the Socio-Psycho Dynamics	185
9.	The Sewa Saga—A Salute to Sagacity	201
10.	Reasons, Rights and Required Reforms	233
11.	Credit Women with Sense and Finance	257
12.	Our Neighbours, NGOs and Enterprises	287
13.	A Rural Mosaic for Reform	305
14.	Political Perceptions	325
15.	Gender Bias or Gender Farce	341
16.	Holistic Health	363
17.	The Downtrodden Dalits	383
18.	Dalit Awakening	411
19.	History of Warfare:The Introduction of Women in the Forces	447
	Annexures	465
	Index	487

PREFACE

The cause of the upliftment of women all the world over is swiftly assuming increasing importance. This is significantly projecting them to the forefront of a newly emergent socio-economic order where they will occupy their rightful place. Social activist Ela Bhatt has rightly said:

> We not only want a piece of the pie,
>
> We also want to choose the flavour,
>
> And know-how to make it ourselves.

But the path to socio-economic equality and freedom is fraught with numerous inherent hurdles e.g. of overcoming societal prejudices and anomalies which exist within many an economic set-up; bureaucratic red tape in setting up co-operatives and similar venture most suitable for large segments of the underprivileged class of women. For as a natural corollary to imbuing women with an importnt sense of self-worth and economic independence, an automatic process of self-awareness and "education" will develop. Education which may not span mere theoretical acquisition of knowledge but a more valuable practical implementation of independent, entrepreneurial endeavour.

I propose to cover this vast canvas of socio-economic change relating it to both NGOs and other ventures which have made significant strides in already laying down the ground rules for women's upliftment; relating them to an unconventional "educational" process. In other words, a comprehensive docutment which sincerely attempts at not only improving women's place and status in society, as an active contributor towards economically viable projects, but also as an integral force in propelling the workforce of rural, less privileged women to the forefront of our economy; to an acceptable and respected place in society; and most important of all, as individuals of an independent India with an ever increasing sense of dignity and self-worth, which will spur them on to contribute within an ever-increasing ambience of diligence and economic viability.

To conclude, I take the liberty of quoting from a well known book on Women's Studies *Women In A Changing Society* by Anjana Maitra-Sinha; wisely recalling Subramanya Bharti's stirring call, motivating and inspiring women across the length and breadth of the country to drink at the fountain of knowledge, to challenge the hitherto unexplored realms of pure male domination with determination and to play an active and decisive role in the enlightening and emancipating process of self determination and progress thus :

The realm of knowledge we shall explore,
We shall not lag behind men,
Knowledge shall be ours as well,
We shall join in the making of the laws,
We shall grow food for the world,
We shall beget Gods for the world.

Dr. Vinita Kaul

FOREWORD

Vinita is a prolific writer. Every article, essay or book that she has written, has been after extensive study and research. She gets completely involved with whatever she is writing about. And till she completes the work, it is priority one for her. That is the making of a good writer.

Her book *Women and the Wind of Change* is typical of these characteristics. She got completely immersed in the work and has written with feeling and facts. She has always stood up for the underdog and fearlessly taken up cudgels against injustice. Anyone who reads this book can see how diligently she has researched the subject, dealt with each aspect logically and brought out all aspects clearly, giving detailed historical background.

Not many people know some of the important events in women's movement narrated by her, and those who knew have probably forgotten them. To quote just one example, in 1930's, a National Planning Committee was instituted by the Indian National Congress with Pandit Nehru as Chairman. It delegated to one of its sub-committees the task of examining the role of women in a planned economy. Rani Lakshmibai Rajwade was the President of this sub-committee and Mridula Sarabhai its Secretary. Their recommendations were bold and even revolutionary for the times. These included legislation on abortion to control population, no restrictions to be placed by law or customs on illegitimate children, monogamy, amendment of Civil Marriage Law so as to enable people to enter into matrimony without any formal declaration of their religion and formulation of a uniform civil code for all citizens. Alas, most of these measures still remain to be implemented. Even the reservations of 33 per cent of seats for women recently proposed has been shelved. It seems our male politicians are really afraid of women acquiring their legitimate rights.

This book is an objective study of the injustice done to women and how, over the centuries, their place in society was progressively eroded by selfish and short-sighted men and how over long periods, women themselves acquiesced in their ill-treatment. It then describes 'the wind of change' - what brought it about, and the gathering momentum of women's fight to restore their due position and rights in society and have full scope and opportunity for using their talents. It also brings out the help in this movement given by some enlightened men. A very important aspect clearly brought out by the author is that throughout this movement, women fought fearlessly, took great blows, even physical ones, with absolute calm and dignity and yet kept the movement totally peaceful and non-violent, unlike many other movements which turned violent sooner or later.

When God—if there be a God—or nature or the process of evolution created man and woman, they were to be equal and complementary to each other—physically, emotionally and in every other way. Had this been realized and implemented, human progress would have been faster and the world and the home a place of peace and harmony. Alas, this is not so. Men and women in every country need to realize this and fight to attain a state of equality, mutual respect and complementarity in society as well as in the political, economic and cultural fields.

I should like to congratulate the author on her work and hope her book will contribute to social, economic and political legislation to enable women to make their valuable contribution to the building up of our country in all spheres.

T.N. Kaul

1

BACK TO THE ROOTS

The word patriarch comes from the Latin word 'Pater' or father. He was the leader and father of his tribe or people. 'Patria' which means fatherland or one's own country, comes from the same Latin word. You know that in French it is 'Patrie'. In Sanskrit and Hindi, we think of our country as the mother or the motherland—which do you prefer?

Jawaharlal Nehru

The above was a letter written by Pandit Nehru to his daughter Indira Gandhi. It reflects the dilemma of duality, of according woman an equal, if not elevated status *vis-à-vis* her male counterpart which has dogged religious thinkers, political philosophers *et al*, since time immemorial thus perpetuating the urgent need to resolve once and for all, the anomalistic connotations surrounding this enigma.

Our ancient religious texts are replete with instances of non-duality. The learned sage Sri Ramakrishna Paramahansa maintains in the *Bhagavad Gita*: "It is my Cosmic Mother who has become everything. She of omnipotence has become the Universe and the beings in it. She reveals herself as the body, the intellect, the virtuous path and the spiritual pursuit. *Sakti* and *Brahman* are one. In the manifest state she is Sakti and in the absolute state, Brahman. Without knowing the Sakti, Iswara cannot be known."

The core philosophy or central teaching of the Upanishads is Advaita or non-duality. As summed up so succinctly by Dr. S. Radhakrishnan, the Upanishads proclaim the identity of the macrocosm (Brahman) with the microcosm of the human self or Atman. *Tat tvamasi* 'That art thou'. intimates that the unity of all that exists is confirmed by science in our space age. As the learned Professor Yash Pal so rightly said: "It has become clear from science that myself, all my cells, all my constituents and those in this table, or in a piece of stone - that all this material at sometime past was 'cooked' together in the same star. Does not this have any implication for questions like our essential relatedness, about ecology? And does it at all conflict with the very beautiful, holistic inspiration of all the great religious teachers?" Indeed not, when one considers the numerous instances, the abundant examples when our seers accorded the 'female' aspect of divinity, a venerated position in the Hindu pantheon. Beginning with Usha, the Goddess of dawn, celebrated in a hymn of the Rig Veda. Eulogizing her multitudinous virtues, a translation by A. A. Macdonell describes her thus:

> The light has come, of all the lights the fairest,
> The brilliant brightness has been born effulgent
> Urged onward for god Savitar's (sun's) uprising.
> Night now has yielded up her place to morning.
> Daughter of heaven, she has appeared before us,
> A maiden shining in resplendent raiment.
> Though sovereign lady of all earthly treasure,
> Auspicious Dawn, shine here today upon us.

Thus affirming the unity of all beings, this Rig-Vedic hymn signifies the presence of feminine deities of later Hinduism. But this inclusion of feminity in the concept of divinity is in striking contrast to the denigration of women in the traditions of the three Semitic religions. However, thinkers of the pantheistic age, both in Greece and India "recognized the unity of life". They, unequivocally, gave women a place of dignity and equality, beginning with Aphrodite, the Greek Goddess of Love and Usha, the effulgent Goddess of dawn of the Vedic pantheon. Creating an ambience of undeniable pagan pantheism symbolizing, as it were, not only the elemental forces of nature but also of life and death. Alongwith Indra, the Indian God of rain, Apollo the Greek sun-god, Yama the Indian God of death and Pluto the Greek God of the underworld, the aforementioned Goddesses received oblation, adulation - call it what you may - from the peoples of their ancient civilizations, in equal measure as the male manifestations of Divinity. Unlike the theologians and law givers of the institutionalized religions of later times - whether Brahmanical Hinduism, Christianity or Islam which lacked the wisdom to acknowledge the common humanity of man and woman.

Gradually the days of the Vedic and other gods and goddesses receded into the background and hard and abstruse philosophy took their place. But in the minds of the people, these images still floated, companions in joy and friends in distress, symbols of their own vaguely felt ideals and aspirations. And around them poets wrapped their fancies and built the house of their dreams full of rich embroidery and lovely fantasy. Many of these legends and poets fancies have been delightfully adapted by F. W. Bain in his series of little books containing stories from Indian mythology. In one of the books of this series, *The Digit of the Moon*, we are told of the creation of the woman.

> "In the beginning, when Twashtri (the Divine Artificer) came to the creation of woman he found that he had exhausted his materials in the making of man and that no solid elements were left. In this dilemma, after profound meditation, he did as follows : he took the rotundity of the moon, and the curves of the creepers, and the clinging of tendrils, and the trembling of grass, and the slenderness of the reed, and the bloom of flowers, and the lightness of leaves, and the tapering of the elephant's trunk, and the glances of deer, and the clustering of rows of bees, and the joyous gaiety of sunbeams, and the weeping of clouds, and the fickleness of the winds, and the timidity of the hare, and the vanity of the peacock, and the softness of the parrot's bosom, and the hardness of adamant, and the sweetness of honey, and the cruelty of

> the tiger and the warm glow of fire, and the coldness of snow, and the chattering of jays, and the cooing of the *kokila*, and the hypocrisy of the crane, and the fidelity of the *chakravaha*; and compounding all these together, he made woman and gave her to man." As an inseparable, indivisible entity of himself!

The mutuality of man and woman in the Indian tradition strikes one as an early intuition of the finding of modern science that masculinity and femininity are matters of degree rather than bipolar; that human beings are bisexual, possessing both male and female hormones and characteristics, though distributed very differently! A fascinating manifestation of this phenomena was self-evident in none other than our Bapu or Mahatma Gandhi and as an all - encompassing love flowed out of his noble heart and embraced the whole of humanity without any distinctions of colour, caste, religious creed or other man-made barriers. B. R. Nanda analyzed the feminine traits in his character thus:

> The strongest formative influence on young Mohandas, however, was that of his mother Putlibai. When there was sickness in the family, she wore herself out in days and nights of nursing. Something of her maternal love he came to possess himself, and as he grew, it flowed out in an ever-increasing measure, bursting the bonds of family and community, until it embraced the whole of humanity. To his mother, he owed not only a passion for nursing which later made him wash leper's sores in his *ashram*, but also an inspiration for his techniques of appealing to the heart through self-suffering... a technique which wives and mothers have practiced from time immemorial.

Alva Myrdal, the Swedish writer, recalls Jawaharlal Nehru remarking to her: "I think the world would be much better off if men became a little bit less masculine."

It is being increasingly recognized by modern students of human personality the world over that it is a combination of what are generally regarded as masculine characteristics (such as strength and self-confidence) and the feminine virtues (like patience, forgiveness and self-effacing service) that makes the finest human beings. An ancient truth regurgitated perhaps more forcefully in the modern age. For not only did Socrates and Plato, the most outstanding among the philosophers of ancient Greece, affirm the equal status of women with men by holding that "those of both sexes having the requisite aptitude" should be guardians in the ideal republic receiving the same education and training for guardianship (including military training), but our own manifestations of Godhood prove it beyond doubt. Take for instance one of the most remarkable figures in the Hindu pantheon —*Ardhanarishwara* (half man and half woman). The significance of *Ardhanarishwara* is reinforced by such appellations as Sitarama and *Umamaheshwara*, *Lakshminarayana* and *Radhakrishna*, in which the divine consorts are compounded inseparably into one entity. "Half of one's own self is she, the wife", says the Satapatha Brahmana, a prose commentary on the Yajurveda.

With the acceptance of such a premise, only befitting in the cosmic plenitude of cycles of existence, it would be only fair to proceed to create an environment — economically energizing, socially unshackling, for the underprivileged, uneducated woman of today, to attain a modicum of self-respect for herself and become an active contributor to a more equitable, independent India; or Bharat Mata, as Panditji so evocatively addressed her in the decades gone by, lost in the cosmic vibrations of a world fast hurtling forward, propelled by the catalytic forces of renewal, upheaval and change.

References

Asaf Ali, Aruna, In association with Raghavan, G.N.S., *Resurgence of Indian Women*, Under the auspices of Nehru Memorial Museum And Library, Published by Radiant.

Chidbhavananda, Swami, *The Bhagavad Gita*, Tapovanam Publishing House, Tiruchirapalli Dt, Madras State, 1967.

Narasimhaiah, C. D., Abridgment by, (of Jawaharlal Nehru's) *The Discovery of India*, Indian Council for Cultural Relations, New Delhi, 1981.

Nehru Jawaharlal, *Letters From A Father to his Daughter*, Children's Book Trust, New Delhi. First published in 1929.

Moore, Charles A., Ed., *A Source Book in Indian Philosophy*, Princeton, 1957.

2

EMERGENCE OF WOMEN'S ORGANIZATIONS PRACTICE AND PREJUDICE

Men and women, like plants and flowers, can only grow in the sunlight and fresh air of freedom; they wilt and stunt themselves in the dark shadow and suffocating atmosphere of alien domination.

For all of us, therefore, the first problem that presents itself is how to free India and remove the many burdens of the Indian masses. But the women of India have an additional task and that is to free themselves from the tyranny of man-made custom and law.

Jawaharlal Nehru

Synonymous with the powerful nationalist movement in India preceding Independence, was the emergence of women's organizations throughout the country. They were neither incidental nor coincidental in the context of events which influenced the process of a more liberalized approach towards women but were the logical outcome of the cogitative process by reformers who belonged to the newly formed religious associations. They were possessed of a visual acuity far beyond their times in relation to resolving the multidimensional complex issues which were rooted in societal practice and prejudice and in the deeply ingrained attitudes of male domination granted sanction through the centuries.

But even before launching of the freedom movement, the presence of other colossus in the field of free thinking had made itself felt. Men like Raja Rammohun Roy, Maharishi Karve and Swami Dayanand Saraswati initiated the reform movement which had an impressive effect on the social status of women.

Raja Rammohun Roy wanted to give a dignified place to women in social life and waged a relentless war against the barbaric institution of Sati. Maharishi Karve was responsible for arousing awareness among women by promoting female education. Swami Dayanand Saraswati accorded them a place of equality in matters of religion and assiduously worked for their emancipation. Thus, we see that unlike the women's movement of the West which has some obvious aggressive political overtones, the women's movement in India emanated from the broader social reform movement. It did not encourage any confrontation or war between the sexes but aimed at evolving cooperation between them.

Thus, for the first time in the history of the nation, women began to communicate with women outside their families and local committees. A process which was greatly facilitated by the increasing number of women 'literate in the vernaculars'. This enabled them to learn about women's issues in the women's journals of the times. Greatly encouraged by their male guardians to "move with the times" they joined new clubs and associations formed particularly for women.

From small local clubs and women's auxiliaries of the Indian National Congress and the National Social Conference came a variety of organizations and associations that reflected women's concerns. By the eve of Independence in 1947 a coalition of national women's organizations could rightfully claim that it was the second most representative body in India. A fora for articulating women's opinions, these institutions evolved simultaneously as a viable platform for grooming women and in successfully acquiring qualities which would later enable them to assume pivotal roles of leadership, both in the political sphere as well as in social institutions. And such institutions played an important role in the construction of the Indian nation in an interconnected process of evolution and change.

Forming a nexus between unarticulated aspirations of women and the hitherto unchallenged domain of male domination, the inherent dichotomy of the situation could not escape one. For here were a handful of enlightened men coming forward in their attempts to liberate womankind from the suffocating, regressive ideologies which placed them as undeniably subservient to the male species. While in Bengal the charismatic leader of the Brahmo Samaj, Keshub Chandra Sen, developed educational programs, a women's journal, prayer meetings and a Bharat Ashram which, when literally translated, means "Indian Hermitage," where whole families lived together and emulated the lifestyle of the English middle-class; many such similar organizations sprung up in other parts of the country too. Before long, other members of the Samaj unanimously concurred that Keshub was far too conservative and they broke with him to form the Sadharan (General) Brahmo Samaj. Members of the Sadharan Brahmo Samaj, motivated by the ideal of male-female equality, formed new associations for women of their families.

The Prarthana Samaj did similar work in Bombay. Those men who were closely involved with the Samaj from the beginning, especially the famous Prarthana trio — G.R. Bandavarkar, Narayan Ganesh Chandavarker, and M.G. Ranade — were concerned with social reform, principally improving women's status. When Pandita Ramabai Saraswati arrived in western India in 1882, Justice Ranade and his friends helped her to set up the Arya Mahila Samaj for the general uplift and enlightenment of women. Ramabai, whose laudable goal was that the Samaj provide a support network for these newly educated women through weekly lectures, etc., envisaged that with an increase in self-confidence, they would gradually begin to define the role of the educated women.

The mechanics for the emergence of the 'New Age Woman' had surely but subtly been set in motion. The multi-pronged movement which would ultimately challenge 'male supremacist predilections' had begun to gather momentum, as awareness of their rights grew among women. Initially the women attended meetings of various (women's) auxiliaries to educate themselves about the problems which needed to be resolved. The main topics on the agenda continued to center around female education and the imminent need to abolish such prevalent social ills as child marriage, dowry and neglect of widows. Definitions of women's roles in altering their own destinies, still remained tentative.

The most eminent among women's auxiliaries was the Bharata Mahila Parishad (Ladies Social Conference) of the National Social Conference. While the National Social Conference (NSC) was formed at the third meeting of that august body - the Indian National Congress - in 1887, the Mahila Parishad was inaugurated only in 1905. The NSE was formulated basically to provide a forum for the discussion of social issues.

Within the Parsee community, the major organization for women's social work, the Stri Zarthosti Mandal (Parsee Women's Circle) emerged from plaque-relief work done by the family of Mr Naoroji Patuck. Deeply touched by the hardships suffered by women, Mr Patuck set up a work class in his home. By 1903 there were over 50 women to join them in forming an organization. Miss Serenmai M. Cursetjee became the first president and remained at the helm of the Mandal for the next thirty-six years. During this time, the organization expanded its agenda to include medical care and education and successfully sought funding from the wealthy Parsee philanthropist Sir Ratan Tata. Equally important, the organization served as a training ground for women who became active in a wide range of activities and organizations in the 1920s and 1930s.

Predictably enough, these organizations received publicity, which spurred the formation of new organizations for women.

As Begum Jahan Ara Shah Nawaz, a prominent and influential member of national women's organizations in times to come, herself pointed out, the first ladies society that she joined was the brain child of her uncle Shah Din. The pioneering efforts of Shah Din within his extended family circle or Mian family wherein he urged the womenfolk to not only stimulate awareness and discussion on female education, but also encouraged them to do active social work among the rural poor, was fuelled, initially, by an urgent need to ensure that Muslim women should not be left behind in measures of 'reform and refinement'. But, what began as a laudable experiment within the family, gradually led these women to initiate a larger organization and ultimately Begum Shah Nawaz's mother, Amir-un-Nisa, became a founder-member of Anjuman-e-Khawatin-e-Islam (The Muslim Women's Association) in the Punjab. And by 1915, the women of the Mian family were undoubtedly playing a leading role in the All-Indian Muslim Women's Conference.

While male-inspired and male-guided organizations for women did invaluable work in educating women and providing them with their first experience of public work, they also imposed certain limitations inherent in the system. Specifically, male reformers regarded the household as the primary focus and fundamental arena of activity for women. Their wives could assist in nation-building not through political agitation but by building institutions to ameliorate the worst situations arising from social customs.

In a rather unusual precedence set by the issuance of a Royal decree by Queen Victoria (in response to a special appeal) the marriage of Rukhmabai to Dadaji Bhikaji was dissolved and the former saved from disastrous consequences. But to trace this explosive issue to its inception, it would be relevant to mention here that 'British support for female education did not extend to issues of autonomy.' The highly publicized Rukhmabai case (actually a series of court cases between 1884 and 1888) proved unequivocally that British law could be used to force women to submit to the most onerous of patriarchal customs. Thus, when Rukhmabai, married at the tender age of eleven to

Dadaji Bhikaji, refused to join her husband and continued to pursue her education from her father's house, Dadaji sued for restitution of conjugal rights. Rukhmabai won but when Dadaji appealed, the court issued an injunction that either Rukhmabai go to live with her husband or go to prison. What is even more shocking is that one of our foremost Indian social reformers and an ardent opponent of the British domination in India, Tilak concurred with the British verdict, justifying it on the basis of our Hindu *dharma shastras* (texts on morals and law and manuals of human conduct).

As a predictable outcome of taking women-based issues out of the closet, from within the suffocating confines of social and religious dogmas, another significant development took place. Women became bolder, they began defining their own interests and needs; they proposed solutions for the resolution of some of the ills which had become an intrinsic part of our custom and practice. They strongly advocated recourse to action, only after forming their own associations. Thus, various women's organizations sprung up all over the country in the nineteenth and twentieth centuries. Known by various nomenclatures, and hampered somewhat by geographical limitations, these organizations were, however, firmly unified by a singular aim. The aim, specifically, of bringing women together to discuss women's issues. And Sarladevi Chaudhurani, critical of women's meetings held in conjunction with the Indian National Social Conference, propagated the idea of a permanent association of Indian women. Thus, the Bharat Stree Mahamandal (the large circle of Indian women) came into existence and held its first meeting in Allahabad in 1910.

This august body systematically established its branches in different far-flung areas of India such as Lahore, Allahabad, Delhi, Karachi, Amritsar, Hyderabad, Kanpur, Bankura, Hazaribagh, Midnapur and Calcutta to bring together "women of every race, creed, class and party on the basis of their common interest in the moral and material progress of the women of

India". They envisaged 'Purdah' as a major stumbling block. In their basic conceptualistic approach being assimilated by the affected women, in the depth and context of its aims as well as the widespread ramifications it was bound to have within a somewhat rigid societal framework. To overcome this problem, teachers (many of whom had prior experience of working with the earlier male-dominated women's organizations) were thus sent to the home of women to impart instructions in such skills as reading, writing, music, sewing, and embroidery. The expansion of opportunities beyond the home necessiated the acquisition of more broad-based skills, public speaking being one of them. But since the key women of such organizations did not necessarily share the same economic base as the women they ostensibly represented, the usefulness of these organizations was somewhat limited.

National Women's Organization

Significant national women's organizations, however, emerged during the years between 1917-27; systematically organized bodies committed to social and political enlightenment. As well as to the propagation of education and the ethics of religion, in more liberal ramifications of a systematized and enlightened approach. The three major women's organizations which thus trace their origin to the decade between 1917-27were: (1) the Women's Indian Association (WIA) (2) The National Council of Women in India (NCWI) and (3) the All India Women's Conference (AIWC).

It is interesting to note that the WIA was founded by an intrepid Irish woman, Margaret Cousins, possessed with a vision far beyond her times and a feminist, theosophist and musician to boot. She arrived in India in 1915, and was invited to meet with a number of women by the Theosophical Society in Adyar. Cousins' subsequent discussions with Dorothy Jinarajadasa (an Irish feminist again, married to the highly respected Singhalese theosophist C. Jinarajadasa) were of immense relevance and led to the subsequent formation of the WIA, whereupon Jinarajadasa, anxious to encourage the formation of auxiliary branches, wrote to the Theosophical Lodge secretaries throughout the Madras Presidency explaining that a local branch of WIA could play a key role in effecting the regeneration of India.

The women who formed this organization decided to name it the "Women's Indian Association" because membership was open to both Indians and Europeans. Annie Basent became the first President with Margaret Cousins, Dorothy Jinarajadasa, Mrs Malati Patwardhan, Mrs Ammu Swaminathan, Mrs Dadabhoy and Mrs Ambujammal as honorary secretaries. By the end of the first year there were thirty-three branches ; within five years, forty-three branches , twenty centres and 2,300 members. Each branch accepted the major aims of the association but remained self-governing. This made it possible to mobilize the branches to express women's opinions.

The WIA, which encouraged non-sectarian religious activity and spurred their various branches to set up adult classes for literacy, sewing and first aid, had, however, been politically active from the beginning. From the time when "they sent a delegation to meet the secretary of state Montagu in 1917 to request the franchise for women. The fourth area of work — philanthropy - involved feeding the poor, setting up shelters for widows, and providing relief for disaster victims."

It may be mentioned at this juncture that Margaret Cousins who generally helped every good cause, was also a co-founder and the guiding spirit with Dr Muthulakshmi Reddy, of the Women's Home of Service. She was also instrumental in getting the Madras Children's Act passed. A staunch believer in women's rights, she not only helped the Madanapalle Theosophical college grow (as its principal) but at various important milestones in India's pre-independence saga, took up cudgels for the enlightenment and improvement of the Indian women.

Kanuben C. Mehta, an equally intrepid Indian, founded the Surat Branch of the WIA and was instrumental in urging the reluctant among women to attend its meetings. Realizing the need of the hour, she soon learnt English herself and by the end of 1921 she had organized lectures on franchise, hygiene and child welfare.

While the WIA did much creditable work in the seminal stages of women's social and educational emancipation, its competition with the self-respect movement limited its appeal to basically high-caste women. "The self-respect movement had a larger agenda than women; its goal was to establish a society free from the domination of the priestly caste, with justice and equality for all human beings. Ideologically more radical in its critique of existing gender relations and particularly of the role of religion in assigning women a subordinate position, the self-respect movement found it difficult to fight issues of property ownership, caste privilege, and gender discrimination all at the same time. In the final analysis, the self-respect movement rejected brahmanical symbols while it retained the same limited definition of women's roles."

With the conclusion of World War I and an era of comparative peace that followed, the women of Bombay, Calcutta and Madras utilized the networks developed during the war, to link their various clubs and associations into a new council. Thus, by the year 1925, the National Council of Women in India was formed, fructifying the efforts of dedicated and influential women who had contributed commendably to the war effort and were now copiously drawing upon connections and contacts established in the course of their noble work. In the same year, the NCWI was established as a national branch of the International Council of Women, upon the invitation of the Marcheoness of Aberdeen, President of the International Council from 1922 to 1936. This august body, namely, the International Council of Women, had convened its first meeting in Washington DC as early as 1888 to advance women's social, economic and political rights.

Lady Mehribai Tata, daughter of the well-known educationalist H.J. Bhabha and married to the scion of the famous Tata industrialist family, Sir Dorab Tata, did much to promote the cause of female emancipation both in India and abroad. In her view, purdah, caste differences and lack of education prevented women from working to change social conditions. As a necessary first step, she urged men to support female education and freedom of movement for women. The two colossus of India's chequered political destiny, Mahatma Gandhi and Jawaharlal Nehru also campaigned vigorously against the custom of "*purdah*". "Chastity", said Gandhiji, is not a hothouse growth. It cannot be protected by the surrounding walls of *purdah*. It must grow from within.It must be a very poor thing that cannot stand the gaze of men. Men to be men, must be able to trust their womenfolk, even as the latter are compelled to trust them.... Let us then tear down the *purdah* with one mighty effort. In attempting to trace the genesis of this abhorrent custom,Gandhi went on to say, "I am of the opinion that the *purdah* in India is a recent institution and was adopted during the period of Hindu decline. Gargi could not have held her discourses from behind the *purdah*. Nor is the *purdah* universal in India. It is unknown in the Deccan, Gujarat and Punjab. It is unknown among the peasantry.." And indeed Gandhiji`s perceptive analysis of the genesis of the *purdah* system was entirely right, substantiated as it was by evidence in that most famous document *Glimpses of World History* by Jawaharlal Nehru wherein he says that though Arab women did not observe *purdah* in the beginning, " success made the Arabs imitate more and more the customs of the two old empires on either side of them, the eastern Roman and the Persian. They had defeated the former and put an end to the latter, but they themselves succumbed to many an evil habit of these empires. Gradually the harem system begins, and men and women meet each other less and less socially. Unhappily this seclusion of women became a feature of Islamic society, and India also learnt it from them when the Muslims came here." Decrying this self-limiting practice most vehemently Panditji, who hailed from a family far ahead of its times and with an irrevocable commitment to the betterment of the masses, maintained in anguished lament in *Glimpses of World History*: "Whenever I think of the women in *purdah*, cut off from the outside world, I invariably think of a prison or a zoo! How can a nation go ahead if half of its population is kept hidden away in a kind of prison?"

That Lady Tata's voice was heard and taken cognisance of, both nationally and internationally, owed itself to the fact that she was a bridge between two vastly alien and different cultures — the British and the Indian — with their widely divergent views and rules on social, political, economic and legal issues and other norms pertaining to the education, enlightenment and emancipation of their respective populations, especially their womenfolk. Her social position, wealth and poise and the synthesis she epitomized in terms of 'dress and address' while abroad, won Lady Tata a respect that was rare. While she was aided in her laudable endeavours by many other women (particularly in the Bombay Presidency) married to wealthy and influential men in industry and banking, the interests of individual members (of the Council) determined its work. Standing sectional committees were formed to deal with art, labour, legislation and the press. Generally, the committees collected information, prepared memoranda, and presented these to the proper authorities. Of all the committees established, the one devoted to dealing with legislation to improve women's status, was definitely the most active. This was largely due to the efforts and leadership of one Mithan Tata Lam, the first Indian woman to pass the bar exam and practise law in India, and partly because this was the kind of "social work" that could be carried out without any fear of losing status.

However, the council failed to grow due to its elitist nature and could not attain the status of a national organization. Though this was not the sole contributory factor responsible for the failure of the Council in acquiring a national stature. Other reasons which were partly responsible for somewhat limited scope and nature of the NCWI were that the succursal councils were politically and socially conservative in outlook. Because of its connection with the British and the immense wealth and status of the leading members, the NCWI remained aloof from the struggle for independence. The NCWI which, at its inception, had three life patrons, namely the Dowager Begum Saheb of Bhopal, Maharani Saheb of Baroda and Lady Dorab Tata, had other women of distinction in important positions, on the executive committee as well. These included India's first woman barrister, Miss Cornelia Sorabji, Maharani Sucharu Devi of Mourbhanj-a daughter of Keshub Chandra Sen, Mrs Shaffi Tyabji, a member of one of Bombay's leading Muslim families and others. Being affluent women they could easily undertake (and afford) the extensive travelling required of the council's leaders, but there were many other women worthy of joining the organization, who simply could not afford it. They simply did not feel comfortable in the presence of these affluent and titled women, which was one of the reasons why the NCWI did not "take of" as Tarabai Premchand so succinctly put it. A certain modicum of inflexibility had also crept into the functioning of this august organization, preventing its members from re-evaluating their techniques and modifying their style of operating. Instead members of the NCWI demanded that the conditions for village work be improved. Most of them refused to follow Lady Tata's advice to visit the slums but there were, however, a few deeply committed ones who did. Among them was one Maniben Kara (1905-79), a social worker who became a leading trade unionist. This intrepid social worker had secretly visited chawls with foreign friends and what she had seen there, had shocked and ashamed her. It spurred her on to study social work in England. Upon her return to India in 1929 and back in Bombay, she organized the Sewa Mandir (Service Organization) to work among the poor. She recalled that while Communists accused her of sabotaging a revolution, women from the slums asked if she had nothing better to do with her time. And therefore, chided by those she wanted to help, Maniben became a member of M.N.Roy group of radical humanists and redirected her energies towards organizing workers.

By far the most important of the women's organizations and the most truly Indian of the three was the last to be formed. The All India Women's Conference (AIWC) first met in Poona in January of 1927, followed by more than six months of serious work on the part of Margaret Cousins and other women belonging to the WIA. The first president of the AIWC, the Maharani Chimanbai Saheb Gaekwad of Baroda, underlined the need for a special type of education for women, compatible with their nature. Delegates to the conference included over 2000 men and women who attended as observers and a large number of professional educationalists, social reformers, women associated with the nationalist movement, and the wealthy and titled. The majority of the women at the conference agreed that the educational system should concentrate on producing educated wives and mothers but they also wanted women doctors, professors, and lawyers. Regardless of whether the curriculum was home science or natural science, there was a general agreement that education should complement gender roles.

Sociological interpretations of historical facts, namely, that inhibiting social customs — particularly child marriage and *purdah*—resulted from foreign invasions and prevented women from receiving instructions, became both the legitimizing factor behind the organization as well as the thrust of its programs. By the year 1928, the AIWC on Educational reform decided that there could be little progress in educational matters unless the harmful social customs and practices were eradicated. While in the 1930s came the civil disobedience movement and the organization's decision to remain apolitical, by the mid -1930s the list of sub-committees of the AIWC included labour, rural reconstruction, indigenous industries, textbooks, opium, and the Sarda Act. At the same time their resolutions ranged from advocating film censorship, to urging widespread instructions in birth control. The leaders were aware that their work was taking them in two directions: one that would benefit women specifically and one aimed at helping the entire nation. Their work on behalf of women was increasingly focused on legal disabilities while concern with the welfare of the nation led them towards Gandhi's program of reconstruction and social action. Their interest in women's status in law propelled them towards collaboration with British officials and members of the legislature, while the Gandhian emphasis on village uplift and untouchables involved work at the grass-roots levels as well as a totally different interpretation of the dynamics of social change.

Amrit Kaur, one of Gandhi's devoted followers, wanted the organization to emerge as a political force for women to reckon with. This proposal was vetoed as the AIWC was committed to a comprehensive legal bill for women.

By the year 1940, the AIWC was establishing itself as the premier organization representing women, complete with a central office and permanent staff. With the organizational details now complete and in perfect synchronization, they could devote their energies to two major tasks: publicity and propaganda for women's issues, and exhaustive research to provide a comprehensive and useful data base on women in India. Numerous provincial branches were infused with a new zeal during the war years and many of them addressed local issues with a fervour which was laudable, supporting peasant movements, teaching untouchables, encouraging political involvement, etc. They reached out to women hitherto ignored by the central body, though it proved an immensely difficult task.

However, a central reform issue against which the development of the various Indian women's national organizations, their efforts to cooperate with one another and their interrelationships with various males, British officials and British women can be viewed in the latter half of the 1920s, is the Child Marriage Reform Issue.

"Efforts to secure passage of the Child Marriage Restraint Act taught these women lessons about competing agendas and the difficulties of collaborating with their apparent well-wishers. At the same time they learned to distinguish between effective petitioning and effective action. In many ways their work on child marriage was a rite of passage into a world where every act had political meaning."

Earlier protagonists of the Age of Consent Bill included eminent personalities such as R. Raghunath Rao, R.G. Bhandarkar, M.G. Ranade and Gopal Ganesh Agarkar, those who violently opposed it had among them such social reformers and conservatives as Lokmanya Tilak, Sir Romesh Chand Mitter, Sir T. Madhawa Rao.

A fierce controversy raged between these opposing forces on the death of ten year old Phulmani through forcible intercourse with her lawful Bengali husband, Hari Mohan Maita, in 1890 and his subsequent acquittal of rape. Sir Andrew Scobie urged for legislation raising the Age of Consent from ten years of age to twelve years. "Both Tilak and Agarkar carried on the acrimonious debate over this issue in their weeklies *Kesari* and *Sudharak* respectively. Agarkar, inspired by J.S. Mill, lashed out against the orthodox and the conservatives who defended the practice of disfiguring widows or supported the ban on widow marriage. He was in favour of State interference in such matters and believed that the Government had the right and duty to protect female children from immature prostitution and from premature cohabitation."

A revival of interest in the age of marriage and age of consent can be traced to discussions in the League of Nations.

Concern with traffic in women and girls led to consideration of the age of consent and to proposals in the Indian Assembly. Various bills addressing these complex yet vitally important issues, were introduced, discussed and debated upon and ultimately defeated. Until 1927 when Rai Sahib Harbilas Sarda introduced his Hindu Child Marriage Bill — a well thought out and comprehensive document the acceptance of which was indirectly hastened by Katherine Mayo's devastatingly vituperative attack on both Indians as well as Indian customs in her publication *Mother India*. Using hospital records, offical accounts and personal interviews, Mayo wrote a "pot boiler" that both shocked and titillated the American and British reading public. Mayo berated Indians for their treatment of women of all ages, focusing particularly on sexual behavior and lingering on accounts of child brides "raped" by their older husbands. She concluded that social customs accounted for the weakness of the Indian race and made it clear that these people were not ready to "hold the reins of Government". And whilst some Indian men termed the attack as scurrilous, there were others who argued (maybe with a modicum of truth) that British officials had prevented them from eradicating these social evils. Whatever the truth of the matter, government officials eager to escape blame began telling the Assembly and "the world at large" that they supported beneficent social legislation.

The assembly, which referred the famous Sarda Bill to a select committee of just ten people, chaired by Sir Morophant Visavanath Joshi, had the redoubtable Rameshwari Nehru as its sole women representative. Recommended by the WIA, Shrimati Brijlal Nehru as she was originally known, was one of the famous aunts of the Nehru family, a devoted nationalist and a freedom fighter. Therefore her appointment and placement on this committee considering such a crucial issue, was of great significance for not only was she an ardent champion of women's issues through her magazine called *Stridarpan*, but also a member of a number of social welfare institutions such as the

Indian Women's Association, the Delhi Women's League, the All India Women's Conference, the Children's Aid Society in Delhi and the Association for Moral and Social Hygiene in India, at various times during India's chequered history.

Once appointed, however, the committee moved swiftly to gauge public attitudes, sent out approximately 8,000 detailed questionnaires and announced a tour to hear testimony from a wide range of witnesses.

The various women's organizations swung into action with an almost missionary zeal, doing their utmost to promote this legislation at every stage. They not only generated propaganda against the hotly debated child marriage issue but also commented on proposed bills. They petitioned, met with the Joshi Committee and lobbied earnestly to secure passage of the Child Marriage Restraint Act; they worked immensely hard, after its passage, for legislation to make it a meaningful Act.

The subsidiary branches of the All India Women's Conference organized meetings throughout the length and breadth of the country. Such meetings became an important fora for the discussions of women's issues and women expressed their opinion rather vociferously on divergent (women's) issues. They refused, and rightly so, to confine their comments merely to the burning issue at hand - namely, that of child marriage. This was only one of the many customs that "crushed their individuality and denied them opportunities for education and development of mind and body." Various women who came forward courageously to share their experiences with others so that large segments of the women's population might benefit, were subconsciously trying to fulfil the prophetic tones of an epiphanic Egyptian verse which ran thus:

> I am the pure lotus
> Springing up in splendour
> Fed by the breath of Ra
> Rising in the sunlight,

Out of soil and darkness,
I blossom in the Field.

An Egyptian Song
(Translated by Rebert Hillyer)

Muslim women in no way lagged behind. Begum Sharifah Hamid Ali, who organized a special campaign to support the Sarda Act and was herself the mother of seven female progeny, urged that the minimum age for women should be eighteen. Married herself at the age of twenty-five, she said while addressing the Muslim women in Sind, that two of her own daughters had been victims to the abuse of child marriage. Drawing from these experiences, she had delayed the marriages of her remaining daughters to a reasonable age and she exhorted others to act in a similar way in the future.

Another time, another place and another enterprising woman — Mrs Diwan — hundreds of miles away, reiterated the urgent need to change consciousness among women and rid them of certain inherent complexes, thus:

> It is very essential that the outlook of women should undergo a radical change. Today women themselves believe that it is proper for them to do certain work and improper to do others... (and) that it is dangerous to remain unmarried. This inferiority complex must be got rid of.

However, it was cautiously considered solutions, resolutions, petitions and viewpoints that were normally channelized to reach government officials.

The members of that august body, the All India Women's Conference who met the Joshi Committee, concentrated on negating the arguments put forward by their opponents rather than establishing parameters of individual choice in determining whether or not they should marry, whom to marry and when. They denied that women favoured youthful marriage, that later marriages would lead to immorality, that all men supported child marriage, and that child marriage was a part of Vedic religion. Instead they concentrated on securing a later age of marriage and couched their support in favour of it "in terms of preparing women to fit biologically determined roles."

When the Sarda Bill, passed in October 1929, finally evolved into the Sarda Act in April 1930, women's organizations throughout India rejoiced. While the NCWI was the most cautious in its praise saying this was the first campaign in the battle against social evils, but not a victory, the WIA was more forthcoming and convened a meeting forthwith to congratulate Sahib Harbilas Sarda, the brain behind the Bill. Sarda's Bill, wherein the Joshi Committee had recommended fifteen as the minimum age of marriage and twenty one as the age of consent, was ultimately passed with a compromise; whereas the minimum age of marriage for females was set at fourteen, that for males was fixed at eighteen and the age of consent was not even mentioned. Be that as it may, there can be no doubt of the influence of world opinion on both Indian and British Legislators. In America and Britain the proceedings of the legislature were followed as if the outcome would prove or disprove Mayo's conclusion. British officials had no intentions of letting the charge of reformers and nationalists gain credence, namely that foreign rule inhibited social reform.

But while the congratulations continued to pour in, with the AIWC reacting the most positively, calling the Sarda Act a "great achievement" and a "personal triumph", the euphoria was short lived. Zealous Muslim leaders, who had violently opposed the Bill even before it had been passed and threatened dire consiquences, now threatened to break the Sarda Act as well as other laws by joining the Mahatma and Congress in their anti-government campaign. While they demanded that the Act be amended to exclude Muslims' women's organizations tried to combat this move in a number of ways. The AIWC claimed that they spoke for all women in India, including Muslim women members presenting a memorial in support of the Sarda Act to the Viceroy and said:

> We, speaking also on behalf of the Muslim women of India, assert that it is only a small section of Muslims who have been approaching your excellency and demanding exemption from the Act. This Act affects girls and women far more than it affects men and we deny their right to speak on our behalf.

Suffice it to say that the government did not amend or repeal that Act as British officials realized that doing so would be tantamount to an admission of weakness. Therefore, since it was an important consensus issue, the Child Marriage Restraint Act had a far-reaching and profound effect on women's organizations and enabled women from different regions and communities to work together with facility. It also made it possible for the three national organizations to coordinate their activities without any major problems.

In the decade preceding India's independence which also coincided with World War II and especially during this period of bloodshed and violence, "the women's organizations emerged as fully mature entities able to respond to the most important national and international issues of the day. Their hegemony was short-lived but in the meantime they participated in almost every major committee or planning group meeting to discuss India's future. They decided not to form a separate women's party but continued to work for a new civil code that would recognize women's rights."

Both their successes and failures can be attributed to social feminism which served as the ideological base for their demands. Although many of the participants in these women's organizations decried the term "feminism", equating it with man-hating and suffragette violence, they sought greater autonomy for women. When they petitioned for education, the vote, and amelioration of social evils it was "to enable women to fulfil their social obligations to the family and nation".

They deserved a degree of respect and honour as members and contributors of a larger social order. But while a few women in these organizations evinced a desire for and demanded complete autonomy for women, this was not practically possible for the following two reasons : firstly these organizations had matured with valuable male support and flourished in partnership with male-dominated nationlist parties. To give the need of women top priority in such an existing scenario, over and above everything else, would not only have been antithetical to their construction of the Indian woman as nurturing and self-sacrificing, it would have forced them to choose between nationalism and feminism. The development of a social feminist ideology made possible the peaceful coexistence of feminism and nationalism in a new shape that Margot Badran has called "feminist nationalism."

A large number of middle-class women who greatly benefited in terms of experience gained in working with these organizational structures and in learning the dynamics of the political world (partly from other women), put their newly acquired knowledge and experience to good use as they fought for women's franchise and women's legal rights. In assessing and analyzing the contribution and usefulness of these women's organizations, it is vital to remember that their attempts to change the social reality for women were played out in an environment that could be especially cruel to women who did not conform. Hence the history of these social organizations is one of the notable accomplishments and severe limitations.

References

Basu, Aparna and Ray, Bharati, *Women's Struggle: A History of the All India Women's Conference 1927-1990*, New Delhi: Manohar, 1990.

Chitalika, K.J., Ed. "Arya Mahila Samaj". *Directory of Women's Institutions*, Vol. I, Bombay: Presidency, Bombay, Servants of India Society, 1974.

Forbes, Geraldine, *Women in Modern India*. The New Cambridge History of India Vol. 2, published in South Asia by Foundaton Books, New Delhi. First Indian Edition 1996. This edition of Geraldine Forbes: *Women in Modern India* is published by arrangement with Cambridge University Press, Cambridge.

Gandhi, Mohandas Karamchand, *Young India*, 3 Feb. 1927.

GOI, Home Dept, Judicial File Nos: 272/31, F73/31, 793/32, 76/32.

Heptulla, Najma, 'Development Strategies for Women: Need for Political Will', In Najma Heptulla (ed.), *'Reforms for Women - Future Options*.

Lady Tata to Miss Serenbai Maneckjee Cursetjee (March 3, 1931), *A Book of Rememberance*.

Lakahmi, C.S., "Mother, Mother-Community and Mother-Politics in Tamil Nadu", *EPW*, 25, Nos. 42 and 43.

Legislative Assembly Debates, January 29, 1929, Vol. 1: 197; Sept. 10, 1929, Vols. IV and V,: 679-80; Sept. 19, 1929, Vol. IV and V,: 1110.

"Life Sketch of Maniben Kara"(unpublished) originally kept with Western Railway Employees Union, Bombay.

Mayo, Katherine, *Mother India*, New York: Harcourt Brace, 1927.

NCWI, *Third Biennial Report*, 1930-32, NMML

Nagpal, B.R., Thy Name is Woman!, Book Review in *The Hindustan Times*, 14 June, 1998.

Nehru, Jawaharlal, *Glimpses of World History*, Asia Publishing House, 1962.

Nehru, Jawaharlal message to the Prayag Mahila Vidyapitha, 12 January 1934.

Ramusack, Barbara N., 'Women's Organization and Social Change: The Age of Marriage Issue in India', In Black,

Naomi and Cottrell, Ann Baker (eds.), *Women and World Change: Equity Issue in Development*, Beverly Hills: Sage Publications, 1981.

Rani, Prabha, "Women's Indian Association and the Self-Respect Movement in Madras, 1925-1936: Perceptions on Women," paper delivered at the Women's Studies Conference, Chandigarh (October, 1985).

Report of the Age of Consent Committee, 1928-1929, Calcutta, 1929.

Sarkar, Tanika, "Rhetoric against Age of Consent Resisting Colonial Reason and Death of a Child Wife", *EPW* 28, No.36 (September 4,1993), P.Ws 1870.

Shastri, Sivanath, *History of the Brahmo Samaj*, 2nd Edn. Calcutta Sadharan Brahmo Samaj, 1974.

Singh, Shanta Serbjeet and Sabharwal, Jyoti, Ed. *A Feminine Critique : The Fiftieth Milestone*, New Delhi: Sterling Publishers Pvt. Ltd.

Smt. Akilabai, Speech on, "Child Marriage Bill", The Hindu (clipping, N.D.), DRP.

The Indian Quarterly Register, 2, Nos . 3 and 4 (July-December, 1929) (Calcutta, N.D.) pp. 395-96.

WIA Appendix D, "Muslim Ladies Defend Sarda Act", *Report*, 1930-31.

Women's Indian Association, *Quinquennial Report*, 1917-1922, WIA papers.

3

EMULATION AND EMANCIPATION

"There can be no civilization in which man and woman are not equal partners. There can be no nation which has not been built up by their joint efforts. There can be no unity for which both man and woman have not worked and planned together, and there can be no freedom unless man and woman march forward together and achieve it."

Vijaya Lakshmi Pandit

It is impossible to make an authentic estimate of Mahatma Gandhi's struggle for India's independence through the pursuance of pacific methods, without an appreciation of the heroic role played by woman workers under their leaders like Annie Besant, Sarojini Naidu, Kamladevi Chattopadhyay, Maniben Kara, Mridula Sarabhai, Aruna Asaf Ali, Rajkumari Amrit Kaur and others, to mention just a few. Kamla Nehru and Vijayalakshmi Pandit, of course, were almost an integral part of the freedom movement, linked to it by destiny and choice. All these heroic women (besides many more) were responsible not only for revolutionizing thought and theory in those crucial pre-independence decades, but also for transmuting them into hitherto unenvisaged platforms for the emancipation of women and the *Azadi* of India. Women of substance all, they played stellar roles in suscitating the masses (of women especially), rousing them out of a passive, somnolent slumber and energizing them not only to carve a permanent place for themselves in the glorious struggle for freedom, but to simultaneously articulate their own aims and aspirations. The period between 1914 and 1918, especially, is of great significance in the history of the national struggle because it was for the first time that a woman, the legendary Annie Besant, led the national movement and "she wrenched Indian politics out of its automatic and placid theorizing, making it a living and vital issue before the country and the whole Empire."

The period also witnessed the birth of a few major national events i.e., reunion of the Moderates and the Extremists in the Indian National Congress in 1916, an alliance between the Muslim League and the Congress, the outcome of which was the Congress League Scheme (Lucknow Pact, 1916), and, most important, the inauguration of the Home Rule League and the Home Rule Agitation which shook the nation from deep slumber and increased the tempo of national life.

These years are of far greater importance in the history of the women's movement and an organized and concerted effort by Annie Besant for their emancipation. As the first president of the Women's Indian Association founded in 1917, this intrepid Irish woman, born on October I, 1847 in London, adroitly channelized the need for the emancipation of women into an organized movement. Such an organized and balanced movement also automatically became the fora through which the demand for the recognition of political rights of women was established. Her leadership, thus, not only gave strength and encouragement to the women of the land to come forward fearlessly, but also inspired them to participate in the national life of the country and to join the national movement in which women have played a prominent part.

Annie Besant, who came to India in 1893 and at different periods of time concerned herself with the upliftment of the Indian masses in the field of religion, education, social reforms and political awareness, came under the influence of Charles Bradlaugh at an early age, while abroad. A co-editor with Bradlaugh on his *National Reformer*, she often demanded justice for the weaker nations, as well as political status for women and equality in all spheres on the basis that if they were inferior they would not be able to withstand open competition. But it was only after a major illness when she was forced to temporarily take leave of her public and professional activities, that she seriously cogitated upon a wider and more far-reaching plan of action. She decided, as she said, "To give myself wholly to propagandist work as a free thinker and a social reformer, and to use my tongue as well as my pen in the struggle. The desire to spread liberty and truer thought among men, to war against bigotry and superstition, to make the world freer and better than I found it - all this impelled me with a force that would not be denied." It was fortunate that such noble sentiments were translated into reality with a persistent perseverance so typical of Annie Besant's mode of functioning.

The closing years of the nineteenth century were a period when both western education and western domination were manifest. Attitudes towards both were vastly different. There was one segment of society which prided itself on emulating the social and educational idioms of the west whereas the more conservative among Indians evinced a certain resentment towards the same.

Annie Besant not only acquainted herself with the religion, philosophy, customs and prevalent conditions in India but also dealt with the conservative element of Hindu society by opening schools and colleges; by speaking of theosophy and Hinduism and associating herself with Sanatan Dharm Paliani Sabha in Benaras founded by Colonel Olcott (one of the founders of the Theosophical Society) with the aim of revitalizing a sense of Aryan spirituality.

This intrepid Irish woman raised her voice vociferously against such prevalent evil practices in the Indian social system as the caste system, child marriage and untouchability. She maintained, "You complain, and justly of the harsh and rude manners often shown to you by your English rulers, but are they one-hundredth part as insolent to you as you are insolent to this race whom you in the past have brought under your yoke."

Propelled forward by boundless energy and an earnest sense of commitment, she began her crusade for education which she vowed would be " an education founded on Indian ideals and enriched not dominated by thought and culture of the West." Under the auspices of the Hindu College at Benaras where she worked devotedly for two years, she was instrumental in bringing out publications on Hinduism better known as the *Sanatam Dharm Series*; a truly remarkable series, the likes of these had not been published earlier. Her valuable contributions in the sphere of education included the opening of various schools and colleges for girls such as the Central Hindu Girls School in Benaras, Madanpalla High School and College and Adyar National College. With the spread of women's education came a modicum of learning and enlightenment; a diminishing of prejudices and practices ingrained in the female psyche since time immemorial and sanctioned by certain religious dogmas.

Not content with the numerous beneficial projects she generated for the upliftment of women and the removal of social ills, in 1906, Mrs Besant organized within the Theosophical Society the 'Sons of India' and the 'Daughters of India' to work for social reforms. Fuelled by her spirit of emancipation and evolving as a natural corollary to her enlightened aims and programmes for reform, in 1911 the ' Order of the Rising Star' appeared on the scene. Annie Besant founded this organization "for the protection of the good, for the destruction of evil doers, for the sake of firmly establishing righteousness."

The year 1913 was significant in the sense that it witnessed the birth of a number of organizations which not only embodied the spirit of the times but carried it a step further by its pragmatic and practical implementary activities. One was a junior branch of the "Order of the Rising Star" which consisted of people below twenty-one years of age; its membership was primarily for the benefit of those who wished to be trained in the special kind of service which the spirit of the new age demanded. In the same year, the new body of the Theosophical Stalwarts appeared, each member taking a solemn pledge to dissociate himself from certain customs. By 1914 it had evolved into an order of the 'Brothers of Service' with the more specific pledge taken by its members to disregard all caste restrictions.

While Mrs. Besant preached and propagated the use of Swadeshi from an economic standpoint, the Intelligence Department very cleverly labelled this as political propaganda.

Political Pulls and Pressures

The political ambience around 1914, when Annie Besant plunged headlong into the political arena, mirrored a restlessness, a feeling of uncertainty and change; when change was imminent, the situation getting more explosive and yet there were not too many concrete, tangible and constructive changes. As she herself observed, expanding on the reasons for entry into politics, " It is not possible that I should have never jumped into political work, had not increasing repression by the authority, narrowing of liberty, the ill-treatment of students, and the danger of revolution forced me into the field."

The Minto-Morley Reforms and Muslim Separatism

Political conditions in the country at this juncture remained quite disturbed. The Minto-Morley Reforms which were announced in 1910 by granting separate representation to the Muslims, further widened the chasm between the two major communities and subsequently weakened the national front against the Imperial Government. It would be relevant to briefly recapitulate the Muslim scenario within the wider ambit of the Indian political context. Prior to the evolution of the aforementioned reforms and soon after, Syed Ahmad, a reformer from Aligarh, with 'his sharp analytical mind and his acute sense of the working of historical forces in the shaping of contemporary societies' was a trail blazer and ' by far the most prominent advocate of an Anglo-Muslims rapprochement'; perceptively recognizing the change and movement in history and the immediacy with which his Muslim brethren needed to be rescued from a sharp downward spiral, he advocated the adoption of western ideas and institutions. The practical implications, which the new ideas from the west justified, were more closely related to Indian circumstances. They were not to live as the British themselves lived, but to carve out a place for themselves within the establishment. Not so much to imitate the west as to 'accept only some of its values as at least a second-best substitute for the vanished Muslim glories.' Ultimately, after some strong criticism and resistance, Syed Ahmad's modernist agenda was acclaimed and endorsed by a new generation of Muslims — including Ansari, Mohamed Ali, Iqbal, Hasrat Mohani — who were alienated by the formalism of the traditional theologians. They were convinced that pursuing modern education and the raising of intellectual standard would not undermine but vindicate the message of Islam.' Inspired by 'his eclectic world-view', the educated Muslims founded notable educational centres of learning like the Madarsatul-Islam in Sind and the Dacca College, modelled on the lines of the most remarkable colleges of those times, the Aligarh College.

Thus, it was under Syed Ahmad's influence that 'sections of the intelligentsia broke loose from the shackles of orthodoxy and buttressed the cause of reforms and reinterpretation of orthodox doctrines.' However, while Maulana Azad paid him a moving tribute by comparing him to that great Hindu reformer, Raja Rammohun Roy, and many of Syed's contemporaries were imbued with a similar reformist zeal and were not unduly upset over Britain's political hegemony, "serious differences in attitudes and approaches came to the surface and caused an open breach in the ranks of the *Ulama* and the liberal intelligentsia." This rather unpleasant rift in ideological thought and action came about because the overriding concern of Ahmad's contemporaries, for which the former had scant sympathy, was to resist the West's cultural penetration. Some notable thinkers from the traditionalist and modernist persuasions took on the burden of this responsibility within a specifically Islamic framework and, in doing so, relied heavily on the neo-traditionalism of the Wallullahi school. This tug of war between the two 'warring' groups was temporarily halted early in the twentieth century when the political landscape was changing in response to major national and transnational developments and Deoband's Dar-ul-ulum,'embodying the spirit of orthodox resistance to foreign rule' and Aligarh College, 'seen as symbolizing political and cultural capitulation to the British' decided to cooperate in the context of securing a place for themselves 'in the political arrangements being hammered out in Delhi and Whitehall'. Their spirited endeavour, for which they revitalized an otherwise defunct Muslim League, was to locate wider communitarian concerns outside the framework of Congress nationalism. Once the *Ulama* and their erstwhile *bete noire*, the Western-trained professional politicians, put their heads together, they came up with a definition developed in the context of colonial institutions and their own scripturalist rhetoric. They sought to create a corporate identity and set Muslims apart from their own class region and linguistic units. They thrust an Islamic identity on Muslims, many of whom were not accustomed to living in accordance with the *Shariat* or the diktat of the theologians. This was not all. The coming together of the men of religion and the modern-day publicists was counter-productive in so far as it stifled liberal, reformist and secularizing currents.

The British government had no reason to challenge the Muslim League so long as it could be pressed into service to counter nationalist aspirations. Having created a Muslim identity in Indian politics through the Acts of 1909 and 1919, they could draw comfort henceforth from Jinnah repeating, at the height of his popularity, much the same arguments that had prompted Morley, Minto, Montagu and Chelmsford to concede to the

Muslims separate electorates, weightages and reservation in the councils and public services.

To make matters worse the Ghadar Conspiracy was unearthed and those found guilty prosecuted. Bhai Parmanand was convicted and sentenced to transportation for life. Seditious and revolutionary activities were rife. Despite the liberal minded British Viceroy-Lord Hardinge's famous Despatch of 25 August 1911 to the Home Government supporting the aspirations of Indians for provincial autonomy, a bomb was thrown on him when he made his State entry into Delhi later in the same year. This, predictably enough, led the Government to tighten the provisions against the press. The partition of Bengal, a 'settled fact' was unsettled in 1911 after a tremendous amount of agitation. It was annulled, but it came too late and could not really be appreciated much. The beginning of the second decade of the twentieth century was marked with upheaval and violence and the portents were sure to spill over into later years.

India was somewhat rudderless in 1915 and desperately in need of a 'General'. "The veterans of Indian freedom of the standing of Gopal Krishan Gokhale and Sir Pherozeshah Mehta were no more. Dinshaw Edulji Wacha was too old to do any active work; S.N. Banerjee was not in line with the latest thought and M. K. Gandhi had not yet taken the rein of political work in his hands. Lala Lajpat Rai was virtually exiled in America. Bal Gangadhar Tilak was released in 1914 after a long term of imprisonment, but he was in shattered health and thus unable to carry on the work - 'a circumstance which stood in the way of his undertaking energetic propaganda throughout India, moving on the wings of time and electrifying the people by an appeal to their emotions. This was left to be done by one older than himself in age, frail in sex, but enjoying a better start in life, not being under a cloud in the scene of her operations, better known to the world and endowed with that dynamic energy which knows no fatigue and seeks no rest.' Annie Besant not only blamed England for ruling India on Western lines, she also "attributed the famines to the financial drain of the 'Home Charges' and the huge bureaucracy and partly the destruction of the manufactured goods of India for the profit of Lancashire." She staunchly and unswervingly maintained that India must be governed on the basis of Indian feelings, Indian traditions, Indian thought and Indian ideas.

Mrs Besant mooted the suggestion at the 1913 session of the Indian National Congress, to sponsor a national movement embodying a wide body of reforms, namely, religious, educational, social as well as political and upon her election as a member of the Congress the following year, she demanded for the citizens of India political equality with other peoples of the Empire. In fact, she went one step further and asked for self-government not as a reward for India's loyalty to the British during the war, but as a right. To better educate the people and make known the demand of a nation in political ferment to the ruling power, she not only acquired ownership of the *Madras Standard* in 1914, but changed the title to *New India* and wrote a series of articles on self-government and her intention "to lead a political campaign in favour of 'Swaraj'." Though her methods were considered as highly inflammatory and rousing racial passions, she remained steadfast in her aim of securing Home Rule for India and stated with a vehemence characteristic of her intent to pursue a cause, in the seminal issue of the *Commonwealth,* that In political reforms we aim at the building up of complete self-government from village council through district boards and provincial legislative assemblies to a national parliament, equal in its powers by whatever name they may be called, also at the direct representation of Imperial Parliament, when that body shall contain representatives of the self-governing states of the Empire.

The Home Rule Agitation

The necessity for the formulation of the Home Rule League was felt because "the Congress showed little activity between its annual session" and the need for 'an active propogandist body' was thus imminent. "The words Home Rule were chosen as a short public cry, making the fact clear that the struggle was not against Great Britain, but for liberty within the Empire."

'Home Rule' which did not necessarily constitute a democratic government but 'a nation which by its own free vote voted an autocracy, will still be a self-governing nation.' It had a pointed star of the Indian Empire with Home Rule in red engraved in the center. The colours were red for Hindus and green for Muslims. Membership of the League was open to both men and women over eighteen years of age and the rules of the organization were simple. A few people interested in working for Home Rule formed themselves into a small composite group, elected one of their members as their representative who, in turn, communicated with the secretary of the Home Rule League. Copies of all the relevant literature were sent to the selected representatives who distributed it to the various members to enable them to do the propaganda, by placing them in reading rooms, libraries and local clubs. So that the branches formed in every town and village would be affiliated to the Provincial Congress Committees with a view to sending as many delegates as possible to the Congress platform and to ensure that the Congress of 1916 declared that "Home Rule was the immediate necessity." And when the Congress and the Muslim League failed to ratify the Home Rule League programme at a joint meeting in August 1916, Annie Besant went on a whirlwind lecture tour and delivered a series of lectures in Calcutta, Lucknow and Allahabad. Finally, the Home Rule League was inaugurated in September 1916; she was even able to persuade Mohammad Ali Jinnah to become one of the secretaries of the Home Rule League.

Mrs Besant was insistent that the Indians should "have a promise that when the war was over, India would have her place in the Council of the Empire and that Indians would be the masters of their own motherland." Therefore, taking full advantage of the opportunity offered by the war, she launched a vigorous propaganda indeed for the Home Rule. In this way the Home Rule League and the League started by Tilak, through the latter's daily *Kesari* and weekly *Marathi* and Mrs Besant's popular weekly *The Commonwealth* and daily *New India*, advocated the cause vociferously and in uncompromising terms. Whether through the press or through speeches and addresses, Mrs Besant decried Britain's foreign policy, the policy in regard to home charges, the method of recruitment in the army, industries, the land tax and education.

However, after several warnings issued to Annie Besant by the Government and Lord Pentland, Governor of Madras, the *New India* continued to be an organ of active propaganda and its owner as indefatigably committed to India's political emancipation as before, undeterred by the threat of arrest or the dangerous consequences of her anti-government campaign. Finally, when all else failed, the Government used the Defence of India Act and an order of internment was issued on the 16th of June, 1917. This order was comprehensive in that it forbade Annie Besant, Arundale and Wadia to attend meetings. It also provided for censoring their correspondence. All the three refused to disassociate their political work from their religious work.

She was finally arrested and the internment of Annie Besant by Lord Pentaland, Governor of Madras in June 1917, played a prominent part in rousing the spirit of women, and awakening them from their lethargy into active participation in the women's movement. Her subsequent release four months later, in September 1917, galvanized women all over the country into action and they accorded her a rousing welcome. Before she was elected as the first woman President of the Congress in 1917, Annie Besant had toured tirelessly and extensively, inspiring women everywhere. Now, inspired by her personal noble example in conjunction with those of Sarojini Naidu and Margaret Cousins, women came forward in large numbers to work for the emancipation of women and the national cause. And thus the Women's Indian Association was born, affording a common platform for women to air their grievances and demand their rights. While Cousins insisted that there should be equality between men and women and an "equipoise of male and female cooperation," it was Sarojini Naidu who stood at the helm of this long and arduous struggle; and while throughout the fight the women, who had been inspired by the aggressive suffragette movement in Britain, remained strangely docile and peaceful in their movements in India, they were nonetheless insistent in their demands.

One of the very first activities of the women's movement was to send a deputation of eminent women, committed to the women's cause, to wait on Edwin Montagu, the Secretary of State for India, who had come to India in 1917, to discuss the coming reforms, including an appraisal of India's claim for Home Rule. Commenting on this, Margaret Cousins wrote: 'I knew the ins and outs of approaching responsible Ministers of State. When week after week my husband and I read in daily papers of a never-ending stream of men going on deputation to the Viceroy and the Rt. Hon. E. S. Montagu and never a mention of the voice of an Indian woman, all my training in organizing, in taking hold of psychological moments could not be curbed, and I approached about twenty of India's best known women in public life, most of whom I had met through the Senate meeting of Prof. Karve's Indian Women's University. Eventually I was privileged to organize and carry through the one and only women's deputation calling for Indian Reforms'. Mrs Sarojini Naidu was spokesman of the fourteen women who waited on the Viceroy and Mr Montagu in Madras city on 18th December, 1917. Among the ladies in the deputation were such well known figures as Ramabai Ranade, Saraladevi Chaudhrani, Uma Nehru, Herabai Tata, Cousins and a supporter by telegram-Lady Abala Bose. This august delegation included representatives from such important women's organizations as the Women's Indian

Association, the Seva Sadan, the Mahila Seva Samaj, the Indian Women's University, the Women's Home Rule League and other institutions and organizations.

This `meeting with Montagu' which was ultimately to acquire great historical significance and constructively effective results, had its genesis in a letter written two months prior to his visit to India, by the concerned representatives from the Indian Women's University. Urging him to meet with a delegation of Indian women seriously concerned with the business of securing some post-war reforms considered absolutely essential for women. While such reforms initially referred to highly enhanced and wider opportunities/facilities for Primary and Secondary Education for girls, when Cousins learnt that only political subjects were to be considered by Montagu, 'opportunities for political service' were also included on the agenda and Cousins included the subject of women's franchise. Thus began the clamour for votes for women and the impetus for women to combine social and political progress. An address was presented by the All India Women's Deputation to Lord Chelmsford and E. S. Montagu which stated that women supported the claim of the people for Self-Government within the Empire, and Gandhi's scheme for reform drawn up by the National Congress and the Muslim League. It demanded that members of the Council should be elected by the people and the franchise should be extended to the people. Women should be recognized as people and there should be no sex disqualification. Local self government should be granted and women should be represented. As a perfect example of a national political body which meted out just treatment to its women, was the Indian National Congress. In 1917, a woman — Annie Besant — was elected almost unanimously (all the Provincial Congress Committees voted in her favour except Bengal) as the first woman President of the Congress. Her presidential address was not only a charter of national liberty when she touched upon with commendable patriotic zeal on almost all subjects of national importance, but she also focused on the various causes of the awakening of the New India spirit thus:

(a) The awakening of Asia.

(b) Discussion abroad on alien rule and imperial reconstruction.

(c) Loss of belief in the superiority of white races.

(d) Awakening of merchants.

(e) The awakening of women to claim their ancient position.

(f) The awakening of the masses.

Another great heroine of India, Sarojini Naidu, was to echo Mrs Besant's view on the awakening of Asia in these unforgettable words: "Asia is awake," she asserted, and "Africa is awakening. There is certainty of a federation of the coloured peoples of the world with which the European nations will have to deal as one unit. That is what I believe", she underlined. She thus exhorted Britain to take a more farsighted world view of the future and to fulfil her initial task in ensuring Asiatic fellowship and friendship by not witholding any longer from India her birthright of freedom which will not be a gift to India but the restoration of what is her own.

In the face of such impassioned nationalist sentiments, the womenfolk of India, in general, could not help but be imbued with similar patriotic zeal and the Home Rule movement acquired tremendous momentum by the addition of large numbers of women to it. The Home Rule League had already adopted the tricolour by the time the Congress session of 1917 took place. This Congress session was important for formally raising the question of the national flag. The committee appointed by this Congress never met, so in actuality, the Home Rule League's flag now virtually became the Congress flag, with the distinctive 'Charkha' added to it later on. In 1931, the Flag Committee substituted saffron colour for red.

In 1918, the First World War ended with the Indian populace rightfully expecting significant changes (as a fitting 'reward' for having endured innumerable hardships during the course of their support to the British government in these trial years) leading towards the building of self-government. However, the ensuing Montagu-Chelmsford Report published the same year, and the reforms envisaged therein, were a sad comedown and extremists like Tilak and Besant both denounced them. The Moderates approved of them and were in favour of giving them a trial, thus creating a rift in the ranks of the Congress once again.

A special session of the Congress was, therefore, convened in August of 1918, in Bombay, to modify the Montagu-Chelmsford Scheme and to find a via media whereby both sections of the Congress i.e., the Extremists and the Moderates, could be reconciled and brought closer. The Congress passed a resolution that a fully responsible government should be introduced in the provinces.

It is indeed heartening to note that when the Congress assumed the responsibilities of government in the provinces in 1937, a reasonably large number of women were included — eighty to be precise — in such important positions as ministers, speakers of the Legislatures and members of the Assemblies. A National Planning Committee instituted with Nehru as its chairman, delegated to one of its sub-committees, the important task of examining the role of women in a planned economy. Two eminent women, Rani Lakshmibai Rajwade and Mridula Sarabhai, were its president and secretary respectively. It is commendable that this Committee , "not only reiterated the declaration of Fundamental Rights adopted at the Karachi Congress but went further. Some of its recommendations seem in retrospect extraordinarily bold and even revolutionary". One of the recommendations of the sub-committees related to legislation on abortion for the purpose of population control; another that no restriction be placed either by laws or custom on illegitimate children. Monogamy, amendment of the civil marriage law so as to enable people to enter into matrimony without any formal declaration of their religion, identical standards of morality for men and women and a formulation of a uniform civil code applicable to all citizens, were some of the other laudable recommendations put forward by the sub-committee. On another platform i.e. the franchise issue for women specifically, a non-violent fight continued unrelentingly during the British regime, and won its victory only after India became independent in 1947. After independence, women were granted universal adult franchise with one stroke of the pen by the Indian Government after it took over from the British and the futility of all the fuss which the British Government had created to grant this simple and at the same time most essential political right became apparent. It is to India's great credit and to the even greater credit of her progressively mature and enlightened electorate of women, that they have exercised this important right in a responsible and discriminate manner. But while the women fought for their rights, they did so in a totally non-violent fashion and using perfectly democratic methods. As Frank Moraes maintained quite rightly," The women's battle for equal rights has been a highly civilized affair-persuasive and persistent; insistent even but never violent, or aggressive. The 'Indian-ness' of it all is quite extraordinary." And of all the heroic women of those times, Sarojini Naidu was, undoubtedly, the most outstanding of them all. She staunchly and unswervingly 'kept the faith' with her sisters; it was almost as if she was prescient about the struggle ahead when she, alongwith the other *satyagrahis*, would have to uphold the banner amidst hardships and tragic circumstances as "One after one, the men were taken to prison after the Salt March in 1930. Until prison doors closed on them also, the women, with their leader Sarojini, upheld the banner."

References

Besant, Annie, *Wake up India, Quoted in West*, Geofry, op. cit.

Hasan, Mushirul, "Redifining Boundaries: Modernist

Interpretations And The New 'Intellectual Structures", *Legacy of A Divided Nation*, New Delhi: Oxford University Press.

Home Political Confidential Proceeding No. 247 and K. W., March 1918.

It was in her speeches in Nagpur in 1915 that she explained as to what she meant by Self-Government: "that the country shall have a Government by the Councils, elected by all the people with the power of the purse and the Government is responsible to the House. There should be elected element in the Imperial Council, the holders of portfolios should be responsible to the elected House. The Provincial Parliament shall also be elected with ministry responsible to the Parliament and that the Governor would act as the King acts in England. In the District Councils and Taluqas and in Municipalities and in Village Panchayats- the one need is elected element who shall be responsible to the electorate which places them where they are." (Home Political Confidential Proceeding No. 652-556 Sept. 1915).

Kaur, Manmohan, *Women in India's Freedom Struggle*.

4

THE WINDS OF CHANGE - THE FIGHT FOR FREEDOM

In a national war, there is no question of either sex or community. Whoever is born in this country ought to be a solider.

Pandit Jawaharlal Nehru

Elsewhere, Mahatma Gandhi emphatically maintained that "in order to play her full and destined role in world affairs, in the solution of conflicts by non-violent means, women must extend their hearts and interests beyond the narrow confines of their homes and family and embrace the whole humanity."

True to their enlightened views, the real breakthrough for women came when, in an earnest fight for freedom, Gandhi launched the civil disobedience movement, and with unerring instinct exhorted the women to come out of their hearths and homes to take part in it shoulder to shoulder with their menfolk. Armed with an astute perception into the psyche of 'warring' masses, he correctly gauged that while men might get swayed occasionally towards violence, a preponderance of women would lend the movement a more pacific modus operandi. Other factors which facilitated the active participation of women in large numbers was that this movement was an all-pervasive movement and one in which womenfolk could participate wherever they were — in villages, towns and even cities — working mainly with crowds of men and women with whom they were already familiar with as their neighbors and acquaintances. They proved themselves particularly effective in picketing liquor and foreign cloth shops "because it would be a poor specimen of man who would break through the cordons and the moral barriers put up by their own womenfolk." The civil disobedience movement made it possible for women to join it without any great fear of physical violence beyond that of the occasional lathi blows or imprisonment — punishments which they bore cheerfully and without complaints in their noble endeavour to shake off foreign yoke.

Indeed the Indian National Congress had realized the importance of women's participation even before when those two national colossus - Gandhi and Nehru - appeared on the firmament of Indian politics, imbuing them with an inspirational energy that was as unique as it was remarkable. As early as 1885, at the time of the inauguration of the Indian National Congress, A.O. Hume had said that, "the political reformers of all shades of opinion should never forget that unless the elevation of female element of the nation proceeds with equal pace with the work, all their labor for the political enfranchisement will prove in vain."

In September 1920, the non-cooperation resolution was put forward before the Congress session at Calcutta. It was ratified at Nagpur in December of the same year. In the first non-cooperation movement, women in the different parts of the country joined the processions and propagated use of khadi and charkha. Some of them left government schools and colleges. The diminutive Mahatma Gandhi in his broken Hindi gave stirring speeches to large gatherings of women, inspiring and motivating them; giving the freedom movement a new direction, a dynamic fulcrum of functioning, a dimension and scope which only he, with his experience of South Africa behind him and his subsequent awareness of the potentialities of women as passive resisters, could have done. Comparing British rule to Ravana-rajya, Ghandhi maintained that just "as Sita did not cooperate with Ravana, so the Indian people must not cooperate with this *Rakshasi-Sarkar*." Addressing numerous public meetings in different parts of the country, he appealed to women to donate their jewellery for the national cause and help him make collections for the Tilak Swaraj Fund. Almost a decade later, Pandit Nehru was to remark about the instinctive almost compulsive response to Gandhi's call to the womenfolk of India, thus:

> Women had always been there of course, but now there was an avalanche of them, which took not only the British Government but their own men-folk by surprise. Here were these women, women of the upper or middle classes, leading sheltered lives in their homes, peasant women, working-class women, rich women, poor women pouring out in tens of thousands in defiance of government order and police *lathi*. It was not only that display of courage and daring, but what was even more surprising was the organizational power they showed.

Sushila Nayar recalls a meeting held at Rohtak where the hall was filled to its capacity with women in *lehangas* and rustic clothes and Gandhi with his outstretched hands received money and jewellery for the Tilak Fund. Renuka Ray recalls how she heard Gandhi's speeches in Calcutta in 1920 and what a profound impression they made on her. The girls of Diocesan College, of which she was a student, went to a women's meeting where the Mahatma asked them to give up their jewellery. Renuka Ray gave hers and was followed by a large number of women. Many of these girls, including herself gave up their studies and joined the non-cooperation movement. Vijaya Lakshmi Pandit describes the first impact of Gandhi on her when he visited Allahabad and stayed at Anand Bhawan, in these words:

> I sat on the ground with my cousin and the little figure began to speak. He was quite incongruous. He spoke very bad Hindi and yet the interesting thing was that none of these things seemed to matter after the first few minutes. He was saying something which was gripping everybody. He was compelling people to look at him, to

listen to him. He ended by appealing to women to give him something.

There was a sudden spate of concerted activities and actions characterizing the spirit of national fervour with which the people were infused, a vociferous denunciation of foreign goods. Meetings and satyagrahas which symbolized the changing content of women's attitudes, and their urgent desire to play a meaningful role in shaping the destiny of the country and liberating it from foreign yoke, were in full spate. Physically and psychologically, they were attuned to playing out in real life, the prophetic vision of the German thinker/poet Hugo Von Hofmannsthal:

Many indeed must perish in the keel
Chained where the heavy oars of vessel smite;
Others direct the rudder on the bridge,
And know the flight of birds and charted stars.

(Translated from German by Jethro Bithel)

Basanti Devi accompanied her husband, Deshbandhu Chittaranjan Das in his tours of Bengal and even asked women to boycott foreign goods. Some members of the family were even arrested but released soon afterwards. Under the leadership of the women of C. R. Das's family, women volunteers went about the streets of Calcutta selling khadi. Basanti Devi presided over the Bengal Provincial Conference at Chittagong in April 1922. In the same year Kasturba Gandhi presided over the Gujarat Provincial Conference and appealed to women to take to spinning and wearing khadi. In Lahore in December 1922, Kasturba presided over a meeting where the President of the Reception Committee was Lala Lajpat Rai's wife, Radha Devi. In Allahabad, Rameshwari Nehru started a "Kumari Sabha" to encourage girls to talk and debate and take part in public discussions. Mrs Pandit was a frequent speaker at these meetings and Jawaharlal used to give her the points for her speeches.

There were stalwarts like Hemprabha Majumdar, who in the face of physical violence and *lathi* blows, remained undaunted. In fact, she was so courageous that C. R. Das called her "the only man outside jail." Women in various other parts of the country made their contributions to the movement. The women of Contai district, Midnapur helped Birendra Nath Sasmal's movement there and the indomitable Bee Amman, the mother of Mohamad and Shaukat Ali, boldly discarded her veil and addressed meetings all over India, advocating the use of khadi and Hindu Muslim unity. Despite all this, women's participation in the first cooperation movement was not on a mass-scale and was mainly confined to those whose husbands, fathers, brothers or sons had already joined the struggle and were in jail.

The Borsad Satyagraha of 1923-24 was marked by a massive turn-out of women. Even the Mahatma remarked that he had never seen such huge gatherings of women for each meeting addressed by him in Borsad, Auklao and Kaithar which had women attending in thousands literally to listen to him. Alaras created a record of sorts for almost every woman in the village left her hearth and home to attend Gandhi's meetings. Predictably enough, they displayed far greater courage than the menfolk when the police confiscated their cows, buffaloes and other property.

While in the Bardoli Satyagraha of 1928 no women were seen at first, from April onwards they not only outnumbered men in political gatherings but held separate meetings of their own as well. So deep was their sense of commitment in fact, that Sardar Patel, the "iron man" of Indian politics, remarked that they were far better than men in steadfastness of purpose, simplicity and purity. Such women thronged to his meetings singing patriotic songs and ultimately the peasants of Bardoli were forced to leave their land and their cows and buffaloes were confiscated. However, they were stubbornly adamant not to pay taxes. The women supported the men fully. Manibehn Patel, Mithubehn Petit and Bhaktibehn Desai fixed their tents and huts on the land declared to be sold by the government. Bardoli set a new precedent as this was the first time that simple, unsophisticated rural women participated in the freedom struggle, though they belonged to the well-off peasant sections, who owned the land they cultivated.

The year 1930, which began with the pledge of Independence, was to witness a momentous event. In March the same year, Mahatma Gandhi declared his intentions of breaking the salt law and manufacturing salt at Dandi, a small coastal village 241 miles away from his Ashram at Sabarmati. The famous Dandi March which commenced on 12 March 1930 and comprised a batch of 79 marchers only, excluded women completely. For the Mahatma did not want it to appear as if he, along with his daring band of followers, were taking shelter behind a bunch of women. It was a well known fact that the British would not touch women, just as Hindus would not kill cows. But this seemingly unnatural division of the sexes in a non-violent campaign, was both unacceptable and abhorrent to the awakened consciousness of the new Indian woman, emerging triumphant on the firmament of Indian nationalism. They felt that no demonstration of solidarity, no action denoting opposition to foreign rule, should exclude women. Therefore no marches, no imprisonment's, no demonstrations should ever take place without them. Two patriotic young women from high class families defied orders and jumped into the fray — both were arrested at Ahmedabad. These were none other than Dadabhai Naoroji's grand-daughter, Khurshedbehn who had written an angry letter to Gandhi asking him why he was preventing women from joining him, and Mridula Sarabhai, then a student of Gujarat Vidyapith. Ms Sarabhai jumped into the struggle despite Principal Kaka Kalekar's orders to the contrary.

However, women turned out in large numbers along the route to greet him. At the village of Abhrama on 10 April 1930, in an audience of nearly five thousand, nearly half were women.

It must be mentioned here that all the women were not attracted by Gandhi's popular doctrine of non-violence, some believed him to be an incarnation of "Ranchodrai" or Lord Krishna and came in thousands because they were eager to have his darshan. Whether politically or spiritually motivated, Gandhi steadfastly lectured to the women all along his route, exhorting them to picket liquor and toddy shops and stores selling foreign cloth. He told them to refuse to carry *chatties* of toddy and attached great importance to all these activities though to the women themselves such anti government action seemed rather secondary. According to him, "Drinks and drugs sap the moral well-being of those who are given to the habit. Foreign cloth undermines the economic foundations of the nation and throws millions out of employment. The distress in each case is felt in the home and therefore by women."

The valiant band of marchers, with the indomitable Gandhi at their head, finally reached Dandi on 13 April 1930 and were received by over 500 enthusiastic women there. In fact the Mahatma had nominated the famous poetess and ardent freedom fighter, Sarojini Naidu, to lead the raid on Dharasana after he and Abbas Tyabji were arrested. And she steadfastly kept her faith with him, never allowing violence to break out at any stage. Accompanied by Manilal Gandhi, she marched at the head of a peaceful army which was stopped near Dharasana. The volunteers, severely beaten and suffering from intolerable hunger and thirst in the scorching summer heat, were cordoned off by the police, menacingly armed with sticks and guns and determined that the women would advance no further in their proposed raids on the Dharasana Salt Works. Unperturbed, Sarojini Naidu sat amidst them on a deck chair, ever smiling and encouraging her army.

Webb Miller, a renowned foreign correspondent for the United Press, who had seen two "serious riots at the Wadala Salt Pans" near Bombay and was informed by a "Gandhi sympathizer" of the impending non-violent demonstration — led by Sarojini Naidu — near the big salt pans of Dharasana, gives a fascinating eye-witness account in his book, *I Found No Peace*. When he finally reached Sarojini Naidu's assembly armed with his own copious supply of victuals and bottled water, he was welcomed and taken to her where she sat, the famous Indian poetess, stocky, swarthy, strong-featured, bare-legged, dressed in rough dark homespun robe and sandals. Welcoming Miller she explained "that she was busy marshalling her forces for the demonstration against the Salt Pans and would talk with him at length later."

Miller says in his book: "Mme. Naidu called for prayer before the March started and the entire assemblage knelt. She exhorted them: 'Gandhi's body is in jail but his soul is with you. India's prestige is in your hands. You must not use any violence under any circumstances. You will be beaten but you must not resist; you must not even raise a hand to ward off blows.' Her words were greeted with wild cheers."

The half mile march to the salt depots then commenced. The marchers cried *Inquilab Zindabad* as they proceeded. Half a dozen British officials guarded the salt pans with 400 Indian policemen who carried *lathis*. Miller then describes sickening sights of physical violence on the marchers who never resisted:

> At times the spectacle of unresisting men being methodically bashed into a bloody pulp sickened me so much that I had to turn away. The Western mind finds it difficult to grasp the idea of non-resistance. I felt an indefinite sense of helpless rage and loathing almost as much against the men who were submitting unresistingly to being beaten as against the police wielding the clubs, and despite the fact that when I came to India I sympathized with the Gandhi cause.

Soon thereafter, the intrepid Indian poetess was arrested by the Indian police. As she stood conversing with Miller and directing the sub-leaders of the *satyagrahis* to contain the people from responding violently to the inhuman beatings and kickings, one of the British officials approached her, touched her on the arm and said 'Sarojini Naidu, you are under arrest.' She laughingly shook off his hand and said: 'I'll come, but don't touch me.' The crowd cheered frantically as she strode with the British officer across the open space to the barbed wire stockade, where she was interned. Later she was sentenced to prison. Manilal Gandhi was also arrested. But the raids and beatings continued all over India for days.

Not only did women give their active support to the Satyagraha movement but they turned their own domestic world into shelters and sanctuaries for Congress workers. They also insisted on making contraband salt and started an intensive non-co-operative movement. They sold small packages of salt at street corners, picketed foreign cloth shops and prevented men from entering liquor shops. The leaders marched to the dealers themselves and asked them to abandon their trade interests. They preached the virtue of the spinning wheel, and the glamour of wearing home-spun khaddar.

In Bombay, Kamaladevi Chattopadhyay, Sarojini Naidu's sister-in-law, and Avantikabai Gokhale were among the first women to defy the government monopoly of salt manufacture and, thus, break the salt law. Kamladevi recalls that on April 1930, thousands of women strode down to the sea like proud warriors. But instead of weapons, they bore pitchers of clay, brass and copper; and instead of uniforms, the simple cotton saris of village India. One watched them fascinated and awe struck. How had they broken their age-old shell of social seclusion and burst into this fierce light of open warfare? What had turned their ancient quietude and turned them into militant rebels? Undoubtedly the women turned this struggle into a beautiful epic. When the police raided the Bombay Congress House where salt pans had been prepared, they found their way blocked by Mrs Perin Captain, Mrs Jamnabehn Ratanabehn and five other women volunteers. Kamaladevi Chattopadhyay also stood by the Police Superintendent who politely asked her to move away but she refused. Soon, Sewa Dal camps were opened in all parts of India to train women in the technique of Satyagraha and in political work and the fierce flame of obtaining Azadi that the Mahatma had ignited, was inextinguishable and shone like a beacon in those extraordinary times. As is abundantly apparent in the eloquent statement released to the press on this occasion, she said:

> A powerful Government could have paid no more splendid tribute to the far-reaching power of Gandhi than by the manner of his arrest and incarceration without trial, under the most arbitrary law in their statute book. It is really immaterial that the fragile and aching body of the Mahatma is imprisoned behind stone walls, and steel bars. It is the least essential part of it. The man and his message are identical, and his message in the living heritage of the nation today will continue to influence the thought and action of the world, unfettered and unchallenged by the mandate of the most autocratic government of the earth.

The indomitable Hansa Mehta, along with a few others had formed the Desh Sevika Sangh which was largely instrumental in organizing picketing in Bombay. In fact the picketing it organized was so highly effective that at one stage the government declared it as illegal. Thus, through that long, hot summer of 1930, day by day, the streets of Bombay would be livened in the early morning with songs of freedom sung by troupes of patriots rousing the people to action. Women would be found all over the city, sitting outside the liquor shops and foreign cloth shops, playing their little 'spinning wheels' (called *taklis*), silently warning every Indian that he must not buy from the shop.

Women stalwarts including Kamaladevi, Sarojini Naidu, Jaishri Raiji, Manibehn, Hansa Mehta, etc., organized a procession on Lokmanya Tilak's death anniversary on 1 August. Since the processions were banned in Bombay's Fort Area and the police refused to let them proceed, they sat through the whole night determinedly out in the open and in pouring rain.

The Satyagraha Movement was gaining momentum rapidly, snowballing into a nationwide crusade for freedom, which had committed leaders and participants in every corner of the country. In Madras the Salt Satyagraha Movement had leaders such as T. Prakasam, Nageswara Rao Pantulu and the remarkable Durgabai. Among some of the most fervent satyagrahis were the women from Karnataka,they not only provided food and shelter to Congressmen who were carrying on their work incognito, but often acted as messengers fearlessly ferrying secret information from one camp to the other. Among the scores of Karnataka Women who participated whole-heartedly in the struggle for freedom were Kamaladevi Chattopadhyay, Umabai Kundapur, Krishnabai Panjikar, Ballari Siddama and even Gowramma and her co-workers to a lesser extent.

In Bihar also many women came forward courageously. Among those in the frontline were Mrs Hasan Imam who not only addressed several meetings of students in Patna but alongwith her daughter Mrs Sami and Mrs. C. C. Das as well as several other women at Patna, organized a procession in the city to inaugurate an intensive campaign of boycott of British goods. During the week ending 25 July 1930, Patna witnessed two demonstrations in which nearly 3000 women took part and the leaders courted arrest. Mirabehn toured Bihar extensively, carrying on a successful propaganda for the use of charkha and women leaders were also advocating non-payment of the *chowkidari* tax.

In the East, in Calcutta a Ladies Picketing Board was formally formed and "various women's organizations such as the Nari Satyagraha Committee, Rashtriya Mahila Sangh, Nikhil Jatiya Nari, broke the salt law and sent batches of women for picketing and courting arrest." In the North, in the Punjab, a massive procession of approximately five thousand like-minded women inaugurated the civil disobedience movement. *Prabhat-pheries,* picketings and meetings became the order of the day. Prominent among the leaders of the movement in Lahore were Lala Lajpat Rai's daughter, Parvati Devi and Lado Rani Zutshi, a close relative by marriage of Pandit Jawaharlal Nehru. On 10 April 1930, at a mammoth rally held under the auspices of the city Congress Committee at the Municipal Gardens outside Mori Gate in Lahore, the huge gathering of 40,000 people were briefed in detail about the programme of civil disobedience which was to begin in Lahore the next day. Elsewhere in the Punjab, in Jullundur to be precise, the satyagraha campaign against the salt law was inaugurated on 17 April, 1930 by Raizada Hans Raj in the presence of an impressive gathering of 20,000 people. A procession consisting of 400 women and 20,000 men marched to the Gandhi Mandap. Women performed the tilak ceremony. Then the volunteers manufactured salt.

Lord Irwin's address to the Central Assembly on July 1930 was marked by picketing on the first day by a specially chosen group of twenty-seven women volunteers drawn from Lahore, Ambala and Simla. Assembled outside the Central Legislative Assembly Hall, they waved little black flags on his arrival and chanted in unison "Irwin, go Back." Then off they went, singing national songs, marching in an orderly procession. Meanwhile, back in Lahore, Lado Rani Zutshi's daughter, Manmohini Sehgal, the president of the Student's Union, organized a series of student's strikes and picketing at college gates and was ultimately arrested along with some of her companions. The list of eminent women freedom fighters then interned in Lahore jails read like an impressive 'who's who' and included such well-known personalities as Mrs Zutshi, Kamala Nehru's mother Smt Rajpati Kaul, Parvati Devi, the redoubtable Aruna Asaf Ali and Satyavati from Delhi. The grand-daughter of Swami Shradhanand, Satyavati's role in awakening women in Delhi was indeed remarkable. She not only led women to picket shops but also urged the affluent ladies who came to bathe in the waters of the Jamuna, to abstain from wearing foreign clothes.

However, it was in Gujarat, the home State of Mahatma Gandhi where women's participation was the largest and perhaps the most impressive. Special classes were started in the Sabarmati Ashram to train women *Satyagrahis*. Mridula Sarabhai who was the moving force behind this venture, was later arrested and sent to Belgaum jail. A women oriented organization, the Rashtriya Stree Sabha carried on an intensive propaganda for the widespread use of Swadeshi. Kasturba, Saraladevi Sarabhai, Mridula Sarabhai, Indumati Sheth, Mithubehn Petit (the grand-daughter of Sir Dinshaw Petit), Nandubehn Kanuga and Khurshedbehn Naoroji (Dadabhai Naoroji's grand-daughter and a full time worker), were among the leaders in Ahmedabad. On analyzing the composition of the leadership we find that most of them were either from the families of millowners — Sarabhais, Kasturbha Lalbai, Ranchodlal Chotalal or from the Sabarmati Ashram. But apart from them, thousands of other women who joined the *prabhat-pheries*, processions and picketed shops, whether they be students, teachers or just plain ordinary housewives, not all of them were educated, sophisticated women. Some, like Gangabehn Vidya who had been widowed at the tender age of sixteen, had read about Gandhi's heroic struggle in South Africa, met him in Bombay when he advised her to learn spinning at Manibhawan and later become an inmate of Sabarmati Ashram. On 21 January, 1931 she led a procession of 1200 women in Borsad. The procession was lathi-charged, Gangabehn was severely beaten up and bled profusely, but she did not give up the tricolour she was carrying. She was in and out of jail till 1934, when she settled in Bochasan doing constructive work in the rural areas.

Similar episodes of unprecedented courage and intense patriotic fervor were etched in blood and sweat on the vast topographical map of India. More than 80,000 people were arrested during the Salt Satyagraha and more than 17,000 of these were women. Writing from Naini jail, the pride evident in his words, Pandit Nehru said: "... I had a special feeling of satisfaction because of the activities of my mother, wife and sisters, as well as my many girl cousins and friends; and though I was separated from them and was in prison, we grew nearer to each other." Indeed the role of the Nehru women in the freedom movement is legendary and need not be repeated here in detail. Suffice it to say that they were in the forefront of the national movement and had spontaneously responded to the Mahatma's call to join the civil disobedience movement. Pandit Nehru's sister, Vijaya Lakshmi Pandit, recalls how the great Gandhi transformed their lives. For not only Vijaya Lakshmi and Krishna but the aged Swarup Rani and the ailing Kamala Nehru were in the frontline of leadership in Allahabad, organizing processions, addressing meetings and picketing foreign cloth and liquor shops. Once when the police lathi charged a procession, frail Swarup Rani got a blow on her head and fainted. She, along with her husband, the dynamic Motilal Nehru willingly forfeited all their luxuries and suffered untold hardships, undaunted. No other family, as a unit, fought harder or sacrificed more for India than the Nehru family. For three generations, men and women stood side by side and formed a strong bulwark of national warfare, falling in entirely with Mahatma Gandhi's ideals of non-violence; but staunchly contributing their own brilliant ideas and service to the nation.

In October 1940, Mahatma Gandhi, undeterred by the punishing physical experiences he so cheerfully bore for the sake of the national movement, inaugurated the civil disobedience movement and women courted arrest by the dozens. One of the first women to be imprisoned was the indomitable Sucheta Kriplani who had been in charge of the women's department of the All India Congress Committee since 1939. In fact, Gandhi's Quit India Resolution in 1942 meant a renewed period in jail for men and women leaders alike. When he himself was arrested on 9 August, 1942, the Quit India movement was practically leaderless as all the senior members of the Congress had been put behind bars. However, as the news of all these arrests spread, the people of India rose as one united nation and spontaneous hartals took place all over the country; women actively participaed, taking out processions, holding meetings and demonstrations and organizing strikes. "Renu Chakravartty was a student leader with a strong Communist bias, and there were countless young women in Bengal who had taken part in the earlier terrorist movement of the 30's and others again who had joined the Labour movement."

In Assam, a young teenage girl courageously led a procession of five hundred and was subsequently killed in the police firing. Whereas in Midnapur district in Bengal, women played a notable part and were, distressingly enough, the victims of police atrocities. In the west of India, in Bombay to be precise, Usha Mehta played a stellar role with her daring underground broadcasts. Operating an underground radio station, the "Congress Radio" news broadcast at precisely 7.30 pm every evening, continued from August to 13 November 1942 with Usha herself broadcasting the news, till she and her colleagues were all arrested and sentenced to four years' rigorous imprisonment and sent to Yeravada jail, where she found herself among 250 women political prisoners. Usha Mehta belonged to a group headed by none other than the highly respected Dr Ram Manohar Lohia.

Aruna Asaf Ali another "tigress of nationalism", went on to become a romantic revolutionary and one of the most important figures of the 1942 movement. For four long, glorious years she remained underground, evading arrest, publishing bulletins and editing, along with Lohia, the *Inquilab*. The British government desperately wanted to arrest her and the then princely sum of five thousand rupees was announced as a reward for her capture. Yusuf Meherally was to write in later years that if "the heroine of 1857 was the Rani of Jhansi, that of the 1942 revolution was undoubtedly Aruna Asaf Ali."

While hundreds and thousand of women all over the country eagerly responded to Gandhi's call for taking up the cudgels for India's freedom, there were some who could not accept his creed of non-violence. During the Swadeshi agitation in Bengal in 1905, some women helped the revolutionary leaders. A force to be reckoned with was Sarladevi Chaudhurani, who not only maintained close ties with the Suhrid Samiti of Mymensingh and toured extensively in the Punjab, but also opened Arya Samaj branches for women where many of the members sympathized with the revolutionaries. There were yet other women outside India who were active supporting Indian revolutionaries. Perhaps the most prominent among them was Madam K. R. Cama who came in contact with one Shyamaji Krishnavarma. Her main activity was to send to India, what the British regarded as seditious literature and assist revolutionaries financially. She started a monthly journal *Bande Mataram* in 1909 from Paris and opposed the Press Act and censorship imposed by the British in India. In fiery language she encouraged revolutionary sentiments. She was also associated with Savarkar's Abhinav Bharat Society.

Revolutionary organizations sprang up in various parts of the country but those in Bengal with Dacca, Comilla and Chittagong as the storm centers, were particularly active and connected with potentially explosive activities. Young college girls who joined these secret societies, fearlessly spearheaded daring raids. Two such courageous women were Kalpana Joshi and Preeti Waddadar, both were associated with the Chittagong armoury supplementary trials and ultimately sentenced to transportation for life.

An important training and recruiting ground for future revolutionaries "The Chhatri Sangha" or Women Students Association started at Calcutta in 1928, enrolled girls from prestigious educational institutions. Thus, we find students from Brahmo Girls' School, Victoria School, Bethune College, Diocesan College and Scottish Church College joining the Chhatri Sangha, organizing study circles, taking lessons in *lathi* and sword play and even learning motor driving and how to fly an aeroplane. Bombs were smuggled in surreptitiously in small tin or leather suitcases to be kept in the hostel or delivered to different people.

In Delhi, seventeen year old Roop Vati Jain was in charge of a bomb factory under Chandra Shekhar Azad. Run under the pseudonym of "Himalayan Toilets", this factory on Qutub Road produced picric acid, nitro glycerine, gun-cotton and other ingredients for bombs. Sushila Devi, yet another keen revolutionary worker, associated fearlessly with such well-known revolutionaries as Bhagat Singh and Batukeshwar Dutt and deliberately cutting her own finger, put blood tilaks on the foreheads of both men on 9 April, 1929. Because of her association with Bhagat Singh to whom she sent letters, rakhi and food, she was arrested and imprisoned. She was declared an absconder in the Delhi and Lahore conspiracy cases and served a number of jail terms.

In the early forties, the formation of certain strongly supportive organizations outside the country, broadened the base of the fight for India's freedom. An Indian Independence League was formed in January 1942 in Kuala Lumpur and Indian women in South-east Asia worked for the cause of India's emancipation from the abhorrent British rule. Two months later, in March the same year, a women's section of the League was started and Indian women from Malaya, Thailand and Burma enlisted as volunteers. Events rapidly gathered momentum and in the month of July, Subhas Chandra Bose addressed a meeting and his clarion call to women to share in the burden of the battle for Azadi, infused the movement with a new spirit and heightened enthusiasm. Subsequently, a purely women's regiment, the "Rani of Jhansi Regiment, was formed with

Lakshmi Sahgal Swaminadhan as the Captain. She was Minister of Social Welfare and Medicine in the Azad Hind Government."

In February 1946 widespread disturbances broke out in Calcutta to protest against the sentence imposed on Captain Abdul Rashid of the Indian National Army and the police opened fire on three different occasions in different parts of the city. In the same month, on the 12th of February to be precise, a huge mile-long procession of over one lakh people, including women paraded through the Dalhousie Square area as a mark of protest against Captain Rashid's sentence. Following close on the heels of this massive public protest, the Bombay naval ratings went on strike. Thousands of railway workers, textile workers and students took out processions and went on strike. In Bombay there were repeated clashes between the police and military on the one hand and defiant crowds on the other. There were students' and workers' strikes in Calcutta and Madras to express sympathy with the demands of Royal Indian Navy personnel and to protest against the repressive policy of the government in which women participated.

To sum up, there were a few important and vital factors which greatly influenced women's active participation in the Indian struggle for freedom and their valuable contribution to it. Most women joined the freedom struggle because, like the men, they were inspired by patriotism and wanted to see the end of foreign rule from their motherland. However, women from such distinguished families such as those of Motilal Nehru, C.R. Das, Jamnalal Bajaj or Lajpat Rai were automatically motivated to join the national movement and to share in the privations and sufferings of their menfolk. In homes where a nationalistic atmosphere prevailed, it was but natural that the women were influenced by the ambient patriotic overtones and wished to become an integral part of the struggle for India's freedom. Bina Das's father was a teacher and a friend of Subhas Bose. Kamala Das Gupta recalls how her father was connected with the Swadeshi movement in Bengal. Sucheta Kriplani's family had been wearing and using Swadeshi since the 1920s. Books played no mean role in inspiring the Indian women; while Annie Besant's autobiography influenced Kamaladevi, thought-provoking novels such as Saratchandra Chatterji's *Pather Dabi* motivated some of the Bengali revolutionaries. But undoubtedly, the most vital factor which influenced such impressive numbers of women to join the national struggle for freedom and to fight with an impassioned zeal which was as selfless as it was admirable, was the overpowering influence of certain key personalities. While student leader Dhiresh Mazumdar Surya Sen exercised a great influence over young girls who subsequently joined extremist groups in Calcutta and Chittagong, others like Subhas Bose in Bengal, Vallabh bhai Patel in Gujarat, Rammanohar Lohia, Jawaharlal Nehru and, above all, Gandhi were influential in drawing women into the political arena. According to one eminent freedom fighter, namely Sucheta Kriplani, Gandhi's personality inspired confidence not only in women, but in their guardians-husbands, fathers, brothers who did not object to their womenfolk coming out of their sheltered homes to march in the streets. It was his letters to such highly respected women as Manibehn Patel, Prabhavati Devi, Gangabehn and others which revealed in depth how he understood their strengths, hopes as well as ambitions. Firmly asserting that women were the true *satyagrahis*, he not only gave them due importance but also the necessary sense of direction by allotting to them specific tasks. His program thus had a special appeal for them for his non-violent modus operandi required such intrinsic qualities as tolerance, the ability to suffer and of course, courage — qualities possessed by women in abundant measure.

Initially, political awakening among women as among men in India, was somewhat limited and confined to the cities, and largely to those with middle-class backgrounds, namely, the professional, business and educated classes. The widening of the nationalist movement brought into its ranks participation by industrial workers and certain sections of the peasantry; patidar peasant women of Ras, Borsad, Bardoli, Karadi and Matwad were active in the satyagraha movement in these areas. From the politically conscious area of Midnapur, many village women joined in and actively participated in the freedom struggle. Some Muslim women shed their *purdah* and with it certain inbred inhibitions and joined the struggle and even a few Parsee women became a part of the movement under the leadership of Gandhi. It would be relevant to mention at this juncture that many more women participated in the Salt Satyagraha and the Civil Disobedience Movement than in the Non-cooperation Movement. In 1942 only a few brave women like Aruna Asaf Ali, Sucheta Kriplani and Usha Mehta carried on underground activities.

In conclusion it must be said that political upheavals help in bringing about social change, and it is doubtful if a century of preaching and social work would have brought about the same change in the position of Indian women as was achieved in the wake of the two decades of political struggle in India. It is by their earnest participation in the political movement of the country that Indian women helped their own struggle for liberation, far in India feminism and nationalism were closely inter-linked. As the national movement gained momentum, the goal of independence became the only concern for both men and women. The cause was Indian; the goal India's freedom. The women's movement in India had none of the man-woman antagonism characteristic of women's movements in the West. In India, women were accepted as political comrades and given equal opportunities for participation in the freedom struggle and they have a record of which they might well be proud of.

References

Asthana, Pratima, *The Women's Movement in India*, Delhi: 1974.

Baig, Tara Ali, ed., *Women of India,* New Delhi: Publications Division, 1958.

Bhat, Usha, Role of Women in the Freedom Struggle in Ahmedabad, unpublished Ph.D. thesis, Gujarat University.

Gandhi, Mohandas Karamchand, *Young India*, 10 April, 1930.

Gopal, ed. *Selected Works of Jawaharlal Nehru.* Vol. V.

Medh, Sushmita, ed., *Jyoti Vikas Yatra*, Ahmedabad, 1971.

Mitra, H.N, ed., *The Indian Annual Register* Vol. I, Jan-June 1930, p. 36.

Nanda, B.R.,ed., *Indian Women—From Purdah to Modernity,* New Delhi: Vikas Publishing House Pvt. Ltd.

Navajivan, 28 November, 1920.

Nehru, Jawaharlal, *The Discovery of India*, New Delhi, 1964.

Patel, Manibehn V., *Borsad Satyagraha* (Gujarat) Ahmedabad, 1972.

Sengupta, Padmini, *The Story of Women of India*. New Delhi: Indian Book Company, 1974.

5

EDUCATION AND ENLIGHTENMENT

In the words of Buddha, "That country is the best which trains the minds of its people"- his wisdom manifest in this all encompassing statement.

It is more important, if there can be any comparison, for the women of a nation to be educated than its men. I say it by way of emphasizing the importance of the mothers, daughters and sisters of a nation. One of the truest measures of a nation's advancement is the state of its women. For out of the women comes the new generation, and it is from their laps that it begins to learn. Political revolution is important and economic revolution is still more important, but the most important of all is the social revolution in the people. It is in the measure that the social revolution succeeds that it provides the basis of the economic stability and progress. Women play the most important part in the social revolution.

Jawaharlal Nehru

(Speaking on the centenary celebrations of the great reformer Maharishi Karve on 18 April 1958).

The nineteenth century reform movements were the first organized all-India response to the challenges posed by colonial rule. They were initiated by the urban educated elite who, although they were a small proportion of the population, made extensive use of modern means of communication and thus came to acquire a widespread social, political and ideological hegemony. There was a great deal of questioning about the existing status of women in Indian society. The questioning, in turn, was generated by two concurrent but diverse streams of thought. One, known as Revivalism, objected that the existing status of women was not in keeping with the very ancient tradition, which was far more liberal. This group spoke of an Utopian past and desired a return to it. They considered that emancipation or, rather, liberalization of the Indian women was to come as a gift from the male section of the community and stressed on the gentle and submissive qualities inherent in a woman. But it was the second group, very aptly known as the Reformers, who did not possess such a passively fatalistic viewpoint, who strongly objected to the subordinate position of women as they believed both in the equality of the sexes and individual liberty. Obviously through a process of deductive logic, they reasoned that a society in which its women possessed a subordinate or subjugated position in respect of its male component, could not but be an unhealthy one. As well as an unbalanced one. Impressed by the humanism and application of rational thought in the European philosophy of the eighteenth and nineteenth centuries, they were greatly interested in the speculations of European intellectuals on society and social patterns and the works of Mill and Bentham were greatly favoured by this group. Fully convinced of the imminent need for social and political reform in India, the Reformers firmly believed that such reform was the only means by which India could once more emerge, with a civilization that she could justifiably be proud of. There emerged such outstanding reformers as Rammohun Roy 'the man who launched the ideological movement for the modernization of India' and along with his supporters, championed the cause of abolishing in-human practices such as the burning of widows. Roy also demanded that the inheritance laws be changed so that women should have the right to inherit property. His was not mere rhetoric but a purposeful and peaceful campaign. He published his own journal in which he freely and fully discussed his ideas and explained the controversies that were current at the time. In 1928, he founded the Brahmo Samaj whose members possessed an ideology similar to his own. Ranade, who was another remarkable reformer, fought to change public opinion on the issue of the Age of Consent of marriageable girls. He not only vociferously attacked the abhorrent practice of Child Marriage but also the ban on the remarriage of widows. While the orthodox were willing to grant that a girl widowed before reaching puberty, could be permitted to marry again, they were against widow remarriage of any other sort, considering any woman who indulged in the said act, as an adultress. Not withstanding this orthodox line of thought, a total of 138 cases of widow remarriage were recorded between the years 1860 and 1901, which in itself was a remarkable achievement. Another supporter of widow remarriage was the novelist Premchand who was regarded as among the most outstanding writers in Hindi and Urdu during this period. His novels and short stories, generally carrying a theme in support of social reform, were another factor in influencing public opinion.

Ranade, however, was very keen that there should be an organization devoted solely to promoting the cause of the emancipation of women, so that the movement should cease to be a local battle in certain areas, and should become a national cause. This laudable aim was achieved to some extent when the National Social Conference was inaugurated in 1887. And the founding of this worthy organization was assisted by the emergence of another aspect of the main problem namely, the demand for education for women.

The lack of facilities for the education of women had already caused a great deal of controversy and eminent thinkers like Vivekanand were of the firm opinion that women should be fully educated so that they could participate in social reforms and assist those who were propagating these reforms. His argument and a very valid one at that, was that women themselves were the most suitable judges of what was good for them and in which areas reforms or changes were required most urgently. In 1875, the Arya Samaj was founded by Dayanand Saraswati who felt that without education women could not distinguish right from wrong; behave themselves agreeably towards their husbands and relatives; beget children properly; train, nurture and bring them up well; do or see domestic duties done as they ought to be done. Dayanand advocated compulsory education for both boys and girls. Thus, despite its traditionlist (Revivalist) leanings, the Arya Samaj mobilized opinion in favour of reform and "education for women" was one of its pet slogans. The intellectual mentor of the movement and its prime mover, Dayanand, insisted that all girls should be educated until the age of 16. It is interesting to note, however, that his was not a narrow definition of education but a broad-based perception which decreed that the girls receive comprehensive instruction in languages, sciences, practical handicrafts and physical fitness. It did not seek to limit their education to the mere imbibing of domestic science alone, but strongly advocated an all-round educational background, similar to that given to men.

Tracing the genesis of his amazingly liberated ideology regarding women's education and the subsequent educational institutions established for the purpose, we go back to the sphere of Hindu religion. In this sphere, unlike Manu, Dayanand's interpretation of the Vedic tradition upheld the right of all individuals, including those from the most oppressed groups in Hindu society — women and Shudras — to enter into direct communion with god. It was from this laudable premise that the great reformer progressed and went on to champion the cause of women's education for he felt that all men and women (i.e. the whole mankind) have a right to study. He was of the firm opinion that an ignorant wife certainly could not participate as an equal partner with her husband in discharging her various social and religious obligations in the desired manner, as the women of the Vedic age did. Other reasons advanced in favour of women's education included: 'If the husband be well-educated and the wife ignorant or vice versa, there will be a constant state of warfare in the house.' Basically the message of

Dayanand's reform movement and all the constructive measures for the upliftment of women that he advocated were that 'women must not be ill-treated because they are the custodians of the family and the repositories of its honour'.

Providing large-scale education for girls was hampered by one very vital factor — that of early marriages. Thus, the spread of education among the female sex in India was inextricably interlinked with one of the burning issues of the times i.e. raising the age of consent of marriageable girls and having it enacted into a law with the utmost expediency. An amelioration of the abhorrent social practice of marrying young girls off when they had not yet reached puberty, would definitely lead to an increased time-frame in which to equip them with the requisite education and more broadminded perspectives.

Traditionally, if women were given schooling at all, it ceased at the primary level stage. However, the nineteenth century saw the opening up of a few private institutions for girls through the commendable efforts of such societies as the Brahmo Samaj, the Arya Samaj, as well as by certain Christian societies which were rendered somewhat ineffectual by social prejudices and the lurking fear that no girl from a respectable family was allowed to attend them, lest she be subjected to conversion to the western faith of Christianity. It was not until much later i.e. about the second decade of the twentieth century, when a 'European-type 'education became a definite asset in upper-class society in India. Convents and mission schools began to enroll a large number of girls from respectable families.

There were other predominating factors which were responsible for the stunted growth of female education in India. The Education Commission of 1884 discovered that there were only 1029 girl's school which came under the purview of the government for inspection purposes, in 1865-66. These declined to a dismal 317 in number in the next decade and a half i.e. by 1881-82. Indigenous schools were dying out with the destruction of the traditional elite which patronized them and the government was taking scant initiative to fill the vacuum. Colonial administrators noted with regret that 'if there is any one class of natives who might be considered as practically excluded from the benefits of Government primary schools for girls, it is the higher class who keep their women in strict *purdah,* which was another social practice which proved to be an obstructing force in the liberalization of the Indian woman and subsequently, the slowing down of her literary emancipation.

The situation was similar in both the Hindu and Muslim communities. The nineteenth century saw a number of Muslims, prominent among them Sir Syed Ahmad Khan, advocating more educational facilities for women and epitomizing an enlightened literary 'mien'. But such consciousness took a somewhat longer time to mature in Muslim society and penetrate its multi-layered structure of orthodoxy or religion and restriction and the concession were, therefore, granted at a later period. Indeed the stereotypical figure of Syed Ahmad as the architect of Muslim separatism, mesmerized by the British, remains 'unaffected by the knowledge of his contribution to introducing rational thought and English education in the last quarter of the nineteenth century. Similarly, the pioneering role of Hali, Maulvi Nazir Ahmad and Sheikh Abdullah, engaged in a project of 'reforming' Muslim women, finds little mention in communal histories and critiques of nationalism or separatism. Presumptive explanations are forwarded to delineate their conduct, maintaining that they were imbued with reactionary or communal tendencies. Unfortunately, unchanging scholarly perceptions and attitudes, derived from colonial knowledge and worldwide Islamist assertions express themselves in different ways and one is reminded time and again of 'the pervasive impact of Islam on its adherents, their enduring transnational links and their obsessive concern to defend Quranic values.

The Spirit of Renaissance

The nineteenth century, commented Maulana Abul Kalam Azad, 'marked a spirit of renaissance for the Indian spirit and

Aligarh was one of the centres of such renaissance'. And the erudite Zakir Husain, author of the *Wardha Scheme of Education* and a long serving Vice-Chancellor of Aligarh university, said to Jawaharlal Nehru on the latter's visit to the campus in November 1955: 'The way Aligarh works, the way Aligarh thinks, the contribution Aligarh makes to Indian life will largely determine the place Mussalmans will occupy in the pattern of Indian life.' Such predominantly magisterial assertions/generalizations, while they do not stand the test of historical scrutiny, definitely are a pointer towards the role assigned to the university in the great intellectual resurgence that took place in the last quarter of the nineteenth century — a phase undoubtedly dominated by the enlightened Syed Ahmad Khan and the Aligarh movement.

The post-mutiny era witnessed two very different generative thought processes or two kinds of reaction — one, a traditionalist backlash, sometimes militant but more often mute; the other a modernist response, represented in the 'Delhi school' and 'Aligarh movement'. First and foremost, the followers of Shah Waliullah attributed the political, social and moral 'decline' to Hindu and Shia accretions, to the Western concept of life which, with its extravagant individualism and materialism, was the antithesis of basic values formulated by the Quran. The message from the *Mujahidin* in the north-west frontier region and the *Faraizis* in rural Bengal, as indeed from their counter-parts in Eygpt, Sudan and Turkey, was that a programme of religious purification, together with religious education and Islamic conscientization in the form of publications, was an alternative to the 'degenerating' Western ideologies which had plunged the *Umma* into crises.

While the Muslim teachers of the Delhi college, subsidized by the British since 1825 and headed by a British principal, made strenuous efforts to demonstrate the compatibility of Islam with Western thought and values, elsewhere too significant educational trends were being established. These affected both Muslim men and women. While the Madarsa-i-Aliyah which flourished in Calcutta produced such luminaries as the historian Syed Ameer Ali (1849-1928) and Abdur Rahim (1867-1947), a judge turned politician, the nexus *vis-à-vis* repressive women's issues and a more enlightened approach was slowly but subtly undergoing a definite change. In the presidency town of Bombay, the tone was set by the Tyabji family whose head, Tyab Ali was the first Muslim to send his sons abroad for education, and the ladies of the Tyabji-Fyzee family first left *purdah* in 1894. His son, Badruddin Tyabji was the first Indian barrister in Bombay, the first Indian judge on the 'Original' side of the Bombay High Court, and the first Indian to act as Chief Justice of the Bombay High Court.

Greatly inspired by Muslim scholarship from Al-Farabi to Ibn Khaldun and Mohammad Abduh, a number of discerning writers came forward to address issues ranging from the social to the theological, applying an unbiased and discriminatory critical analysis of the topics in question. Thus Hali devoted his *Majlis an-nisa* to the plight of Muslim women. Syed Mumtaz Ali commented on polygamy, the age of marriage, *purdah* and the empowerment of Muslim women. Nazir Ahmad, a civil servant, set a model for writers in the *Mirat al-urus* (The bride's mirror) detailing the evils of polygamy and the virtues of female education and widow remarriage. Justice Shah Din in Punjab advocated training for Muslim girls, if not in scholarly pursuits then at least in the basic skills of reading, writing, arithmetic, hygiene and home economics. He was the first president of the Muhammadan Educational Conference in 1894, and he and Mohammad Shafi were the first Muslims to send their daughters to study at the Queen Marry College in Lahore. The liberal minded Badruddin Tyabji, first helped found and then successfully ran an educational foundation in Bombay. The major focus of his career was, undoubtedly, liberal education for both Muslim boys and girls. He also campaigned vigourously for the Age of Consent Bill which was adopted in the teeth of both Hindu and Muslim opposition and at the Muhammadan

Educational Conference in 1930 he pleaded for the abandonment of purdah. Earlier, Syed Ameer Ali stated at the All Indian Muslim Education Conference in 1891 that female education should advance at the same pace as male education. Spurred by an ambience of enlightenment and change, by the early twentieth century, a host of papers and periodicals edited by Muslims which adopted a liberal stand on women's education, appeared on the scene. These included the *Mussulman*, *Nabanoor*, *Mohammadi*, *Al-Eslam*, *Sadhana*, *Bulbul* and *Saugat*. In a nutshell, the activities of the likes of Ameer Ali and Badruddin Tyabji were spurred by the models of European women and European criticism of the treatment of women in Islam. This influenced the very issues they chose to address as well as their own interpretations. Reformist ideas in the early twentieth century were stimulated by the social and cultural transition and the intellectual ferment in Turkey, Egypt and Iran. For once, new models of conduct were found worthy of emulation, new icons replaced old ones in the temple of learning, and fresh ideas were imbibed and adapted to suit the Indian environment.

In Days Gone by

A certain similarity existed between the Muslims and Sikhs regarding the existing 'diktat' for the education of its women. While boys in the Punjab of pre-annexation days received secular, religious and even some vocational trainings, 'for girls learning was confined to the reading of religious texts.' Among the Muslims and Sikhs, the imperative to read the sacred texts made female literacy socially acceptable. The females of the upper-caste Hindu families received education, such as it was, in the relative privacy of their homes. Rarely indeed were they taught how to write, for this was considered an accomplishment which only the superior class of courtesans were supposed to be adapt at. Therefore, even the few women (other than courtesans) who were conversant with writing skills, were understandably hesitant to admit to their accomplishment.

Khan Ahmed Shah, Extra Assistant Commissioner, Hoshiarpur, summing up upper caste opinion on a suitable form of education to be provided for women, said:

> With the exception of a few books especially compiled for girls, the course of instruction is the same as that followed in primary schools. Such instruction is not liked by the people, and the existing schools are not popular among the respectable classes. In fact, to render these schools really useful and popular,religious instruction is indispensible. Neither would it be so impracticable, as in the case of boys, as there are separate schools for Christian, Muhammadan and Hindu girls.

Orientalists like Leitner also subscribed to the view that women's education should be esssentially religious. His underlying reasons for holding this view were motivated purely by the interests of colonialism. But the logic was not very different from that of the others operating in the field of female education. Working on the firm conviction that 'it was the women in the joint family who were the bulwark of religion, fear of god and fear of authority' he felt it would be absolutely ruinous to give them an education similar to men. While the nationalist ideas of the educated youth might be tolerated by his female relatives at home, the moment he questioned the supremacy of religion or god, he would, in all probability, be 'slapped on the mouth with his mother's slipper.' In the long run, therefore, Leitner felt it would be far more advisable to have girls instructed in indigenous schools, by the scholarly Pandits and Mullahs; or, alternatively, to let them pick up a smattering of education at home, so that religious dogmatism should continue to be the dominant colour of women's mental world.

Lala Mulraj, the Extra Assistant Commisioner, reiterating very similar ideas on behalf of the Punjabi elite, said:

> As to the girls' school for Hindus and Muhammadans maintained by the Missionaries, perhaps they are doing

> more harm than good to the country by trying to shake the faith of the girls in their religion, which is so intimately connected with morality, and by teaching them to sing Christian songs in the vernacular. If the primary girls' schools maintained by the Government and the Missionaries were closed, it would make a great saving of resources and be productive of no harm. Female education, at least among the Hindus, can be left alone.

Thus, the content of female education was suspect not only due to the underlying fear of Christian proselytization especially where the teachers constituted low class women converts, but also due to certain other reasons. Government schools, with their quota of male teachers and inspectors, were invariably associated with a relatively freer mixing of the sexes which was more prevalent among the lower castes but totally taboo among the upper caste families. Because of the dismally low wages given to women teachers in girls' schools and the existing discrimination between the salaries paid to male and female teachers in schools, very few good women teachers were available. Often male teachers had to be employed for girls schools. As W.M. Holyrood of the Punjab Education Department so succinctly summed up; 'Frequently an incompetent old man is employed when no female teacher is available... If (salaries) were on the same scale as those provided for boys' schools, all other difficulties might perhaps be surmounted.' Not only were most of the students in government and Mission schools for girls were from the lower (caste) strata of Indian society — Punjab Education Report of 1869-70 cites a predominance of Muslim women of low castes in schools for women - but so were the majority of men and women in normal schools who were trained to be teachers. They comprised largely of the lower caste women and those women from the upper caste of society who had no (other) means of earning a decent living to support themselves and who were taking to education at this time, even though the education imparted in these schools had very little relevance to their life conditions. Basically, therefore, they turned to these institutions for the very same reasons that they readily accepted the charity of the missionaries — these were among the very few options available to them in which they could earn a meagre livelihood.

Educating and elevating to a certain social strata of acceptability, the lower and less privileged classes of Indian society, should, logically, have been a worthy campaign, worthy of adoption and emulation on a national basis. It is ironical, therefore, that the upper, suppossedly 'liberated' classes of society subscribed to certain ideological prejudices which propelled the issue of female education to the forefront of the national arena and made it a highly explosive issue. There were many reasons responsible for this as the following statement amply illustrates:

> The upper classes look upon indiscriminate extension of education with disfavour. They consider education as their sole birthright and privilege and any extension of it to the lower classes as destroying that distinction which they formerly enjoyed. They also say that education unfits the lower classes because of their position and occupation in life, and makes them discontented.

A woman from a lower caste who had the opportunity of acquiring a modern education and automatically moved into a 'respectable' profession, was viewed as a threat to both the caste and the sex hierachies. From time immemorial, sexual harassment and exploitation of the lower caste women had been the prerogative and the privilege of the so called 'chaste' men of the upper crust of society. Prostitutes were obviously women from the lower classes but even those women who were in the performing arts, were considered 'fallen women'. Not to mention those who were proficient in the literary art of writing. Unfortunately, practices were irrevocably linked to professions and class. They were seen through a miasma of superciliousness and a strong sexist bias. If we attempt to analyze this somewhat rigid stratification of society or caste bias, we would, in all probability, unearth a deep seated feeling of insecurity. Thus, the hitherto unchallenged shell of superiorty with which the upper castes (of men especially) surrounded themselves, was being shattered into smithereens by the spread of education and enlightenment. No matter what be the originating or catalytic forces responsible for such a change. Once again Leitner, the confirmed orientalist, comes to our rescue when he puts forward his perceptions thus:

> The female education given by us was avoided by the more respectable, because it too closely resembled that enjoyed by a class, which, if not criminal, to which our system is now reducing it, was not reputable, although under the caste system which prevents society being gangrened, it confined vice and made it hereditary, if not respectable.

The hotly debated topic of female education with the tussle between the Punjabi elite, on the one hand, and the government and missionary forces on the other, continued, triggering off the efforts of the Arya Samaj for reform in women's status, with women's education at the core of their emancipation.

The partriarachal family structure, hitherto the pivot of Indian society and the source from where all forms of authority and sanction flowed, now seemed to be threatened and strengthening of the patriarchal family, therefore, was an important motivating factor behind the reforms suggested. Various prevalent social evils such as the inhuman practice of child marriage, the brutal life that came with compulsory widowhood, prostitution (especially when its tentacles began to reach the women of upper caste homes) and the increasing estrangement between husband and wife were all posing a threat to the stability of the patriarchal family of the upper castes and classes. Therefore, the question of reforms in the status of women from these sections of society became one of the central questions in the movement to reform Hindu society.

The Arya Samajists sought to effect reforms on multi-level platforms and did commendable work through preaching their doctrine of widow remarriage. Adopting the ingenious mode of pamphleteering, such literature, often dramatic in style, 'presented Samaj ideology in numerous forms as lectures, dialogues, moral tales, poetry, offering didactic entertainment to the literate Hindu'. Thus Munshi Jiwan Das in his tract *Sadah-i-Haq* (The Plain Truth), Pandit Lekh Ram in *Risala-i-Nawid-i-Begwan* (A Treatise Containing Glad News For Widows); Atma Ram in *Masala-i-Niyog* and Munshi Chatar Bihari Lal in *Risala-i-Dharm Mitra,* stated the various Samaj arguments in favour of widow remarriage. Campaigning basically for "virgin" and child widows, they succeeded in denting public opinion by the early twentieth century and it is indeed heartening to note that 'the Vedic Magazine reported that between 1895 and 1901, a total of 400 such marriages were conducted by the Arya Samaj.' Assuming that marriage was the sole aim of a woman's life and the perfect panacea for all ills besetting her, they sought the institution of marriage as the most desirable way of integrating widows into society and negating the treat to the family that these unattached women represented.

But since complex issues such as those of widow remarriage and ban on child marriage required mainly propagandist work which simultaneously entailed the condemnation of social evils prevalent in the community, it was the question of women's education that seemed to be centrally significant. "Much of the constructive effort for the betterment of women came to centre around the question of women's education because through it the reformers could concretely demonstrate their vision of women's role in a reformed society."

Though upper caste women were its main focus when the Arya Samajist championed the cause of female education, they were successful in bringing about a certain overall acceptability to the process. The curricula in Samaj schools which received generous financial support from the commercial and trading classes, catered to the perceptions of men regarding the education required by women of their castes and classes. And included, per se, a heavy dose of both religion and domestic economy along with general education. For the course was geared towards the production of a 'modernized' educated housewife rather than equipping women so educated, with any professional capability. The question is, or was, as to how educated a wife does an educated man really desire. In a study done around the mid-twentieth century by Margaret Cormack, the researcher/ author draws the line at matriculation. Maintains Ms Cormack:

> The tradition is growing that 'a girl must go to school if she wants a chance for a good marriage.' Hence even modern education remains for the Hindu girl, a road to marriage. All informants agreed that a girl betters her marriage chances by going up to Matriculation (roughly the equivalent of high school) but that increasingly the penalty of higher education is the decrease of marriage chances.

A certain level of education, thus, became a desired qualification in the middle-class marriage market and corresponding to such a trend, the attendance at government schools also began to alter in terms of both caste as well as class composition. That apart, even the very nature and content of education in such schools began to change and adapt itself along the lines laid down by the Samaj schools. The Education Department greatly encouraged this trend and lower caste girls were adroitly channelized into mission schools. Such mission schools, set up specifically for the purpose of educating low caste students, came into existence at around the turn of the century.

It is important to note that while the reformers advocated women's education, they viewed it chiefly in terms of the traditional role definitions for women which were in consonance with the prevalent overall attitude of those times. Women, whether Indian or British, should be trained to be excellent wives and mothers. The government also possessed similar views, a fact which is amply reflected in the1913 Resolution of the Government of India, which stressed the need for a special curriculum of "practical utility" for girls. In keeping with the spirit of the times, the obvious preference of western educated Indian males for educated brides further strengthened the *raison d'être* of women's education and motivated parents to send their daughters to school. Therefore, similar to 'the *Zenana* set-up, schools not only provided the girls with the basics in reading, writing and arithmetic, but also taught them hygiene, needlework, embroidery and cooking i.e., those subjects that would prepare them for their future roles'.

Moral education which imparted the value of inculcating such values as obedience, chastity, patience and the joy of motherhood, also formed an intrinsic part of the curriculum. In fact, as Karlekar so succinctly sums it up, "the liberational role of women's education emphasized by radicals was clearly subordinate to the wider social goal which stressed willing acquiescence and not a questioning and enquring mind." The entire issue of a separate curriculum for boys and girls, in fact, gained momentum in the 20's and 30's and the majority view as expressed both in the Hartog Committee (1929) and the Basic Education Committee (1938-39), supported differential curriculum for boys and girls, in support of the arguments given above. Even the All India Women's Conference on Educational Reform (1927) demanded specialized education for women to fulfil their "peculiar" role in society. The prestigious Lady Irwin College, founded in 1932, was the result of this long standing demand.

Earlier, towards the close of the nineteenth century, various Stri Samaj Associations sprung up in response to the Arya Samajist movement for women's reforms. Flourishing under the auspices of the Arya Samaj, they provided valuable support for the Kanya Mahavidyalaya exoeriment during its crucial early years. Even though the KMV management was predominantly controlled by men, the success of the venture became increasingly dependent upon the active involvement of the female staff and students. Mai Bhagwati, the editor of *Sahayak*, the first Hindu magazine devoted to the cause of women's education to come out of the Punjab and Guru Bibi Devi were two of the most indispensable workers in the early days of the KMV. It would be pertinent to mention that Bhagwati's *Sahayak* was not only a sister publication of *The Regenerator of Arya Varta* but, its specific and laudable aim was to 'propagate the idea of women's education and call upon men to uplift the condition of women.' Savitri, a child widow and the first Acharya of the KMV, worked with single-minded devotion for the KMV being the moving spirit of the foundation of the Vidhwa Ashram or Widows' Home in 1907. Lajjyawati, a spinster, was a powerful orator and completely committed to spreading the KMV message far and wide. She, who saw the KMV through three eras, efficiently headed this remarkable institution as its principal for many years. Another remarkable woman and perhaps one of the most versatile of Samaj pracharikas, was Pandita Surender Bala, an excellent exponent of *bhajans*. She proved to be extremely successful in addressing public meetings in many different places, spreading the message of women's reform.

The KMV thus became a centre of gravity for educational efforts in the entire province and the *Panchal Pandita*, its organ since 1897, became an instrument to carry the message far and wide. It carried valuable information about the experiments being conducted at the KMV to different Samajes, almost all of which opened *pathshalas* and by 1918, more than 104 *pathshalas* followed the syllabus laid down by the KMV. Even some government schools included the books devised by the KMV in their syllabus, as well as the *Panchal Pandita*. It was, thus, well on the way to fulfilling the objectives with which it was launched: 'Of furninshing good reading matter to our sisters, cultivating their mental faculties by widening their interests by giving them a view of the world outside the closed Zenanas, and of infusing in them liberal sympathies and elevating ideas.' The KMV's role therefore, as a nucleus of educational activity in Punjab and North India, is nowhere more apparent than in its initiative in producing fairly copious literature for women such as *Pahli Pathawali*, *Doosri Pathawali*, *Akshar Dipika*, *Patra Kaumudi*, *Katha Vidhi*, *Balodvan Sangeet*, etc (mostly written by Devraj), which were translated into Marathi, Telugu, Gujarati and various other languages. While a Sahitya Bhandar run by the KMV, facilitated the distribution of such literature, the KMV itself was able to fulfil its aim of playing a central role in the spread of women's education as, since its very inception, it had addressed itself to the task of training teachers. Devraj's noble message that each one of the girls should become a Pathshala by herself so that not a single girl in the country should be left illiterate, constructively compounded the process of women's enlightenment.

However, while women's education did become the central question of the movement, it was ultimately envisaged only as a means towards an end and education in the KMV became an added qualification for girls in the urban middle class marriage market. The following excerpt amply illustrates the predominant underlying motive of KMV education:

> The aim of all education besides book learning, is to build up character and efficiency. This is particularly so in the cases of girls who have to adapt themselves to the environments into which their marriages carry them. She is a householder first and everything else afterwards.

> She must not only live but also believe and think like her husband before she can be happy. She must realize the future of her children and must sympathise with the system of education which is to bring them up as bread earners in the modern world.

Such was the justification offered as late as 1935-1936 when the KMV decided to introduce university examinations for its students. While this organization i.e., the KMV maintained the emphasis on subjects of 'feminine interest' in its curriculum until 1947, after independence the government put pressure on it to make the curriculum conform to the general university curriculum whereby, men and women are prepared for the same stultifying examinations.'

However, with the onset of India's independence in 1947, education, at least in principle, was seen in a new and different light. It was taken out of its conventional role model of 'inculcating and reaffirming values akin to the traditional role definitions for females,' and was now perceived more as a means for 'providing equality to women and enabling them to play multiple roles in society.' Social justice in the form of providing equal opportunities for all (one of the important tenets of the Indian Constitution) along with the 'agency of education was expected to reduce the existing disparities in our society.' Perhaps what India really required could best be summed up in the eloquent words of Abdul Mannan Syed: "Pragmatism and secularism in place of spiritualism, individualism in place of emotionalism, a spirit of critical enquiry in place of unquestioning acceptance of tradition and authority". A scrupulous adherence to such principles, and earnest and practical implementation of such noble renaissance traits would perhaps resolve the deplorable condition of women's literacy in the forties as enunciated by the poet Kazi Nazrul Islam. In an excerpt from a letter to Shamsunnahar Mahmud who, defying all odds, successfully appeared for and cleared her Masters examination as a private candidate in the turbulent years of the Quit India Movement in

1942, and then went on to become a writer, educationist, teacher, social worker and, later, a parliamentarian in East Pakistan, he very clearly says:

> The fate of our countrywomen is indeed lamentable. I have seen so many women of great promise wasted under the cares heaped on them by society and by the household. They are imprisoned by the demands of the household as if by an impregnable wall. That wall will never crumble unless women themselves revolt. Where is that brave woman who will launch the attack? Her destiny beckons.

The first woman to launch a systematic and uncompromising campaign for women's education was Rokeya Sakhawat Hossein (1880-1932). She was born into a zamindar's family in Payrabad, Rangpur. A pioneer of the women's movement in Bengal, she was a writer, an educationist, social worker, and a visionary who worked unceasingly for women education which she considered the first pre-requisite for emancipation. Abdul Mannan said in a glowing tribute: She was the forerunner of our modern sensibility and contemporary awareness, of our emancipated intellect, not just the pioneer of the women's movement alone. Rokeya's abiding contribution was in the sphere of education:

> She was too well read and observant to overlook the fact that women in patriarchal societies are exploited and oppressed but her immediate deep concern was for the group to which she belonged and which she knew best, Bengali Muslim women.

Herself a victim of the suffocating practice of *purdah* since the tender age of five and a keen observer who noticed that 'the separation between the public world of men (the *Bahir*), and the private world of women (the ghar) was particularly sharp in the Muslim community and maintained by the ideology and practice of *purdah* or *abarodh* (strict seclusion)' she fought determinedly to get the girls out of the darkness of seclusion and ignorance and established the Sakhawat Memorial Girls' school in 1911, in Calcutta. Undaunted by narrow-minded, stifling prejudices and practices, Rokeya had to go from door to door, entreating guardians to send their wards to school, guaranteeing security and *purdah* by offering covered transport for the girls. Rokeya's bold formulation of women's emancipation as laid down in her numerous writings, specially in *Stree Jatir Abanati* (The Degraded Condition of Women) and *Ardhangi* (His Other Half) is as relevant today, almost 70 years after her demise, as it was earlier. To her, women's emancipation meant the establishment of equal rights for women in the educational, economic and political spheres. That alone would ensure a just society where men and women could work side by side in harmony, like 'the two wheels of a cart'. Rokeya won, despite her orthodox Muslim detractors and the school established by her had a host of well-wishers, male and female. Men and women from the Brahmo, Hindu and Muslim communities from all over India congratulated Rokeya and lent her support. The prestigious *Amrita Bazar Patrika* along with liberal Muslim dailies and periodicals, supported the cause of women's education. A prolific writer herself, "in *Sugrihini* (The Good Housewife), Rokeya emphasizes the domestic role women have to play in society and the need to be equipped for this through proper education which included cooking, nutrition, nursing, chemistry, mathematics, and horticulture. Rokeya often used the 'perfect householder' argument to promote female education and induce parents to send their daughters to her school." And while we may not be ever able ot translate her feminist fantasy *Sultana's Dream*, her only piece of literary writing in English in which she vividly depicts '*Ladyland*' , a realm where women assumed the public role and men stayed indoors, into reality, we can and must propagate her 'perfect householder' concept in an innovative manner to consistently break down deeply entrenched prejudices and provide a minimum basic education for each and every 'new Indian woman'. For it is only when even the lowliest of the low - the woman in the village and field - is lifted out from her quagmire of ignorance and illiteracy (and subsequent misery) and provided with the quintessential knowledge of the 3 R's, to a level where she is able to function independently to an extent and articulate her basic requirements with confidence and dignity, would we be fulfilling her rightful destiny and imbuing her with the courage to follow the path of perseverence in acquiring greater knowledge and shaping herself into a worthwhile Indian woman capable of contributing to the country's progress.

Superior notions of patriarchy, the myth that girls are inferior to men and only suited for child-bearing and domestic duties, the widespread belief that girls don't have the aptitude and the intelligence to pursue studies, particularly in subjects like mathematics and science are only different facets of the same problem and not in the least tangential to each other. Firmly rooted in the Indian (predominantly male) psyche since time immemorial, such an ideology has received social and religious sanction through the centuries. But, with the cataclysmic forces of change challenging old, outdated norms and practices and striking violently, inevitably at rigidly defined gender roles, new and different permutations/combinations are emerging in the work field, at home, between men and women; women dare to articulate their individual dreams and desires and not all of them have to do with marriage and motherhood. In fact, among the educated and urban elite, there are many women who voluntarily choose to remain single, unwed and hassle free. Devoted to specific careers in which they achieve hitherto undreamt heights of power, fulfillment and fame.

Change is evident in spheres of both attitude and practice at certain levels; whereas previously parents from the lower and middle income stratas of society would not have been particularly keen to educate their daughters beyond the basic minimum requirement to make them reasonably articulate and independent, today the predominant reason given by parents from lower and middle-classes for educating their daughters is that education' especially higher education, is a necessary preparation for their economic security. Though an encouragingly increasing segment of this society may genuinely view it in terms of making their daughters economically viable and independent, more often than not it is linked to the issue of marriage marketability and her ultimate role as wife and mother. Therefore, even at this level, we need more sweeping attitudinal changes across the board; piecemeal reform will no longer do. The decision to pursue education, especially higher education, need not however be based on its implications in terms of marriage alone. Other perceived benefits such as prospective employment opportunities and the enhancement in social status may determine female access to education as well. The urge for knowledge or pursuing education as an end in itself is another reason cited by the upper income groups of society. Noble precepts these, they need benefit of those greater media publicization for the hovering tentatively on the verge of a more liberal approach but bound by custom and convention.

Amongst the lower rungs of society, one of the principal reasons which keeps many girls out of the schools especially in the rural areas is that they are required to work at a very young age in various domestic chores. They collect firewood, fetch water from near and far flung areas, carry food and water to parents at their places of work, look after their younger siblings, besides being responsible for many other activities. Unfortunately many of these girls are compelled to work at a very tender age, either as paid or unpaid workers. A substantial number of girls, more than boys are employed at an early age. Research on child labour has revealed that the survival of poor families often depends upon the work and income of their women and children. Therefore, attending schools *inter-alia* implies foregoing the opportunity to earn or help in the home. For the poor, the immediate costs of income lost as a result are often too high. Equipping the young girls with education that will ensure for them a brighter future, is thus, sacrificed at the altar of bare family subsistence and dire economic necessity. Poverty converts choices into compulsions and confines the mind in an iron cast of short-sighted immobility, incapable of perceiving the long term multiple benefits of learning and education, such as earning on a regular basis and being a source of greater familial support. Solutions present themselves in the guise of stringent as well as philanthropic measures which, if implemented scrupulously and simultaneously in all those areas where the abysmally poor exist carving out a meagre living for themselves, can at least alleviate poverty and illiteracy, if not eliminate it. For elimination on a national scale will require consistent, concerted effort and will on a massive scale. First, minimum basic education must be made compulsory for every child from at least five years of age onwards, with particular emphasis on the girl child and such an educational scheme be positively linked to attractive economic incentives for the family, thereby automatically encouraging the parents to send their daughters to school. It would be laudable if an alternative could be worked out whereby such parents were exposed to regular spaced out sessions with social workers imparting impartial and constructive advice about the child's future and the social and economic benefits about educating the girl child. But before we formulate socio-psychological and governmental programmes and policies for the education and uplift of the girl child specifically in rural areas, let us dwell upon and concretize certain physical parameters to make such a dream, a living reality.

The launching of 'Operation Blackboard' a scheme to provide minimum essential facilities in primary schools like two teachers, two rooms of 30 sq metres dimension, toilets, blackboards and chalks, etc., in 1986, was an acknowledgement on the part of the government that the majority of the primary schools (leaving aside the secondary schools) did not have adequate facilities. Approximately forty per cent of the primary schools in India don't have *pucca* buildings and about fifty-five per cent don't have drinking water. While the percentage of toiletless secondary schools in the rural areas is mercifully low, middle and primary schools in such areas suffer from an acute shortage of toilet facilities with as much as sixty-five to eighty per cent being without such an essential basic amenity. For children of a younger age group it can be very discouraging since it does not help them either to get toilet trained or develop superior habits of hygiene and cleanliness as compared to what they experience in the dismal conditions of their own homes. There is likelihood of schools exclusively for girls being more ill equipped, than those for boys or schools which provide co-educational education. Urgent remedial measures need to be taken to at least lessen if not eliminate this disparity. Obviously disparaging attitudes towards girls' schools *vis-à-vis* those of their male counterparts, can and must be discouraged and put a stop to with the utmost expediency. Impartial, periodic governmental surveys of schools in rural areas, district-wise, with the findings assiduously forwarded to relevant governmental authorities, in a position to ameliorate dissatisfactory infrastructural conditions for education of the under-privileged, would go a long way towards improving the general (and specific) scenario in such areas and encourage more parents to send their children to school.

Another important and vital issue directly linked to the socio-psychological deterrents in sending girls to school is the relatively low percentage of female teachers in such rural areas. There are always dangers of female and child abuse. The omnipresent threat of an innocent girl being molested by her male tutor, etc., many parents, no matter how used to they may be to such problems which come to light oftener in the uninhibited ambience of the rural culture, will hesitate to expose their offspring to such a real danger. Despite the recommendations of several commissions like the Education Commission (1964-66) for a rapid expansion in the number of women teachers, and their suggestions regarding the provision of special allowances and accommodation to attract female teachers in rural areas, only 28.8 per cent of all teachers are female. The lack of amenities like medical care, proper accommodation, transport and toilets deter women from taking up teaching in the villages. Moreover, it is not unusual for women teachers to face resistance from their families and to feel apprehensive themselves about working away from home.

Coeducation has and will be a controversial issue till Indian society evolves a homogenous level of modern concepts and liberal ideology. Certain orthodox notions of gender bias being so deeply ingrained in the psyche of the average affected Indian, this is not a phenomena likely to occur in the forseeable future! schools exclusively for girls have for a long time been argued as an essential ingredient for enhancing female participation in the Indian setting. Given the prevailing attitudes towards women, it is perhaps judicious to provide institutions only for women in areas which register the maximum resistance to coeducation. Nonetheless, the mere setting up of such schools certainly would not be enough; it would only be the first step towards creating a suitable infrastructure. It would be equally important to ensure that these schools are well-equipped and are run on standards at par with those of boys or co-educational institutions.

The all-pervasive evils of gender bias have inevitably permeated the all-important domain of policy making with reference to the formulation of curricula for males and females, and no matter how judiciously policy planners have attempted to combine a curricula for women with the democratic goals of education, many shortcomings have occurred. Therefore, we find that "inadequate and substandard provisions are not the only deterrents to women's education." Ironically, that which seeks to "liberate" and "empower" (viz. the educational system) has deliberately or inadvertently sustained traditional prejudices against women. Educationists and policy planners of modern India have had to grapple with the conflict between the regular ideals of womenhood i.e., the stereotype of the home-maker wife and mother, and the democratic goals of education i.e., the creation of the spirit of enquiry, the freedom of thought and expression, notions of equality, etc. The resulting policies have, by and large, reflected the ambivalence regarding the roles of women and the purpose of their education, especially in relation to the curriculum.

While the recommendations of the University Education Commission set up shortly after 1947, argued that much of the education between boys and girls could be common, it did, nevertheless, embody typical attitudes towards women's education and their role in the society and firmly believed that since the greatest profession of women is, and probably will be that of the home maker, it was essential that her education should make her familiar with the problems of home management and skilled in meeting them. Similarly, the Committee on Women's Education set up in 1958, felt that some of the subjects taught were not related to the aptitudes, interests and needs of the girls and advocated the introduction of courses in the fine arts, needlework, cooking, etc., from primary level onwards. The principle of the provision of courses of special interest to girls such as home-science, painting, music, etc., continued to be implicit in later Councils and Commissions though both the National Council for Women's Education (1961) and the Kothari Commission (1964-66) were more emphatic in their recommendations for a common curricula for both boys and girls. The Kothari Commission, specifically, 'suggested many measures that if implemented, would favour female participation'. Therefore, education was expected to prepare women for the other role-options (part-time or full time jobs), that they may want to consider in addition to their principle role (not clearly stated, but implied nonetheless) as home-makers.

The report of the Committee on Status of Women in India (1975) expressed concern over the failure of many states to adopt the modern curriculum. It held the schools which "reflect and strenghten the traditional prejudices through their curricula, the classification of subjects on the basis of sex, and the unwritten code enforced on their "pupils" as responsible for sustaining the existing gender and class inequalities." It is worth noting that even the National Policy of Education (1986), 'acknowledged the presence of sex-biases in the curricula, and the educational system as a whole,and has advocated measures to reduce these inequalities.'

It is indeed lamentable that very often our children are consciously presented with conflicting images regarding the roles, nature and capabilities of males and females in their classrooms. Relatively recent research in particular, highlights the hidden or implicit role of the textbook in reinforcing sex-based stereo-types and role models. Two established authors, Kalia (1978, 1979) and Nischol (1976) in their studies on school textbooks found "that the females portrayed were invisible: they had few largely familial roles. Girls were shown to be non-achievers, passive and timid and rarely in roles associated with economic activity and independence. Boys, on the other hand, were couragaeous and high achievers." While Kalia in his later textbook observed that while 93 per cent of the various occupations undertaken performed by the male characters in the textbooks fell into the category of what one considered "high prestige" occupations such as lawyers, doctors, engineers, etc., a major percentage (eighty-seven per cent to be precise) of those occupations pursued by women, fell into the "low-prestige" category. Nischol's findings were similar and corroborative of the above deductive conclusions. Women were portrayed in the "sex appropriate" occupations: in addition to mothers, wives and daughters, they were shown as teachers, nurses and domestic servants. However, textbooks alone and the stereo-types projected therein, cannot instill convincing gender (biased) roles in the minds of young learners. Teachers play a pivotal role in such major gender projections, both implicitly as well as explicitly. Teachers are believed to be largely conservative in their outlook and don't necessarily realize the need to teach or preach greater equality between sexes. In fact, quite often we find that there is no difference in the way teachers, male or female, approach the issue of gender equality in the classroom. This is because irrespective of their sex, most have internalized the role models and value systems that the society has projected as appropriate for women. One of the results is differential attitudes towards boys and girls. Therefore, unless serious and determined efforts are made to address the inequities within the educational system itself, the role of education as an agent of change, as a social equalizer and intellectual determinant and, most importantly, as an agent of liberalization, mutual tolerance and respect, irrespective of narrow considerations of caste, colour and creed, will be seriously hampered.

Viable alternatives, partly as interim measures to bridge the gaps that exist between the literate and the totally non-literate, underprivileged sections of society, as well as meritorious alternatives in their own specific capacity, would be non-formal education (NFE) schemes. Now that it is increasingly evident that the formal educational system eludes many children, especially those who have to work for a living, either on a paid or unpaid basis and that girls constitute a significant proportion of these child workers. This, coupled with the 'failure to curb the incidence of dropout and stagnation, even among those who make it to school further elucidate the need for viable educational alternatives.' Therefore, the NFE programme launched by the Government in 1979 in as many as nine educationally backward states, aimed at providing relevant and need based education to out of school children between the crucial ages of nine to fourteen years, is laudable indeed! Presently, it is indeed heartening to note, that there exist approximately two lakh centres, 90 per cent of which are of primary level. To ensure the success of such a wide-based and worthy programme, it is not only mandatory that the teachers are imbued with a unique sense of commitment, reaching out to the hungry minds of those eager to learn, with patience and understanding, but the syllabi must be apprepriately tailored to meet their needs. The objective should be to define a practical, work oriented and need based curriculum so that it covers various important aspects of a child's learning and proves to be educative in the true sense of the term. Moreover, the community at large needs to be involved at all stages of programme planning and implementation.

The Adult Education Programme is another worthy alternative to formal schooling. The launching of the National Literacy Mission, just over a decade ago, was a tangible attempt on the part of the government then to promote literacy among the masses. The constant, urgent requirement for mass literacy efforts has always been emphasized by the various august bodies connected with education and the National Adult Education Programme of 1978 was the outcome of the various Committee recommendations. Despite these interventionist measures, the number of illiterates in the target group 15 to 35 years have been steadily rising from 91 million in 1951 to 110 million in 1981. The majority (63%) of these are female.

With an increase in female literacy and greater awareness of one's rights as well, it was felt that the educational level of illiterate children would automatically come down once mothers perceived the multipronged benefits of education. With the perpetuation of relative knowledge and enlightenment, very likely the infant and child mortality ratio along with the fertility rates would also come down, thereby actively enhancing women's self-confidence and self-image. However, for such campaigns to meet with a significant measure of success, it is absolutely necessary that the primarily academic curricula be linked 'to the satisfaction of their basic needs (primarily the enhancement of their learning potential)' or else there is a heavy percentage of dropouts making the campaign a non-starter. While many grassroot organizations have taken cognizance of this vital factor and have come up with successful packages that focus on income generation, awareness building and the three R's, the government has, by and large failed to do so. Nowadays although, more emphasis is being laid on providing information and training techniques in subjects which constitute 'alternate forms of employment and create social awareness', another criticism of governmental programmes has been 'the persistent middle-class bias which alienates the target group even further... the curriculum for women, blatantly or subtly supports the traditional role definitions. It addresses conventional topics such as child and maternal health, home management, nutrition, etc., and provides occasional training in sewing and embroidery.'

A perusal of the Tables 5.1 to 5.4 will only validate one's conclusion that "the advances in female educational participation belie the gender based inequities that persist" be they in the more blatant forms of unequal access and utilization or, in the subtle and often invisible form of miscommunication within the classroom. If we earnestly desire to see the fructification of education as the agent of basic change in the status of women and as a trail blazer altering the destinies of those living in the darkness of ignorance into a meaningful existence, we will not only have to shed our rigid gender- biased norms willy-nilly but also evolve radically enlightening views which will treat with compassion, resolve with dispassion and change with persuasion the downtrodden women and their all important issues.

Table 5.1
Literacy Rates (all ages) in 1981 by Residence

States	*Rural*		*Urban*		*Total*	
	Males	*Females*	*Males*	*Females*	*Males*	*Females*
Andhra Pradesh	32.25	14.08	61.89	41.55	39.26	20.39
Bihar	34.38	10.17	62.47	39.81	38.11	13.62
Gujarat	47.85	24.06	68.62	51.13	54.44	32.30
Haryana	43.44	15.37	64.98	47.35	48.18	·22.25
Karnataka	42.06	19.77	64.98	47.78	48.18	27.71
Kerala	74.13	64.25	80.10	72.20	75.26	65.73
Madhya Pradesh	32.91	8.99	64.41	42.26	39.49	15.53
Maharashtra	51.25	24.88	71.80	54.65	58.79	34.79
Orissa	44.51	18.45	65.13	42.72	41.7	21.12
Punjab	41.91	27.63	60.72	49.72	47.16	33.69
Rajasthan	29.65	5.46	60.55	34.45	38.3	11.42
Tamil Nadu	51.16	25.80	72.50	53.99	58.26	34.99
Uttar Pradesh	35.18	9.49	54.73	35.43	38.76	14.04
West Bengal	43.58	22.06	69.08	54.82	50.67	30.25
All India	40.79	17.96	65.83	47.82	46.89	24.82

Source: Census of India 1981, Series I, Part II, Special Reports and Tables based on 5 per cent sample data, pp. 82-83.

Table 5.2

Percentage Distribution of Literate Population by Age, Sex, and Residence During 1981 by Level of Education*

Level	Males			Females		
	Total	*Rural*	*Urban*	*Total*	*Rural*	*Urban*
1. Literate (without educational level)	29.38	33.75	21.00	33.42	39.37	25.91
2. Primary	30.29	33.26	24.58	33.98	37.47	29.59
3. Middle	17.68	17.56	18.79	16.78	15.04	18.98
4. Matriculation or Higher Secondary	17.27	12.90	25.66	12.48	7.05	19.31
5. Non-Technical Diploma or Certificate not equal to Degree	0.09	0.09	0.08	0.09	0.08	0.12
6. Technical Diploma or Certificate not equal to Degree	0.57	0.37	0.94	0.29	0.25	0.35
7. Graduate or above	4.42	2.07	8.95	2.96	0.74	5.75
	100.00	100.00	100.00	100.00	100.00	100.00

*Excludes Assam.
Source: Census of India, 1981 Series I, Part II, Special Reports and Tables based on 5 per cent sample data.

Table 5.3

Total Enrolment in the Educational System (all levels)

Years	*Boys*	*Girls*
1950-51	1,19,42,009	64,00,763(33)
1960-61	3,37,04,897	1,42,59,505(42)
1970-71	5,57,12,623	3,00,30,484(54)
1980-81	7,26,25,002	4,12,06,441(57)

Source : Towards Equality, 1975, p. 240
Education in India, 1981-82, Vol. I, p. 27.
Note: Figures in parentheses indicate the number of girls enrolled per 100 boys.

Table 5.4

Percentage of Institutions Exclusively for Women (all levels)

Year	*Total No. of Institutions*	*No. of Institutions Exclusively for Girls*	*Percentage of all Girls Institutions*
1947-48[1]	1,64,553	17,951	10.30
1950-51[1]	2,86,860	34,829	8.70
1960-61[1]	4,72,655	41,674	8.80
1967-68[1]	7,93,799	2,30,032	29.00
1970-71[2]	6,53,493	93,784	14.35
1980-81[3]	7,69,967	62,645	8.14

Source: 1. *Towards Equality*, 1975, p. 258.
2. *Ibid.*, 1970-71, Vol. I, p. 7.
3. *Ibid.*, 1981-82, Vol. I, p. 34.

However, as India stands poised to meet the challenges of the new millenium, startling new information reveals an increasingly encouraging picture regarding education.

While the Probe report, 1998, highlighted the gender-steeped opinion expressed by the 226 respondents households who had never enrolled their children in schools (in UP), 82 per cent maintaining they kept their daughters out of school for help with the domestic work, there are greys in these stark black-and-white attitudes. Eighty per cent of the total sample size of the parents interviewed by the probe survey team voted for compulsory elementary education. There's no denying the fact that aspirations to education abound in our villages, towns and cities.

Those who've had success in 'translating these aspirations into realities', have obviously defied prescribed text-book solutions to do so. Worthy of mention is the Lok Jumbish who, in conjunction with the state government, is working wonders to attain the universalisation of education in Rajasthan. Small additions and meagre subtractions have changed entire equations here. In Kaman block's predominantly Muslim Bagechi village, only one girl attended school six years ago. Today, in an amazing reversal of situations—of progress—only one girl doesn't attend! A highly flustered community is definitely embarrassed about it. "She'll go too, we're working on it. It's just that her mother is a lazy woman who refuses to manage home by herself." What, then, has prompted such embarrassment among the community towards illiteracy ? Propelling them to strike a welcome blow to the gender issue, if only in the sphere of education. "An educational initiative that does away with rigid systems and addresses geo-cultural pluralities", firmly maintains Anil Bordia, the Lok Jumbish chairperson.

Instinctively realizing that parents would rather send their children to masjid-run *madrasas* than run-of-the-mill government schools, Lok Jumbish workers wisely began befriending the moulvis. Simultaneously, they convinced villagers that Urdu teachers would be provided at each school. Following this innovative two-pronged approach, many a school today has the village moulvi himself teaching Urdu for a small remuneration. Predictably enough, the schools are full of children and enthusiasm.

This novel educational experiment underlines that where curricula are relevant and community need-based, there educational schemes have usually met with some measure of success and worked well. Sometimes it works even better if people "demand" that their needs be met. Much like the Education Guarantee Scheme in Madhya Pradesh whereby "any panchayat that doesn't have a school within one kilometre of the village can demand one in writing and the state government will be obliged to provide it." It is indeed heartening to note that Madhya Pradesh has many innovative schemes going.

Just forty-five kilometres from Dhar, a teacher duo works on 79 students in the small primary school in Chiloor village. It's a modern condition of a *pathshala* or *maqtab* — a commendable multigrade system as against the usual monograde method of teaching in educational jargon. Here a single teacher handles five classes and students are justly judged "on the basis of acquired competencies rather than marks." Leading to the rather unique phenomena that the same child could be in the Class V for a subject and Class II for another. Avers Dhar's collector, Rajesh Rajora : "Over 80 per cent of the country's primary schools have only three teachers on an average : so in a way, they are also following a multigrade system. Here we have formally accepted it and made things easier."

Certainly education should be much more contextually relevant for the community. A point which our education system seems to have ignored miserably so far. Unfortunately for the would-be beneficiaries as well as for the overall progress of the country. Shashank Vira, who heads the R&D wing of the ISCE Board that's 'revamping its curriculum currently', states emphatically that he was amazed to find how not one mainstream board gave its students the option to study agricultural sciences. "This is an agricultural country. We introduced it last year. And made some other radical changes like making mathematics optional even in Class X. Students will drop out if you decide you're the only one who knows all and the rest have to comply with what you think is right for them. There has to be more choice in education."

We should therefore strive towards a ceaseless commitment to the moblization and motivation of relevant agencies to eradicate illiteracy. While achieving amazing results like the North eastern states where tiny Mizoram has overtaken Kerala as India's most literate state. The latest NSSO figures reveal that Mizoram's literacy in 1997 stands at 95 per cent, two percentage points higher than Kerala's 93.

Conceding that Kerala has slipped from its previous levels of literacy achievement, Dr Raghu (Director-in-Charge, Adult and Continuing Education, Kerala University) attributed this to minor fluctuations along with a loss of momentum in the literacy campaign and lack of political will. A major reason for this slip in recent years, according to Dr R.V.G. Menon, President of the Kerala Shastra Sahitya Parishath, is because the latter stages of the literacy campaign didn't go beyond simple literacy goals to skills upgradation or citizenship training for lack of technical inputs. Admitting to a lull in the campaign for the last seven years, he feels there is a resurgence now, with the Literacy Mission being very active. Let us hope then that its ambitious Sree project which seeks to link the illiterate, semi-literate, neo-literate and the literate to the present continuing education project that's being implemented through panchayats, meets with success. But I digress.

Mizoram's stunning success followed by five other north eastern states — Arunachal Pradesh, Meghalaya, Assam, Sikkim and Nagaland recording the highest growth in literacy in the years 1991-97, is remarkable indeed.

Though Meghalaya at 27.9 per cent leads the rate of improvement in literacy between '91 and '97, it is closely followed by Nagaland at 22.4, Assam at 22.1, Sikkim at 22.1 and Arunachal at 18.4. All this despite serious insurgency and fiscal problems in Nagaland and Assam during the period under review. Maintained a deputy commissioner of a district (in Assam) involved in a total literacy campaign "We've been fortunate to keep the TLC unaffected by insurgency unlike other sectors of development." Likewise is the progress in the erstwhile head-hunting state of Nagaland.

Spectacular success in the sphere of education, however, undoubtedly belongs to Mizoram. Maintains Lalrawna, joint director, adult education, Mizoram : "After we shifted to the

'Each one, teach one' method in '89-90, we made rapid progress." Elaborating further on this concept he explained that an effort was first made to identify illiterates in far-flung villages, then a number of volunteers appointed as animators and village adult education committees simultaneously formed. "This method, involving a broad spectrum of people and organizations like village councils, church bodies, teachers and social workers, yielded superb results." Today Mizoram is nearly cent per cent literate but for a large percentage of its minority Chakma and Reang population. A senior government official said: "Among the Mizo, 100 per cent literacy has already been achieved. It's only because of the Chakmas and Brus (the Reangs) that the overall percentage is 95." However, in addition to the Chakma and Reang obduracy, the fact that autonomous district councils have, since 1994-95, taken over TLC in their areas, may have slowed things down.

Even at 95 per cent, the figures are impressive enough though officials at the directorate of adult education maintain that the 1998-99 figures indicate that 96 per cent of Mizoram's seven lakh population is literate. Significantly, Mizoram hasn't stopped at producing simple neo-literates, but also turned its attention, especially in the last two years or so, to the Continuing Education Programme. This aims at making neo-literates and school dropouts acquire knowledge beyond the preliminary. In a commendable move, the Centre itself has sanctioned Rs.45.67 lakh to establish 360 centres and 40 nodal ones across the state. To enable Mizoram to become a fully literate state in the forseeable future.

Figure 5.1 gives composite information regarding various comparative aspects of educational development, sourced from the recently released National Sample Survey Organisation and *Probe*.

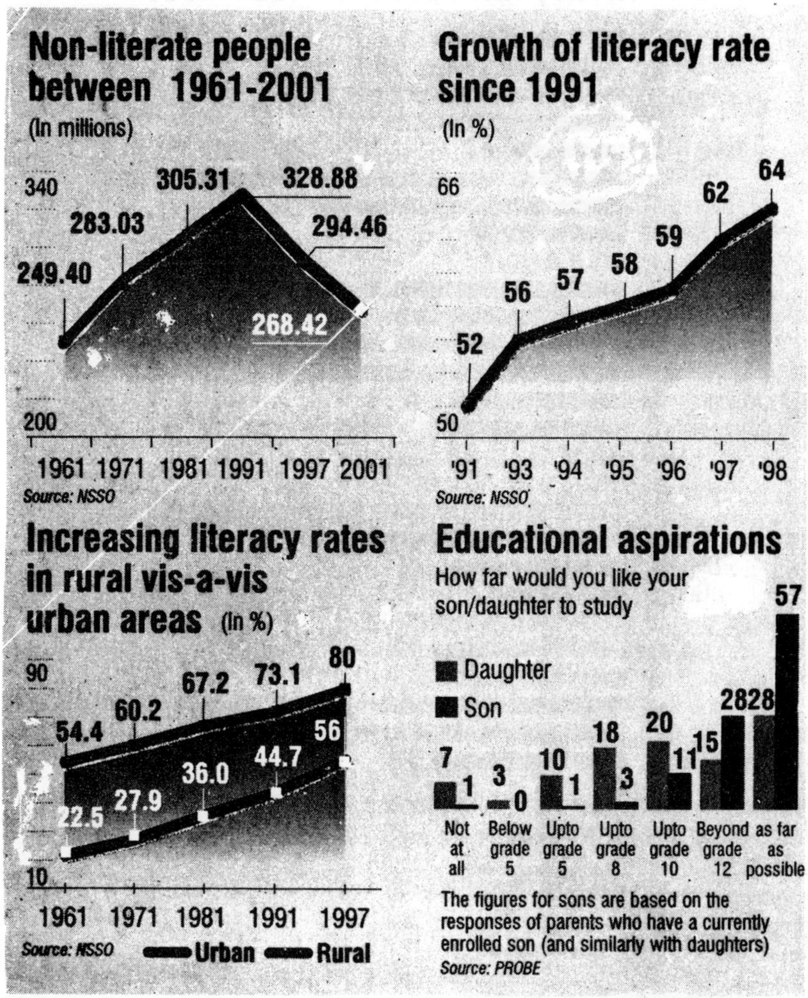
Non-literate people between 1961-2001
(In millions)
340
200
249.40
283.03
305.31
328.88
294.46
268.42
1961 1971 1981 1991 1997 2001
Source: NSSO
Growth of literacy rate since 1991
(In %)
66
50
52
56
57
58
59
62
64
'91 '93 '94 '95 '96 '97 '98
Source: NSSO
Increasing literacy rates in rural vis-a-vis urban areas (In %)
90
10
54.4
60.2
67.2
73.1
80
22.5
27.9
36.0
44.7
56
1961 1971 1981 1991 1997
Source: NSSO
Urban
Rural
Educational aspirations
How far would you like your son/daughter to study
Daughter
Son
7 1
3 0
10 1
18 3
20 11
15 28
28 57
Not at all
Below grade 5
Upto grade 5
Upto grade 8
Upto grade 10
Beyond grade 12
as far as possible
The figures for sons are based on the responses of parents who have a currently enrolled son (and similarly with daughters)
Source: PROBE

Increase in literacy rates between 1991-1997

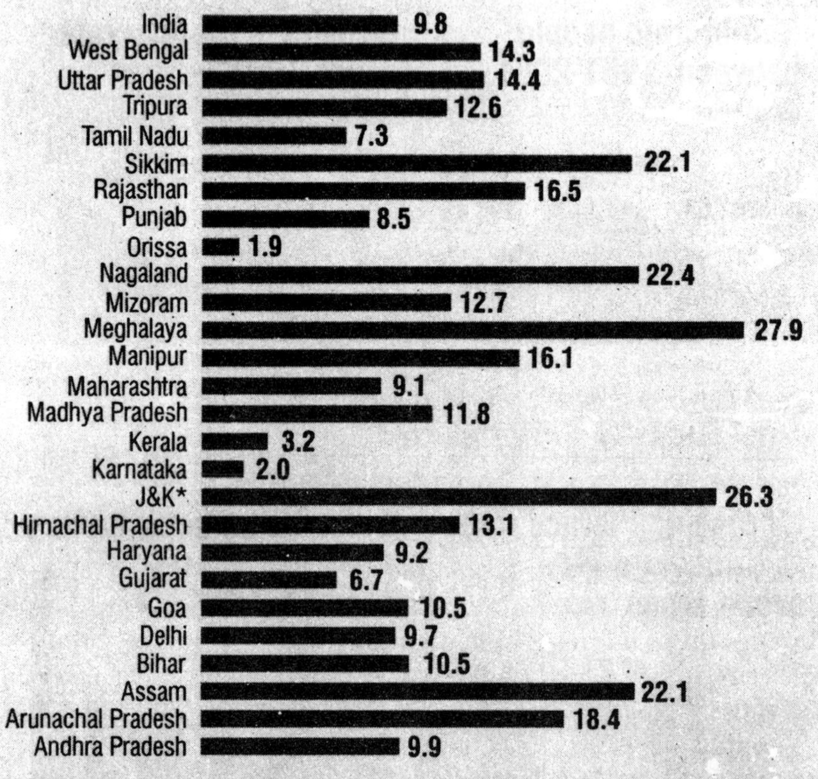

**Census data for Jammu & Kashmir were not obtained in 1991*
Hence the increase is from 1981

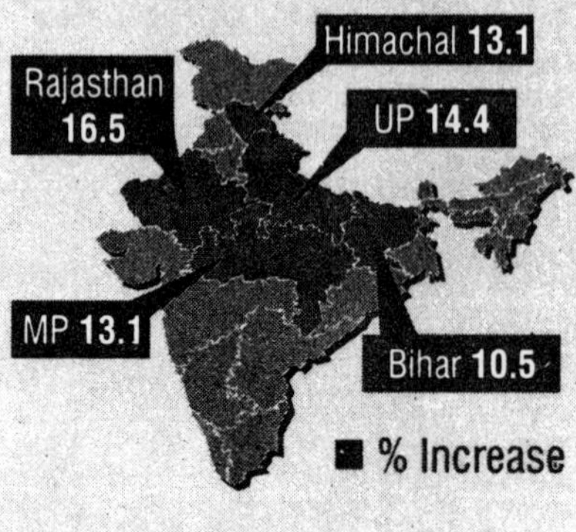

	1991	1997
India	52.2	62
Bihar	38.5	49
Madhya Pradesh	44.2	56
Himachal Pradesh	63.9	77
Uttar Pradesh	41.6	56
Rajasthan	38.5	55

Source: NSSO

The figures are impressive but just how accurately do they reflect reality ? This is an inquiry which will have to be made regularly and at repeated intervals, its findings assessed impartially and with a view to speedily redressing areas of default. By responsible State government agencies in conjunction with National Surveys. Only then can the existing plethora of policies, projects and missions in India—National Literacy Mission, District Primary Education Programme, Education Guarantee Scheme, Operation Blackboard, Education for All, Joyful Learning Programme, Non-Formal Education, Mahila Samakhya, Shikshak Samakhya, SCOPE, Lok Jumbish, Bihar Education Project, Andhra Pradesh Education Programme, National Programme for Nutritional Project, ever hope to succeed.

For as the wizened septuagenarian, Mehti Bi wisely counsels from Rajasthan's Ahelwadi village — a village celebrating the 'event' of seeing the first four girls ever to pass out of class five from this relatively obscure hamlet, much more remains to be done. Remarking on the achievement she cautiously maintains:-

> "It's too little and too early to gloat over ! Now that they've finished with primary school here, will their parents send these girls to the middle school in Ladla, so many fields away? More likely, the girls will be married off. Hurry and convince the parents to send them to Ladla. Say that girls who go to school keep their houses cleaner and take daily baths. Stop this monkey dance on small achievements, think how to make them bigger and stronger ...."

References

Amin, Sonia Nishat, 'The Early Muslim Bhadramahila: The Growth of Learning and Creativity, 1876 to 1839'. In Ray Bharati (ed.) *The Seams of History*, Oxford University Press, 1993.

Evidence of Khan Ahmad Shah, *Appendix to the Education Commission Report* (1884).

Evidence of Lala Mulraj, officiating Extra Assistant Commissioner, Gujarat (Punjab) in *Appendix to the Education Commission Report* (1884).

Evidence of Miss Rose Greenfield, *Appendix to Education Commission Report* (1884).

Gokhale, Nitin, *'An Animated Effort'*, *Outlook*, 14 June, 1999.

In Colonial India, New Delhi: Oxford University Press, 1989.

Jayalakshmi, 'Women's Development: Need for New Approach', *Reforms For Women-Future Options*, Heptulla, Najma, Ed, New Delhi: Oxford and IBM Publishing Co. Pvt. Ltd, 1992.

Light of Truth (or an English translation of *Satyarth Parkash* of Swami Dayanand Saraswati, by Chirangiva Bharadwaj. (Lahore, Kaviraj Satya Vrata Bharadwaj, 3rd edition, 1927)

Kalia, Narendra Nath, 'Why I would be ...to be a woman in today's India : A context analysis of sex role models in Indian school textbooks', *Indian Journal of Social Research*, Vol.19, Apr-Dec. 1978

Kalia, Narendra Nath, *Sexism in Indian Education : The Lies we Tell our Children*, Vikas, New Delhi, 1979

Kishwar, Madhu, 'The Daughters of Aryavarta'. Krishnamurty, J. ed., *In Women.*

Kulshreshtha, Indira, *The War Against Gender Bias*, New Delhi: Sterling Publishers Pvt. Ltd, 1993.

Menon, Venu, *'Who Stole The Crown?'* *Outlook*, 14 June, 1999.

Mushirul Hasan, "Redefining Boundaries: Modermist Interpretations And The New 'Intellectual Structures'", *Legacy of A Divided Nation*, New Delhi: Oxford University Press.

Nischol, K., 'The insurable women : Images of women and girls in school text-books', *Social Action* Vol. 26, July-September, 1976.

Paranjape, Sarina, '*Women's Education Status*'. In Sapru, R.K., *(ed.) Women and Development*,New Delhi: Ashish Publishing House, 1989.

Ward, Barbara. E. ed, *Women In The New Asia*: United Nations Educational, Scientific and Cultural Organization, Amsterdam, 1963.

Wadhwa, Soma, 'When Numbers Lie', *Outlook*, June 14, New Delhi: 1999.

6
CRIME AND PUNISHMENT

The one issue that has inflamed feminists more than any other is that of violence against women. According to one estimate, as many as thirty specific forms of violence against women have been identified. These range from sterilization abuse, through pornography to outright murder. Violence against women is often seen as an assault against her body but more importantly it is a negation of her integrity and personhood. The fear of sexual violence has been a powerful factor in restricting women's behaviour and sense of freedom.

In one of the most ironical dichotomies of the modern era, it is indeed deplorable that, antithetical to the process of progress and modernization, the liberated woman of today is subject to growing acts of criminal violence; a terrible violation not only of her body and being, which the Hindu religious texts endowed with such sanctity, but also a desecration of her individuality, her hard won emancipation and her well deserved status as man's equal in every sphere of life.

Manu, who under the various names of Minos, Mnekes or Mneuis is believed to be the father author of the basic social laws of the Hindus, the Greeks and the Turks and, in fact, for the whole mankind, minced no words about the high status of women in the society. He said, in chaste sanskrit:

यत्र नार्यर्यस्तु पूज्यन्ते रमन्ते तत्र देवताः ।
यत्रैतास्तु न पूज्यन्ते सर्वास्तत्राफलाः क्रिया ।।

On translation, this philosophical dictum meant that the home where there is respect for women is like an abode of gods themselves; but where they are not respected, all other forms of worship are fruitless. For that abode of family sanctity is then reduced merely to a concrete, physical structure, its foundations weak, its physical delienations a constricting, suffocating force, rather than the protective and hallowed precincts within which the woman nurtures and is nurtured; from where the malleable minds and evolving impressions of future generations can be influenced to contribute constructively to the overall national fabric of a country. So high a praise by Manu, the ancient law giver, and by numerous other philosophers, thinkers and authors is not mere rhetoric, but a humble recognition of the central role of women in the very existence of mankind. A modern Hindu writer has stated this quite uneqivocally thus:

> A man's religious life is considered to be essentially deficient without his wife's participation in it. Without a wife the psychological and moral personality of man remains imperfect. She is his constant companion in his religious life, preparing for him the sacred articles used in worship, accompanying him on pilgrimages, present at all ceremonies and finally, in her role as the mother, is regarded as divine, respected many times more than the father and teacher.

Therefore, if as a class, women have been behind the evolution of religion, culture, art and literature, as individuals they have made hitherto matchless contributions towards the development of our social system, enriching the social fabric immeasurably through the numerous roles they have played in the evolution of society through the ages. Women are eulogised as goddesses, revered as the mother figure, protected as sisters and daughters and considered indispensable as the wives and procreators of the human race. It is the special and specific qualities of compassion, selflessness, devotion and a sense of self effacement intrinsically associated with women, that has enabled them to nurture the human race, despite innumerable trials and tribulations. Thus, people have always seen in them a unique blend of all the three forms of godhood, i.e. the creator, the preserver and the destroyer of evil; the 'trimurti' of Indian mythology. It is no coincidence that the ultimate symbols of knowledge, power and plenty are also three female goddesses, namely, Saraswati, Shakti and Lakshmi.

How then has a sexist approach sought to negate the repository of such virtue and subject it to vice, destroying as it were the very visceral form of the source of life? The answers are too complex, too rooted in inherent attitudes of chauvinism, so-called male superiority, alarmingly increasing levels of insecurity among the male dominated world, and a host of other related and inextricable linked factors, to be explained in a simplistic manner. They require to be analyzed systematically, disseminated dispassionately and possible solutions arrived at, keeping various considerations in mind. Over and above considerations of tolerance and justice, it is absolutely imperative to avoid any emotional overtones of judgement. This would not only tend to colour an impartial conclusion, but it would necessarily impede a constructive implementation of remedial measures.

Gender bias, economic disparity, unequal power equations between men and women, are all predisposing factors in the perpetuation of crimes against women. Rehana Ghadially so aptly summed up in her arresting expositions in *Women in Indian Society*, that the struggle against violence is the struggle against the unequal distribution of power—both physical and economic between the sexes. The challenge lies not only in re-defining hierarchical relationships between the sexes but hierarchical interactions in all aspects of interpersonal relationships. People in positions of power—upper caste men, police, labour contractors, military personnel—dismiss violence done to lower caste and class women as insignificant. Women accept the male view of what is important and in violent encounters, end up blaming themselves, the victims, rather than castigate the perpetrators. As Heilbrum states, 'until women adopt a model of action that sustains the primacy of their own claim they will not achieve full equality."

Nearly a decade and a half ago, on 8 March, 1984 to be precise, various autonomous women's groups across the length and breadth of the country celebrated International Women's Day; predictably enough, most of their activities centred around the theme of violence against women, of a preponderance of crimes of many hues continuing to be perpetrated upon the fairer sex. An examination of the reports that these organizations boldly forwarded to a feminist magazine revealed their growing preoccupation concerning crime such as dowry deaths, abuse of amino-centesis procedures, rape, prostitution, sexual harassment and wife beating. In addition to this formidable list of horrors, is the entirely indigenous phenomena of Power rape, i.e. rape of helpless women by men in positions of authority. With the passage of time laws pertaining to rape and even more specifically to dowry, have undergone necessary changes and amendments most often and are mute testimony to the importance of these two central issues in a woman's life. The emotional and psychological barometer of women subjected to such traumatic experiences, registers an unimaginable graph of mental agony and emotional destruction.

The women's liberation movement in India has rallied around the retrogressive issue of rape and brought together diverse women's groups from different parts of the country, urging for a constant update and modernization of rape laws. However another deplorable form of cruelty towards women i.e., wife beating , seems to get camouflaged under the broad term dowry deaths. The deaths which occur within the home are the ultimate manifestation of the violence suffered by most Indian women in varying degrees. "The term 'dowry deaths' is an over-simplification of a far more complex social phenomenon of power relationships within the family. We prefer to call them plain 'wife -murders'. Most of these women are harassed for a long time before they are murdered or driven to suicide and for every woman who dies in her home, there must be a million more who are beaten and harassed, economically deprived and mentally humiliated."

This form of violence, which seems to imbue men with a peculiar sadistic pleasure and provide a suitable vent for frustrations and rage, wrongly suppressed over a period of time, is perhaps, the most widespread and common form of abuse against women. While there seems to be a reluctance on the part of most groups working towards social change, to specifically venture into the relatively private area of domestic violence, social pressures force women to maintain a status quo. Social workers prefer to view the problem of marital disharmony more cautiously, classifying the phenomena of domestic violence and the subsequent degeneration of a matrimonial alliance under the somewhat deceptive terminology 'domestic discord'. The implications are much deeper and more complex and the ramifications of such abuse far more physically and emotionally debilitating than can be imagined. Social workers are, perhaps understandably, reluctant to interfere with personal power relationships though it is imperative that they change their approach now, if this degenerative process is to be checked and further immeasurable harm prevented.

Shattering the myth that middle-class women do not get beaten, it is a regrettable fact that any woman 'who does not accept the traditional role of submissiveness and subordination needs to be 'advised' or 'tamed' into accepting this position and any means including violence is justified in achieving this goal'. The women who are subjected to violent beatings come from all sections of society, belong to different religions, span all educational levels and socio-economic strata of society. But, whereas the working class women are able to talk about wife beating more openly and accept it with greater equanimity because they do not necessarily consider it 'individual' orientated, middle-class women tend to question and doubt themselves much more. The incidence of wife beating is not necessarily higher among people existing in sub-human conditions in slums and chawls, it is merely because these people have practically no privacy and their privations are anything but private. Relatively speaking, middle and upper class women are subjected to beatings behind closed doors, live in total isolation and are further oppressed as they are compelled to keep up the facade of a successful marriage. What is even more shocking is that highly qualified professionals like doctors and lawyers are guilty of committing this disgusting crime. Many of the husbands of middle-class families indulging in this sadistic crime were perfectly sober at the time of wife beating and not in the grip of a drunken alcoholic stupor. True, there are incidents both among the middle and working classes when the husbands were extremely annoyed with their spouses, went out and got drunk, and then returned home and subjected them to a sound thrashing. However, it transpires that these men were not ordinarily violent or abusive or even aggressive in their daily transactions with other human beings. It might be relevant to record an important interpretation of power relationships between men and women in a socio-historical context thus: "It is not just that the structure of power is apprehended only by returning the dominated subject to the stage and locating power in the confrontation between domination and subordination. It is that the very paradigm of margin against centre is unhelpful and hierarchizing, as it does experience," maintains Nita Kumar. Citing Suleri's views in support of such an interpretation thus: "Alteritism represents the detail of cultural facticity by citing otherness as a universal trope, thereby suggesting that the discursive site of alterity is nothing other than the familiar and unresolved confrontation between the historical and allegorical." Whereas, both Foucault and post colonialism seem to posit systems where the inequality of relations (legitimized by the state and by colonialism, respectively) creates a world in which 'things move, rather than people; a world in which subjects become obliterated, or, rather, recreated as passive objects, a world in which passivity or refusal represent the only possible choices.'

Some other causative factors responsible for the cruel practice of wife beating include a man having witnessed wife beating in his childhood or having been subjected to child abuse himself; in both such instances he is likely to assume that physical violence is the acceptable way of resolving marital problems. Child abuse also leads to the belief that one who loves also has the right to beat. While economically dependent and independent women are likely to get thrashed by insecure and frustrated husbands, the incidence of women more likely to tolerate their wretched positions are the ones who are dependent on their spouses for various reasons. The many underlying factors that force the unhappy women to remain trapped within violent marriages include: (a) lack of education (b) economic dependency (c) lack of support structures (d) the difficulties in obtaining divorce/ job/house (e) the burden of child care, etc. Teamed with an abusive and insensitive husband, these problems assume even more monumental proportions and the women become passive, resigned and negative in their approach, adopting the path of least resistance. Inherent societal sanction, though undergoing a slow but definite attitudinal change, towards wife beating and related forms of violence, also push the miserable woman further into her quagmire of misery and prevent a bold breaking away from established norms and practices. A man given to habitual wife beating can, therefore, be relatively sure that his spouse will not desert him and the so-called security of the home, and can carry on his violent aberration with impunity.

To ameliorate the sufferings of women and against women, it would be advisable to adopt some of the measures are suggested below:

a) to create an awareness about the seriousness of such problems is absolutely essential in society, so that agencies crucial to alleviating or at least reducing the agony of severly abused women, can operate effectively in their favour. These include doctors, counsellers, institutions, social workers, and of course that most vital of law enforcing organizations, the police. To inculcate a more sympathetic and unbiased attitude among them towards resolving the many ills being perpetrated upon women, would be a forceful and positive step towards addressing the question of women's violence or more specifically, wife beating! The attitude of the institutions and counsellors should be to make the partners in a marriage more complete human beings rather than to preserve the marriage at any cost."

b) it will be appreciated if a specific law is enacted which can deal effectively with the crime of wife beating . At present no such special law exists and wife beating is covered under the general law for assault. These are sections 319-326 of the Indian Penal Code (IPC). Sections 319 and 321 are non-cognizable offences i.e cases in which the police can take no action against the assaulter.

Sections 320/322 cover 'grievous hurt', which is defined as:

(a) Emasculation

(b) Permanent privation of the sight of eye

(c) Permanent privation of the hearing of either ear

(d) Privation of any member or joint

(e) Destruction or permanent impairing of the power of any member or joint.

(f) Permanent disfiguration of the head or face

(g) Fracture or dislocation of a bone or tooth

(h) Any hurt which endangers life or which causes the sufferer to be, during the space of twenty days, in severe bodily pain, or unable to follow his ordinary pursuits.

Sections 324/326 cover those cases where the assaulter uses dangerous weapons or means.

While wife beating constitutes perhaps the most under-reported crime in the country, police reponse to this deplorable practice is also far from commensurate regarding the seriousness of the crime. All-encompassing changes would not only make a vital difference to the speedy redressal of this problem but perhaps effectively slow down the perpetrators of such crimes when they realize that they can be taken to task. Therefore, it is desirable that not only should a female police officer meet the woman complainant who comes to the police station to report the crime, but in the absence of such a suitable women police officer, the injured party should be taken to the nearest woman's home at the earliest. Furthermore, the police must be empowered to take preventive action i.e., when the woman comes to the police station because she fears an assault, she must necessarily be given the option to stay at the womens' home till the crisis tides over, temporarily at least. The battered woman should preferrably never be interviewed in the presence of her husband and the police should ensure that the wife is not beaten further as a result of their reprimanding the man, thereby injuring his very fragile male ego. The individuals of the police force themselves should be more conversant with the abhorrent practice of wife beating , both in its nature and scope, so that they are better able to handle the problem. Finally, "since the situation of assault of a husband on a wife is quite specific, in that the wife is economically dependent on her husband, so assault occurs in the house in which both reside, it is essential that the police operate under different laws than those which cover general assault. A law such as Domestic Violence Act should cover the points made above and several others".

Dowry deaths constitute another form of rephrensible crime against women. Upon analysis of exhaustive data recorded by researchers over a period of time concerning this grave and horrifying social practice, certain innate psychological similarities emerge between wife-batterers and dowry-seekers. "Like most wife-batterers, dowry seekers also come from all walks of life, want their wives to return when they walk out of the house.They are not alcohol or drug abusers and respond to rigidly defined gender roles. Wife-batterers have low self-esteem, are over concerned about the family's status and well-being and try to control not only themselves but others. When demands of dowry are not met, the seekers feel that the family's status and their sense of power and control are challenged. Son-in-laws in India not only enjoy special status and power in the family but they also act in ways that help them maintain it. Finally, the image of a wife-batterer or that of a potential dowry-death victim's spouse is seriously threatened when there is a change of anticipation of extra responsibility and assertiveness on the part of the wife. While the convention-bound bridegroom and his greedy, grasping family must, undoubtedly, bear the burden of blame for victimization of the bride and the ultimate perpetuation of her death by unnatural means, on no account can they alone be vilified for this crime. We may agree that they are the chief offenders causing the bride untold misery through their unreasonable demands, interference and cruel character assasination which, unfortunately in our puritanical Indian society carries a lot of weight, but by no means are the girl's parents devoid of blame. Scared of societal censure, lacking the courage of conviction to support their daughter in her rightful fight for survival, obsessed by a totally misplaced sense of propriety and unwilling to face the unpleasantness that would undoubtedly result from formal legal proceedings, they compound their daughter's already miserable plight by urging her to "bear everthing quietly, not discuss her misery with others and encourage to go back to a violent home. The increase in violence followed by a compromise, paradoxical as it may sound, has also been observed in case of young married Chinese women." The deterioration in the already exacerbated situation occurs because, in the interim period, not only has the husband's family been humiliated by the negotiations, by the curious questioning of neighbours as word of the altercation(s) inevitably spreads, but the cantankerous mother-in-law has also heard a lot of uncharitable remarks on her equally uncharitable treatment towards her daughter-in-law. It is pertinent to note here, that in a majority of cases neither the dowry victim nor her family reported the matter to the police or took any form of legal action against the demand for dowry which is a punishable offence. It is definitely worth analyzing why such a grave lapse — a lapse, if prevented, that could be instrumental in saving innumerable lives — occurs in the first place. Of all the plausible answers that come to mind, perhaps the following are the most relevant to the issue: a) It is possible that there is insufficient awareness of the Dowry Prohibition Act and its subsequent amendments. Moreover, the Act itself deters families from reporting because it makes the givers of dowry offenders too; b) the woman perhaps rightly, feels that reporting the matter and involving outside agencies in a basically private matter, may further aggravate domestic violence or even result in the breakdown of the sacred institution; c) often, crime victims commonly come to see themselves as helpless, vulnerable and impotent; and d) finally, the victim may well come to believe that even others are ineffective in changing the course of events in their life, thus witholding information from the relevant authorities. Such lack of recourse to immediate action and subsequent remedial measures, has very serious negative consequences for the community.

Social Support Network

"Social support is emerging as the single most important factor in mitigating the impact of highly stressful situations"

(Brownwell and Shumaker, 1984). The erstwhile highly inadequate social support network (of the victim) in dealing with the police and the judicial system, is now, mercifully enough, history. The emergence of more formal social support systems have made it possible for the bereaved families to take action beyond beating their chests in helplessness. The assistance has been emotional, informational and tangible in nature. It has taken the form of public demonstrations, protest marches, slogan raising, giving media coverage, distributing pamphlets, holding exhibitions, enacting plays, assisting parents in filing cases in court, pressurizing the police, pressurizing authorities to amend existing laws and following up cases with police and lawyers.

Perhaps the single most vital factor of such a social support network is that it has been effective in creating wide public awareness of the crime. Such awareness functions on two psychological planes simultaneously i.e. the knowledge that such a system of assistance exists not only 'facilitates our adaptation to socially trying situations' but subconsciously it can act as a possible deterrent for the criminal offender as well if he knows that there exists a network of socially aware (and alert) agencies in taking him to task. But whereas such social support has been overwhelmingly 'crisis intervention' rather than 'crisis prevention' in nature, with bystanders reluctant to interfere for the latent fear of repercussions on their own offspring, it is now an urgent need of the time to evolve and implement effectively, crisis prevention measures which will deal with the crime of dowry demands and domestic violence.

One of the mosts grievous shortcomings which need to be addressed in this connection is police apathy and unconcern, which, in turn, greatly influence a dowry victim or her parents from reporting a crime before it is too late. Police agencies have to adopt a more cognisant, responsible and socially responsible attitude towards speedy redressal of such a problem.

The sheer bulk of the problem is no excuse to treat the issue lightly or in a generalized manner. A sympathetic approach, a sensitive attitude and the necessity to record faithfully the evidence of each aggrieved party on its individual merits or demerits are mandatory steps which can arrest if not alleviate the incidence of this abhorrent crime.

Necessarily in tandem with police awareness and expedient action, would be the facilitation and just redressal of such serious complaints (of dowry deaths) by the Courts. It may be a High Court or the highest repository of justice in our land, the Supreme Court. However, analysis of data collected by various researchers, points towards the fact that a morally unacceptable, dismally low percentage of the accused received their just punishments at the hands of such courts. Among the various reasons forwarded for acquittal of the rest of the crime perpetrators were that the judges doubted the veracity of the woman's dying declaration; found fault in the investigating agency; found the evidence in quite a number of cases to be inadequate or insufficient; refused to accept the medical report of the doctor and finally, misinterpreted facts. "The judges have doubted the veracity of the dying declaration on the grounds that it was a wife's attempt to falsely implicate an innocent husband, that she was not medically fit to give a dying declaration (though doctor certified fitness) and finally why did she wait for the police before giving the dying declaration. In cases of rape, it has been the history of western law that the words of a woman are not to be trusted (Newsweek, 1984). The same seems to hold true for dowry cases in India." Unfortunately, the sexist bias that many judges seem to display at the time of assessment such as accepting the argument that 'women in unhappy marriages are prone to suicide', refusing 'to recognize harassment as abetment to suicide' coupled with faulty investigation and insufficient evidence, are some or the other glaring anomalies that obstruct the expedient dispensation of justice. To compound the problem further and render it 'uncommonly difficult to sustain a charge of dowry murder in court' are quotations of other such complicated arguments by these judges that not only did the investigation turn hostile but also the police did not take possession of incriminating evidence; that the police obviously in a lackadaisical manner of functioning, allowed the accused persons to acquire vital information from the police diary; these and other inter-related factors strongly pointed towards corruption in the police force. In many cases apparently, there was no direct evidence by a witness, the witness was labelled as hostile and unreliable and the accused had tampered with and attempted to destroy incriminating evidence. Some of the ways in which the judges of the land, the guardians and arbiters of justice and equality, can ensure that certain principles are upheld in accordance with the highest traditions in the land, are as follows: Adjustment in attitude, a less discriminatory and more humane approach, a sterner indictment of the criminal offender after more microscopic examination of the evidence offered, a lessening of the incidence of cursorily dismissing evidence, a stricter injunction to the members of the police force to deal with investigations in the spirit of enquiry and information without disruption or corruption impeding the process of justice.

A brief recapitulation of dowry and the law would be pertinent here. While the Dowry Prohibition Act of 1961 was the first attempt by the Government of India to acknowledge dowry as a prevalent social evil and to curb its practice, subsequent legal modifications in 1984 and 1986 were brought about through the vocal and vital efforts of various womens' organizations. The 1961 Act which not only defines dowry but makes both the giving and receiving of such dowry a highly punishable offence, mentions emphatically that in case dowry is given, it will be the woman's property. While the 1984 Dowry (Amendment) Act brought only nominal changes and disappointed the expectations of many feminist groups, it made the dowry issue a cognizable offence and empowered institutions to file complaint of office. Changes were also made in the basic definition of dowry and provisions for getting such dowry back were made far more stringent, by reducing the period of transfer of dowry to the woman or her heir within three months (earlier it was one year) and increasing the punishment in the event of failure to comply with minimum six months and maximum two years imprisonment (earlier it was six months). While the amount of the fine remained unchanged at Rs 1000, this amendment clearly empowered the judge to order the return of dowry and if the girl's husband and or his immediate family failed to do so, a fine equal to the value of the property could legally and legitimately be imposed.

A still later amendment of the Dowry Prohibiton (Amendment) Bill 1986 introduced in the Rajya Sabha, tightened the provisions of the Act and included dowry deaths in the list of offences in the Indian Penal Code. Fortunately for the affected women and, indeed, for society at large, a commendable provision of this Bill has been that it has made the offence non-bailable and raised the minimum punishment to five years and fine upto Rs. 15,000. Furthermore, the Bill provides "that if a woman dies within seven years of her marriage due to causes other than natural, her property would be transferred to her children and if she has no children, to her parents. The burden of proving that no dowry demand was made will be on those who took or abetted the taking of the dowry, the aggrieved person will not be subject to prosecution.

Rape, Its Reasons and Repercussions

The literal dictionary definition of 'rape' reads as, "unlawful sexual intercourse (usually by force) with another person without that person's consent." Of all the atrocities perpetrated on women, rape is the single most reprehensible crime leaving as it does often inerasible scars on the assaulted woman's psyche, not to mention her arbitarily ravaged physical frame. It is a dastardly act of a depraved mind, committed for many reasons — political, professional, personal, a combination of the above and assumes many forms — incest (perhaps the most disgusting of all), marital rape, the rape of working women by their bosses and /or other senior men in power, custodial rape, rape by strangers, the horrifying rape of unsuspecting, innocent children, etc. The last mentioned, specifically, can create such ghastly repercussions that it is capable of destroying the innocent young victim's chances of even conceiving and having a family in later adult life; apart from the obvious trauma to the uncomprehending child's mind which can result in a legacy of deep-rooted complexes and character abnormalities. Inter-caste rape, rape by the government and the military are the other forms of rape commonly occurring in our country.

The socio-psychological reasons for rape are complex and deep-rooted, sometimes defying comprehension, at other times offering barely discernible glimpses into the rape-perpetrator's warped psyche. While the crime of rape is as old as mankind and it is difficult to pin-point a definite reason for its commission, the single most important factor that encourages men to commit it is the popularly held belief that women belong to a weaker species. While there is no scientific basis for this belief, there is no denying the fact that it is universal and is not only shared among men but by and large women have also been given to believe in it. It is indeed ironical that such a weakness is attributed to women mainly for reasons for which otherwise they would deserve extreme respect and appreciation.The fact that a woman can suffer silently and for a long time for a cause which is dear to her, obviously calls for a discipline and make up of the highest order but apparently this is interpreted as a failure to retaliate openly in the defence of that cause and hence a weakness. Her dedication to the cause of the home and the family, which is so total that it forces her to practice control and suppression of her normal desires to venture out, has obviously been taken to be a lack of enterprise and drive in her species. Rape, akin to other crimes like wife-beating, dowry deaths and various other interrelated or individual offences committed against women, all have a basic common factor running through them and that is that: these offences are always one-sided and without provocation and the victim is always an innocent woman. She is in no way responsible for giving rise to the offence and she has also no way of averting it. These offences are also marked by unexplained social apathy." Economic factors play a marginal role, "though the victims in eve-teasing and dowry deaths mostly come from the middle-class and those in cases of wife - beating and sexual murders belong to the economically weaker sections."

But let us discuss this most foul crime in particular specifics, in each broad category of the female sex assault. Its near fatal, homicidal and psychiatric repercussions in certain instances, a total breakdown of self- confidence, peace of mind, loss of self-respect and respect in one's society at the very least in all cases. While physical assault and aberrations of all kinds against women are to be condemned strongly, the sickening assault by an adult, temporarily unbalanced man on the tender, unprepared physical frame of a child, is truly contemptible and assumes the worst form of an act of total perversion, unforgivable cruelty and unqualified and stringent condemnation. It is brutality at its worst and must be crushed at all costs even going to the extent of taking the life of the rapist. If there is one excuse for enforcing capital punishment, it is in this type of crime. For such a nightmarish experience for an uncomprehending child, an act which 'not only militates against all canons of good behaviour' but will also adversely affect her future development as a woman, can create severe mental inhibitions about almost every thing connected with men and put her off normal sex and marriage for life. Unfortunately, there appears to be an increasing incidence of child rape as the following Table 6.1 illustrates:

Table 6.1

Table showing some Important Statistics for Cases of Rape on Minor Girls (under 16 years) from 1971 to 1980 in an Area Around Delhi with a Population of 14 Million

	Number of Cases						
Year	*Registired cases*	*Challenged cases*	*Cancelled*	*Un-traced*	*Acquitted*	*Conviced*	*Pending trial*
1971	15	15	1	1	7	5	1
1972	24	23	-	1	6	17	-
1973	18	16	1	1	5	11	-
1974	17	14	1	2	7	7	-
1975	30	28	2	-	11	15	2
1976	21	19	2	-	7	7	5
1977	27	25	1	-	9	16	-
1978	34	31	3	-	15	15	1
1979	33	31	2	-	9	19	3
1980	53	50	3	-	11	18	21
Total	272	250	16	6	87	130	33

Custodial rape and rape by the personnel of the police force, who, in actual fact, are supposed to be the custodians of the law in a manner of speaking and maintain not only law and order but also the safety of the country's citizens, is also considered quite reprehensible. Indeed the Indian police force, which has the reputation of being extremely corrupt and repressive, are often seen "as rapists and brutes by oppressed groups, as political scapegoats by the ruling classes, as instruments of repression (or hapless victims of the system) by opposition parties. Whether or not they are indeed corrupt, police rape gets more attention than any other form of rape."

Parliament amended the provisions relating to rape about fourteen years ago, to give them more teeth and obviously with the hope that the potential crime-perpetrators would perhaps become somewhat more cautious and hesitate to rape at random and frequently. While there was no clause earlier prescribing a basic, minimum punishment, all that has now undergone a change in favour of the complainant and the minimum now is seven years imprisonment for the rapist. If the rape is committed by the police, a public servant or someone in the management of a jail or hospital, the minimum is ten years. This is called 'custodial rape', because it is committed by someone who has custody or control of the woman. The same minimum punishment is given to 'gang rape' (rape of a woman by several men) and rape of a pregnant woman.

In addition, the same law also provides for that most sacrosanct of trials, an 'in camera trial', which, as the term itself suggests, is not open to the general public and makes it an offence even to publish the victimised woman's name without her prior permission. This is to protect the woman's honour and to discourage the abhorrent practice of 'yellow' journalism. Another significant change which was effected with this new law fourteen years ago, was that "in custodial rape cases, the court would presume that the accused is guilty and it is for him to prove that he is innocent. The normal rule is that the accused is presumed innocent until he is proved guilty by the state prosecution.

A woman who is assaulted with the intention of being raped which, logically, would be tantamount to an active attempt at rape, can, in self-defence, kill or maim her attacker without any consequences because self-defence is considered legal.

For the purpose of completely avoiding any ambiguity of comprehension and consideration of this vital issue of rape, let us briefly recapitulate the legal interpretation of rape. "Section 375 of IPC says: A man is said to commit 'rape' who has sexual intercourse with a woman:

(i) against her will;

(ii) without her consent;

(iii) with her consent, when her consent has been obtained by putting into her the fear of death, or of injury;

(iv) with her consent when the man knows that he is not her husband, and that her consent is given because she believes herself to be lawfully married;

(v) with or without consent, when she is under 16 years. Exception: sexual intercourse by a man with his own wife above 15 years is not rape."

In addition to random rapes and custodial rapes, the police also use rape as a highly effective weapon in the suppression of leftist movements and tribal uprisings. In all such cases, "the police, local upper-caste landlords and the government are all embroiled in a complicated system-by which they all support each other and benefit from the suppression of peasant movements". The methodology used by the police in the suppression of peasant movements is very familiar. The Santhal Parganas being a case in point. The Santhals, a group of tribal people, attempted to reclaim their land by forcibly harvesting it. Mahajans (money lenders, land owners, some of it illegal) promptly called in the Central Reserve Police Force who promptly preceeded to burn, plunder and rape in a terrible spree of vengeance. It is indeed fortunate that since many tribal societies have not adopted private property notions of female sexuality, the tribal women of such societies obviously get much more easily accepted by their own families as well as their communities without the humiliating social stigma that brands others as fallen women' in other rural communities. The Arab women of Jordan, however, are nowhere near as lucky. The horrific practice of "honour killing" which has its roots in the crude Arabic expression "a man's honour lies between the legs of a woman", sanctions the brutal killing of such a female if she dares in any way to dishonour this ancient male-oriented precept. For Arab women, virginity before marriage and fidelty afterwards are considered musts. She does not enjoy the luxury of a broadminded, understanding male ethos like the Santhal women. For it must be remembered that rape is indeed a powerful tactic because raping women is also a way of demoralizing and defeating men, as it has been in patriarchal cultures for thousands of years. And the men in this ancient Arab land are 'expected to control their female relatives'. Whether she is raped or whether she strays from the stringent moral norms and indulges in illicit sex, 'the dignity of the men can be restored only by killing her. In Jordan, the 25 or so cases of 'honour killing' documented every year constitute a quarter of all homicides.'

In every case of rape there must be medical examination of the private parts of both the man and the woman as soon as possible. There are four standard tests: (i) marks of violence about the genitals (ii) marks of violence on the other parts of the bodies (iii) stains of semen or blood (iv) veneral diseases on both. These tests would give vital clues to the crime. If there is no age certificate of the girl, medical tests can generally prove her age.

Comparisons of attitudinal prejudice and practice are essential between societies and peoples of different lands for it is only then that broad parameters of what is considered 'civilized' and would constitute norms which are generally acceptable, emerge and attempt to form a framework within which we can treat the grave malaise of crimes perpetrated against women, universally. By speaking in an informed manner in international fora, by forming 'societies' of social activists committed to articulating the neglected needs of women, by campaigning vociferously for the redressal of grievous wrongs done to them. The director of Jordan's National Institute of Forensic Medicine, Dr Mu'men Hadidi, says that in 80 per cent of the cases in which he conducts a hymenal examination which is routine in Jordan when a girl has gone missing, the same girl will be returned to him soon after as a corpse, even if she is proved to be a virgin. "Once the story is out in the community," says Asma Khader, a lawyer and feminist, "they have to kill." Sirhan, a 35-year old murderer, is cheerful and relaxed and happy to tell his story. He's especially proud to describe the efficiency with which he shot his young sister Suzanne in the head four times last March. "She came to the house at 8.15, " he relates, "and by 8.20 she was dead ." Three days before, the 16 year-old girl had reported to police that she had been raped. "She committed a mistake, even if it was against her will," says Sirhan. "Anyway, it's better to have one person die than to have the whole family die from shame." For his crime, Sirhan served his time at an Amman prison. For similar crimes perpetrated on women — wives and close female relatives discovered in the act of adultery — a man can engage in the brutal practice of "honour killing" without fear of any repercussions or punishement. Women have endured the custom, while legal establishments have tolerated or even condoned it. But as awareness of this barbaric practice is spreading and concepts of acceptability/ morality, etc., changing, various counter measures are being gradually activated to provide distressed women with some form of protection. Victor Hugo very wisely said: "Nothing in the world is so powerful as an idea whose time has come." And the time has come when crippling compromises will no longer suffice.

The following excerpt from a strongly worded letter dated 3 April, 1983, from Pragjoytika Mahila Sangha - an Assamese women's organization, to the People's Union of Civil Liberties, throws ample light on rape by the government and its affiliated agencies:

> "The indignity, violence and infringement of human rights that were perpetuated in the name of conducting 'a peaceful election' by the government with the help of the CRPF (Central Reserve Police Force) and other paramilitary forces drawn from all parts of the country, are beyond the imagination of any civilized person. During the last election period and even now, the CRPF and our own Indian government killed people with bullets, raped women and plundered the belongings of

> the indigenous people of Assam. What pains us most is the fact that the atrocities were perpetuated by the police force of a democratic country on their own sisters and brothers like occupation forces. While many of these victimised women had no connection whatsoever with political events, they were violated anyway. A large number of them, while 'obviously brutally raped and marked for life with savage toothmarks, etc.,' persistently refused to acknowledge that they had been raped or were surrounded by inlaws who fiercely denied that rape had occurred. Even in such bizarre situations when the women are totally blameless, they are petrified of being blamed and vigorously deny the truth. In the far-flung north-eastern states of Nagaland and Mizoram, the Indian army is engaged in a similar systematic terrorizing campaign to suppress freedom struggles.

These are not the only incidents of organized rape which make the government and its institutions a threat to women's freedom. It is also the complicity the government lends to many individual rape cases. The horrific gang rape of Anjana Mishra, an otherwise ordinary housewife fighting for a divorce from her forest-officer husband, Mishra was pitch-forked into prominence in 1997 after she accused former state advocate-general Indrajit Ray of attempting to molest her. She took him to court and Chief Minister J.B. Patnaik was drawn into the controversy for his alleged role in trying to bail out Ray, a friend of his. On January 9, 1999 in an apparent bid to teach her a punishing lesson indeed, Anjana's car was stopped in the picturesque Nandankanan Zoological Park by three scooter-borne miscreants who then "held the driver and a companion at gun point and drew her to a nearby forest where they took turns to rape her." In a nine-page FIR, Mishra described the gang rape as a "pre-meditated act to scare me into withdrawing my charges against Ray." It led to an unprecedented public outcry in Orissa. There were statewide protests as the public organised strikes and took to the streets. Patnaik was away in Delhi but rampaging mobs targeted his official residence in the state capital. Predictably angry Oppostion reactions ranged from the CPI, CPI(M) and Janata Dal jointly calling for a statewide bandh to public denounciations of the Chief Minister and his coterie. While the Biju Janata Dal President Naveen Patnaik maintained that "J. B. Patnaik has lost all moral authority to rule," former state president of the BJP, Debendra Pradhan remarked caustically that "Orissa has become worse than Bihar. The Government needs to be summarily dismissed." While even the worst detractors of the beleagured Chief Minister admit that 'he would not have been as naïve as to have instigated a gang rape', undoubtedly what has stoked passions to a high point of public outrage and demanded his ouster, are his unsympathetic attitude towards Mishra in pursuing the Ray case and his unfeeling remark that he was "not responsible for all dacoities and rapes in the state." Strong evidence points out towards his undeniable complicity in trying to hush up the Ray case. While a former Director-General of police, Amiya Bhushan Tripathy, 'has even filed an affidavit in the high court, alleging that Patnaik had exerted pressure on him to go slow on the case' the former Chief Minister, Nandini Satpathy has gone on record stating that a section of the ruling elite was 'willing to cough up Rs 2 crore to buy Mishra's silence.' Be that as it may, Mishra's supporters maintain that the administration 'was trying to paint the gang rape as a stray incident of crime without hidden motives' hinting that it was a case of robbery that had "inadvertently" turned into gang rape. In her nine page FIR however, Mishra steadfastly claimed that the miscreants were aware of her identity, called her by her nickname, Rolly and even returned her mobile telephone eventually, thereby seeming to discredit the theft theory. Following the barbaric gang rape which has not only the public and the opposition screaming for his blood but even the Congress high command, Sonia Gandhi pressurizing him to pursue the case, 'Patnaik may have little choice but to get things rolling' and ensure that justice, albeit a trifle late, is eventually done. Or else with Assembly elections due within a year, Patnaik's insensitive handling of the Mishra case, could well be the Congress undoing in the state.

Incest, which perhaps constitutes one of the most disgusting and unnatural forms of rape, has very aptly been defined as "sexual intercourse within the prohibited degrees of kindred." While the causative factors for the hardly publicized incidence of incest defy logic, they obviously stem from the deeply warped psyche of a convoluted mind which perceives events and situations through a completely self-centred, selfish miasmic haze. "In most cases the crime is unrecognized and the victims forced to take part in a conspiracy of silence. Incest is one of the implicit reasons offered in support of child marriages..." It is not-so-subtle a manifestation of a complex socio-economic malaise and needs remedial and reformist measures at the grassroots level in an intensified campaign to inform, educate and enlighten the potential perpetrators and victims, of this malpractice, of the highly damaging repercussions it can have. It is thus necessary to make available, centrally, counselling facilities in such areas, in those strata of society where a relatively high rate of incest is perceived to occur. A widespread increase in the general level of education, employment skills and self-awareness also will automaticlly promote greater self-confidence, a more healthy mindset and a more balanced and constructive dissipation of energy. Simultaneously, it is absolutely essential to create a housing infrastructure, whereby large growing families, which are forced to live in cramped quarters, in close proximity with each other and practically non-existent levels of privacy, are able to spread out and live in more congenial conditions conducive to healthy living and healthy thinking, without infringing on the personal and moral rights of any other member of the household. Manifestations of unnatural sexual overtones often occur due to a forced awareness of physical cravings, perceived when existing in abnormal conditions of co-habitation. Coercion and compliance then become strange bedfellows in a complicated game of even more complex filial relationships.

Rape is a universal phenomena and "it is important to remember that the widespread use of sexual violence is not the exclusive prerogative of men in the government, the police and the military... Women are raped at work, on the streets, in the fields, in their homes by men who are their employers, their acquaintances, their neighbours, their relatives, then in-laws and their husbands.... Caste-related rape is important in Indian society where casteism and sexism are both very strong. The rape of lower caste women is a socially sanctioned way to express sex and class domination. Even without casteism, sexism is present in all strata of society and so is rape."

According to the *Manifesto of The Progressive Women*, 1977-1978: "Many women activists have found it necessary to take up issues related to oppression of women like dowry, violence in the family, alcoholism, sexual discrimination of women at their work place, etc." Womens' organizations with a deep sense of commitment towards ameliorating such ills, mushroomed nationwide and attracted lawyers, doctors, professors, students and working women in particular. Like casteism and communalism, sexism is also one of the most effective weapons utilized by the ruling class to divide the masses and to maintain status quo. To combat sexism, the women's movement must evolve a multipronged approach as well as strategies 'to ally with other protest movements, because women's movements cannot sustain themselves in isolation from the wider political movement.' They must address the issues of casteism, class issues communalism and how these various factors affect every woman's life. In order to successfully achieve this aim, it is mandatory for the autonomous women's groups to work in collaboration with various types of mass organizations like democratic rights organizations, trade unions and issue-based united fronts concerning the masses.

Wife beating, dowry deaths, rape cases are all horrendous crimes committed against the discriminated female sex. But they do not, by any means, constitute the only serious offence committed against women. The widespread abuse of advanced technologies which have made sex determination and sex preselection tests possible with a commendable degree of accuracy, as well as the cruel practice of female infanticide, are two of the other grave crimes perpetrated against women.

During the last three decades or so, advanced techniques like sonography, fetoscopy, needling, chorion biopsy and the most popular one, aminocentesis, have increasingly become household names in India and more and more women are coming forward to make use of them and reduce or eliminate the chances of having an abnormal baby. Although Mumbai and Delhi are the major centres for both sex determination and sex preselection tests, the highly popular technique of aminocentesis is utilized even in the clinics of small towns and cities of a number of states such as Gujarat, Maharashtra, Uttar Pradesh, Bihar, Madhya Pradesh, Punjab, Tamil Nadu and Rajasthan. While justification for the use of these techniques has aptly been put forward by a team of doctors of Harkisandas Nurrotumdas Hospital (pioneers in the technique): 'In developing countries like India, as the parents are encouraged to limit their family to two offspring, they will have a right to quality in these two as far as can be assured. Aminocentesis provides help in this direction'. But this practise is often misused. A scientific technique meant primarily for the detection of genetic abnormalities, it has attained increasing popularity in India in detecting the sex of a foetus, with disastrous repercussions. Given the socio-psychological preferential bias towards the birth of a male child, the process of aminocentesis which is conducted after the completion of 16 weeks of pregnancy to rule out several genetic disorders like mongolism, defects of neuotube in the foetus, retarded muscular growth, 'Rh' incompatibility, haemophilia and other types of abnormalities, is being increasingly (mis) used to aid female foeticide. Apart from the Jats and the Rajputs who considered the birth of a daughter as a loss of prestige, 'abuse of aminocentesis for female foeticide was prevalent among all communities'.

Towards the beginning of the eighties, a fierce controversy erupted as a result of several investigative reports published in popular magazines like *India Today, Eve's Weekly, Sunday* and other regional language journals. What shocked everyone, from academics to activists, was that between 1978 and 1983, around 78,000 female foetuses were aborted after sex determination tests in our country. The advocates of population control policy obviously wanted to cash in on the socio-cultural values that considered the birth of a female child as a great calamity and perpetuate the modern method of femicide to have achieved NRRI (Net Reproduction Rate of One) i.e. replacement of a mother by only one daughter (with the help of the sex determination test) by the year 1990 as per the projected claims of the 7th Five Year Plan of the Government of India. Their argument was that if there are fewer number of women, obviously there will be a lower rate of reproduction on the whole and therefore less growth of a runaway population. Be that as it may, perpetuation of 'modern methods of massacre of female foetuses on a massive scale' is not only inhuman but unforgivable. Apart from the obvious trauma inflicted on the expectant mother through the forced expulsion of her child through unpleasant pressure tactics, brainwashing and other related methods of psychological persuasion, it is highly unjust that the woman be subjected to the physical invasion of her body and the emotional invasion of her mind, not to mention the cross-violation of her rights as an individual, to prevent so-called population explosion at some point in the unforseeable future. "Women have always been at the receiving end of all family planning policies. Harmful effects of pregnancy test, contraceptive pills, anti-pregnancy injections, camps for mass sterilization of women with its unhygienic atmosphere are always overlooked by the enthusiasts of family planning policy. Ninety nine per cent of population control research is conducted on women without any consideration of the harmful effects of research to the women concerned."

However, the popularity of sex preselection tests can be even more dangerous, more misused than that of sex determination tests because the former does not involve ethical issues related to abortion. So it gives 'licence' to abortionists and anti-abortionists alike to use this method. Dr Ronald Erikson, who has his chain of clinics conducting sex preselection tests in 46 countries of Europe, America, Asia, Latin America, announces in his handout that,out of 263 couples who approached him, 248 selected boys and 15 selected girls. Which just goes to prove that preference for the male child is not a socio-psychological phenomena confined merely to a Third World country like India but that it is universal. While in Erikson's method, no abortion or apparent violence is involved, still it can lead to violent social disaster if one thinks of its consequences in the long term. Through social consequences of sex selection as well as sex determination tests, the reality shatters the myth of neutrality of science and technology. It is, therefore, vitally important to link science and technology with socio-economic as well as cultural reality to create paradigms which have not only a socio-medico sanction but also an ethical acceptability. Aiming to establish a peregal system between both men and women in this crucial sphere where many, multi-layered moral issues are at stake and where the class, race and sex biases of the ruling elite which have crossed all boundaries of human diginity, can be eradicated. And creating widespread public awareness of such issues with all their implicit manifestations, is another very important, and vital step. Issues important in this regard are those that help in : (i) bringing about a positive change in attitudes; (ii) breaking down age-old prejudices that the birth of a female child is a curse, and (iii) making potential parents believe that to have a daughter is as great a blessing, if not more so, than having a son, because the modern girl has as many opportunities and avenues in which to excel, as her male counterpart. The girl child has proved herself to be equally competent in whatever field of specialization she has chosen.

Another extremely barbaric and brutal way of limiting, or rather, attempting to limit the population of the girl child, is through the age-old practice of female infanticide. An example of this inhuman method of killing was discovered among the Tapirape tribe of the Amazon region; the social structure of the Tapirapes was such that it prevented the tribe from splitting into smaller groups, even when the rationale for the existence of such a practice was inadequate food supply. Another factor which lent credence to this practice was the patriarchal nature of the tribal society.

Well known scholars like Malthus, McLennon, Carr-Sander, and Krzywick have propounded their respective analytical theories linking three important factors ideologically and factually to each other i.e. — 'the basic relationship between population increase, want of essential necessities, and the need for an artifice for restricting rapid multiplication of human mouths.' But while these theories have justified in their own fashion 'the existence of female infanticide at a time when human civilization was still primitive and employed crude techniques and had reasons to eliminate their female members', the advance of civilization, the relative acceptance and emancipation of women as individuals in their own right and (supposedly) more modern thinking, it definitely does not justify accepting this crude and cruel form of female elimination. In fact such an inhuman practice needs to be decried most vehemently, attacked most vociferously and extirpated with the utmost expediency.

There is very little evidence indeed of female infanticide prior to the advent of the British, in India. However, when the

British came to India 'this practise was common almost throughout India: from Gujarat in the west to the eastern borders of Uttar Pradesh, from Punjab in the north to Madhya Pradesh in the south.' Surprisingly though, there were hardly any tribal societies which indulged in this macabre practice, the Nagas of North East India, the Khonds of Orissa and the Todas of the Nilgiri hills of Tamil Nadu in the South, being the only exceptions. According to various sources such as Cave-Brown, Pakrasi, etc, female infanticide is believed to have been practised among several communities belonging to middle or upper classes: the Rajputs who were distributed in almost all the provinces of nothern India; the Sikhs and Muslim Pathans of Punjab; Khatris of northwestern India, Kanbis of Gujarat; Jats, Gujars, Tagas, Ahars, Minas, and Ahirs all of whom were inhabitants of northwestern India.

Several reasons have been advanced for the prevalence of this practice, certain superstitious beliefs such as the one that if you kill a female child, the next one is sure to be a male, that female children bring ill-luck to the family, etc., lending credence to the practise of female infanticide. Superstitions apart, the prevalence of hypergamous marriages, a custom which forbids the marriage of a woman with a person of lower social standing, also contributed in no mean measure to the existence of female infanticide. Such social strictures on formalizing matrimonial alliances invariably led to the giving of large dowry to secure a bridegroom of high social status. The financial burden of marrying off a daughter, and the social stigma of having an unmarried daughter in the house, forced people to kill infant girls at birth. A likely reason for the practise of this abhorrent custom among the tribal societies was inefficient family planning. According to Davis and Blake "female infanticide has the same effect as abortion, the major difference being that, in this case the progeny is being selected according to sex." While the oft-quoted Pakrasi was of the opinion that the Nagas practised female infanticide only 'to avoid raids by their strongest neighbours in quest of wives.'

The fairly widespread practise of female infanticide, however, attracted the attention of the British rulers and galvanized them into action. A notable feature of all the measures taken by them to curb this crude custom was an Act for Suppression of Female Infanticide (VII of 1870). "The British also organised conferences on the evils of infanticide, established a record of dowry deaths, helped fathers to pay for the marriages of their daughters, fixed a norm for the amount of dowry to be paid" according to Miller. Thus, the measures taken by the British Government greatly helped in the decline of this practise and led to its notable reduction in India.

Nearly two hundred years after the practise of female infanticide was first reported, it continues to flourish among the southern societal group of the Kallars. Though the maximum concentration of Kallars is found in Usilampatti *taluk* of Madurai district, they form a minority group in other districts of Tamil Nadu. Once a fierce and turbulent race, famous for their military prowess, like the Rajputs, they ceased to be rulers during the British period, whereas the Rajputs continued their traditional occupation as warriors even during this time. And today they are found in such diverse occupations as: landless agricultural labourers, watchmen, small businessmen, illicit liquor distillers, etc. This radical change in occupation as well as the low level of education among the Kallars, especially their women who play an insignificant role in their economic pursuits, are very likely the contributory factors towards the extant practise of female infanticide, a total antithesis to the rapid strides made in various fields, a complete negation of the process of modernization, emancipation and change.

Government hospitals, private nursing homes, primary health centres, as well as maternity hospitals/centres, all are witness to the shocking trend of nearly 80 per cent of all female babies delivered to Kallar women every year, vanishing with their mothers soon after birth and being reported dead due to natural causes after a week or so by their respective mothers.

The more gruesone methods of doing away with the innocent child include the father stepping on the throat of his infant daughter a few hours after the baby was born while the mother was still unconscious, to 'stuffing a few grains of coarse paddy into the mouth' (of the child). According to Venkatramani, the infant breathes the grain into the windpipe and chokes to death. Other less invasive (but equally condemnable) methods include feeding the female infant with the poisonous milk of a wild plant (*calotropis gigantea*) or the oleander berries known for their lethal poison, with little sugar — the result being instant death. It is also observed that every Kallar household has this plant grown in the courtyard for use at an appropriate time such as the birth of an unwanted female baby. These executions of the unsuspecting, innocent victims are normally carried out by their parents, either on their own accord or forced by the in-laws of the women. Since the preference for sons is so strong among Kallars, a woman who gives birth only to female children is looked down upon by the members of her husband's family. In cases where women cannot bear sons, even divorce is reported to be common. The birth of a female child among the Kallars, especially if it happens to be a continual occurrence between the same couple, spells disaster and unhappiness for the woman — the almost sure death of her baby daughter and an almost certain divorce for her — a fate surely worse than death.

The Economics of Female Infanticide

The deplorable custom of female infanticide among the chauvanistic Kallars (approximately 2 lakh in Usilampatti taluk alone) appeared to be motivated by the relative economic backwardeness of the community and the social importance of males. These motivational factors are almost comparable to 'pride and purse' which underlined this practice in north India in the nineteenth century. In no other community in modern India has such undue importance been attached to the birth of boys or the economic value of male children been as pronounced as among the Kallars. This is borne out by the fact that the existence of this custom has not been reported from any other part of modern India. There are many instances of neglect of female children in education, health, nutrition and clothes, across the Indian subcontinent but none measure upto this custom of outright murder. The practice of female infanticide and the inordinately high economic import of a male child are inextricably inter-linked with the cultural ethos of the Kallar community. One of their hereditary occupations had been dacoity. Their status in the economic front, particularly those who inhabit the villages, has not changed in a major way and the majority of them still work as landless agricultural labourers. Hence, it is not surprising that they are a merciless race as regards the value of human life. Whereas the birth of a son denotes not only the perpetuation of the race with all its inherent valour and adventure, but more male hands also ensure increased physical power to the community, in an age of increased competition for survival with other groups. Another reason that the female child is considered such a liability and her birth viewed with distaste and abhorrence is that the evil nature of dowry among Kallars is similar to that among the castes practising infanticide in the nineteenth century. Quite apart from the institution and practice of hypergamous marriages which entailed substantial sums of expenditure in dowry and marriage expenses, the system of dowry among the Kallars in any case acquires somewhat daunting dimensions for even if the Kallar bridegroom is not of higher status, the marriage still involves a considerable amount of expenditure. Those who cannot afford to pay such an exorbitant dowry, prefer to witness the comparatively short-lived misery of their daughters for a few hours after birth, than to see them suffer in adult life and hence resort to the heinous crime of female infanticide. The expenditures of the girl's family do not cease with dowry and marriage expenses. They seem to be never-ending as the in-laws expect gifts and feasts on all important as well as festive occasions. In conclusion thus, the economic overtones in the form of dowry and post-marriage expenditures rather than the desire to kill, is the real culprit. This has been reflected in the responses of mothers who become emotional and they do not appear ruthless but seem to be unfortunate and helpless victims of desperately cruel circumstances.

Predominantly economic reasons, and social, religious and ritualistic sanctions all form a formidable and complicated web of justifications or the *raison d'etre* of female infanticide. While the Infanticide Act of 1870, instituted by the British and used by them so effictively, still exists and is strong enough to suppress female infanticide, there is no mention anywhere in the literature of female infanticide as to whether anybody has been convicted for this crime as per the Act. The Kallars resent any sort of government and outside interference in their personal affairs and the government officials seem to be correspondingly reluctant to take any cognizable action in the matter even though they are aware of what is happening. With the government's own strong family planning policies, this custom has been ignored for it serves the same goal at no cost to the government. But sooner or later, the government will have to take a stand, identify active infanticide areas and attempt to suppress this barbaric custom. There are examples of successful suppression of this custom in the past. Tightening of the dowry laws, social upliftment of the Kallars, especially their women, economicallly and educationally, all will be positive steps in attacking this evil at its very roots and diminshing its gruesome incidence, if not entirely eliminating it immediately.

Murder, crime, abduction, desertion, cruelty, adultery, eve-teasing run the gamut of mostly macabre crimes against women, apart from the ones already elucidated above. Some horrendous newspaper clippings stand mute testimony to the perpetration of ghastly crimes thus: "Rohtak girl kindnapped by relative", "Journalist murdered in East Delhi" runs another news item, relating to the gruesome murder of 31 year old Shivani, a special correspondent of *The Indian Express*, in her Nav Kunj Apartment residence in Patparganj, on the afternoon of 23rd January, 1999. Describing this heinous crime, *The Hindustan Times* of 25th January states: "A deep incision in the left side of her throat apparently proved to be fatal. There were two other stab wounds in her abdomen while an iron skillet had been used to batter her chest. A yellow electrical wire was also found near her body, indicating that an attempt had also been made to strangle her. Two kitchen knives have been recovered, one of which was still in her neck when the body was found." "Culture of crime" (Comment) by Sumer Kaul in *The Hindustan Times* of 28th January, 1999 says, " A girl objects to eve-teasing by a jeepload of boys and they crush her under the wheels and drive away." Sumer Kaul goes on to say, " Once upon a time, not very long ago the eve-teasers would have confined themselves to some lewd remarks and then fled the scene out of fear of their parents as well as the police"—not so any more. Indeed, contrary to conventional sociology, crime can no longer be linked mostly to poverty and destitution; but it is relatively linked to the privileged sections who now account for the bulk of illegal acts. This enlarged phalanx of wrong doers may still be in a minority but they include the movers and shakers in every field and calling. The *primus inter pares* among them undoubtedly are the politicians. They have created new norms of dishonesty and depravity. The higher and better off you are the fatter is your diary of wrongdoing: from heinous deeds like rape and murder to offences like bribery scandals, scams, money laundering and smuggling. I am not sure the wrongdoers of today believe their doings are wrong. They commit illegalities in the well-founded belief that they will get away with it. Aiding them in their sense of impunity are their counterparts in the police and similar agencies, and a legal system that has many escape routes and other infirmities. The proverbial long arm of the law is not long enough or is easily twistable, and the wheels of retributive justice don't grind at all or grind so slowly as to be farcical.

MY Appeal

AWAKEN ! Politicians sitting in halls of FAME
Awaken to your country's GROWING Shame
LAW KEEPERS, Law givers
Others belonging to the same genre of the game
AWAKEN ! Forget your personal GAINS
Dispense JUSTICE
PROTECT the wronged woman's name
So she may rise
FROM the mire of MISERY
And hold her head up HIGH
WITH PRIDE ONCE AGAIN!

References

Antony, M.J., *Women's Rights*, New Delhi:Dialogue Publications, 1985.

Atray, J.P., *Crimes Against Women*, New Delhi: Vikas,1988.

Banerjree, Ruben, *Sordid Sequel*, article in *India Today*, January 25, 1999.

Beyer, Lisa, *The Price of Honor*, article in *Time Magazine*, January 18, 1999.

Flavia, 'Violence In The Family: Wife Beating' Women in Indian Society., In Ghadially Rehana, (ed.), New Delhi: Sage 1988.

Ghadially, Rehana, Ed., *Women in Indian Society*,New Delhi: Sage 1988.

Ghadially, Rehana and Kumar, Pramod, 'Bride Burning : The Psycho-Social Dynamics of Dowry Deaths; In Ghadially Rehana(ed.) *Women In Indian Society*, New Delhi: Sage, 1988.

Krishnaswamy, S., 'Female Infanticide In Contemporary India: A Case Study of Kallars of Tamil Nadu', In Ghadially Rehana (ed.) *Women In Indian Society*, New Delhi: Sage 1988.

Kumar, Nita, ed., in *'Introduction' to Women Subjects*, Stree, New Delhi.

Patel, Vibhuti, 'Sex Determination And Sex Preselection Tests: Abuse of Advanced Technologies', In Ghadially Rehana (ed.), *Women In Indian Society,* New Delhi: Sage, 1988.

7

AN ECONOMIC PERSPECTIVE

As early as 1890, Elizabeth Cady Stanton had stated "When women can support themselves, have their entry to all the trades and professions, with a house of their own over their heads and a bank account, they will own their bodies and be dictators in the social realm."

The Indian Constitution guarantees equal status to women. Articles 16(I) and 16(2) guarantee "equality of opportunity for all citizens in the matter relating to employment irrespective of religion, race, caste, sex, descent, place of birth.

Indeed, the changing position of Indian women is of a vast and bewildering complexity. An attempt to encapsulate it in a single pithy statement would be tantamount to condensing a multidimensional process into a highly inadequate and generalized system of thought. Yet one important factor emerges from the recognition of this highly complex and complicated socio-economic phenomena, namely that "economic independence is essential despite the existence of considerable variation between rural and urban areas, between classes and finally between different religions and ethnic groups." To effect a stable, progressive and constructive climate in which development can take place and thus enhance both the social and economic status of men and women who constitute its social fabric, a certain broadmindedness and flexibility of approach is essential. For development in its entirety and multifaceted nuances of providing broadbased opportunities for growth and development, includes all dimensions of human life — political, economic, social, cultural — and 'has been conceived as an integral process of economic growth and social progress. This position represents a collective articulation of the desire of the majority of mankind to humanize the conditions of people through the process of development.' Since women constitute not only half of the human resources in developing countries, but also because they have to bear the brunt of the daily struggle for survival in such countries, any development strategy which neglects the need for enhancing the role of women, definitely cannot lead to comprehensive socio-economic development. Therefore, the point of departure is to recognize the role of women as a dynamic factor and a valuable asset for the overall process of development. It is not a burden or cost nor a mere humanitarian concession to a disadvantaged group.

In 1967, the United Nations General Assembly accepted the basic principle that men and women should be given the same rights, obligations and work assignments,as an endorsement of the principle of equality in terms of access to opportunity for both sexes. It was also an acceptance of a fundamental social issue that social, economic and political inequality persist between men and women in contemporary society. The problem of social inequality has two dimensions, a distributive and a relational aspect. The first refers to the ways in which different factors such as income, wealth, occupation, education, power, skills, etc., are distributed in the population. The second refers to the ways in which individuals differentiated by these criteria are related to each other within a system of groups and categories. Social inequality is established over a period of time by a series of economic, social and religious phenomena and interwoven into the fabric of history and embedded in the minds of men and women. It is a persistent malaise which seems to permeate the very seams of the social structure and dwell there stubbornly, preventing women from developing to their fullest potential. "Although women in the 1980's, made conscious of new dimensions in their lives, are steadily recognizing their potential and capabitities beyond the realm of home, social inequality continues to persist between men and women." Thus, whether in highly developed industrialized economies or in developing countries, the omnipresence of such a mentally debilitating and economically restrictive phenomena automatically retards women's unequal access to economic and social opportunities especially in developing societies. Suffice it to say that there are 'two key issues that seem to have a pervasive impact on the creation of gender inequality in developing countries', which in turn influence basic attitudes towards a woman's employment and subsequent progress. They are: (a) norms of patriarchy and (b) the impact of modernization. "While patriarchal attitudes are known to affect the status of women in all societies in the contemporary world, modernization refers to a key process whereby ideas and technologies springing from the industrial economies of the west have been transferred to developing countries."

It may be argued that, "woman's gains in her status in many societies are directly related to her entry into production" and that sharp differences between the male and female segments of society signifying patriarchal superiority, only surfaced with the advent of agrarian societies. The status of women was known to be relatively high in pre-agrarian societies, since both males and females shared in the production process. Writing on women in pre-agrarian Egypt, Petrie concludes that women enjoyed considerable property rights and that their scope of activity went beyond child-bearing and caring for the house. The patriarchal control in subsequent peasant societies is related to major structural characteristics of agrarian production and as with the introduction of the plough, the fields were primarily cultivated by the men, 'his role became more valued and control over resources was put into his hands.' Women eased away from agricultural production, lost their status in relation to men who gained access to power, mainly due to their initial involvement in production. They had rights in religious authority and public office. By contrast, women were regarded as ill equipped for management or control of public life and affairs, though they may be loved and revered within the family and may be accorded a surprising degree of informal authority there. Women continued to 'work' but it was confined to the domestic sphere as such and taken for granted; they did not get the respect they deserved for such 'work' nor was it considered anywhere at par with activities outside the home. Over the past forty years, researchers have repeatedly shown that regardless of personal gifts, background or education, women are strongly and directly influenced in their activities by the marital, child-rearing situations. A commonality among women in all societies is that since the work place is more often located away from the home, she is forced either to carry the "double-burden" of home maker and wage earner or be only the home maker and reconcile herself to the traditional gender role where the "work" has still not achieved the same value as the work performed outside.

Janet Zollinger Giele argues that there is a curvilinear relationship between societal complexity and sex equality. In the simplest societies men's and women's freedom of choice are more nearly equal. It becomes the most unequal at the intermediate level and the position of women in the more advanced economies seem to improve again. But even in such advanced industrialized economies where all the benefits of modernization have been felt and where the development of industrial technology has transformed the home-based family-unit economic activity into an efficient, organized, surplus generating process, significant economic disparities between the two sexes persist, as in the US. Giele explains, women in the US, though sharing with men the benefits of a developed economy, good physical health, high literacy and education and participation in all the major rights of citizenship characteristic of a western democracy, yet in a number of important dimensions there is still a clear and consistent inequality in their status with men. Occupational segregation and low income still resist change. Women's low income which reflects low-paying jobs, remains at about sixty per cent below men. Women on an average earn less than Black or Hispanic men. Persistent discrimination seems to be the major cause for wage differential between men and women. Lenin's statement that "the proletariat cannot attain full freedom if it does not grant full freedom for women", is well known. Engels (1972) in his book *Origin of the Family*, clearly states that "the first condition for the liberation of the wife who was considered to be the husband's property was to bring her into public industry so that she could be an equal partner."

However, the strategy of development via modernization in third world countries, economic expansion and creating equal rights and opportunites for both the male and female components of its society, is a vastly different (and more difficult) proposition than in the industrialized west `where early economic gains preceded most other social and legal reforms'. In the third world country which represents the "have-nots" segment of the world, and where a large percentage of the population is necessarily poor and illiterate, its major problem is to stretch its resources several steps ahead of its exploding population while keeping an eye on its ever increasing economic distance with the advanced west. Therefore, while it aims at improving rapidly the income-generating capacity of society by introducing modern techniques of production and transforming existing social institutions, a fundamental component of the process of modernization has been, at best,only selective mainly benefiting the menfolk.

The Indian Scenario

A review of the economic role played by women reveals that in the traditional agro-based village economy, through centuries, women played a distinctive role in the process of earning the livelihood for the family. In the initial stages of industrial development, most industries continued the traditional pattern of family participation. In cotton and jute textiles, plantation and mines, entire families migrated to the work place, with women and children participating in these economic activities. However, in the post-independence era, both modern as well as organised industries grew rapidly. The year after India attained independence, in 1948, the first industrial policy resolution was introduced with emphasis on industrial growth and development while the Industrial Resolution of 1956 stressed on the acceleration of the rate of economic growth and speeding up of the industrialization process. Successive industrial policy statements of 1973, 1977 and 1980 emphasized high priority, capital intensive industries, foreign investment, promoting competitiveness, technical upgradation and modernization. In this whole process of planning and industrialization, the Seventh Plan perceived women as a resource and a critical input for nation development.

However, to give effect to the various strategies outlined in the Seventh Five Year Plan, the National Perspective Plan for Women published in 1988, aims at 'economic development and integration of women into the mainstream of the economy and securing equity and social justice for all women. The Plan lays special stress on rural women who suffer the worst form of discrimination. The remarkable feature of the Plan is that it does not seek more investment or more resources. It aims at giving a new thrust and responsiveness to developmental programmes at all levels.' Recognizing the imminent need for a holistic approach, it offers sectoral reviews of the situation of women in rural development, employment, supportive services, education, health, legislation, political participation, media and communication and voluntary action while simultaneously suggesting interlinked and covering strategies for the integrated and wholesome development of women by 2000 A.D. While expressing satisfaction about the number of existing programmes, it was however, felt that what is needed is not merely larger resource allocation but technical inputs for greater effectiveness of these programmes and to guarantee better resource utilization. Due emphasis has to be placed on certain crucial, key criteria such as more effective planning, monitoring and evaluation of existing programmes, through a result oriented mechanism operating at different levels. Recognizing the urgent necessity of critical and wider dissemination of information backed by research data and documentation, the Plan proposes to set up a National Resource Centre for Women.

Taking women's economic independence as a critical entry point for development, let us assess the importance of a policy such as full employment which should be the basis of the Eighth Five Year Plan. The right to work, plan or programme incorporating, at the implementational level, a system of generating durable regular employment through the full utilization of the productive forces of the country. It is an established fact that women play a decisive and fruitful role in the production, storage and processing of food and make up one-third of the workforce in the developing countries, but ironically enough, they form the largest group of landless labourers and are unorganised.' Therefore, the mobilization and organization of poor women around issues of common concern, is a prerequisite for sustainable economic and social development. In order that our planning, policies and activities at the grassroots' level meet with a significant measure of success, women should rightfully be represented in the local body, the cooperatives, and the State legislative assemblies and Parliament commensurate with their population. Thus, they can project the developmental needs and shortcomings already existing in the prevailing systems and programmes and constructive via medias to circumvent or remedy such lurking flaws. In ancient Greece, Athens was considered a model in participatory democracy. Any citizen could move a legislation there. With one important precondition, notwithstanding: "before moving the legislation he should stand on a platform, with a rope round his neck. If the legislation was accepted, the rope was removed from the neck. If it was reflected, the platform was removed." A truly laudable practice and one that would be indeed wise for us to emulate to ensure maximum participation, representation and comprehension among that massive body of nameless, faceless women who could form the economic bulwark of our country, but presently constitute a dismally neglected bulk of our unharnessed female population.

Harnessing Human Resourcing

According to Pramila Balasundaram, some valuable practical suggestions to institute a movement for human resource development involving women in the low income areas, are reproduced below:

Establishing a network of organizaitons both non-governmental and governmental, working in areas of low income such as resettlement colonies and slums.

Giving the responsibility of identifying women who have shown the skills and the motivation to act as catalysts of change within the community, to voluntary organizations in the area — all NGOs would be able to identify such women.

Putting in place a system of support through appropriate training for these women and providing the financial and material help required.

In connection with the last mentioned suggestion, it would be extremely useful if an exclusive banking system for women with the concept, 'of the women, by the women, for the women' could be translated from a mere precept into reality. In fact, such a need has manifested itself not merely as a desirable solution but an imminent necessity on a nationwide basis, taking into consideration the lack of exposure and the innate lack of accessability for women in the present banking system. The callous disregard of institutional financing towards the developmental needs of women can be gratified to an extent by a central banking agency to guide, monitor and evaluate the services of all the financial institutions with regard to women. Furthermore, there is no harm whatsoever in taking into confidence the womenfolk of the country in the grip of a financial crisis; on the contrary, it might well prove to be eminently useful since women have proved to be competent in the management of financial crisis at home. They have also proved beyond the shadow of a doubt that they are credit-worthy and capable of understanding financial transactions.

Maintains Jayalakshmi, putting forward innovative suggestions, that, "the unskilled female construction labourers can be trained in innovative cost-effective housing technology, in collaboration with Nirmit Kendras. Deviating from the conventional role of acting as unskilled helpers, women can be trained to become masons,carpenters and painters and can be involved with all aspects of housing. Women, housing and environment go together. This will be a step towards the participation of poor women in development using primarily local knowledge and local resources sensitively."

Of Technological Advances, The Women Work Force and Related Matters:

It is an internationally acknowledged fact that 'technological dynamism' renders human labour surplus and women workers, who constitute by far the most vulnerable and exploited section of the labour force, have always remained depressed and have been discriminated against in spite of ILO's concern for the protection of women workers. However, a shift in technological choices that could `ameliorate the conditions of women by removing the drudgery, reducing workloads, helping income generation and improving health and also understanding the adverse second-order impacts of technology on women is what is urgently required and may be the answer to counter the unwelcome phenomena of labour surplus, judiciously. A greater involvement of women in scientific and technological development would thus require:

(a) Popularization of scientific and technological knowledge and skills in order to enable their further development, by mass media, through changes in school programmes and through all participatory and community development activities (especially in agriculture, etc.). Furthermore, frontier and transdisciplinary technologies can be used in different ways and at different levels. Their use can serve to accentuate the productive role of women relating to them to a number of areas which are of relevance in better quality of life and to the integration of women in development, i.e. food production, clean water supply, improved housing conditions, use of alternative energy sources, in the services, education, etc. Such technologies also stimulate the growth of employment, as they offer a variety of employment combinations. It would be pertinent to mention here that women's access to technological advancement also largely depends on 'the global relations between the technology owners and users and those who try to secure access to new technology and to processes of industrialization. Subsequent exchange of experience on application of science and technology in development, joint research, etc., between such forces would definitely lead to a greater facilitation of women's involvement in scientific and technological advances.

(b) Changes in the traditional attitudes towards women by enabling them to fully participate in scientific and technological development by stimulating their involvement in various forms of education and training.

During the Sixth Plan Review, the laudable scheme of Krishi Vigyan Kendras introduced 'for bridging the gap between the farmer's knowledge and available technology also covered women. Eight Home Science colleges for women attached to agricultural universities were set up to provide training and research facilities'.

Recapitulation, Remuneration and Reconstruction of Policies and Plans

An excerpt from the Sixth Plan Perspective unequivocally states that : The Constitution of India not only provides for equal rights and privileges for women and men but also for making special provision for women. A series of social legislations have been enacted from time to time for raising the status of women in the country. The Five Year Plans have consistently placed special emphasis on providing minimum health facilities integrated with family welfare and nutrition for women and children, acceleration of women's education, their increase in the labour force and welfare services for women in need. Various welfare and development schemes have been introduced to improve the living conditions of women and to increase their access to and control over material and social resources. Various studies show that women are becoming increasingly conscious of their rights and capabilities. However, the demographic features of female population like excessive mortality in female children resulting in persistent decline in sex ratio, low rate of literacy, and low economic status stress the need for greater attention to the economic emancipation of women. The low status of women in large segments of Indian society cannot be raised without opening up of opportunities of independent employment and income for them. Sustained and sincere efforts on a national scale to create such an ambience conducive to the emancipation of women, is the only answer.

Some relevant and thought-provoking remedial measures are put forward by Kamala Sinha who is of the opinion that, "our planners, despite the recognition of women as a potential force in the nation's development process, have suggested no positive, affirmative action programmes to utilize their potential." Given below are some of the more important suggestions:

(a) The planning process must take into cognizance this vast women's resource in the nation building process.

(b) In small and tiny industries, women entrepreneurs and women workers should be given preference.

(c) Women's cooperatives in small and tiny industries should be given priority.

(d) Proper technological, vocational and in-service skill training should be part of the industrialization process, especially for women.

(e) 30 per cent employment quota should be fixed for women and all employment exchanges should be instructed to send 30 per cent women applicants names to prospective employers.

(f) Equal Renumeration Act and all other labour legislations/protective, welfare legislations for working women must be properly and strictly implemented.

(g) Supportive programmes like creches, balwadis, working women's hostels, self-financing cooperative housing schemes for working women, health, hygiene, family planning, motivation, awareness generation and adult education programmes should be taken up.

(h) For the home-based, self-employed women workers, proper marketing facilities for their produce should be made as part of the infrastructure.

(i) Bank credit and ownership of an establishment should be given to women on a priority basis.

(j) In no case should women workers be retrenched. If a woman wants to retire voluntarily, a woman of her family should be given the option to replace her.

(k) Sexual harassment at the workplace should be dealt with separately by enacting a protective labour legislation, which should not remain a part of

Criminal Procedure Code. Onus of the crime should lie with the employer/the floor boss/supervisor and not only on the assaulted.

(l) In all affirmative policy making and implementation processes, working women's representatives (through trade unions) should be involved.

(m) Women should not, by agreement be allowed to be used as cheap labour by multinational companies. Their interests/jobs should be protected by special legislation.

Despite international recognition of rural women's right to own land, (World Conference on Agrarian Reform and Rural Development held at Rome), attempts to incorporate this principle in land tenure and land development policies have been marginal. Forest policy including policies for reforestation has yet to recognize the role of women in forest development even though in some areas, women have initiated major protest movements against deforestation which have negatively affected their ability to feed their families and livestock. Case studies from Asia and Africa indicate that rural women are very dynamic and innovative in these fields when they are given the opportunity to participate collectively in such developmental activities. They also indicate a process of increasing self-confidence among women and an enhancement of their status within their families and the community. However, extension of such experiments to other areas will require incorporation of women as a target group in policies and structures for agrarian reform, and development of forests, agriculture, animal husbandry, silk production, fish culture, land development (including waste lands, etc.

However, the solution to the problem lies in the establishment of long-term strategies and measures to implement them as a matter of national priority in the context of solutions, for example, chronic food problems, deforestation and ecological imbalances, unemployment and poverty, and to enhance the process of corrective and individual self-reliance.

At this juncture, it would be wise to take cognizance of the Directive Principles of State Policy enshrined in the Indian Constitution. With particular reference, of course, to such Directive Principles as those affecting women and their future, in Article 39 of the Constitution. It says:

> "The state shall, in particular, direct its policy towards securing:
>
> (a) that the citizens, men and women equally, have the right to an adequate means of livelihood.
>
> (b) that there is equal pay for equal work for both men and women;
>
> (c) that the health and strength of workers, men and women, and the tender age of children are not abused and that citizens are not forced by economic necessity to enter avocations unsuited to their age or strength."

Let us then briefly trace the position of women as a workforce, taking the mid-nineteenth century as a suitable cut-off point for the purpose of our relatively modern (and pertinent) period of reconstruction.

It is indeed creditable that women formed 25 per cent of the total workforce at a time when cotton textile mills were first to be developed in India in the mid-nineteenth century. Though this percentage remained stable till 1930, thereafter 'began a slow and steady decline of the women workforce. In 1975 only 2 per cent of the total workforce was women'. Nevertheless in 1944, women formed 14 per cent of the total workforce; the decline being more gradual here, six years later i.e., by 1952, the strength came down to 11per cent. Thereafter the decline was pretty rapid - in 1962 it dwindled to 3.9 per cent, finally to less than 1 per cent in 1970.

In the mining industry, in the early decades after independence-between1951and 1971, and thereafter, women's share of employment declined by a massive 47.4 per cent. In coal mines, the percentage has dropped by 66.8 per cent. In terms of overall industrial employment, coal mines, even today, employ the largest number of women. Nevertheless the decline has been phenomenal. In 1919, in the coal industry, women formed 38.1 per cent of the colliery labour force. For every 10 men working underground, there were seven women employed for the same job. In 1939, a total ban was imposed on the employing of women for underground work. The number of women workers dropped to 10 per cent in 1970. This is despite the fact that overall employment has increased considerably in the mining sector, including coal mines.

However, more encouraging statistics are forthcoming in the plantation industry, which is intrinsically labour-intensive. Here women's employment, especially the "nimble-fingered pickers", has remained static over the years and women form as much as 48 per cent of the total workforce (over 4 lakhs in absolute numbers).

But whereas various protective and welfare legislations have also contributed to the decline of women's employment in the traditional organised sector, an encouraging trend has become apparent in the service sector. Over the years, women's employment has grown considerably in this sphere, including school and college teaching services.

Talking in terms of fairly accurate approximations, till a decade ago in the All India Services there were 994 female officers as compared to 15993 male officers, 5.8 per cent of the total. In the IAS (again upto 1988) there were 339 women officers, comprising only 7.5 per cent of the total. In the IPS there were only 21 women officers, 0.9 of all the women workforce, 10 per cent work in the organized sector. Eighty - three percent work in the unorganized, rural, agro-based and construction sector and they work mostly on a piece-rate, casual and /or daily-wage basis. The balance of nearly 7 per cent are invisible twilight zone workers in the informal self-employed, part-time jobs. This is the most exploited, vulnerable group.

While the formulation of the Eighth Plan and its subsequent announcement was awaited, the (then) new industrial policy announced, reiterated that:

> "the Government is pledged to launch a reinvigorated struggle for social and economic justice, to end poverty and unemployment and to build a modern, democratic, socialist, forward-looking India."

In order to achieve this goal, it laid emphasis on a reformatory action plan in the following relevant areas: 'on the privatization of public sector undertakings, possibly banks; the bringing in of new technology; dismantling of the regulatory system; foreign investment and technology collaboration with 51 per cent or more equity share to foreign companies so as to increase export and foreign exchange earnings needed for paying out foreign debts which include interest on the IMF and World Bank Loans.'

A dichotomous situation prevailed. The framers of this industrial policy lacked visionary acumen and the policy did not envisage any measure to protect the organized sector's most exploited section of the workforce — the working women, nor prescribe any panacea for them in the unorganized and informal sector. While imminent technological dynamism and the subsequent investment by multinationals in the country would obviously lead to more exploitation and retrenchment (women being the first to be sacrificed), on the other side of the scale 'inflation, spiralling price rise, family's consumeristic demands, etc., were pushing more and more women into the job market; into low category, subsistence-wage jobs'.

In the free trade zones and in the informal sectors women are in any case widely exploited; whereas the unorganised sector and the home-based informal sectors are, unfortunately, beyond the purview of labour legislation. It is a deep-rooted socio-economic malaise that women workers, whether white-or blue-collared are subjected to varying degrees of sexual harassment at their work places. A serious and sincere incorporation and implementation of the indepth remedial measures suggested by Kamala Sinha, while chalking out long-term policies which will have a significant bearing on women's status and future evolvement as actively contributing citizens of the country, as well as other relevant and timely action, is the need of the times.

Entrepreneurship and Enterprise

The entry of women in organized business is a fairly recent phenomenon. In reality, women have been associated with economic activity since ages. Women have all along participated in outdoor occupations, in the fields and on the farms tending to cattle. They have also played an important part in the production process by working in cottage industries such as handloom, powerloom, pottery, embroidery, handicrafts etc. While such economic participation by women went largely unacknowledged because it was carried on basically within the environs of the home, it taught them the vital art of entrepreneurship; a factor which stands them in good stead today. As regards their entry in small business and trade activities, they are in significant numbers. However, their activities are normally associated with women's requirements, namely, garments, cosmetics, interior decoration and the like. Women entrepreneurs would be particularly effective in increasing exports, especially of the traditional items. To help them achieve this goal, it would be necessary to conceptualize and make available to them design centres to compete in the modern designs of today. Also, as potential entrepreneurs, women face financial constraints and subsequent paucity of capital since both property rights as well the laws of inheritance have always been in favour of men rather than women. It is in this area thus that women urgently require the help of law and society to be placed on an equal footing. As regards credit, women entrepreneurs in particular, especially in rural areas, are denied need-based finance for reasons of inadequate security to satisfy the financial institutions. It is, therefore, suggested that the quantum of credit be raised suitably matching the need-based requirements of the potentially viable woman entrepreneur and her enterprise, and collective enterprises of women entrepreneurs should be encouraged. In an encouraging step forward, the SIDBI produced project files for over 400 items, in consultation with the banks and SFCs. SIDBI should similarly prepare project profiles for women entrepreneurs at the village level and also identify the areas of enterprise under service subsector which is now also declared as tiny enterprises, so that rural enterpreneurs do not find any problem in convicing the financial institutions about the project viability. For identification of the woman entrepreneur, a task force consisting of the various promotional agencies and representatives of the women entrepreneurs should be constituted.

Since people, including women themselves, are still unfairly sceptical about the ability of women to run factories and business establishments, independently and efficiently, suitable steps must be taken forthwith to correct this highly erroneous misconception. Approximately thirteen years ago, in 1986 to be precise, DC (SSI) conducted 28 training courses for women throughout the country which, unfortunately, declined during 1990-91. It was suggested, therefore, 'that the women entrepreneurship training programmes be monitored on a quarterly basis by DC (SSI) in collaboration with the women entrepreneurs association. Special training-cum-orientation programmes for apprising officers of banks and state agencies should be planned to change their biased attitude while dealing with this group'. Also, to further encourage and promote enterprising women to come forward as entrepreneurs, it is imperative that not only should financial institutions extend long-term loans with longer moratoriums but that they should be flexible as well regarding the guarantee terms. Relatively recent trends indicate that the scope of the National Equity Fund Scheme will cover projects upto 10 lakhs for equity support (upto 15 per cent). An extremely viable proposition would be to raise the quantum of support for women entrepreneurs to 30 per cent instead of 15 per cent to the general category of enterpreneurs. Trade union activities should be restricted to units employing above 30 persons for units with power, and 50 persons for units without power, and wage should be linked with production output.

While encouraging change, adaptibility and easier channels of economic assistance to promote entrepreneurship among women, it is also essential to extend counselling support to already existing women entrepreneurs to enable them to run their units better. For this purpose one would like to recommend that special management as well as entrepreneurial competence development programmes be conducted for such existing entrepreneurs. However, infrastructural facilities being quite scarce in most metropolitan and big cities, allotment of sheds and plots on a quota basis would encourage them to come forward and engage in fruitful enterprise.

Entrepreneurship inevitably leads to the woman being the leader of the organization. Due to her inherent qualities of management, among other things, she is also able to engender a feeling of commitment from the workers. Women entrepreneurs who have formal authority and control over vast resources, still share power and information as an asset rather than a liability. They believe that although pay and promotion are necessary tools of management, what people really want is to feel that they have the opportunity as individuals to learn and grow. The women believe that employees and peers perform better when they feel they are part of an organization and can share in its success. Allowing them to get involved and to work to their full potential is a way of maximising their contribution and using human resources most efficiently.

Today, there is increasing emphasis on creating an awareness about entrepreneurship and with this laudable aim in mind, the Department of Science and Technology has taken the initiative in encouraging the introduction of entrepreneurship as a subject in the curriculum of the technical institutions and colleges and also getting teachers trained in the subject. The National Science and Technology Entrepreneurship Board (NSTEBD), set up by the Department of Science and Technology, has thus proved to be a key factor/contributor to the spread of entrepreneurship development in the country. Other institutions like the EDI (Entrepreneurship Development Institute) organized two technical teachers training programmes in Gauhati and Imphal in Jan-Feb 1991 and February 1991 respectively, wherein 20 to 26 teachers (some of them females) attended and valuable inputs were provided to them on EDP processing, motivation and experience sharing along with managerial aspects in various functional areas. A society known as the Indian Entrepreneurs Trainers has also been set up at EDI.

The future is thus expected to provide us with much more valuable and interesting data about the effects of feminization of those areas which were hitherto perceived to be purely male domains.

Rerences

Anand, Indu, 'Economic Independence of Women' *Reforms For Women - Future Options*, Heptulla, Najma, Ed., New Delhi: Oxford and IBH Publishing Co. Pvt. Ltd., , 1992.

Balasundaram, Pramila, 'Poor Women are Our Strength', Reforms For Women-Future Options. In Heptulla, Najma, Ed., New Delhi: Oxford and IBM Publishing Co. Pvt. Ltd., 1992.

Heptulla, Najma, 'Development Strategies for Women : Need for Political Will'. In Heptulla, Najma, Ed., *Reforms For*

Women - Future Options, New Delhi: Oxford and IBH Publishing Co. Pvt. Ltd., 1992.

Samarasinghe, *Vidyamali*, 'Gender Inequality in Developing Countries : A Reiteration of some Leading Issues', *Women At The Crossroads A Sri Lankan Perspective*, Kiribamune, Sirima and Samarasinghe, Vidyamati, (eds.), Published by International Centre for Ethnic Studies in association with NORAD and Vikas Publishing House Pvt. Ltd.,New Delhi, 1990.

8

THE ECONOMICS OF ENTREPRENEURS AND THE SOCIO-PSYCHO DYNAMICS

Government is a contrivance of human wisdom to provide for human wants. Men have a right that these wants should be provided for by this wisdom.

Edmund Burke

In consonance with the ambience of modernization and the ambitious aspirations of women, this hitherto much neglected and thoroughly undervalued segment of society, is also demanding a more equitable system of economic remuneration.

Women all over the world are paid less than men for doing the same work, though several countries like India and England have laws prohibiting such discrimination. An analysis of women in the workforce, conducted over a decade ago by the International Labour Organization, showed that wage disparities increased in as much as 14 western countries. Hence we realize that the disparity is not merely a malaise that afflicts Third World and developing countries; it is manifest in the more developed industrialized economies as well. However, to get to the point, from 1977 to 1982, the difference in wages widened in Australia, Czecholovakia, Denmark, the Netherlands and England. The most marked gap was in Japan, where women received only half the remuneration received by men in certain sectors. In 1982, women's wages lagged behind that of men by 11.4 per cent in France; by 33 per cent in Switzerland; in Japan by 47.2 per cent and the Republic of Korea by 57.9 per cent. These figures refer to only non-agricultural jobs. In agricultural labour, women's position is still abominable. Moreover, women occupy more of the jobs which are less paid.

The year 1975 was celebrated the world over as International Women's Year. Following the year 1975, during the Women's Decade (1976-85), to further strengthen the woman's position and 'ensure that there was no discrimination in pay on the grounds of sex only' the Equal Remuneration Act was passed in 1976. This Act which protects men equally against discrimination, maintains that, "no employer shall, while making recruitment for the same work of a similar nature, make any discrimination against women except where the employment of women in such work is prohibited or restricted by law."

Recognizing the vital role which women play in society and that the processes of change in women's position depend primarily on the interrelations between transformative factors and forces, spontaneous or consciously directed, and the inherited matrix of social and cultural institutions, values, norms and practices, forms of production and distribution which in turn are manifested in the division of resources, labour and power, the Government appointed in 1971 the Committee on the Status of Women. The Committee submitted its report four years later, in 1975 and put forth certain very useful recommendations concerning the rights and status of Indian women. Based on these recommendations, the Mexico Plan of Action and the Resolution of Parliament adopted in 1975, a National Plan of Action was formulated for framing strategies necessary to improve the position of women in our country. Fitting into these long-term strategies as well as to provide special attention to the problem of working in the informal sector, a National Commission on Self-Employed Women and Women in the Informal Sector was appointed in January, 1987. The Government notification appointing the National Commission on Self-Employed Women stated in unequivocal terms that:

"Despite the existence of various constitutional legal provisions safeguarding women's employment, a large number of women workers, particularly in the unorganised sector, suffer from varios disadvantages relating to their working lives as well as in their homes. The coverage of labour laws has not benefited these women workers in many crucial areas especially health, maternity and social security. With the changing social and economic conditions, women's productive roles have assumed new significance but without back-up support and services a healthy combination of women's productive and reproductive roles cannot be sustained."

Experience acquired during the UN Decade for Women, Equality, Development and Peace (1976-1985) has indicated how the process of development can be promoted or constrained by the integration or non-integration of the productive, reproductive and household functions of women into development processes. The decade has also greatly increased the awareness of the continued violations of the basic rights and needs of women, contributed to the knowledge of the role of women in development, 'reflecting the developmental dimension of the problem and stimulating further activities along these lines at the national and international levels.'

Geting back to the vital issue of the Equal Remuneration Act, this act makes provision for the establishment of advisory committees by the government to provide many more employment opportunities for women. The committee, which comprises an equal number of men and women, would consist of a total of ten members. It would undertake to study in each case, not only the number of women employed in each establishment, but also the nature of their work, hours of work, suitability of women for employment and the need / necessity for providing more jobs. Both the employers and employees concerned could make the desired recommendations to such a committee. Thereafter, the government would consider the advice of the committee and issue appropriate directions regarding employment of women.

In case the employer unjustly holds back part of the woman's pay, complaints about unequal remuneration can be made to a labour officer in the locality. This officer, who posseses the power of a civil court, can, after hearing the case of the employer as well as of the unfairly deprived (female) employee, order the employer to pay the woman the amount withheld by him on the grounds of sex. The local labour officer is suitably empowered, and can even ask for the production of witnesses and documents. In case the decision is not in her favour, the female employee can appeal to the higher authority within 30 days.

Every employer, on his part, is duty bound to maintain regularly and in an organized and methodical manner, registers and documents as prescribed by the government. The government is empowered to appoint inspectors to ensure that the equal pay law is being enforced and adhered to in all establishments. As such, these inspectors can enter any building, factory or premises, at any reasonable time, with help if necessary. He can make on-the-spot investigations to check whether the law is followed in the establishment. Not only the employer and his agents can be examined for a judicious corroboration of facts and to rule out any type of fraudulence, but the Equal Remuneration Act also prescribes penalities for those who do not abide by its rules. Therefore, if any employer recruits staff in flagrant violation of these rules and discriminates between men and women against this law, he could be fined as much as Rs 5,000. Furthermore, if he fails to maintain the prescribed registers of his staff or fails to produce the same for inspection or even refuses to give the required evidence at an enquiry, he could be punished and asked to pay a fine of Rs. 1000. Where an entire company, instead of an individual employer, violates the Act, the company as well as all those who are in charge of its business, shall be deemed guilty and punished. Only metropolitan magistrates or first class magistrates are empowered to try an offence under this law and before making a complaint, sanction of the government or an officer authorised by it must be taken. The complaint must be made within three months of the sanction.

However, the Act does not confer or create conditions of equality between the two sexes, which are either absolute or unconditional. Clauses exist which provide certain loopholes, however justified or otherwise. For example, though the law prohibits any employer from making a distinction in economic remuneration between male and female employees, Section 16 authorises certain restrictions regarding salaries if a declaration is made by the 'appropriate government'. Such a clause could work against the interest of women employees as the air hostesses found to their regret, some years ago. Specifically, Section 16 says, "Where the appropriate government is, on consideration of all circumstances of the case, satisfied that the differences in regard to the remuneration, or a particular species of remuneration, of men and women workers in any establishment or employment is based on a factor other than sex, it may by notification, make a declaration to that effect, and any act of the employer attributable to such a difference shall not be a contravention of any provision of this Act." Thus, a government can justifiably use such an interpretation to explain a disparity of wages in any particular given case and the courts have to accept it without enquiry. In fact, if one recollects correctly, in the controversial air hostesses' dispute, the Central Government had issued such a notification stating that the differences in the said remuneration between air hostesses and flight stewards were 'not based on sex'. The Supreme Court took serious cognizance of this representation and issued a judgement which was final and binding in its verdict thus: "The declaration by the Government completely concludes the matter." Hence one perceives that this rule could be used arbitrarily both in terms of public sector undertakings as well as in cases of private employment. All the government has to do is to issue a notification to the effect and shut out a subsequent enquiry by the courts.

Since the concept of 'equal pay for equal work' is (rightfully) assuming increasing relevance in the modern scenario of woman's emancipation today, it would be worthwhile to take a look at the law in an advanced country like England where two Acts have been passed which prohibit discrimination on the ground of sex. The first of these, the Equal Pay Act of 1970, applies to everything in a woman's contract of employment such as pay, holidays and hours of work. The provisions in the Act are implicit and binding, even if there is no written contract. To claim equal pay with her male counterpart, the woman has to prove: (a) that a 'comparable man' has been paid more than her; (b) that her job and his job are either the same or broadly similar with no substantial difference; and (c) that both his and her job have been given an equal rating under a job evaluation scheme.

Although the Act is drafted in terms of discrimination against women, Section I(13) makes it crystal clear that its provisions "are to be read as applying equally in a converse case to men and their treatment relative to women." Cases where the woman is paid more than the man do occur, albeit rarely, in England.

The second English Legislation which applies to recruitment, promotion, training and fringe benefits but does not cover salary or other things in the contract of employment, is the Sex Determination Act of 1975. However, it does cover all categories of jobs, whether temporary or permanent, apprentices and sub-contracted workers. It is mandatory for an employer not to discriminate on grounds of sex in any of the following ways: (a) refusing to employ or consider for job; (b) refusing to give the same opportunities for promotion or transfer; (c) refusing to make equal provision for training; (d) giving less favourable fringe benefits and (e) issuing dismissals. It is strange enough, that while an employer is banned from discriminating against someone on the ground that he or she is married, discrimination against someone who is not married is not considered unlawful. In fact instances of such 'open' discrimination, based on gender bias, are very much in evidence. For example, a potential employer only visiting boys' schools for purposes of recruitment and not even taking the trouble to visit a girls' school, leave alone recruitment of deserving candidates from there; in the eventuality of retrenchment, asking women to quit first; subsidizing mortgages only for male staff and so on and so forth. However, it is considered unlawful for a trade union, professional association or licensing body to discriminate in the matter of admission, expulsion and allocation of benefits.

The Sex Discrimination Act allows certain exceptions; exceptions which, to my mind, are based on *de jure* methods of classification and could be transposed and applied to Indian conditions. These are, as elucidated in the British Sex Discrimination Act (1975), applicable "where sex is a Genuine Occupational Qualification (GOQ) for the job.' Such jobs are:

Where the job needs to be held by a man to preserve decency or privacy, because it would involve physical contact with men in circumstances where men might reasonably object to having a woman present, e.g., massage, frisking, lavatory attendants.

Where the job is in a single sex hospital, old people's home, mental home or other institutions where people receive special care.

The job needs to be held by a man because of the protective laws relating to women's employment e.g., bar on women in nightshift in factories.

Quite apart from such conditions, an employer can discriminate when the job pertains to private household, employment in dramatic performances and in modelling where someone of a particular sex is required, etc. Discrimination could be either direct or indirect. Whereas rejecting a woman for a job and giving the same job to a less qualified man, would constitute a form of direct discrimination. Indirect discrimination includes various indirect ways of applying a test or condition which appears impartial but in reality puts women at a distinct disadvantage and, more often then not, proves to be a skilful method of eliminating them as potential job qualifiers, thus leaving the field open for men. All these job selectors are considered unlawful in England.

The Supreme Court, in a judgement delivered in 1982 (Randhir Singh vs Union of India), has put more force in the Directive Principles declaring 'equal pay for equal work'. The court held that though equal pay for equal work was not a fundamental right, it undoubtedly was a constitutional goal and, as such, the principle could be read into the fundamental rights while interpreting law. Hence the equal pay principle in Article 39(d) can be read along with the fundamental rights to equality contained in Articles 14 and 16. The judgement, almost historic in spirit and import, written by Justice O. Chainnapa Reddy, said; "To the vast majority of people, the equality clauses of the Constitution would mean nothing if they are unconcerned with the work they do and the pay they get. To them equality clauses will have some substance if equal work means equal pay." This judgement can, therefore, be legitimately used to support a writ petition in a High Court or Supreme Court if women are paid less than men for doing the same work.

Some other excerpts of the judgement maintain that "Article 14 of the Constitution enjoins the state not to deny any person equality before the law or the equal protection of the laws and Article 16 declares that there shall be equality of opportunity for all citizens in matters relating to employment or appointment to any office under the state."

An important part of the judgement, of great relevance to the issue at hand, reads thus: The preamble to the Constitution declares the solemn resolution of the people to constitute India into a Sovereign, Socialistic, Democratic Republic. Again the word 'Socialist' must mean something. Even if it does not mean 'to each according to his need', it must at least mean 'equal pay for equal work'. The principle of 'equal pay for equal work' is expressly recognised by all socialist systems of law. Under provisions in Section 31 of the French code du Travail, and according to Argentenian law, this principle must be applied to female workers in all collective bargaining agreements. The Preamble to the Constitution of the International Labour Organization recognises the principle of 'equal remuneration for work of equal value' as constituting one of the means of achieving the improvement of conditions, 'involving such injustice, hardship and privation to large numbers of people as to produce unrest so great that the peace and harmony of the world are imperilled'.

The social and political consciousness of the people, higher levels of awareness and expectations (especially among the women) and the position of women in the economy (of India) increasingly attracting considerable attention because of their participation in the labour market, the highest tenets of equality enshrined in the Indian Constitution will have to be practised and protected for the benefit of the Indian people.

The multipronged women's movement has gained momentum, focusing attention on and attempting to remove deeprooted problems related to gender bias. "Particularly because of the Government's active interest and the concerted efforts of women's organizations, women are now enjoying high visibility in the context of public and parliamentary discussions on the problems confronting women."

Before we embark upon the task of assessing and analyzing the socio-psycho factors which constitute an integral part of their mental make-up and subsequent mode of functioning as successful entrepreneurs, let us first examine the reasons which have brought about such a vital change. There appear to be at least four major factors which account for this trend. Firstly, structural processes relating to changes in systems of large-scale production and administration have created routine and semi-skilled white-collar and manual occupations which have been filled to a large extent by women. Secondly, a number of demographic changes have enabled more women to take up full-time paid employment; they now marry later, live to an older age, have fewer children within a shorter and earlier period of their lives. Therefore, by the time they reach early middle age, they are relatively freer from their responsibilities and able and willing to pursue careers of their choice without unnecessary twinges of guilt. This not only provides them with a viable interest of their own but also helps them successfully get over the 'empty-nest' syndrome once the kids have left home to pursue their future occupations. Thirdly, the rapidly increasing incidence of more and more women acquiring 'qualifications within higher educational institution; have radically altered their perceptions and led to a drastic 'restructuring of psychological expectations' which, subsequently, 'has led many women to search for work-related rather then marriage-based self-identities'. Finally, a rise in the standard of living and the desire to maintain fairly high living standards, have also sent women willy-nilly to seek economic betterment through the avenue of paid employment.

However, many women remain dissatisfied with jobs allocated to them — jobs based on gender bias, the predetermined role of women and so on and so forth, which were not only traditional but limited in scope and opportunities. They dared to venture farther afield and extended their resources toward entrepreneurship. Getting into the fiercely competitive world of business and achieving economic independence, involves considerable effort and risk. This risk is higher for women entrepreneurs, who have the additional problems of operating in a male dominated arena.

An empirical study conducted by the Department of Psychology, University of Delhi, to obtain an indepth knowledge of the psychological characteristics of Indian women entrepreneurs *vis-à-vis* their non-entrepreneur peers as well as to 'evaluate their prospects in the cross-cultural perspectives', yielded surprisingly favourable findings relating to the women entrepreneur group!

In this interesting study, a group of women between the ages of 35 to 55 years with a minimum working experience of ten years, were chosen at random from such significant entrepreneurial bodies as the National Alliance of Young Entrepreneurs (NAYE), National Institute of Entrepreneurship and Small Business Development (NIESBUD), FICCI Ladies Organization (FLO), National Association of Women Entrepreneurs and Executives (NAWEE), and the Ministry of Industry. The women matched in age, job experience, gross personal income of Rs 5000 or more per month, minimum basic qualification (of the entrepreneurs) being graduates and even some diploma holders and were with respondents such as a group of university teachers and medical doctors from a government hospital, in terms of personality, self-concept and sex role orientation.

Personality assessment which was in accordance with the Need Theory of Personality and carried out with the help of T.A.T., was further broken up under the sub-heads of cognitive qualities and orectic qualities; personality characteristics considered under cognitive qualities included the following:

(a) general intelligence
(b) level of organization
(c) reservation and
(d) verbal quality and imagination;

Those considered under orectic qualities involved personality traits as:

(i) generally emotional,
(ii) extroversion and introversion,
(iii) cheerful depressive,
(iv) self-assertive and submissive,
(v) anxiety ridden,
(vi) decision general,

(vii) ambition,
(viii) social consciousness,
(ix) maturity and immaturity,
(x) integration.

For the remaining two psychological characteristics the Self-Concept scale and Bem Sex-Role Inventory were administered and the subsequent responses subjected to relevant statistical analyses.

The results indicated that the women entrepreneurs were significantly better as compared to their non-entrepreneur peers in terms of cognitive and orectic qualities of personality; the former were more organized, imaginative, cheerful, self-assertive, decisive, ambitious, socially conscious, mature and integrated. The latter group was, however, found to be more intelligent. Women entrepreneurs had a significantly higher self-concept than their non-entrepreneur peers. It was found that they possess greater potentialities; self confidence, self-acceptance, sense of worthiness; past, present and future orientation; strong beliefs and convictions; emotional maturity and sociability. Nevertheless, they also showed intense feelings of shame and guilt in comparison with the non-entrepreneurs. By and large women entrepreneurs were found to be masculine while the women non-entrepreneurs were rather feminine in terms of sex-role orientation.

Keeping in view the gradual and inevitable transition in the role and status of women in India, it was considered worthwhile to (further) explore their novel role of entrepreneurs *vis-à-vis* women executives. In order to make the study more broad-based and encompassing a more comprehensive segment of society relevant to the situation, `comparisons were also made between women and men entrepreneurs as also between women and men executives.' The respondents, who were selected with the help of stratified random sampling techniques from the metropolitan city of Delhi, 'comprised a group of successful middle level executives, both male and female, from both public and private sector organizations.' The general matching conditions/requirements for both entrepreneurs and executives were similar here as compared to those of respondents cited in the previous case study, with a few exceptions. The age span was longer, ranging from 25 to 55 years for entrepreneurs as well as executives and the minimum working experience for both groups of people was five years instead of ten, as in the previous analysis. The aim of the study was to investigate the differences, if any, among the successful male and female entrepreneurs and for their non-entrepreneur peers in terms of the following factors:

(a) Sex role orientation; (b) Type-A/B behavioural patterns; (c) Risk taking behaviour; (d) Role stress lifestyle in general; and (e) Motivation (personal, social and influence motivation). Psychological tools employed for this purpose were: Bem's Sex-Role Inventory, Jenkins Activity Survey, Yousuf's Choice Dilemma Questionnaire, Mehta's Thematic Apperception Test and Pareek's Organizational Role Pics. In addition, it was also possible not only to delve into their experiences and problems but also to gain an insight into their attitude and beliefs, value system, work and lifestyles with the aid of interviews and case history methods. The data was subjected to appropriate statistical analysis and the following salient findings recorded;

Results

Both the groups of female entrepreneurs (70 per cent) and female executives (40 per cent) attributed a majority of their occupational problems to "sex role stereotypes". However, they showed no regrets for: (a) starting their own business and (b) or working in an organization. On the other hand, they sought to combat gender-related prejudices and "sex role stereotypes" at the work place by adhering to Type-A lifestyle and by opting for the approach strategies of coping with the role stresses. As opposed to female entrepreneurs in their overall behaviour pattern, male entrepreneurs were found to conform generally to Type B pattern. And despite the differences in their overall behaviour pattern, both the groups, however, were found to be patient, dedicated to their work, hard driving and competitive. Marked differences were noted in their risk taking behaviour and they were found to be optimal risk takers. They adopted different coping styles in different situations. Nevertheless it was assessed that the entrepreneurs (irrespective of their gender) preferred the approach strategies to cope with stress, resolved from role ambiguity, role stagnation, self-role distance, interrole conflict, role inadequacy and role erosion. Their dominant coping style was found to be intropersistive in nature while the back-up style was defensive in nature.

Of the wide gamut of 15 comprehensive factors studied in this investigation, as many as 11 factors were found to be significantly discriminating between the four groups of male entrepreneurs, female entrepreneurs, male executives and female executives. These factors, which threw light on broad-based psychological dimensions of differing variables, were "feminity scores, overall type A/B behaviour, pattern, speed and impatience factors, hard-driving and competitive factors, and a few role stress coping styles for example, impunitive, intropunitive, impersistive, extrapersistive-interpersistive styles.

The emergence of women as a viable force on the economic scene, as entrepreneurs specifically, is a significant development in the emancipation of women, securing for them a permanent place in our society — a society they can serve at large by opening new vistas for the educated, unemployed youth, needy women and handicapped people. In addition, the active association of women with economic enterprises should also usher in an era of clean business ethics.

References

Antony, M.J., 'Equal Pay for Women', *Women's Rights* Dialogue Publications, New Delhi, 1985.

Pujari, Premlata and Kaushik, Vijay Kumari, 'Women and the Development Process', *Women Power in India - Institutional Systems For Women's Development*, Vol 2, Delhi: Kanishka Publishers, Distributors, 1994.

Sen, Anima, 'Problems and Potentials of Women Entrepreneurs: An Indian Perspective', *Reforms For Women: Future Options'*, Heptulla, Najma, ed. New Delhi: Oxford and IBH Publishing Co. Pvt. Ltd., 1992.

9

THE SEWA SAGA - A SALUTE TO SAGACITY

Women are poorer than men amongst the poor. They are the worst victims of all socio-economic decay, degradation, and distortions. Yet I envisage poor women as being in the vanguard of development processes and movement.

Ela Bhatt

This is the dream that Ela Bhatt, a woman of extraordinary courage and vision, dreamt for the miserable millions of downtrodden and oppressed women of India. These are the bold views she dared to articulate in an interview upon accepting the appointment to the Central Planning Commission, in December 1989, in the firm belief that somehow, some day, they would surely be translated into an unbelievably beautiful reality. A reality that would not only gently uplift the persevering Indian woman from her quagmire of pitiable penury, but restore her to her rightful status in the context of the Indian ethos and, indeed, the world. As a woman who had found herself and could rightfully contribute towards making the nation a contendable force in the constellation of countries worldwide. As the famed poet Walt Whitman so rightly said:

An individual is as superb as a nation when
he has the qualities which make a nation superb.

The Beginning of SEWA

SEWA, an acronym for Self Employed Women's Association, was founded in 1972, with the intrepid Ela Bhatt as its chief founder and guiding light. Based in Ahmedabad, the largest city of India's western state of Gujarat, and working under a name which translates as 'service', SEWA successfully integrates a complex myriad of lives, occupations, and issues into one union. Essentially an organization today, "of the women, by the women, for the women", under its common and all encompassing banner, women have forged, "a new model of what a trade union can be a Third World model, which defies conventional conceptions about who unions organize and what they do for their members. Most unions in the world organize workers in one kind of industry, who share one fixed workplace. SEWA organizes women who work in their homes, in the streets of cities, in the fields and villages of rural India, with no fixed employer, carving their small niches in the economy, day by day, with only their wits to guide them against incredible odds of vulnerability, invisibility, and poverty." This unique capability of SEWA to start a movement for women — psychologically, occupationally, financially, socially and geographically and transform it "from the private, individual, circumscribed world to a broader consciousness of collective, public, political worlds spanning successfully the delicate transition from traditional to modern worlds" and from verbal interactions of highly sophisticated technologies, overcoming the vile and debilitating forces of communalism and fundamentalism, has turned it into a world role model.

Three years after its inception i.e., in 1975, SEWA played an important role in the globaly growing women's movement. And Bhatt, who attended the all-important Mexico City Conference in 1975 on the occasion of the United Nations International Women's Year, who was on various panels, shared the experiences of the union and banking work, as SEWA was one of the few groups represented which had some experience, and which made a vital contribution to the women's cause for posterity. With the subsequent decade for women, this conference 'marked the beginning of international organizations turning to SEWA as a resource in the women's movement.' Another significant event at the conference proved to be Bhatt's meeting with Michela Walsh, a US Wall Street investment broker. Based on inspiration generated at that meeting, Walsh went on to launch Women's World Banking (WWB), which has been extending loan guarantees to women around the world since 1981. Therefore both SEWA and Bhatt (who was nominated as the chairperson of the WWB's Board of Directors) have had a long lasting working relationship with the WWB.

The Ideology behind the term 'Self Employed'

SEWA's choice of the term 'self-employed' to denote the large sector of workers — over 35,000 from diverse trades, religions, ethnic backgrounds, living environments and even differing trade aptitudes — brought together by a common ideology and goal, was a conscious attempt to give this underprivileged segment of society, a modicum of dignity; a positive status as diametrically opposed to their hitherto negative labelling as 'informal, unorganized, marginal or peripheral' sector labourers. For only 6 per cent of India's census recognized female workforce is in regular employment, 94 per cent of working women are self-employed. In the last decade (since this evaluation was made) it is possible (and probable) that the percentage of women regularly employed, has gone up somewhat from 6 per cent and is marginally more. For the purpose of clarification and to avoid ambiguous interpretations at a later stage, 'self-employed' is a broad term covering all the workers who are not in a formal employer-employee relationship. It denotes women who work at home — as weavers, potters, garment and quilt stitchers, patchworkers, embroiderers, bidi rollers, incense stick makers, milk producers, spinners, basket and broom weavers, metal workers, carpenters, shoemakers, painters, sculptors and toy makers. It also includes those women 'who sell or trade their services or labour' such as agricultural workers, headloaders, hand-cart pullers, waste paper collecters, acrobats, cleaners and construction workers, as well as the multitude of hawkers and vendors who carry out trade in the streets and markets from their baskets or cartloads of wares.

Thus we find that both traditional and modern occupations come under SEWA's definition of self-employed, from the bartering of goods to capitalistic piece-rate work.

The SEWA Woman of Toil

Struggling for survival in a world where the physical resources they have traditionally relied upon for survival and subsistence, dwindling and disappearing rapidly in the face of intense population growth and accelerating industrialization, the SEWA women have their own method of coping with emergent problems countrywide. First and foremost, women are much better fighters than men against poverty. Combining their intrinsic managerial skills with incredible ingenuity in combining domestic work and income earning activities in order to make both ends meet, they are often able to ameliorate a desperate situation. Through their enterprising endeavours of combining many jobs and occupations simultaneously, bringing in small amounts of cash, trading for foodgrains and clothing, exchanging services for access to a small hut, vending small quantities of consumer goods, collecting wood or fruits or recyclable waste from common lands, and using what specialized skills they possess to earn wages. Secondly, whatever little they do earn, they plough into the home front, for domestic betterment, be it for food, clothing or to improve their meagre shelter. SEWA women confirm this fact but countless other resilient downtrodden women throughout the country function similarly, with the same prioritiies. Thirdly, what emerges very forcefully, is the women's concern about their children's future. Determined to give them a much better and brighter future, they toil tirelessly working for 12 to 20 hours a day, in order to effect such a change. However they reveal a surprisingly balanced outlook despite their desperate need for financial resoures, as well as an exceptional ecological consciousness. While their menfolk often opt for cash income from wood crops, women organizing across the country insist on protecting trees, or planting trees which will provide fuel and fodder and be a long-term resource rather than a cash crop. They increasingly understand the effects of deforestation, droughts, soil erosion, and saline encroachment on both the land and their families' live as they lose the local resources that they depend upon.

These self-employed women, because of the unique nature and scope of their economic existence, need a very different type of union to oversee and fulfil their various requirements. Thus, SEWA came into being as a result of their intense needs for fair credit, maternity protection, fair wages for whatever work they are engaged in for they have to shift occupational skills as the season or market demands and do not have formal jobs of the formal sector to fulfil their needs, skills training, year round work, and legal help when they are exploited or abused. Thus, SEWA attempted to address not only the gender issue but also the poverty and equity issue.

Organizing Women from all walks of Life

A few members of SEWA, especially those women who pulled freight on carts and headloaded textiles between markets, when they saw the advantages the textile unions were gaining for their members, approached the Textile Labour Association (TLA), India's largest union of textile workers, and were directed to Ela Bhatt. Bhatt, the lawyer was then heading the TLA's Women's Wing and had been dealing with labour issues for nearly a decade and a half. Though dealing with organized labour primarily, she was constantly exposed to the realities of the poor working class and was familiar with the host of problems which afflicted the masses of unorganized workers in India. She responded to their appeal for help thus: "You need to organize yourselves if you want to get some of these benefits."

They did organize themselves with women from diverse occupational skills, coming together under a common banner, fuelled by a common need. Soon the ranks of the SEWA organization swelled, encompassing 'tribal, Hindu, Harijan, migrant and Muslim women; tattooed Vaghari women, women in purdah; sinewed muscular smiths; sun-darkened cart-pullers and agricultural labourers; young nimble girls, bidi rollers with their mothers and grandmothers, progressively more thin and bent due to years of sitting over their rolling work; street-wise and bawdy vendors alongside of women timidly emerging from homebound communities; all in different dress; speaking different languages and dialects'. Women who had boldly migrated to the cities for textile mill jobs, had to face retrenchment and were reduced to picking recyclable waste from the city's garbage dumps. They had several ideas how to alter their dismal circumstances and they came to the union for service and support. Also those women persecuted for demanding legal wages for their work in the tobacco processing plants, for legal assistance. But all these developments took place only after the first two dozen or so women, acting upon Ela Bhatt's sage advice, came together and pooled a few paise and took some decisions to demand that their wages be regularized. Thereafter the floodgates automatically opened. Agricultural workers came to discuss how they could actually get the minimum wages under the law and used-clothes and vegetable vendors wanted to become a part of the organization, for protection from police brutality and extortion.

It was Ela Bhatt's initial encounter with the headloaders in 1971, when they approached her for help with Gal Baji, their contractor, that set the tone for the future working ideology of SEWA and won her the prestigious Asian Ramon Magsaysay Award for the successful implementation of her strategy. Bhatt shrewdly assessed that though the *thekedar* was well aware that the women were living on the street, he was still very obviously controlling them. He wanted charity, not justice. The initial advantage that Ela gained from this situation made her realize 'that the best way to change situations of poverty was through struggling for justice in women's work lives' and this has proved a powerful organizing tool which eliminated any sense of charity in the organization; the second admirable principle which formed the basis of SEWA's two-fold functional ideology was 'that women from all levels of society join together to plan with rather than planning for poor women'. To concretise this latter philosophy, in the 28 years of SEWA's existence 'over 46,000 women have joined Bhatt's work, dedicating their individual skills to facilitate interfacing the formal and informal worlds. The majority of SEWA's organizers are working class women. Some with special leadership qualities have come to represent their trades in the union. A few middle-class and elite professional women leaving outside jobs in business management, as physicians, and lawyers, to contribute their skills to the organization. Others have come from various parts of India with skills of organizing union, public health management, and economics, to settle down in Ahmedabad specifically to work with SEWA.

Intrepid and enterprising women come from distant shores, dedicating their valuable time and energies towards imparting skills. One such was Martha Stuart from New York who began the process of training self-employed women in the use of video equipment, so that they could communicate their work, life and struggles to the larger world from their own special perspective. From this laudable start, SEWA has begun extending training to illiterate communities all over the world. The inherent strength of the organization is in its membership, which, in turn generates the understanding and ideas which the middle-class women can help convey. They provide their services while they pass on their skills, this dual purpose action taking place more or less side by side. The underlying idea here is holding hands in mutual respect while they shift control. Out of this superb ideology, have emerged 60 women from various trade groups who are now providing basic health care services to their communities. Out of this methodology of functioning, have emerged other self-employed women who are learning to prepare and represent their own legal cases. Artisans have grown from exploited piece rate workers, to partners in business in their own cooperatives. From these cooperatives, certain women have risen as managers of the cooperatives. Through this kind of interaction and growth, SEWA has paved the way for putting self-employed workers on the world labour map. However, while labour unions in the west were lobbying against putting out work into workers homes, SEWA realized the unsuitability of such a system in India and recognized that 'centralized industrial modelled workplaces would never suit their need'. Therefore, they vocalized demands to be legitimized and protected at home and the International Labour Organization (ILO), which sets standards for international labour laws, and the International Confederation of Free Trade Unions (ICFTU) which represents an impressive 96 million workers in 81 countries, responded to their demands and initiated an ILO Convention in 1990 for the recognition and protection of home-based workers.

The SEWA Bank

Akin to the Working Women's Forum (WWF), an NGO started in Tamil Nadu initially as a response to urban poverty and the acute malaise afflicting poor women in the informal sector SEWA too, initially 'acted as an intermediary between the poor women's groups and the nationalized banking system'. While SEWA inevitably guaranteed the loans, the bank granted loans at 4 per cent but failed to understand the workings of the informal sector. Despite SEWA being a reliable intermediary, the poor women's groups however, ran into numerous difficulties relating to time consuming banking procedures, needlesslly complicated application forms, the banking hours and attitudes of male bank staff. In addition, it became increasingly clear that credit alone did not solve the problems of these poor women and that it was necessary for SEWA to generate alternative forms of production and opportunities for creating new kinds of work and income generating activities.

It was imperative therefore, that SEWA should concentrate on certain social and financial anomalies and shortcomings first, to facilitate a smooth flow of finance, independent of restrictive and obstructive irritants. In 1974, barely two years after its inception, SEWA recorded a major achievement and registered its own bank - the Mahila SEWA Sahakari Bank and the Women's Co-operative Bank with deposits and share capital from its members. Thus, even the poor women habituated to saving for their needs to survive, as in the 'Chit System' found no difficulty whatsoever in understanding and operating a simple credit society. Both SEWA as well as the SEWA Bank are governed by the Cooperative Act and the Banking Regulation Act and at the same time, accountable to both. The bank, which was launched with an initial total capital of US$ 5,500 with members purchasing a Rs. 10 share, in one year had built up as many as 9000 depositors and increased the capital to exactly six times the original i.e. US$ 33,000. This helped to meet some part of the accrued overhead costs. The repayment rate on SEWA Bank loans is nearly 90 per cent.

The SEWA Bank, which proved to be an immensely viable financial unit, revolutionized the lives of poor women with its constructive and farsighted ideology and made them credit-worthy. Free from the evil exploitation of money lenders and no longer confused by the mind boggling constraints of the formal banking system, they were able to utilize the income they generated, for the benefit of their families and for themselves. In formal banking procedures, photographs replaced signatures for identification purposes, a different kind of informational input was required to establish credit needs, and loan appraisals made through the less intimidating methods of dialogue and personal contact. The entire system based on trust, even judgements about the respective credit-worthiness of loan aspirants and loan amounts, were made using new norms and new kinds of information. The SEWA Bank, which reviews the borrowers case in its entirety and with a modicum of compassion, does not see the loan as a pure economic, commercial transaction and makes adequate provision for providing repeat loans, in cases of a crisis and to cover unforseen calamaties and needs.

Thus, ensuring the staying power of the borrower until the loan is repaid. This process is aided by the fact that invariably women save more. The borrowers now also have an additional cushion for unforseen calamaties from their savings, which earlier were expropriated in one way or the other by the money lenders, traders, and others who had power over them. The SEWA Bank, whose aim is to reach out and provide financial aid to as many poor women as possible, follows these principles for charging interest: the Reserve Bank fixes the rate of interest on savings at 6 per cent for Primary Co-operative Banks and the SEWA Bank also observes the same rule. The RBI also fixes the upper limit on loans and advances at around 17.5 per cent (subject to revision as and when the situation demands) and within this limit SEWA has a differential rate depending upon the size of the loan. The lowest interest rate poor women paid to the money lender was 12 per cent per month or 120 per cent per annum and sometimes the rate went up to as much as 300 per cent per month, obviously exacting a burden of payment which the already economically deprived women found excruciatingly difficult to meet. SEWA does not have large borrowers to cushion the process and since profit is not the major criteria here, their margin of profit is also much less. The rate of interest is also not the chief issue here. For subsidized rates are not necessary and reasonable commercial rates are acceptable as the women are prepared to pay normal rates of interest.

Before we discuss the broad infrastructure and the various supportive measures which contributed so substantially towards making the SEWA banking process such a stupendous success, let us digress briefly and examine the all important administrative mechanics of this formidable organization. Jayshree Vyas, the SEWA Bank's Managing Director who began her career with a nationalized bank and has an insider's understanding of the problems of poor women, maintains that 'people accept the government loans which are heavily subsidized, and they also temporarily increases their assets. Without all the other supportive services, these loans do not usually improve a woman's life. Everyone knows that they are vote-gifts, and can be written off. Self-employed women pooling their own money, on the other hand, feels like well-balanced fields. What they take out, they put back in, looking seriously after their field and their crops, as they mean not only this year's survival but also their long-term ability to generate a living for their family'.

Organization

SEWA Bank oversees their finances beginning with the Board of Directors, which comprises 10 long-standing trade leaders from different self-employed occupations, four organizers with professional training, and one cooperative manager. They take the major decisions about the bank, and sanction all the loans. The trade leaders have an insight into both the financial and psychological workings of the self-employed, while the professionals have the skills and literacy to link the trade leaders' insight with banking economics and the formal guidelines and cooperative regulations of the Reserve Bank of India, from which the bank receives its authority. Furthermore, and this is of vital significance in the socio-psycho dynamics of loan recovery, the Board does not hire well-educated personnel for this purpose. Instead, it very wisely seeks the help of union organizers and group leaders and hires women already well experienced in self-employment, who live in the neighborhood of the borrowers themselves, who speak in the same dialects and wear the same clothes, and most importantly, who understand the constraints and unpredictability of the trades and lives of the self-employed. Armed with this understanding and sensitivity, and supported by the other services of SEWA, they have shown self-employed women to be excellent credit risks.

Again, reverting to the success of the SEWA banking process, such a thing would not have been possible without close supervision, self-monitoring through participatory processes and building of a collective consciousness, and cooperative values among the SEWA groups. In addition, proper training and technical inputs to improve the efficiency of the activities were also necessary. With this in mind, in 1975 SEWA established the SEWA Mahila Trust to cater to the training requirements, technical inputs, legal aid, maternity benefits, death benefits, widow benefits, health, creche, group insurance and other follow-up needs of members and borrowers. This was followed by the establishment of their own producer cooperatives so that they could purchase their own raw materials and also market the produce thus avoiding the middle-men who appropriated a large share of the surplus.

Holistic Health Reforms

Two of the important interrelated issues, namely health and maternity benefits, which are essential not only for the well-being of the poor women but also crucial to the success of their economic venture and to enable them to pay the loan in time, were taken care of by SEWA. SEWA initiated its own maternal protection scheme. Strongly of the opinion that society as a whole should assume the responsibility of the nation's children, not only of the poor mother, SEWA registered a newly pregnant woman under the maternal protection scheme, charging a very nominal fee of Rs15. Thereafter, SEWA linked her to prenatal services appropriate to the area where she lived and worked and at the time of delivery, she was given a stipend of Rs.100 and a kilo of ghee, a high energy food traditionally consumed by *post-partum* women. In addition to such helpful and health conducive measures, SEWA also conducted useful training courses for midwives in the rural areas where they work, imparting to them the importance of using sterilized tools and maintaining sanitary conditions. Within a surprisingly short period of time, the highly successful results of this scheme were evident in the health and survival rates of both the mothers as well as their children. After several years of expansion of this programme, SEWA still believes that the government should provide this service to women, but not as a welfare service. The health activities of SEWA's first decade developed mainly along the maternity protection benefits and the 'Know Your Body' classes under the wise and compassionate guidance of the veteran women members of SEWA's Community Health Committee and the first participants in SEWA's Jagruti (Awareness) Community Health Programme. A more comprehensive programme was developed when Mira Chatterjee joined as SEWA's full-time Health Coordinator in 1984. Since then, health awareness classes, prenatal and maternity benefit services, a child care programme which includes sick and well child medical care, an increasing number of community health centres and their linkages with government care centres, and an occupational health research team have been linked into one programme.

Maternity Benefits

However, the health team's first major policy goal was met in 1987 when the maternity benefits which SEWA had supported from almost a decade earlier (1978) were finally adopted statewise by the Labour Ministry to cover landless agricultural labourers and Gujarat began implementing the Maternity Protection Scheme. These labourers constitute 75 per cent of the state's female population, and through this programme they are eligible for antenatal care, four to six weeks of wage compensation, a safe delivery kit, one kilogram of clarified butter, and well baby care for their newborn. The state's adoption of this scheme marked the first shift in the policy balance which historically has been weighted heavily in favour of the urban organized sector. In 1986, only 2.28 per cent of Indian working women were receiving proper maternity benefits.

Family Planning

Linked to these health issues was yet another issue of vital significance, the controversial family planning issue which needed to be handled with immense care and sensitivity so as not to unnecessarily hurt the deep-rooted preconceived notions and practices of the people. Mira Chatterjee, speaking from her experience as SEWA's Health Coordinator, said, 'Most women-especially in the slums-do not want to have many children. But they are pressured to have sons. Two sons. That is why as feminists, we are opposed to the whole focus on only women. Fertility is rarely in an individual woman's control. Often it is the husbands and mothers-in-law who dictate what size family is necessary'.

As regards creating awareness about the issues which are related to women's health, including family planning, SEWA continues to conduct 'Know Your Body' classes for its members and their daughters; and Ranjanabehn Desai, who initiated SEWA's early health work, travels around and conducts such training sessions in many villages and poor neighbourhoods of Ahmedabad. Working in conjunction with local midwives, she has reached literally to hundreds of women, listening patiently to their problems and offering the options available to them in terms of family planning and other health services. While SEWA helps women in knowing family planning choices.

SEWA has done praiseworthy work in the field of health, extends far beyond the conventional aspects of health problems, and attempts to revolutionize custom-bound restricted ideologies and practices. It has crossed the barriers of human calling, to fulfil human needs which hold the human body sacred, its violation in any manner blasphemous as Kantibehn, an agricultural labourer expresses in these poignant words:

> 'This body is my only asset. On days I work, I earn. When I am sick, I cannot earn. My fire stays cold those days. There is no other body, no other asset to fall back on ..'

Therefore, SEWA has initiated and implemented a novel scheme whereby its health workers and a team of young, literate women from self-employed trades have been trained to work together, conducting occupational health studies among their trade groups. They collect in-depth data on occupational hazards which range from postural problems for women who work long hours transplanting paddy or piece-rate production work like bidi and agarbatti rolling; to women's *exposure to noxious substances* like chemical dyes, fumes, tobacco, silicon and chilli dusts and cleaning chemicals; *to work environmental problems* due to lack of lighting and ventilation, is a common problem for piece-rate workers at the extreme end of the continuum of poverty. The most obvious hazard they have documented arises from the cycle of extended work hours, low wages and poor nutrition.

Thus, SEWA has discovered, through a series of its own informal experiments conducted practically in diverse occupational fields, that while the workers are not ready to compromise on the high quality of their finished product, they are open to accepting via medias which will reduce their health hazards. For example, women like incense rollers or handblock printers will not use gloves to protect themselves from chemicals, because it slows down their work or affects the quality of the product they sell on a piece-rate basis but that they have been eagre to substitute less toxic chemicals for the noxious ones. Likewise the well known SEWA embroiderers of Lucknow perceived it as a distinct work advantage to get spectacles and regular checkups, as the majority of them suffer deteriorating vision from years of fine stitching work in extremely poor lighting conditions.

The SEWA Health Workers :
A Vital Link for Health Related Issues

SEWA's intense lobbying on these issues has resulted in the National Institute of Occupational Health establishing a Women's Cell, and they have worked in close collaboration with the National Institute of Design (NID) and the ILO on the serious postural problems afflicting women workers. Subsequently, the women workers and NID researchers have jointly come up with new designs for freight carts with brakes, for sewing machines built to heights corresponding to women's frames, for stools or tables which relieve the back stress of bidi or incense workers, and for waste pickers protective collection treatment.

The SEWA community health team members have not only proved to be vital links in recognizing the many chronic symptoms of workers linked to their occupational hazards such as postural problems of work, exposure to hazardous substances and even poor nutrition, but are also aware of some useful interventions to alleviate the symptoms and exposures. Unlike the doctors who work at the clinics and dispensaries specially set up for workers, like the Bidi Welfare Clinics. Not only are such clinics chronically understaffed and undersupplied with the requisite medicines but many of them have been found to have supplies of drugs banned by the World Health Organisation. Not only that, the medical practitioners often possess very little training or experience in the work related to health problems of the self employed (especially women).

The SEWA health workers, apart from spotting chronic health symptoms quickly, also use in their clinics 'safe, inexpensive generic drugs on a 'rational' basis, meaning that they discourage 'shotgun' treatment and use of injections, tonics and vitamins which many physicians push as cures at great expense to patients'.

Discouraging the high incidence of over-prescription of expensive drugs and converting it into 'safe drug therapy on a wide scale' the SEWA Community Health programme has as its cornerstone vast respect 'for the positive aspects of traditional belief systems in combination with safe modern medical practices.' For example, while SEWA supports the practice of traditional birth attendants, it, nevertheless, ensures that they all receive proper training in sterile birth practices with periodic refreshers from time to time; it even issues sterile birth packets to each women who registers for maternity benefits.

In addition, SEWA health workers are doing sterling work in the field of grappling with community discrimination against women and rescuing women from punishing treatments of exorcism procedures. Women are frequently accused of being 'possessed' by evil spirits, a condition which elicits 'exorcism' in the form of being locked in dark rooms without food, being forced to breathe the smoke of burning chillies,beatings, electric shock, etc. These dedicated health workers have not only defended women in other equally disturbing situations over which the poor individual has no control, but at times also prevented serious victimization from taking place.

Teams of SEWA health workers have painstakingly discussed with neighbours and members exhaustively about the epidemics which frequently break out in their slums, and why their children die from diseases which middle-class families survive. The proof that they have made some headway, lies in the fact that many communities have now logically concluded that their foolish practices of denying measles stricken children food or drink or access to proper, informed medical opinion, are indeed detrimental to the child's health and in severe cases, can often have serious and debilitating repercussions.

The SEWA Pharmacy

SEWA opened a pharmacy in 1989 in central Ahmedabad near the union headquarters, which through retail sales of the reasonably priced generic 'Low Cost' drugs manufactured in Baroda, generated such profit as was able not only to help and maintain the local SEWA community health centres but also go towards meeting expenses of the Health Community members' monthly salaries.

SEWA physicians also regularly visit all the clinics on a weekly basis. SEWA has extremely adroitly entered into an exchange programme with an Ahmedabad Medical College for their students who require rural internship training. This works on a dual level with maximum benefits for all concerned parties.

While the interns provide curative care at SEWA clinics and child care centres, the local health workers share their experiences of preventive care, occupational health problems, and village life with the interns. This practice establishes an experiential base for doctors, with poor and rural clientele.

Gradually, the goals articulated by the SEWA women in the early years after their inception, in a small pamphlet entitled 'Profiles of Self-Employed Women' published by them, came to be realized one by one. Given below are the four basic goals or Four-Fold Path towards better living and economic progress, as enumerated in their pamphlet:

There are certain practical truths they (self-employed women) need to realize in their own interests, (1) to be healthy in order to avoid loss of work days, (2) to be literate enough to avoid being trapped into corrupt practices, (3) to improve their skills by better training in the modern sense, in order to increase their bargaining power, and (4) to learn to save in order to build their own capital or to make use of credit facilities for productive purposes. Not only was it considered necessary to identify such definite goals to give the underprivileged and ignorant women, dominated by the dictates of a male bastion, a collective ideology and sense of purpose, but organizing around these goals helped hundreds and then thousands of women come together as *workers* to begin shattering the myths of their isolation. They stopped reiterating fictitious middle-class perceptions that 'women are in the home,' and that 'women do not work'. They stopped believing that they were at the mercy of the contractors, or passively accepting the violence and harassment of the police. They started believing that through their struggle they could stop police harassment or secure minimum wages, or get other relevant demands met."

Cooperative Ventures

From the Organizing Song of SEWA composed in Gujarati by Anila Dholakia, contained in the chapter entitled Women's Cooperatives: A Lever for Change in Kalima Rose's seminal full length work on the SEWA Movement (*Where Women Are Leaders*), we can visualize the background and spirit of the women in SEWA, thus :

> We are poor women in a hostile land
> With no foodgrains in our vessels
> Droughts come often and
> Unemployment is rife.
> We have neither land, nor work
> Our houses are small as our hands
> And our needs are many.
> We are women, illiterate women
> Coming together in Nalkantha villages
> We are women, poor women
> Coming together to make a union.
> We started spinning thread
> To earn some grains for our families.
> We then wove cloth
> To bring cash into our palms .
> We defied the drought with our thousand trees
> And began milking our cattle together.
> We are illiterate, but so what?
> We challenge everyone with our strength:
> The landlords who paid us so little
> The men who would not let us out.
> We have come together to fill
> the village pond with milk
> We have contained it with the
> Strength of our union.

Muses Lalita Krishnaswami, SEWA's veteran cooperative organizer, "until women have extensive exposure to new ideas and technologies, their desire and ability to assume responsibility are big constraints to making our cooperatives successful." Warming to her theme, she further elaborated that at first the emphasis was on training them only in the specific skills of their occupation, like finer weaving, or block printing, or veterinary care. "Women had to struggle to learn administrative and management skills each time a problem came up. Now we have an entire human resource development training programme for women in cooperatives. It includes training in cooperative management, legal issues, functional literacy, marketing, and communications. It includes repeated exposure to both new places and new knowledge. It is a systematic way for them to learn cooperative and business skills as well as the trade skills."

Enterprising, imaginative and systematic as the SEWA organization is about its very realistic and farsighted ventures for the upliftment, development and progress of the poor and rural women's population, it has organized skill training for its members through numerous channels: government extension, the Labour Department, voluntary agencies, vocational schools, village council training institutes, universities and industrial boards, cooperative unions, handicraft boards, and their own skilled artisans. Usha Jumani, SEWA's very efficient Management Consultant, believes that self-employed women have very specific needs for training which must 'directly relate to their daily problems of work and survival or they will not be interested'. She believes that they must be financially compensated during their training period for the work they are missing and that development of interesting and innovative training material/ training aids like audio visuals etc., are a must as the bulk of the women who undergo training are illiterate. We all wish to achieve what Joseph Conrad articulated in the following words:

> I don't like work-no man does-but I like what is in work, The chance to find yourself. Your own reality-for yourself, not for others-what no other man can ever know.

SEWA's cooperatives span a plethora of diverse trades and services. Besides building up and steadily sustaining the successful cooperative bank which has facilitated a diginified means of sustenance for hundreds of hopelessly poor women. The successful banking venture has inspired SEWA to pursue organizing more cooperatives. Women have formed artisan cooperatives, vendors cooperatives, land cooperatives, and labour and service cooperatives. Urban members belong to only one occupational cooperative. The various cooperatives are described as follows:

(a) artisan cooperatives include *chindi* stitchers, weavers and cloth block printers;

(b) service cooperatives include child care or health care services provided by the self-employed women for the member community;

(c) vendor's cooperatives include kerosene vending, fish vending, vegetable supply service to government hospitals, schools, and jails; and

(d) labour cooperatives provide industrial cleaning services to large institutions on a contract basis, and collect recyclable waste materials from government insitutions.

In the rural areas, however,women are engaged in diverse seasonal occupations and often they are members of more than just one cooperative. Simultaneous membership in land-based, artisan, and/or dairy cooperative can provide the necessary resources to keep women employed throughout the year. Wage earners include landless, poor, and low caste women who tend animals, work in the fields, and do domestic duties for other households; artisans who work on a piece-rate for a contractor; or women who migrate for several months every year in search of agricultural or construction wage work. As such, self-employed women not only raise and sell crops from their own land or from sharecropping of others' land, some of them raise animals to produce milk, clarified butter, meat, eggs and wool which they sell. They also hire out animals for ploughing. The poor and needy women often render services in exchange for goods: They clean cattle sheds in exchange for grains; care for cattle in exchange for their calves; and trade home produced pottery, cloth, grain winnowers, rope or tools in exchange for foodgrains or other goods.

SEWA'S Intervention in NDDB in Favour of Women

Just six years after its inception, in 1978, SEWA recognized a glaring anomaly, namely, that the National Dairy Development Board's (NDDB) programme to create a market economy of the rural poor through milk, targeted men, whereas it was women who did the bulk of the dairy work. Obviously incensed by the sheer injustice of the situation, SEWA approached the NDDB (whose headquarters are in Gujarat) with the somewhat revolutionary concept of imparting training to women to form cooperatives. After some initial reluctance, the NDDB did impart training and a total of 12 cooperatives were formed. This, however, was followed by six long years of a protracted, tumultuous struggle to shift the control of women's occupation from men to women, and to shift profits from middlemen to the actual producers. Furthermore, since the advent of the NDDB's 'Operation Flood' and its widespread introduction of high yielding cross-bred cattle, dairying predictably shifted from being a largely subsistence activity to becoming the most lucrative commercial enterprise after agriculture, in many villages of the Dholka taluk which is drought-prone, saline, thorny scrubbed land. The attitude of the men is as hardened and unyielding as the fallow baked fields which stretch out behind the teams of endlessly toiling men and women as they dig pits along the roadway, as government drought relief work for daily wages and grains. It would be relevant to mention here that, before the women's cooperatives were organized and set up here, the existing male cooperatives were controlled by the dominant caste or village political leaders. Women rarely belonged to these male dominated cooperatives and rarely, did they ever receive any income from the dairy work. In fact whole families used to be often indebted to the milk trader, resulting in low rates for their milk. However, with 'Operation Flood' the entire scenario underwent a sea change. Unlike crops, milk kept income flowing to the village almost the whole year round. Predictably enough, the milk traders and male political leaders of the 12 villages where SEWA first organized dairy cooperatives, did not condone women channelling so much of the village finances and, ultimately, only four of the original 12 cooperatives set up by SEWA, survived.

Setting up of Women's Dairy Cooperatives

After these initial losses and adverse male reaction, SEWA did succeed in setting up as many as 18 women's dairy cooperatives with 50-400 members in each of two districts of the state and revived 35 defunct men's cooperative in Banaskantha district, into women's or mixed cooperatives. SEWA's all-women cooperatives represent women's first significant economic and decision-making participation in the dairy movement. Like the union, these cooperatives provide important models of modern organizational forms which defy old gender, class, or caste power hierachies by including women from many communities.

When forming new dairy cooperatives, SEWA did it in an extremely organized and systematic manner. It first organized all the village women who wanted to participate, but catered especially to the poor landless and small landholding women by creating and making accessible, an integrated package of training and supportive services. Such a package includes all the essentials from procurement to practice, linkages to obtain a loan, a good quality animal, cattle life insurance, as well as training in animal husbandry, dairying, and veterinary skills. Gathering momentum, the women's dairy movement in India has, thus, expanded during the eighties through other NGOs, there being over 500 all-womens' cooperatives today.

Until 1988, SEWA Bank lacked rural jurisdiction, thereby limiting its ability to extend credit to its rural members. While nationalized banks were under government pressure to give loans to the rural poor, they were reticent about extending financial assistance to assetless women who approached them. Finally after much stalling, refusals, etc, SEWA was compelled to deposit Rs 50,000 in cash with a nationalized bank before it could get loans sanctioned in women's names. Even then, loans were delayed, women lost other buyers, loan sanction dates and repayment rates did not match milk reproduction cycles. Further exacerbating credit problems were cooperative laws, which hinged membership on individuals selling milk to the cooperative for 90 days, to qualify for membership. Women without cattle, obviously could not fulfil the condition, yet their ability to get a loan sanctioned relied on their having the legitimacy of cooperative membership, thereby further complicating matters. Undaunted, SEWA almost simultaneously channelled international economic aid into revolving loan funds to help members purchase cattle, and got the cooperative bye-laws amended to allow future cattle owners membership. SEWA also fought to get members access to the subsidized government loans offered under the Integrated Rural Development Programme (IRDP), and to change IRDP loan policies to cover two animals with alternating lactation cycles so that women could continue to meet repayment schedules even if one animal was not producing.

Obstacles Faced by Womens' Cooperatives

Attempts to register the various cooperatives met with formidable resistance as it was tantamount to vying almost openly, with vested interests in the region and a direct clash of interests. Some of the obstacles encountered included (1) SEWA's paperwork circulating endlessly through a maze of bureaucratic red tape, (2) milk traders wielding political power, pressuring officials to reject SEWA's applications over petty wordings, and (3) chauvinistic registrars rejecting applications on the basis that women were illiterate, or that they were not workers. Once their first milk Cooperatives were actually registered and women began selling milk through them, the traders and Sarpanches launched an attack. The process seemed to be never-ending harassment and obstacles the order of the day. Vested interests manifested themselves in many ways such as: sanctioning cooperative loans to family members who did not even belong to the cooperative; issuing false receipts for loan instalments while pilfering the women's money; and simply extorting profits by under-reporting and underpaying milk collection and underpaying members.

The quintesssence is that difficulties continued to plague the cooperatives for a few years more until SEWA developed a strong relationship with the district dairy and National Dairy Development Board and pressed the NDDB on its commitment to bring higher returns to producers and help cooperatives survive as democratic units. With such an alliance, SEWA now had the requisite leverage to pressurize Sardar Dairy that they would buy milk only from legitimately registered cooperatives. Since only one cooperative per village could be registered, this radically altered SEWA's position. The formerly intractable traders suddenly came to the organizers' feet, begging the cooperatives to purchase their milk.

In order to overcome the various manifestations of similar difficulties that all the cooperatives were experiencing, SEWA organized intensive training programmes for two levels of dairy organizers through the Sabarmati Ashram Gaushala Project. Six SEWA organizers and an accountant from outside the villages received training for Secretary from the Dairy, and local women leaders from each village were trained in milkfat-testing, as payment is made on the basis of milk quality. SEWA thus very wisely focused its attention on developing a strong female leadership.

Land Issues

While SEWA was busy developing artisan and dairy cooperatives to help women supplement their agricultural labour income, organizers also focused specifically on agricultural issues concerning women. According to the 1981 census, 79.4 per cent of female workers are engaged in agricultural work, mainly as labourers. Many SEWA women reported that since, following the deep-rooted system of patriarchy and its inherent rigidly defined practices and sanctions, they did not hold land titles, the husbands usually mortgaged the family land arbitrarily without consent of their women, who complained that not holding title to their husband's land, led to their being forcibly evicted from it by their in-laws after his demise. Research has also shown that even in those cases where the women did claim their husband's land, their ability to make the land productive was dependent on access to assets such as bullocks, plough, and irrigation facilities. In addition, 'Chen's data also revealed that households headed by women in Devdholera have recorded the higest percentage of sale and mortgaging transactions in the village', thereby indicating that they experience more difficulty in holding on to their asset.

SEWA's involvement in the burgeoning dairy movement raised other land based issues relating to women and brought them within its purview. SEWA's major goal of helping stabilize year-round income with milk production was inevitably hampered in the case of landless women who could not grow their own fodder due to increasing pressure on the drought-prone and already degraded common lands as village herds increased. For such women, fodder collection meant wearily trudging long distances to collect from common lands, or sacrificing part of their coveted daily labour wages in exchange for green fodder from the landlord for whom they so painstakingly laboured.

Fuel Crisis and Degradation of Resources

The problems of the rural women's fuel crisis came to SEWA's attention when it took up a massive *chula* (cooking stove) building project nearly 14 years ago, at the behest of the Forest Department in 1985. Organizers who trained women subsequently built an impressive 15,000 smokeless stoves in three districts of Ahmedabad, Junagadh, and Mehsana districts. A major incentive for SEWA was its interest in reducing health hazards to women constantly exposed to wood smoke. While many of the women who used the new stoves, appreciated breathing less smoke, they pleaded that what they really urgently required, was wood, preferrably near the villages. With ecological problems manifesting themselves at an increasing pace, forests receding and common lands increasingly degraded, landless women walked up to 10-20 kilometres to fetch wood.

While most rural women do collect fuel for their own use, 'head-loading' jungle wood can also constitute an income generating activity for them. An interesting case study shows that in Junagadh district, SEWA has 700 Baravali members who sold the firewood they collected from the Girnar forest for their livelihood. Collection, which is an extremely arduous process requiring about eight hours, demands a daily round-trip walk of 10 to 20 kilometres, climbing over 2000 feet of trailless, steep, slippery slopes. These women carry wood between 20 to 35 kilograms a day to a contractor who pays them the paltry sum of Rs 10 to Rs 20 per load. However, since most of these women are the sole supporters of their families and their earning are so low, they are compelled to carry on with this back-breaking work even during the rainy season or when they fall ill — or else go without food that day. To further compound the problem, in 1983, with the forest under extreme deforestation pressure, the Forest Department limited entry to the forest for firewood cutting, though a large part of the problem was due to the large timber contractors and mining erosion. This, in turn, sparked off a severe conflict between the forest officials and firewood cutters who depended on this occupation for their survival and though SEWA intervened and succeeded in getting its members licences to cut one headload of wood per day, it also saw the long-term need of orienting members towards other income earning activities.

With women in the dairying industry lameating the need of fodder access, with poor landless labourers clamouring for land access, and with an imminent need to regenerate fuel resources, SEWA recognized that if the rural women's situation was to change on a long term and sustainable basis, it certainly could not be achieved in isolation from land access. So, without further ado, SEWA swung into action and launched several innovative experiments to help women deal with their land constraints. Firstly, the women developed their own fodder plantations in the two villages where SEWA had purchased land for cooperative centres. Secondly, SEWA somehow lobbied the Forest Department to provide training to women for running nurseries and the Baravali headloaders were the first to be trained by the Forest Department; they subsequently started a nursery on the Gujarat Agicultural University land, raising seedlings to sell to the Forest Department for its reforestation of the Gir.

Common Property Resources and Cooperative Acquisition of Land

Since the majority of SEWA members are landless, cooperative acquisition of land for women seemed the logical goal. SEWA cooperatives operate on the principle that members can pool resources in the form of share capital and acquire assets which they could not get as individuals. Therefore, in 1986 SEWA undertook a large survey of all existing wastelands in the areas it was working, and petitioned for land leases to be extended to women's cooperatives by whichever governing body controlled the land viz. village, panchayat or state. Chen, who studied CPR or common property resources in the Dholka village of Devdholera where SEWA's rural headquarters are located, found that benefits are tapped from CPRs by women as a buffer against seasonal shortages. CPRs contributed to rural equity for the landless because the physical products of fuel, fodder, fruits and honey derived from those lands supplemented their income and employment.

With most wastelands thus facing increasing degradation, SEWA's aim was to develop models for women to regenerate both subsistence and income resources on such wastelands as a way to reverse environmental degradtion and women's poverty. Wasteland regeneration obviously requires substantial capital investment and it must be mentioned here that SEWA's efforts to acquire wastelands for women and channel capital and development support from state, central, and international programmes, make an important case study of women's roles in both ecological and social change.

The list is endless, the beneficiaries numerous. SEWA's stupendous success in placing the entire process in women's hands has considerably altered the dynamics of power in favour of women. It has definitely changed the power relationships for many categories of artisans that SEWA has organized and subsequently linked to training and cooperatives. Originally, women block printers only undertook to do just a fraction of the entire block-printing process for the contractor i.e., the actual stamping of the dye on the cloth (which is all they knew). Once they acquired training, however, in how to make dyes, design blocks, prepare the cloth, and make more sophisticated designs and garments, they confidently broke their relationship with the contractor, controlling the entire process themselves and selling through the cooperative. Women in other trades such as weavers or basket-makers who participated in the crucial steps of the process but had no control over the income from that process (because their husbands sold or bartered the product themselves), have acquired some control of the family income through their cooperative membership.

Labour and Service Niches

While SEWA attempts to reorient policies and priorities of development to support decentralized occupations and to support local labour for local improvements, it has been quick to appreciate and fill any new niches and job requirements which may have evolved or surfaced as a direct or indirect fallout of changes in economies and the rapid industrialization taking place in the country. Therefore, its labour and service cooperatives which are the most recent cooperative forms, have struck highly innovative chords in women's organization.

SEWA's unionized paper pickers systematically organized alternatives to the haphazard, untidy practice of street scavenging, through two kinds of labour cooperatives. While Pethapur Cooperative collects waste paper from government offices and mills on contract, Saundarya Safai Co-operative takes on contracts to clean industrial complexes. The majority of Saundarya's 200 members work on a part time basis, filling the gaps and hours when the regular employees of each particular institution do not work.

Truly in consonance with the underlying meaning of the acronym SEWA service — SEWA itself continues its advocacy role on behalf of the masses of self-employed women. In 1980 it was at SEWA's insistence that the Government of Gujarat established an unorganized labour board to give the same protection to self-employed women as is enjoyed by industrial workers. In 1986, as a result of a resolution in the SEWA Annual Conference of the preceding year, the Prime Minister appointed a Commission for Self Employed Women with the head of SEWA as the chairperson. The report of the Commission is entitled *Shrama Sakti*.

Other feathers in the cap of SEWA are its collaboration with the Women's World Bank setting up affiliates of WWB in the four states of Gujarat, Rajasthan, Maharashtra and Madhya Pradesh and the SEWA experience, alongwith other similar programmes, contributed in the setting up of the DWCRA programme of the Government of India. DWCRA was a response to the evaluation of the Integrated Rural Development Programmes (IRDP) under the Sixth Plan and is for the most part, an integrated programme of delivered services for women and children, and under it, banks are required to ensure that 30 per cent of their loans should go to women. After the DWCRA programme started, SEWA did a survey for the government entitled 'Economic Activity of Women in Rural Areas' and prepared a block level plan with poor rural women's perspectives as the starting point." For a more beautiful tomorrow. With the dawn of EMANCIPATION.

References

1. Jhabvala, Renana, 'Women's Struggles in the Informal Sector : Two Case Studies From SEWA,' *Struggles of Women At Work*, In Gothoskar, Sufata, (ed.), Under the auspices of Indian Association for Women's Studies, New Delhi: Vikas .
2. Rose, Kalima, *Where Women Are Leaders - The Sewa Movement In India*, New Delhi: Vistaar Publications, 1992.
3. Wignaraja, Ponna, 'Innovative Approaches in South Asia,' *Women, Poverty and Resources*.

10
REASON, RIGHTS AND REQUIRED REFORMS

He who will not reason is a bigot; he who cannot, is a fool; and he who dares not, is a slave.

Lord Byron

A woman who thinks that she is intelligent demands equal rights with men. A woman who is intelligent does not.

Colette

"Our women have more rights than women of other countries, but there are large areas wherein women are suffering, where, may be they are not conscious of their rights," said Indira Gandhi, erstwhile Prime Minister of India, in April 1975. Her reference may well have been to certain provisions in the Constitution of India relating to equality of the sexes and universal adult suffrage. The preamble to the Constitution claims, ideologically at least, of bestowing equipollence of status and opportunity on both the male and female segments of its society. It also speaks of securing to all citizens of India social, economic and political justice, equally, without bias. And although the directive principles are fundamental in the governance of the country and are to be applied in enacting legislation, they are not judicially enforceable. In this context, one of the provisions of the Constitution is of special significance. After having laid down that the state shall not discriminate against any citizen on grounds of sex, among other things, it provides that nothing in this article shall prevent the state from making any special provision for women and children. Thereby imbuing the provision with a modicum of inescapable equivocality and ambivalence. Endowing with validity a Constitutional Provision in India which sanctions the state to discriminate in favour of women, if such discrimination is found necessary'.

Women claim to be the largest minority in India with a mind-boggling list of social and economic disabilities, disparities and inequalities hindering them from exercising their human rights and freedoms in society as free, equal and independent individuals living in a supposedly democratic society. Here we examine some of the more important legislations enacted by the Central legislature in India to ameliorate certain unhappy conditions in which women, particularly Hindu women, found themselves. Occasionally, there is talk about ameliorating the conditions of our Muslim sisters as well but, certain political considerations invariably stand in the way of effecting any substantial reforms in that sphere. For it must be kept in mind at all times that Muslim personal laws are considered to be an intrinsic part of the religion of Islam and the Indian government generally considers it prudent not to interfere in matters pertaining to the delicate issue of religion and its somewhat subjective societal interpretations and ramifications.

Marriage and Divorce

Hindu law endows the union of marriage with a sanctity beyond compare. Early marriage or the practice of child marriage has a fascinating and somewhat complex *raison d'etre* for its genesis which goes back to the beginning of time and is linked inextricably to the vital issue of property.

Apparently, the patriarchal form of family organization exercised a stronger hold on the *Manusmriti* society than it did on that of the *Arthashastra*. The inheritance of personal property by a male heir, therefore, had a key role to play in the transformation of women's status in society, requiring a readjustment of customs and institutions. A definite pattern of life for women emerged in society now. From that perspective, the customs like pre-puberty marriage, *varna* endogamy, sacred forms of marriage, polygamy, *putrikaputra*, *niyoga* and adoption (amongst whom again some were preferred over others), became increasingly important, as they all assured the transmision of property through the male heir. The last two customs particularly (that is, those of *niyoga* and adoption) assumed a greater proportion in the *Manusmriti* with the limitation set on the eligibility of heirs.

This also must have been the chief underlying reason as to why such an inordinately high degree of importance was given to the physical chastity of women, both before and after marriage. In fact the virginity of a bride was of such paramount importance that, interestingly enough, for Kunti and Draupadi it was arranged through divine help, because in their case it was absent. To completely eliminate all possible risks, however, early marriage, in fact child marriage, was strongly advocated, so that there could not be any doubt whatsoever about the parentage of a child. As a precautionary measure, it was enforced that women should be protected by their father, husbands and sons, and always live under their domination. This obviously led to the perpetual tutelage of women and male domination in society.

Whatever be the reasons for its existence, once liberal Hindu reformers realized what a great impediment early marriage was towards the proper education of the girl, snowballing at a later date into an alarmingly illiterate and uninformed segment of society, they campaigned against it vigorously. In 1926 the Child Marriage Restraint Act was passed declaring it an offence if a man under the age of 18 years married a girl below fourteen years of age. However, this socially motivated legislation has been made relatively ineffective by maintaining that a marriage celebrated in violation of the stipulation regarding age, would nevertheless be valid. Very much the same restrictions regarding marriageable age are to be found in the Hindu Marriage Act, 1955.

There is a provision in this Special Marriage Act, for obtaining a decree of divorce by mutual consent, provided the parties have lived separately for a year and three years have elapsed since the date of marriage. Apart from the common grounds on which either party to the marriage may obtain dissolution of a marriage performed or registered under the Act, the wife may sue the husband for divorce on the ground that he has committed rape, sodomy or bestiality. Whereas both in Hindu and civil marriages any spouse can seek divorce on the ground of not having lived together for a year after there was a decree for judicial separation. In Parsee law, on the other hand, only the party who sought judicial separation can seek divorce, provided there was no cohabitation for one year. The Indian Divorce Act applicable to Christians is, however, totally silent on the consequence of not resuming cohabitation, or living together as husband and wife. In the provisions of the Indian Divorce Act which applies to Christians however, there is a certain degree of discrimination between the sexes in the matter of grounds for divorce. A single isolated act of adultery on the part of the wife is a valid ground for granting a divorce on the petition of the husband but, if a wife has to be successful in her petition for divorce, she has generally to prove against her husband not only adultery, but also an additional ground such as desertion or cruelty; commission of rape, sodomy or bestiality by the husband, are also grounds enough for obtaining a decree of divorce.

Like judicial separation for over one year, disobedience of a decree for restitution of conjugal rights also gives grounds for divorce to both parties after one year, according to Hindu law and under the Special Marriage Act or civil marriage. However, there are specific and special grounds, albeit very few, in each case which grant additional reasons for divorce. For those governed by the Special Act, undergoing imprisonment for seven years or more for a criminal offence, validates the innocent party (spouse) in legally seeking and obtaining divorce. Such a reason is not found under Hindu law.

Although Hindu law has two special grounds of its own, which validate divorce. The first is, conversion of one spouse to another religion other than Hindu, Jain, Sikh or Buddhist. Only the Hindu spouse can seek divorce - one cannot convert oneself into another religion and seek divorce because of one's conversion. However, this reason is often misused by a husband who wants to marry again and where there are no valid grounds for divorce, he merely converts to Islam and marries the woman of his choice, as Islam sanctions bigamy. However, the first marriage does not automatically dissolve on his pre-mediated, wily conversion to Islam. Only the Hindu wife is empowered to seek dissolution or bear the indignity and insult in silence.

The second ground, and this is available only to Hindus, is in the unlikely event of renunciation of the world by the other spouse, by entering a religious order formally, with the conduct of proper and appropriate ceremonies. A person does not become a sanyasi or sanyasin by a mere vocal declaration or donning of saffron or other coloured robes, as the case may be. According to Hindu law, a person who thus renounces the world "dies" in law and is not entitled to inheritance and his or her property passes on immediately to the heirs.

Divorce without Recourse to Court: In certain Hindu communities, as also among most tribal groups, it is possible for the husband and wife to obtain divorce without recourse to court. They are required only to follow some customary practices, like making a declaration before the elders of the community or the headman of the tribe that they no longer desire their marital relationship to continue. A unique practice is prevalent among the erstwhile proud warrior race of the Kallars of Tamil Nadu. A race which lays great stress on the birth of sons and even practises the inhuman custom of female infanticide, the absence of a son commonly leads to divorce. As a token of divorce 'a kallan gives his wife a piece of straw in the presence of his caste people'. In Tamil, as used by Kallars (unheard of among other caste groups), the expression 'to give a straw' means 'to divorce', and 'to take a straw' means to 'accept divorce. Even today, the question of divorce among Kallars is reported to be the least complicated social issue.

It is extremely well known that among Muslims, while the husband can unilaterally and without assigning any reason divorce his wife by pronouncing talaq three times, his wife has to get a judicial pronouncement of divorce on specified grounds. Although rather rare, it is, however, possible for the wife to have the power of divorce delegated to her by the husband at the time of entering into the marriage contract. For instance, it may be stipulated that if he takes a second wife, he should have the option of repudiating her marriage. Considering the fact that the Indian Constitution makes provision for the equality of the sexes, it would be worthwhile to give appropriate judicial recognition to the practice of *fasaq* by means of which a Muslim wife is equally empowered (as her male counterpart) to 'unilaterally repudiate her marriage'. However, an excellent opportunity for such recognition was lost when the Kerala High Court in 1975 ruled that the right of Muslim women to obtain divorce is exclusively governed by the Dissolution of Muslim Marriages Act, 1939 and that it is not permissable to go beyond it.

The Indian Divorce Act, 1955 `was modelled after English enactments for matrimonial reliefs adopted about the middle of the last century. Over a hundred years later the United Kingdom prescribed by legislation, a single valid ground for divorce, that is irretrievable breakdown of marriage'. Ideally, if irretrievable breakdown of marriage is made the only ground for judicial declaration of divorce applicable to all communities and religious groups in India, there will be equality of treatment not only between men and women but also between various religious groups. Thereby actually creating a completely just and non-discriminatory climate in this vital sphere of human relationships. Perhaps one has to bide one's time and wait for the opportune time for the adoption of a civil code for such a welcome unification of laws. However, in the meantime, if the Indian

Divorce Act could be amended making grounds for divorce identical for both men and women, preferrably adopting the provision regarding irretrievable breakdown of marriage as the sole ground of divorce as laid down in the (British) Divorce Reform Act, 1969, a major hurdle would be removed regarding attitudes of gender bias.

It is not always the spouse who seeks dissolution of the marriage, who is eligible to move the court for maintenance. For instance, if the husband has sought a divorce, the wife can seek maintenance and expenses in the case from the husband till it is decided. If, on the other hand, it is the wife who is desirous of obtaining a divorce, she can simultaneously seek maintenance and court expenses from her husband. It is advisable to put in an application for maintenance — lawyers term this as maintenance *pendente lite* — as early as possible, in order to meet the various expenses incurred during litigation. Also, if application for such maintenance is delayed, it provides convenient leverage for the other party to argue that one is well able to look after oneself. However, since there is no formula for award of court expenses, some courts invariably grant very nominal amounts to the affected party. This is highly unrealistic for, in these times when court expenses are very high, it is the duty of the courts to take into account all necessary expenses (court fees, cost of judicial papers, typing expenses, process fees, diet money for witnesses, commission fees, fees for medical or other expert witnesses, lawyer's fees and the like) and award a realistic amount. But the court must ensure at the same time that such a provision is not misused and, as one judgement said, "a husband should not be saddled with mounting expenses because a cantankerous wife adopts such an attitude. It is quite conceivable that a husband of poor means could be well nigh ruined in a given case by a litigous wife."

During the pendency of a suit under the Indian Divorce Act, a wife may apply for alimony and the court may grant an amount not exceeding one-fifth of the husband's average net income. While passing a decree for divorce or judicial separation, the court is empowered to order the husband to pay a lump sum or make periodical payments for life to the wife, taking into account various important and pertinent factors such as her fortune, the means of the husband and the conduct of the parties. There are similar provisions which safeguard the interests of the wife and provide her the same benefits mentioned above, in the Parsi Marriage and Divorce Act, 1936. The spirit of equality envisaged in the Constitution finds clear expression in the Hindu Marriage Act. For it makes provision for the grant of expenses of matrimonial suits and a monthly allowance for the support of either spouse during the pendency of legal proceedings; providing the spouse applying for the expenses and allowances thereof lacks sufficient income to support herself or himself as the case may be. The Act also has a provision for making an order for permanent alimony and maintenance in favour of either of the spouses. An order of maintenance can be enforced through the Civil Procedure Code. And action of 'contempt of court' could also be taken against a man disobeying such an order. On remarriage, however, the affected spouse loses his or her right to maintenance. Furthermore, if the recipient of the alimony happens to be the wife, she is required to remain chaste. If maintenance is being granted to the husband, 'he is enjoined from having sexual relations with any other woman'.

In the case of a Hindu woman, there is yet another law which grants her maintenance, namely, Section 18 of the Hindu Adoptions and Maintenance Act, 1956, which deals with maintenance of a Hindu wife by her husband. This provision and the one dealing with a divorced wife in the Hindu Marriage Act are, however, independent of each other and one does not shut out the relief obtained under the other one.

However, there are some loopholes in the Hindu law. Although a Hindu daughter-in-law is entitled to maintenance from her father-in-law, he is not obliged to maintain her if he has no ancestral property; and if he has only such properties as were acquired by his own efforts. In the latter case too he is under no obligation whatsoever to look after the widowed daughter-in-law, minors and destitute family members. Also, in the event of the father-in-law's demise, it does not automatically devolve upon the mother-in-law to take on the responsibility of the now deceased man towards his daughter-in-law. It is thought desirable to confer on the widowed daughter the same right to claim maintenance from her parents as is enjoyed by unmarried daughters if she is not maintained by her husband's family. Another practical problem which relates to both Hindu wives and others whose husbands have been missing, absconding, imprisoned or have deserted them, is that they cannot claim maintenance from their fathers-in-law because their husbands are, in effect, still alive. The wife has a right to maintenance for life. She need not forfeit this right even if she lives separately from her husband on certain specific grounds such as the husband's cruelty, desertion, keeping a concubine or having another wife, his suffering from a virulent form of leprosy, his conversion to another religion, or any other cause justifying her living separately. She, however, forfeits her right to maintenance if she is unchaste or ceases to be a Hindu.

Prior to 1955, divorce was considered absolute anathema by women of the higher castes; after the passing of the Act, however, it is the women of the higher castes as well as the rich and educated in urban areas, who petition the courts for divorce. A dramatic change in social and moral values, freer mixing of the sexes, long absences necessiated by job responsibilities, a greater degree of competitiveness and subsequently greater pressure (both physical and mental) on the person concerned as well as an increasing incidence of wives and mothers taking up full-time, professional jobs, have all contributed greatly towards a rising divorce rate among the urban population of India. The glaring need remains though to educate the poor, ignorant women in the villages who have no recourse to obtaining such information as to what their rights are and how they can successfully file for divorce and be rid of their misery in cases where they are being subjected to harassment, beatings, dowry demands or any one or more of the many ills which plague the so-called weaker sex. Probably the illiterate women in the rural areas do not even know that there are legal provisions for divorce apart from those enshrined in the customary law of certain communities or tribes.

Property

Let us take a journey backwards in time briefly and examine what conditions — social and otherwise—prevailed then and not so subtly influenced property issues subsequently. Because of their superior birth and knowledge of the sacred texts, the Brahamins alone were deemed capable of making and /or interpreting law for all. They became increasingly ambitious and powerful, or at least appeared to be so and endeavoured to impose their ideology and 'way of life' on the entire population, not just a particular or privileged segment of society. The underlying propensity definitely was 'to bring the varna society to a stage where the brahmanical ideology would be more effective, than otherwise (e.g. the prescription of the gandharva for all, especially for the vaisyas and sudras and then its elevation to the group of 'sacred' marriage category). Socially too, one may assume, the brahmins were coming to the forefront and the position of women as recommended by Manu bore the brahminical imprint to a very great extent. They enforced on the whole society the customs and institutions needed, primarily by them. That Brahminical influence played such a decisive role in reshaping and influencing the evolving position of women in a different manner, did not for a moment, escape the attention of the astute jurist, Maine, who remarked: 'These inquiries pushed much further, have shown that the Hindu laws, religious and civil, have for centuries been undergoing transmutation, development, and , in some points, depravation at the hands of successives Brahmanical expositors, and that no rules have been so uniformaly changed — as we should say, for the worse — as those which affect the legal position of women'. So it came about that with the brahmins taking the lead, the rich people — the varnas and economic classes coalescing in this case, were responsible for the downward movement in the status of women. A condition which has inflicted untold misery on them by virtue of the inequalities generated, many of which persist to this day and difficult to eradicate because they are so deep-rooted. In the downward spiral of women's status, both religion and property played important roles and the *Manusmriti* combined them effectively. "Our evidence also shows that whenever property and its inheritance was in question, everything else was sacrificed and significant changes were made in favour of property and its inheritance."

An individual family with its well-defined property rights became the dominant feature in society. A family consists of a man, his parents, wife/wives and children and wealth would preferrably be concentrated within that unit. Manu aimed at a greater concentration through the law of primogeniture (among sons born of the same mother) although he did not press it further. The house, tiller, cattle, etc., were not to be divided. They went to the sons of a *samavarna* wife of a brahmin alone.

Those married under the Special Marriage Act and even those persons married under other forms but having subsequently registered their marriage under the Special Marriage Act are, in matter of inheritance, governed by the Indian Succession Act, 1925. Therefore, when a man to whom the Indian Succession Act applies dies leaving a widow and lineal descendants, the widow is entitled to one-third of the property of the deceased and the lineal descendants to two-thirds. Under the Act, in the case of Christians other than Indian Christians, a widow in the absence of lineal descendents will get the entire property of the husband provided its value does not exceed Rs 5000. If it does, she will receive Rs 5000 and a share in what remains along with the kindred of the deceased according to the specific rules laid down in the Act." Therefore, some people, especially women, definitely prefer to be married under the Special Marriage Act because of its beneficial provisions regarding divorce and intestate succession. These provisions were more beneficial to women, be they Hindus, Muslims, Indian Christians of Pondicherry or Indian Christians in those areas of Kerala which once upon a time comprised the princely states of Travancore and Cochin, provided they were not governed by the matrilineal custom. Prior to the adoption of the Hindu Succession Act in 1956, when a woman succeeded to the divided property of a deceased Hindu male, she took only a very limited interest in the matter. For she was denied the legal capacity to be a co-partner in a Hindu joint family. The Hindu Succession Act of 1956 changed all that. This Act, "which applies to Hindus, Buddhists, Jains and Sikhs, determines the heir on the basis of consanguinity or affinity without any discrimination on the grounds of sex." It gives a woman full ownership in the property inherited or acquired by her. Thus, the widow, the mother and the daughter now not only inherit property along with the son but also take an equal share with him. Parsee and Muslim women, however, are entitled to only half the share of the brothers or male heirs in the family.

Though the Indian Succession Act is generally applicable to Christians, there are various regions in the country where the Act is not applied. Likewise, there are also certain Christian communities to which it is not made applicable such as particular tribal Christian communities and those who are governed by the matrilineal system. Since the Act is not extended to the Union territory of Pondicherry, Indian Christians living in this territory are governed by traditional Hindu Law (i.e. Hindu Law as it was in force in the region before certain changes were effected by the Indian Parliament in 1955 and 1956) in the matter of inheritance with all the disadvantages and disabilities imposed on women.

In the erstwhile princely states of Cochin and Travancore, there are certain local enactments in operation relating to the vital succession issue among the Christian communities residing in these states. Unfortunately, they appear to be gender based and discriminatory towards women. Under the Travencore Christian Succession Regulation, 1916, the share of the widow in the estate of the husband is a life interest, terminable on her death or remarriage, except where she gets the whole estate in the absence of certain specified relatives of her deceased husband. Under the Cochin Christian Succession Act, which works somewhat differently, the widow gets a share equal to two thirds of the share of a son, if the deceased is survived by a son or lineal descendents of a son. Under the Travencore Regulation, 'which seems to discriminate against daughters who can take only one fourth of the value of the share of a son or Rs 5000 whichever is less', the maternal relatives are excluded completely from succeeding to the intestate if there are paternal relatives surviving the deceased man. In the Cochin Act, however, 'no maternal relatives are included among the heirs'. The Travancore Regulation does not apply to the small body of Indian Christians residing in the taluk of Neyyattinkara or the erstwhile princely state who follow *marumakkathayam* (matrilineal descent). Nor do the Roman Catholic Christians of the Latin rite and certain non-catholic Christians living in a few southern taluk of Travancore come under the purview of the Travancore Regulation. They follow their customary usage 'and among them male and female heirs of an intestate share equally in his property.'

The areas where the two enactments, namely, the Cochin Christian Succession Act, 1921 and the Travancore Regulation apply, are quite remarkable in that that they have an extremely high rate of literacy among the females and a large number of highly educated women. The awareness and education factors notwithstanding, if these women happen to be Christians who come within the purview of these enactments, they are entitled to only one quarter of the share of a brother in the property of their deceased father. The question remains whether these erudite women would at any stage consider reverting back to their matrilineal system for the sake of a more equitable and just distribution of family property. It is a question which will remain unanswered until and unless these women are desirous of committing themselves to bring about a change.

Adoption

In a country of such ethnic and religious diversity, where even among sub-castes of a particular community different customs and practices prevail, it is no wonder that there is no law of adoption covering all the peoples in the country. The Hindu Adoption and Maintenance Act 1956 deals with adoption by Hindus, Sikhs, Buddhists and Jains only. The government has attempted several times in the past (since independence) to pass a uniform, secular bill for the whole country, but a section of the Parsees and the Muslims offered specific peculiar objections to the various bills introduced in Parliament. Let us briefly examine the post-independence scenario where other signs of change were evident in the debates on the emotive and contentious issue of reforming Muslim family laws. What needs reform in the Muslim Personal Law? Is the Islamic law a product of human intelligence and adaptation to social needs and therefore amenable to modifications and changes or is it of divine inspiration and therefore immutable? If so, what lessons should be drawn from the history of reform in Muslim countries? Or what weight should be given to the views of Muslim thinkers in India, such as Iqbal who believed that the Muslim liberals were perfectly justified in reinterpreting the fundamental legal principles 'in the light of their own experience and the altered conditions of modern life?' No simple and straightforward answers seemed to be forthcoming especially because at the International Congress of Orientalists in Delhi in 1964 and a subsequent seminar five years later, the key issues discussed "related to the divine and a sacrosanct character of the Shariat, the preservation of 'Muslim identity' and fear of Hinduization." Traditional or conservative opinion, articulated by the Jamaat-I Islami and the Jamiyat al-ulama, was indignant at the prospect of changes in personal law. Modification of law based on specific injunctions in the Quran or *Hadith* was 'unimaginable'. Quranic regulations were considered authoritative and final for all occasions and all epochs and those wanting to tamper with them were enemies of Islam and its followers. Maulana Asad Madani a Jamiyat-al-ulama leader, viewed the plea for reform as 'a mask for the Jana Sangh's sinister designs to exterminate the Muslim community from India'.

However, A.A.A. Fyzee, Oxford-educated and a scholar of Islamic jurisprudence, held the view that Islam had ceased to be dynamic and that its vitality was sapped by totalitarianism. More important, he positioned himself against the traditional belief that in Islam law and religion are coterminous. He believed that law is a product of social evolution and must change with time and circumstances. He was convinced that 'gradually all individual and personal laws, based upon ancient principles of governing the social life of the community, will either be abolished or so modified as to bring them within a general scheme of laws applicable to all persons, regardless of religious differences'. Such a development, he pointed out, will not destroy 'the essential truth of the faith of Islam'. Addressing the Maharashtra State Muslim Women's Conference in Poona on 27 December 1971, he earnestly proclaimed that the Muslim Personal law as practiced under the Shariat Act had brought untold miseries to the community and must be discarded in favour of a uniform civil code. Some of these ideas were inspired by Azad's Tarjuman-al-Quran and his emphasis there on the rudiments of religious pluralism. Fyzee regarded this as the only pragmatic solution for the Indian Muslims, and for the preservation and progress of Islam in a composite society. M.H.Beg, a distinguished jurist, boldly suggested that Muslim jurisprudence could contribute valuable ideas in formulating a uniform civil code of personal laws. Muslim jurisprudence 'has acted and could still act as a part of that common stock of juristic ideas which have acted and reacted upon each other to produce a composite culture in this country which sustains the secular state'. W.C. Smith, who succinctly summed up the situation in all its complexity and analysed the strong oppostion to 'the liberal and secular credo', maintains: 'Indian freedom they saw rather as the unchecked opportunities for their enemies to hold them down or indeed to crush them' and concluded that 'only in very limited numbers did Muslims evaluate with true appreciation the ideals and announced objectives of the nation to which they belonged'.

There were various meaningful Acts passed under Hindu law which had a bearing on large segments of women in Indian society. The Hindu Minority and Guardianship Act, 1956, also bestowed certain additional rights on Hindu women. It provides that though the father may appoint by will a guardian for his minor children, any such appointment will not take effect during the lifetime of the mother if she survives the father. It will take effect only on her death, provided she has not appointed a guardian by her own will.

A Hindu mother is entitled to act as the natural guardian of her minor children if the father ceases to be a Hindu or renounces the world by becoming a hermit or ascetic. The Hindu widow and the Hindu mother, entitled to act as natural guardians of their minor children, are empowered under the Act to appoint guardians for them by will.

In 1956 substantial changes were effected in the law of adoption applicable to Hindus (since these enactments which are considered part of a Hindu code, apply to Hindus, Buddhists, Sikhs and Jains, so that a reference to Hindu women in this context includes Buddhist, Sikh and Jain women as well). The Hindu Adoption and Maintenance Act, 1956 has invested the Hindu woman with certain rights of adoption which she had not enjoyed before such as the privilege and right to adopt a son or a daughter. Previously, an adoption could only be formalized to a male. Furthermore, under this Act, a married man cannot, unless under certain very special circumstances, adopt a child without the prior consent of his legally wedded wife. Under the previous law, her consent was totally immaterial but under the new legislation, her consent is not necessary only under such circumstances as her having 'renounced the world or having ceased to be a Hindu or has been judicially declared to be of unsound mind.' It is indeed heartening to know that a Hindu woman who is not of unsound mind or a minor, can now legitimately adopt a male or female child, 'provided she is a spinster, divorcee, or widow or one whose husband has finally renounced the world or has been judicially declared to be of unsound mind'. In general, during coverture it is only the husband who can adopt. If a woman is desirous of adopting, she must not have any direct male lineal descendants living who are Hindus, whether it be a Hindu son or a Hindu great-grandson and so on and so forth. A further stipulation is that the adoptee should be at least twenty-one years younger than her. Similarly, if she wants to adopt a female child, it is mandatory that she does not have any Hindu daughter or son's daughter living at the time of adoption. Corresponding requirements have also to be met by the man desirous of adopting a son or daughter. If, in the case of a couple belonging to two different religions, for example when the man belongs to the Christian religion and the wife to the Hindu religion, the couple cannot be termed as parents of the child but its guardians, the court empowers the child when he or she is eighteen years of age to decide if he wants to continue living with his guardians or not.

Employment and Education

More and more women are now realizing the importance of earning for themselves and thus building up not only their confidence but also a sense of economic independence and self-worth. The rising cost of living, higher age of marriage, smaller families and increase in the life span of women, have all contributed to the steady rise in women taking up jobs.

Factories Act

The provisions of the Factories Act 1948 will indicate the extent of protection given to women at their place of work. It is as exhaustive as it is important and discussed below are some of its more important salient features. The main purpose of the Factories Act is to improve the working conditions in factories and to provide for effective steps and welfare of the workers. It deals with working hours, leave and wages and employment of young persons in great detail. The various provisions deal with the following: standards of cleanliness inside a factory, ventilation and temperature, control of dust and fumes, lighting, overcrowding, drinking water supply, separate toilets for males and females, fencing of dangerous machinery, precautions in case of fire, maintenance of buildings, first aid facilities, place for washing, rest rooms and canteens. Section 27 has injunctions banning the employment of women and children in cotton pressing. If they are employed at all, specific measures to safeguard them have been set forth and have to be complied with. Section 48 provides for the establishment of creches with clean, well-lit and well ventilated rooms, if the factory employs more than 30 women. The women workers can then leave their infants and kids here under the charge of a suitably trained woman. State governments, in addition, are empowered to make further rules for the provision of suitable staff for the washing, cleaning, changing and feeding facilities of such children.

The Factories Act, 1948 not only empowers state governments to prohibit employment of women in dangerous operations but a few enactments lay down the general rule that women should not be permitted to work between 7 pm and 6 am but this rule is relaxable in certain circumstances. For example, in situations when raw material might get damaged if there is delay as in the case of fish canning plants, etc, the state governments can exempt factories from this rule. But even then, no woman shall work between 10 pm and 5 am. Section 79 lays down in detail the facility of annual leave with wages. Elaborating on the term "dangerous operations" mentioned above, it is, specifically, Section 87 which states that where the 'serious risk of body injury, poisoning or disease' are present, the state governments can make suitable rules regarding the problem. It can prohibit or restrict the employment of women, adolescents or children in such dangerous operations. Provisions for maternity benefits for women have been incorporated in the Employees State Insurance Act, 1948 and a number of state enactments. While Maternity Benefits in coal mines is governed by the Maternity Benefits Act, 1961 women workers in factories and plantations are entitled to maternity leave according to the maternity benefit enactments of different states.

The relevant issue of equal pay for equal work has already been discussed in detail in a separate chapter and need not be elaborated upon here.

Only 13 per cent of Indian women, according to the 1971 census, may be regarded as workers, i.e., those who are engaged in some form of economic activity. Although about 80 per cent of these women are engaged in agriculture, only 12 per cent of the total employees in central and state administrative services and public sector undertakings are women which may not be unrelated to their education or lack of it. Only 18 per cent of Indian women are literate. Though one of the directive principles of the Constitution requires the state to provide free and compulsory education for all children under 14 years of age, the directive is generally followed with callous disregard of its spirit and its significance for the country. Coupled with the general apathy to women's education, this indifference to put in practice a constitutional directive results in greater social and economic deprivation for girls than for boys.

Statistics indicate that at the very vital primary school level, as many as 97 boys out of a hundred attend school. The corresponding ratio for girls is significantly and discouragingly, lower, which is about 62 girls out of every hundred attend school. Further, out of 100 girls who enter the first grade, only as small a percentage as 26 go to the fifth grade. It is only about 2 per cent of women who are able to benefit by the opportunities provided for higher education. In the years 1971-1972 it was found that only 36 girls were under any formal, meaningful instruction at various levels of education compared to a hundred boys. If in 1971 about 18 per cent of women were literate this may appear to compare well with only 8 per cent literacy for women on the eve of independence in 1947, but an increase of 10 per cent in the not too short span of about three decades is hardly something that should make us complacent.

Abortion

There are certain other types of social legislations which seek to protect interests and benefits that are of special concern to women. The Suppression of Immoral Traffic in Women and Girls Act, 1956, as its title indicates, is intended to protect helpless women and girls from a typical mode of exploitation not altogether unknown in the country and is vital not only to the well-being and health of the women, but its strict implementation can also prevent venereal diseases and the dreaded AIDS from spreading rapidly and claiming lives, killing innocent victims. The year 1956 also saw the enactment of another important piece of legislation, namely, the Women's and Children's Institutions (Licensing) Act. This was subsequently superseded by the Orphanages and Other Charitable Homes (Supervision and Control) Act, 1960. The chief object of the enactment was to regulate the activities of these institutions and to prescribe a proper standard to which the treatment and the training of the inmates should conform. Such a measure was found to be absolutely necessary for, while there are a large number of good and properly managed charitable institutions, there are many others "run with the objective of exploitation as their main and sustaining inspiration."

The Medical Termination of Pregnancy Act, 1971 may also be mentioned in the context of social legislation relative to women. Before the government embarked upon its family planning programme with full gusto, law in India dealt with abortion as a crime. According to the Indian Penal Code, causing miscarriage and injuries to an unborn child were crimes and the Criminal Procedure Code dealt with procedures for trying these crimes. But in 1971, Parliament very sagaciously passed the Medical Termination of Pregnancy Act to make abortions a lot easier and free from unnecessary complications. Four years later, in 1975, the government made several rules and regulations regarding abortions with the result that abortion facilities exist almost everywhere. However, when the MTP Act was passed in 1971, one of the underlying causes was also to promote the method of abortion as an effective means of birth control. Whatever be the case, the enactment seeks, among other things, to protect women's interests. It has a few provisions which, it is clear, were enacted with the sufferings of women in the legislator's mind. Such legislation provides that a pregnancy may be terminated where the length of the pregnancy does not exceed twenty weeks, if two medical practioners are of the (same) opinion that the continuance of the pregnancy would involve a risk to the life of the expectant mother or of grave injury to her physical or mental health. Two lucid explanations are offered in the enactment itself as to what exactly constitutes grave injury to the health of the pregnant woman. The first explanation reads as follows: "When any pregnancy is alleged by the pregnant woman to have been caused by rape, the anguish caused by such pregnancy shall be presumed to constitute a grave injury to the mental health of the pregnant woman."

In this case the anguish is definitely, undeniably "palpable". "The second explanation is more intriguing in that "anguish" is given an extended application" It states: "Where a pregnancy occurs as a result of failure of any device or method by any married woman or her husband for the purpose of limiting the number of children, the anguish caused by such unwanted pregnancy may be presumed to constitute a grave injury to the mental health of the pregnant woman."

Though the promotional slant of the government's family planning programme may be perceptible in this explanation, it is evident that the Parliament certainly cannot be blamed or held responsible in any way 'for any lack of solicitude for the largest minority in the country'. This solicitude may be even more evident in another provision of the Act which stipulates that in determining whether the continuance of a pregnancy would involve grave risk to the health of a pregnant woman, account may be taken of her actual or reasonably forseeable environment. This enactment has been hailed as a major landmark in India's social legislation, and a far-reaching measure assuring the women of India freedom from undesirable and unwanted pregnancies.

Since abortion is not purely a medical affair, but involves moral and legal questions as well, it is a subject of controversy practically worldwide. There are right-to-life movements in the West which defend the rights of the unborn child. Not only that, medical scientists are generally in agreement that life begins from the moment of conception and height, weight, intelligence, blood group and all identifying traits are decided at that very moment in time. In 18 days of conception, the heart begins to beat. In six weeks "quickening" (movements in the womb) starts. The brain also begins to function and is measurable by electrocardiogram. Electrocardiogram (ECG) can also record its movements. In 12 weeks, it begins to feel pain, breathes fluid, sucks thumb, sleeps and wakes. Nothing new develops now, only further maturation and increase in size takes place. It is at this stage that most abortions also take place.

According to that unchallengeable encyclopaedia of knowledge and information, *The Encyclopaedia Britannica*, "after abortion, the likelihood of abnormal pregnancies, premature births, illness in the woman or even sterility is increased. Abortion can be followed by feelings of guilt, disturbed sexual relations, and psychologically induced illness. Studies show a high proportion of abortees to be maladjusted. In a study in Yugoslavia, only 24 per cent were considered well balanced."

In cases where legal abortion has been denied, the children may suffer. One study revealed that children born after refused requests for abortion showed a high incidence of delinquency, social maladjustment, educational failure and need for psychiatric help. For purposes of birth control, medical opinion strongly favours contraception over abortion.

Various provisions in the Act deal with the various complex aspects of abortion and its wide ranging repercussions. Whereas Section 313 deals with abortion without the prior consent of the mother - an unpardonable crime to my mind - and stipulates that the punishment for such a heinous act could even be life imprisonment, Section 314 maintains that whoever causes the death of a woman, inducing abortion, may be sentenced upto ten years in jail and also pay fine. Referring back to Section 313, a woman cannot give "consent" under fear of injury, or if she is under a misconception, or if she is of unsound mind or in an intoxicated state, etc. Each provision must be examined carefully in the context of that aspect of abortion to which it refers. The penal code also makes it a crime to conceal birth by disposing of the body before or after birth.

The Central Government has set rules in 1975 for approving a place for abortion. This is to maintain safe and hygienic conditions and the rule prescribes also the minimum equipment necessary at the place as well as the qualifications of a doctor who is qualified to conduct abortion. Furthermore, those who set up clinics or hospitals for abortions must apply in the prescribed form to the chief medical officer of the district and the officer will visit and inspect the place to check its suitability within the prescribed norms. The Supreme Court has also explained in detail the duties of a doctor in a case decided in 1969 and maintains that 'a breach of any of those duties gives a right of action for negligence to the patient'.

"Human rights activists and champions of women's rights were appalled by the revelation of international trafficking in foetuses for experimentation and use in cosmetic industry. At a meeting of the International Association to Combat the Exploitation of Human Foetuses, it was stated that traffic in foetuses has been going on for several years in great secrecy. Foetuses are taken out from willing mothers, frozen and used for laboratory research and for commercial use." Shocking! Bizarre! But unfortunately all too true. And raising even newer and more controversial medico-legal and ethical issues than before. Issues which must be dissected conscientiously, with humane considerations in mind and strong measures taken to prevent and completely ban such horrific malpractices, which amount to butchering and bartering precious human life.

References

Antony, M.J., *Women's Rights*, New Delhi: Dialogue Publications,1985.

Krishnaswamy, S., 'Female Infanticide In Contemporary India: A Case-Study of Kallars of Tamilnadu', In Ghadially Rehana (ed.) *Women in Indian Society.* New Delhi: Sage 1988.

Minattur, Joseph, 'Women and the Law: Constitutional Rights and Continuing Inequalities', *Women In Contemporary India*, Souza.

Mukherjee, Prabhati, *Hindu Women - Normative Models*, Calcutta: Orient Longman, First Published 1978, Revised Edition 1994.

11
CREDIT WOMEN WITH SENSE AND FINANCE

Men are dependent on circumstances, not circumstances on men.

Herodotus

The Lace Makers of Naraspur

Housewifisation ... is the process by which the ideology of the housewife, the woman sitting in the house provides the necessary subjective and sociocultural element for the building-up and maintenance of such a system. In fact, the ideology of the housewife in the case of the lace workers has assumed the character of a material force. It has found its institutionalization in the sexual division of labour in society, in the exclusion of women from other productive activities and from trade, in the marriage system and the caste system. It would be wrong to treat this ideology simply as ideas, values and consciousness. The women are caught in this system by a number of very real compulsions and constraints, the major one being their economic dependence on a man and their responsibility for the ongoing subsistence production - Maria Mies in *The Lace Makers of Narasapur*.

So the housewifisation of the lace-makers of Narasapur of "the little girls, beautiful young women, old withered women...busy at their crochet hooks, framed in a door or window..to catch the best light...victims of an ideology of male supremacy" took place. In the distant district of west Godavari, where, in a project supported by the ILO, one visualized the implementation of this exquisite trade as "thousands and thousands of female crochet lace-makers, six to sixty, largely upper caste (the Kapus), forced to work indoors plying their crochet needles endlessly because of their men and their ideology-'good' women remain at home", created beautiful articles to take your breath away. To make the deeply exhausting work of lace-making spending long-long hours of work sitting hunched over the tyrannical ball of thread and crochet hook and then being paid an absolute pittance for it, "steady foreign (export) orders and credit" were absolute necessary, said the then Secretary of the cooperative, Hemlata. Amplifying that only if the women were sanctioned loans, could they get out of the lace merchants hands. But till then, they were forced to take loans from him and, therefore, work for him. It was only when Viji Srinivasan, who worked in the Ford Foundation's New Delhi office and developed a part of their women's programme, specially working on women's roles in eight key economic sectors of the Indian economy—agriculture and forestry, dairying, sericulture, fisheries, khadi and village industries, handloom, handicraft, small animal and bird husbandry, took some lacework samples from Narasapur and did some aggressive marketing, that the fortunes of the toiling workers of Narásapur changed. Central Cottage Industries placed a small order, an individual placed a small order but the break really came with Trade Aid, New Zealand, an Alternative Trading Organisation (ATO) placing an initial order and then buying steadily from the lace-makers cooperative at Narasapur. The initial order was for the sum of Rs 8750.

But the problem of access to credit, as articulated by Hemlata, still remained and the possibilities of the Working Women's Forum setting up a credit programme in Narasapur especially designed for the situation of the lace-makers caught in a whirlpool of poverty and exploitation, were explored. An application for the "replication" in a rural area of the WWF's work in Madras city was forwarded, accepted and implemented, the replication being of the Forum's work in Madras city, in Narasapur. Not only that, but one Mr Parameswaran of the Bank of India opened an entirely separate branch in Narasapur only for the Working Women's Forum. The Chief General Manager of one of the leading banks in the country spent the entire evening and night meeting with group after group of the poorest of lace-makers in various villages and talked with them patiently and earnestly in the light of the oil lamps - the long flickering shadows throwing the poverty of the lace-makers into sharp relief. In the context of such an ambience it was not difficult to believe in the ideology and subsequent implementation of bank nationalisation and its socialistic impact, even in the concept of the "system" and the "establishment".

But after several months of trying to work with the branch at Narasapur and failing to leverage loans, the Working Women's Forum were compelled to set up and register their own credit cooperative society. Over a period of time it transpired that the Working Women's Forum and the Godavari Delta Women Lace Artisans Cooperative Society Ltd., as Hemlata's society was called, were unable to work together amicably but may be that should have been anticipated as their functions were different. However, Vi Cottrell of Trade Aid in New Zealand continued to place orders with Hemalata's cooperative... At an ILO-sponsored workshop at Mahabaleshwar, Vina Mazumdar of the Centre for Women's Development Studies reiterated that the WWF could not organize the lace-makers of Narasapur for the lace-merchants would have stooped to anything - "threats, even murder" to prevent the success of the enterprise.

When in 1991 Dr R.J. Rao, an erstwhile colleague of Viji Srinivasan, went to Narasapur to investigate and assess how both the Godavari Delta Cooperative and Working Women's Forum were doing-earlier Jaya Arunachalam of the WWF had confirmed that loans had been given to 38,000 lace-makers since he could only visit Hemalata's cooperative due to paucity of time. The result of his findings were truly impressive. He discovered that not only was Hemalata working assiduously with 250 members in 40 villages but that the turnover was an impressive Rs 700,000 (Rs 7 lakhs) in 1990 - 1991 and expected to be Rs 10 lakhs in

1991-92. Four Alternative Trading Organizations were "placing orders regularly-Oxfam-Bridge in the United Kingdom, SERRV in USA, Trading Partners in Australia and Trade Aid in New Zealand." Displaying excellent organizational and training skills, Hemalata had initiated a skill-training programme so that high standard quality lace was produced.

Therefore, as the 'housewifisation' of the lace-makers of Narasapur took place and women of all ages painstakingly created their individual versions of exquisite workmanship, such 'housewifisation' went beyond the concept of just 'male supremacy'. It was a process by which women, though sole supporters of their families, though sole income earners, were thought, "by their husbands, male planners to be housewives, or at the most, supplementary earners." Thus low wages were justified and dowry kept high (for she had to be supported by the male to have the luxury of being a housewife).

In the Godavari Delta Cooperative and Working Wömen's Forum, there were two different strategies. There were two or three markets. The first being that of domestic/local demand - at the shandies and at home; the second being that of the local exporters and both being 'cheap' markets. It was possible that the exporters would buy at the shandies. The Working Women's Forum presumably gave loans to those women who sold their goods in these markets. Since it was a 'missing-piece' approach, it could reach 38,000 women.

The third market was that of the ATO's. Since the ATO's policy was to enhance advances, hence these women didn't need loans. Since this was time-consuming work, the Godavari Delta Cooperative could only reach 250 women as it was not possible for the ATOs to give orders for 38,000 plus women.

Some questions, however, remained to be answered. Such as in which case was the 'housewifisation' being reversed —in the Godavari Delta cooperative or the Working Women's Forum? It was obvious that the ATO's could be 'controlled' by a grassroots group. But under what conditions would working together in the cooperative's premises be the answer? Questions with some interesting challenges - challenges to be met and answered at another time, another place. As of now enough challenges had been made to the housewifisation of the lace-makers of Narasapur.

Brief History, Growth and Development of the Society

Nestling on the bank of the Vasista Godavari river at the confluence of the Godavari river and the Bay of Bengal, is the small town of Narasapur. And crochet lace-making, originally introduced in the delta area of Narasapur and its environments by one Mr and Mrs Macrae of Scotland a century ago 'to afford part- time employment to the poverty-stricken ladies of the area', is 'one of the important handicrafts with a highly artistic appeal'. Unfortunately, however, the lace artisans are mercilessly exploited here by the middlemen who, by paying these artisans pitifully meagre wages and exporting the laces to distant shores, are not only amassing tremendous wealth but since they play an important role in the production and export of these products, they effect an indirect monopoly in the lace business by exploiting these artisans. Because their employment by the middlemen-exporters depends upon the orders they secure from their buyers. Therefore, Hemalata, also a lace artisan and founder member, former President and designer of this Society, having experienced the exploitation of these middlemen-exporters, approached the All-India Handicrafts Board for help and she was advised by the Board to form a Co-operative Society along with the women artisans and to seek financial and other help from the Board to overcome and get over the difficulties which would be useful for the uplift and betterment of the member artisans. Therefore, after extensive touring of the villages and explaining to the village women the imminent need for getting out of the clutches of the middlemen and securing just and equitable conditions of work and remuneration for them, as well as after encountering numerous trials and tribulations (both technical and otherwise), Hemalata, having gathered the women artisans as potential members, 'applied for registeration to the government as Co-operative Cottage Industrial Society'. Finally, the matter had to be resolved at the ministerial level and the society was registered under Regn. No. IND Q 88.

Aims and Objectives of the Society

1. To raise funds required for business;
2. To purchase raw materials, other appliances and instruments and transform the raw-material into finished goods;
3. To impart technical training to members;
4. To encourage self-help, mutual aid and cooperative spirit and to strive hard for the betterment and uplift of the downtrodden members economically and socially;
5. To provide better wages and profits to its members;
6. To do all such acts as may be conducive to the betterment of the members.

As originally contemplated, no financial assistance could be harnessed either from the All-India Handicrafts Board or from the Andhra Pradesh State Government and it was only after the visit of Viji Srinivasan of Ford Foundation in 1980 and her efforts in bringing 'the entire history of the Society to the notice of Mrs Marty Chen, the Field Representative of India and Bangladesh of Oxfam America' that Chen, possessed of a good and kind heart lent her helping hand for the uplift and development of the Society by granting generous help, by contributing handsome donations. With the grants made by M/s Oxfam America during the first year, the following programmes were conducted:

> The Society sponsored training classes to two batches, each batch consisting of ten candidates; The Society established a rented office with minimum furniture and staff;
>
> Lace articles were manufactured to a tune of Rs 21,350 and sales were also made to an extent of Rs 15,000.

Better wages were paid, profits distributed to the member artisans. While the wages at the time of starting the business for making rounds of 60" was Rs 24 paid by exporters, the Society paid a wage of Rs 70 for the above size for making one piece. The parities between the wages of the Society and the middlemen-exporters were incomparable.

On 17th September 1982, Chen visited the Society and was satisfied with the progress made and the work in progress, which was assessed after exhaustively interviewing several artisans in the neighbouring villages with the help and support of M/s Oxfam America for three consecutive years to the Society. The Society progressed by leaps and bounds, not only in terms of economic standards but also in its membership strength which increased from 100 to 600. Apart from rendering valuable help and support to the society, Oxfam also introduced it to trading partners in the United Kingdom and New Zealand by extending support to the latter by placing orders with the Society and marketing the merchandise produced by it.

In 1992, when empirical knowledge was garnered regarding this issue, the Society was doing business with the following Trading Partners:

M/s Oxfam Trading, Licester, United Kindom;

M/s Trade Aid Importers, Christ Church, New Zealand;

M/s Trading Partners, Australia;

M/s Serve Self-Help Handicrafts, Windsor, U.S.A.

The Batik Women of Desia Nagar

Let us now narrate the story of Desia Nagar where, back in 1991, the enigmatic Batik women dwelled. But their story too has a beginning with 'once upon a time' - only their's was no fairy tale beginning. Chosen for their dyeing skills as well as for their willingness to work and their need to work, many were from the Scheduled Caste, Adi Dravida (I think an 'honourable' name for the '*Paravas*' which had a derogatory connotation....the women were called *Parachis*). Mallika, Indrani, Sivagami, Chokkammal, Govindammal, Krishnaveni, Elsa - they had been pavement-dwellers in Old Slaughter House Road. In the winter of 1961 they were picked up by the police, men, women, children, animals, chickens and dropped in Desia Nagar, Ashok Nagar and Cherian Nagar, adjacent 'Sites and Services' urban community development projects just outside Madras city, far away from their places of livelihood. Because it was on the seaside, it was cold. Children got very ill and died. In these circumstances, the Swallows from Sweden and Denmark began to work there, their volunteers lived there. Collaborating in the project was Service Civil International (SCI). Josephine a refugee from Burma, transposed dreams into the colourful products for the Swedish market — as they patiently completed the time consuming batik process — waxing, dyeing, wax removal - so that they could see the process in its entirety and develop their own individual roles. As the fascinating, typical *batik* filaments emerged in colour in the cloth, an artistic and unmistakable folk art style came to life. The talent of these persevering women was unmistakable, but at that time in the early sixties, to market such talent and learn from the marketing experience was the crucial issue.

The women of Desia Nagar had all, in the initial stages of being brought there, completely lost their livelihood opportunities though some of the men and women, it must be mentioned here, had come with a little cash. Capitalizing on their relative financial superiority and cashing in on the desperate monetary needs of others, these enterprising people overnight became moneylenders, charging Rs 12.50 interest per Rs 100 per month and became rich overnight too. One such woman was Parvati Ammal. Also Adi-Dravida,her dark fat body was full of folds of flesh. Every month, when the 'batik women' got their stipends, Parvati and hordes of other such women and men who had lent money to the 'batik women', sat outside the thatched hut and as the women emerged, snatched their money.

Most of them went home with Rs 10 only (out of Rs 250). She also sat outside the harbour and caught hold of the men harbour — workers (carrying bags of wheat, etc) as they came out of the entrance and did the same!

After discussion of the relevant personnel with one Pandiarajan, a young lawyer who also worked in the same area in collaboration with the Swallows, through an organisation called Service Civil International and possessed an indepth knowledge of the area and its problems and the causes of poverty, and a study of the existing laws of money-lending, a detailed report was sent to the Swallows. All the debts of the existing 17 *batik* women were listed therein. The Swallows very generously met the entire debt of Rs 17,000 which had been forwarded to them.

Over the next eventful month, every day, the lawyer and the concerned women personnel systematically visited the moneylenders of seventeen women, (there were around 82 transactions, not necessarily 82 moneylenders), apprised them of the laws "you need a license, you can charge only 10 per cent interest per year, if you transgress these laws, you can be imprisoned for six months or fined Rs 1000". All of them accepted less than what they claimed, and signed release documents for they were mortally afraid that the finances would run out.

Over the next year various other innovative support programmes were developed — consumption loans; insurance (life). Here LIC proved to be extremely helpful suggesting some of the women personnel becoming their agents so that the agent's commission could be used as a Revolving Fund for the women. This was done without further loss of time, so if a batik woman died, her children would get Rs 1000. A lot of extremely beneficial community education programmes against expensive weddings and funerals were organized, to instil in the people a judicious use of finances, and avoidance of unnecessary and usesless expenditure.

Ultimately, the time came for the most difficult and heart wrenching operation of all, the most difficult strategy in the NGO world, that of handing over. Bjorn Eder, a teacher and adult educator and an individual with a comprehensive understanding of the complex modalities of handing over, came from Sweden for this purpose. He got 'the handicrafts' registered under the Government's Industries Department as an Industrial Cooperative — the Swallows Handicrafts Industrial Cooperative Society Ltd. He got the Swallows in India to give the building to the Swallows Handicrafts Cooperative at a reasonable rent, and transfer all the assets including stock, sewing machines.

After much judicious deliberation, resource personnel were fixed up, 'mock' elections were held and there were several 'trial' Boards of Directors. This way everyone got an opportunity to try out the cooperative. A Disciplinary Committee was also tried out and Quality Controllers and Stock Controllers, etc., were trained (from among the women) explaining to them simultaneously the trade and control of Alternative Trading Organisations (ATO) as it contributed 90 per cent of the orders.

Despite various teething problems and other difficulties, this Society was the only one in Madras which was exporting. The turnover during 1991 was as under:-

1988-89	Rs 6 lakhs
1989-90	Rs 8.8 lakhs
1990-91	Rs 12 lakhs

But for export orders, the Society is dependent on bank credit. Since there is a lack of working capital, there is a delay in purchasing raw materials ....58 members are getting a steady income. All have advances as Education Advance, Debt Releasing Fund, Festival Advance, Bonus Advance. The workers express satisfaction that there no longer exists hunger, lack of clothes, there is credit-worthiness and there are expectations and the children of the workers are educated.

In the 1960s, there was no concentration, no focus on women. An attempt to draw attention towards their miserable plight only elicited a response from the Swedish and Danish "volunteers". In the outside world there was no resonance. Would they, (the women), be better off if we had conscientised them? Would they be better off if we had resorted to community (mass) education? These are some of the thought-provoking issues that one must ponder about at length.

Yet, in spite of these issues, the Swallows Handicrafts has certainly vindicated the possibility and viability of handing over. It has also demonstrated the possibility of developing an entire project based on Alternative Training Organisations. It has contributed to our understanding of handicrafts as an economic sector.

Community Service Guild (CSG) in Cuddalore — Dec. 1991

"Sand-dunes of white-brown sand leading to the bright blue sea of Cuddalore in South Arcot district of Tamil Nadu ... green coconut trees waving frantically in the cool breeze and causing shadows to undulate on the sand ... grey thatched houses, as low as two feet from the ground ... thatched houses made out of coconut leaves... intertwined with skilled nimble fingers...blue nylon threads spread out in the stark white sand like a wave from the Bay of Bengal, being repaired by the same nimble fingers... mats are spread in front of a grey green coconut tree... in the shade quickly women gather..." Behold the fishing hamlet of Devanampattinam.

The 'leader' who was President of the Community Services Guild's Self-Employed Women Cooperative Society until the Government of Tamil Nadu superseded all elected Boards of Directors and placed special officers, was a dark, thin married woman of Tamil Nadu, called Nayakam.

From the traditional fisherfolk community Parvata Raja Kulam, she and other women like her, follow the following trades — dried fish, fresh fish, dried fish auction, cigarette shop, sweet shop, grocery, *idli*, *vada*, *puttu*, *appam* (snacks). She tells her story of how they came to the notice of the CSG and how the latter organization came to their aid. Since the fish caught by their menfolk was not enough, the women were forced to buy fish to take to the market, sell it and earn an income, however meagre. For this purpose they had to borrow money from moneylenders (often Muslims), the system being for every Rs 100 loaned, the moneylender deducted Rs.3/- straight away; subsequently Rs 12.50 per week had to be paid for ten weeks. The payment of the interest obviously posed hardships, to cirumvent which Nayakam, along with two other colleagues, approached various bank including the Punjab National Bank, where the Collector offered to stand security for them but all to no avail! Except for the Indian Bank where they took some cognizance of the women's pitiable plight and advanced them Rs 300 each. Which they repaid in record time, thereby vindicating the trust placed in them.

"At the Indian Bank we met Mr. Babu of CSG. He agreed to our request and came to our hamlet, held a meeting of all the women; after all formalities were completed, he gave 12 of us Rs 600 each as loan, in two groups (six members each)." Gradually more and more women joined us. The number rapidly multiplied and finally there were as many as 100 women, many of whom took loans repeatedly as many as six times or seven times or even eight times. Then CSG developed their new Sangam, the Society was registered and every member contributed Rs 170 as share capital.

The dried fish trade is a seasonal trade. The women earn from Rs 90 to Rs 200 at a time. For example, if the fish is bought for Rs 500, the gills removed, the fish cleaned and dried and then sold to the merchant of dried fish, he could pay as little as Rs 590 or as much as Rs 700 for the lot. Not such a phenomenal amount when you consider the amount of trouble the fisher women go through in first drying the fish in an area called the 'salt space' which also happens to be the cremation ground. The entire process from putting the fish into salt at night, carrying it in a basket to the sea to wash it the next morning, carrying back the washed ware with the smelly salt water dripping all over them, is nauseating at the very least. During the rains, when the fish is infested with worms and insects, then the fish has to be sold for less than half the price. There are other problems such as the vexatious disputes between the launch fishermen and cattumaran fishermen, with loss of business and injury to the fishermen often being the outcome. Though this problem has been successfully ameliorated with the formation of the Owners Association when, in the case of such an occurrence, the Association investigates the matter and then awards suitable compensation. The owners are generally Muslims, Christians, Naidus, etc., while the caste fishermen are mostly 'labourers' on these launches.

While the Sangam established by the CGS has succeeded in reducing the interest rates of the moneylenders from Rs 10 per Rs 100 per month to Rs 5 for the same amount, their laudable objectives being the removal of women's difficulties and their advancement in life, the fisher's cooperative society, unfortunately, only belongs to the men. In Village Women's Development Committee — the committee members get training of two days per month; also a Thrift Scheme where the women save Rs 10 per month for three years.

Many problems exist, having roots in the peculiar social and cultural ethos of the area, such as the men being heavy drinkers and not going out to sea unless they infuse sufficient quantities of liquor and the economic repercussions, etc. The women need, essentially, a modicum of economic emancipation and freedom from interdependece upon their menfolk for a regular income. So the members of the Community Services Guild advanced tentative suggestions for their breaking the shackles of male domination in a society, a ruthless society where the ills of ruthless racism and pitiless poverty prevail all too obviously.

Evidence of the CSG's helping hand seem to be prevalent everywhere. The leader of the flower-sellers group, Nangai who, along with her husband has a shop in the Nagammal temple at Tirupapuliyur in Cuddalore, took seven loans — ranging from Rs 250 to Rs 1800-from the Community Services Guild. She buys flowers every morning, around 9 am at the Floriculturists Union at Tirupapuliyur — flowers come here from Salem, Thanjavur, Dindigul, etc., beautiful multihued blooms in all their pristine beauty-pink oleander, green scented *maru* leaves, yellow chrysanthemums, golden marigolds, blushing roses and so on and so forth. She spends about Rs 200 every day, including the money spent on the procurement of jasmine buds from the Devanampattinam market. On Thursdays and Fridays she buys more, also at the time of weddings, Hindu and Muslim, temple festivals, etc. Contrary to expectations of women handling more of the jobs of garland- making, hair-ornaments and other skilled jobs, it is the men who make garlands and handle other 'intricate' work. Women do the monotonous lengths of flowers, tied together by banana fibres, measured by the forearm length and sold; they also sell from house to house, men sit in the shop. Belonging to the Gounder caste—notorious in Tamil Nadu for patriarchy, dowry and female infanticide—Nangai employed others to help her tie the 24 seers of flowers per day and had an impressive list of regular clients to whom she delivered "forearm length" flowers every day. Floriculturists from the village of Vellakkarai have also been identified by CSG and helped according to their needs.

Till 1992, the women assisted by CSG in Cuddalore were of the following trades:

Wosem (Cuddalore)

Sl. No.	*Trade*	*No. of Women*
1.	Fish	128
2.	Dried fish	103
3.	Coir	100
4.	Eatables, tiffin	104

5.	Idli	125
6.	Paddy straw	12
7.	Rice	56
8.	Vegetables, fruit	210
9.	Flower	16
10.	Tea shop	28
11.	Sari, cut piece	125
12.	Confectionary	121
13.	Poultry, eggs	15
14.	"Petty" shop	65
		1258

In addition, around 400 women were awaiting loans, after becoming CSG members. Various questions arose as the decade of the eighties came to a close. Questions as to whether 'models' could be repeated , reproduced or 'replicated', arose and were debated upon exhaustively at the Ford Foundation in New Delhi. Finally, if voluntary effort or even NGO effort cannot be replicated, then how to upscale them? Anyway, to cut a long story short, finances had been taken from out of the Women's DAP to support the Community Services Guild's (CSG's) 'replication' of the Working Women's Forum credit 'model' called Wosem (Women's self-employment) in Cuddalore and Salem. This began in 1984 and was termed the Delegated Authority Project.

"...But because CGS doesn't have a charismatic leader, nor a leader with political power, nor having direct linkages to donors in Europe, etc., it gets neither the attention nor the funds it deserves, let alone for replication, it doesn't get the funds it deserves or needs for Wosem in Cuddalore or Salem. This relates to the problems of administrative costs", one such problem being that "voluntary agencies" should, essentially, have "volunteers". "With increasing specialization and professional needs, this becomes impossible; and another problem is how long can a donor provide support to the same organization." The Ford Foundation is almost the only exception. The Foundation's grant to CSG was almost entirely for administrative costs, the breakdown of such expenditure being as follows :

Budget Breakdown of Ford Foundation Grant to CSG

1.	Staff support	$14,200
2.	Study tours	$300
3.	Local travel costs	$4000
4.	Office expenses including rental	$1250
5.	Survey and evaluation of project	$2000
6.	Central office	$3250

An advisable line of action therefore would be, "that the Ford Foundation explores the whole issue of administrative costs and develop models for at least 15 women's development organisations in the country."

However, the affirmative action problems of CSG still remained. A feature written by Viji Srinivasan (for internal circulation) in Ford Foundation in 1983, about the difficulties of the affirmative action in practice, is reproduced below. Subjective case studies at the interim part of the report have, however, not been considered relevant to the issue here and have, accordingly, been deleted.

Affirmative Action in Community Services Guild

This feature is based on field visits in February 1983 and July 1983.

The women's access to credit programme of the Community Services Guild is now well-established. Though as yet it is not large enough nor participatory enough (compared with WWF), it is a planned replication effort which is very successful. Recovery rate is 100 per cent. The project has steadily built up a base, women's groups have been formed, and there is effective and indepth interaction between the project staff and the constituency. One illustration of the indepth interaction is that the fishermen and fisherwomen of Madras city are notorious for not repaying loans (other organisations have not been able to collect loans from fisherwomen in Madras city) but CSG has been able to get 100 per cent recovery rate. The replication effort demonstrates that many development agencies can take up the 'facilitator' role in women's access to credit programmes from institutional sources.

Community Services Guild (CSG) has had many problems in getting and retaining women staff members. I have therefore thought it worthwhile to describe CSG's affirmative action attempts in details.

Table 7.1

Affirmative Action Statement

	M	*F*	*Total*
Governing Board	7	2*	9
Administration	5	-	5
SWELS Project Officer	1	2	3
Organisers	1	5	6
Health Staff	1	3	4
Kalwods project	2	9	11
Wosem project	-	2	2
Research project	-	2	2
	17	23	42

*These 2 women are representatives from the constituency.

This is a guarantee which has genuinely tried affirmative action and now has 23 women project staff out of 42 project staff. But they have had so many problems that I think it would be worthwhile to record them.

First of all, they had problems in getting women candidates. They adveritsed eight times in newspapers that only women candidates were required for working with low-income women. Apart from that, they wrote to three colleges in Madras, one in Madurai and one in Coimbatore, asking for candidates. In spite of that, they got very few candidates.

The SWELS programme began in August 1981. In the course of those two years, the staff (male and female) have organised low-income women's groups, low-income youth groups (male), self-employment schemes, placement schemes, production units. But in the course of these programmes, the young women project staff have had so many problems; consequently, a lot of the administrative staff's time, including the Director's time is spent in trying to solve these problems.

However the problems arising from such case studies are symptomatic of the social change taking place in Madras city where a lot of interaction is taking place between young people and religion/caste/class barriers are breaking down. Thus, it has given rise to some thought-provoking questions. These questions are reproduced, verbatim, as below:

1. Are not the NGOs in Bihar (or elsewhere) right in saying that it is better to have all male staff (even if the constituency is of poor women) to avoid "problems"? The problems would probably be worse in Bihar which is a more feudal, more caste-ridden society.
2. Are not the women's NGOs right in saying that they prefer to have all-female staff? (though they say it is to get women staff and constituency to participate fully in meetings, they also add that it is to avoid 'problems').
3. Is the approach of the CSG possible in Indian society now? For example, one of CSG staff's observations is that the low-income Youth Clubs (young men) expect the women's groups and the women's Youth Clubs to be "under" them and to be controlled by them. According

to CSG staff, the male chauvinistic approach is prevalent among the low-income-groups also, and one of CSG's aims is to get all the groups to participate in a spirit of equality and hand over the project to them. I know of very few groups of this nature among 'development-oriented' NGOs, and therefore, is not such an attempt worth supporting further, in its aim of equality of gender participation among the constituency? However, CSG is too small, and Indian society is perhaps not ready for it. Can the mixed-gender approach work in our society? Are we too glib in talking about mixed-gender approaches without thinking through the problems at the micro-level of affirmative action? Would not women - only organizations work better?

Women Self-Employment Scheme

Report for the Period January-June 1986 (Written by CSG)

The Women Self-Employment Scheme (WOSEM) was started by the Community Services Guild (CSG) in November 1982 in Salem (Salem District) and the next October (1983) in Cuddalore (South Arcot District). The WOSEM was started with the idea of relieving the poor self-employed women from the clutches of moneylenders. Those women, who either had very little money or no money at all, had to depend on the moneylenders or wholesalers for seeking credit. Thus, most of the earnings were eaten away by these people by way of interest. Hence, in spite of the hard labour at business, the left over earning was nothing but a very meagre profit which could hardly sustain them with one meal a day (of totally undernourishing food).

Seeing their plight, the CSG had planned the WOSEM scheme to assist these women with an institutional credit delivery system and hence to maximize their earnings. With this intention the CSG had started WOSEM scheme, which presently covers 12 areas in Salem and 7 areas in Cuddalore. The enthusiasm of the CSG was often put to test by the nationalized banks with whom the CSG started working for arranging the credit delivery for these poor women. Though the rate of interest through the nationalized banks was very much less (4 per cent under differential interest rates), the CSG had to face lot of problems with these banks as these banks have gone back on their word in the issuance of loans; this was happening in spite of all efforts including lobbying at different levels.

All these women, before the introduction of this scheme, were under the mercy of moneylenders who charged them an interest which most often happened to be anywhere between 200 to 240% per annum. Otherwise they would be under the mercy of wholesalers, seeking credit; without any bargaining capacity and accepting the rate quoted by them. Further, these people had to face the harassment of local police and petty officials of the civil bodies, on various grounds. Most of these women had to work more than 8 hours per day outside their economic activities. Apart from this, they have to shoulder the responsibilities of buying the needed provisions, cooking, attending on their children, etc. This mostly led to the deteriorating health condition of these women.

The following were the objectives under which the Project was initiated. To arrange institutional credit facilities through banks initially and later on, help them towards forming their own Thrift Society to help them to be aware of their existing condition and assist them to overcome the same, help them to increase production/sale and expand /diversify business by arranging required training facilities; assist them in getting into formal groups and organizations; help them to become economically self-reliant and empowered, thus, towards reducing the gap of inequality between sexes.

Between January-June 1986 there was not much improvement in the assistance from these banks, in spite of the assurance given by them for more loans every week. During this period, there was assistance only for 200 members in Salem and 213 members in Cuddalore. This had led the staff and the members of the WOSEM scheme to jointly decide on the need for savings by the members towards creating of a thrift programme and revolving fund. So a Credit Cooperative Society was formed.

This period (January-June 1986) saw good people's participation. Due to the new idea evolved by CSG towards the group system and group responsibility and the identification of needy and feasible new members by the already existing groups, this system has curtailed the earlier problem of delay or occasional default in repayment of this credit by the individual members (who were of course selected by the CSG during initial stages of this scheme). The new plan of getting formed into small groups of 5 members each (for each group) and all these groups jointly meeting twice a month to discuss their problems both common and individual has helped the women to understand each other well and come closer.

Hence these women members, due to their active participation in the group meetings and village meetings are able to understand the situation clearly — both working and living. This leads them to start thinking of the ways to overcome the same. Also, this helped them in discussing various problems they face including their husbands' alcoholism, wife-beating, son's or daughter's marriage, dowry, etc. These women began using methods such as role-play, towards finding a solution.

As mentioned earlier, these people were able to see the need and the urgency for a thrift programme and thus begun planning for savings. During the first six months of this year, 324 Saving accounts, 3 Time Deposit accounts, 2 Recurring Deposit accounts were started by the members of Salem area and by 29 members in Cuddalore. However, all these women members were asking the CSG to start its own thrift programme where eachone of them would become members.

Presently women involved in the business of vegetables, flower, fruit, incenses-stick production, papad, soaps, sarees, fish and dry fish, petty shop, small snack shop, idli shop, coir, small canteens, bakery, tea shop, thatching materials, carpentry and so on were being covered under this scheme.

Now these women's groups, with assistance of the staff of WOSEM are able to take their problems to the Government officials seeking redressal. During this period they have made several representations for problems like drinking water, water for other purposes, toilets, street lights, etc. They were using different methods to make their voice heard, starting with a few regular petitions with mass signature, followed by picketing, mass rally and so on.

Though they are still in a loose network, without a formal organization for themselves, they are able to see the usefulness of collective/united action. On a few occasions they were able to send their group leaders to meet police and other government officials against certain harassments like not being permitted to sell in a particular place, local water problem and luggage charge by transport owners, etc., and were successful in attending to certain family problems like wife-beating through collective action. Further, thanks to deliberations in their group meetings, the members realized the need and importance of making regular savings through banks. All these efforts made them realize the need for having a formal organization of their own.

Till December 1985, 705 members secured credit assistance through banks and 119 members from the small revolving fund of the CSG.

The main setback of this programme is the discouraging attitude of the nationalized banks, as credit assistance is the back-bone of this scheme. Hence in the near future it is planned to create the scheme's own Revolving Fund with the members contribution added to it. Also, plans are under way to give a comprehensive outlook by arranging health care, functional literacy and night schools as sought by these members.

Hence WOSEM had to expand its programmes and activities from arranging credit delivery from banks to the following:

1. Arrange institutional credit delivery for self-employed women.
2. Help them to be aware of their existing conditions and assist them to overcome the same.
3. Help them to increase production/sale and expand/ diversify business.
4. Assist in getting themselves formed into formal groups and organizations.
5. Help them to become economically self-reliant towards their development, thus reducing the gap of inequality between sexes.

Since the Ford Foundation's assistance had come to an end for this scheme by the end of June 1986, the CSG had approached SIDA, who were kind enough to support WOSEM from July 1986 onwards. Also, a revolving fund was arranged with Rs.75,000 for Cuddalore, on an experimental basis. The CSG is working on the modalities to form a separate society for a thrift programme towards catering to the needs of the WOSEM members.

Mahila Vikas Sangh and Tasar Silk

The tensile strength of the woven material, of homespun and handspun khadi, in dignified creams or the warm colours of the earth, the earth of Gandhiji and his followers where mud and blood mingled inextricably giving shape to India's birth, staining khadi fabric with its warm and vital hues - of browns and ochres and crimsons, now flowing, now fading, now merging with each other in a tantalizing, vibrant medley of colours. On cushion covers, on saris, on multi-use materials scattered randomly for use. In bold, kaleidoscopic form they unravelled their own saga of formulation and how they coalesced into symbolizing not only one of India's most colourful and fascinating industries but also an ideology of (village) self-sufficiency and gainful self-employment.

Khadi; beautiful gossamer silk; all woven by dextrous, nimble-fingered women, skillfully integrating arduous processes with a fertile imagination to create versions of infinite beauty and colour...

Meanwhile many many years ago, the Ford Foundation Representative, because of a project of the Family Planning Association of India in collaboration with Gram Nirman Mandal, a voluntary agency located in Sukhodeora Ashram, an Ashram near Kawakole in Nawada district, where JP spent a lot of his time and where, through bhoodan, several hundred Scheduled Caste families were flourishing agriculturists, had met the President Tripuri Sharan who very wisely suggested that Ford Foundation's relatively small budget would 'be better spent in a few States', especially in the poorer States. Subsequently, a meeting of Tripurariji and Thakurji (of the Sarvodaya organisation's Vanasvi Seva Kendra) was organised, the seed sown, but naturally, for a 'joint' programme and organization in Bihar. Both the esteemed men, greatly enthused by the potent possibilities of such an idea, judiciously suggested that "the new organisation should have a member-agency with experience of 'commercial' khadi and marketing, technical aspects of charkha-making etc." And suggested the Bhagalpur Zilla Khadi Gramodyog Sangh in Bhagalpur, nominating to call the organisation Mahila Vikas Sangh.

Thus, Mahila Vikas Sangh came into being, the bye-laws were drawn up, with a federal structure and it was decided that the member-agencies would 'send' five members each to Mahila Vikas Sangh's Governing Body. An experienced and benevolent looking woman President has been appointed. "Leelaji has for a long time been 'working' and running Tilouthu Mahila Mandal. She has been running a balwadi and an applique training centre with the assistance of the State Social Welfare Advisory Board" and possesses adequately sufficient experience of development.

One Mr Pandey, Secretary of Gram Nirman Mandal, was also elected Secretary of MVS. Having previously worked in the tribal areas of Nawada and the adjoining Munger district - Jhilar and Pratappur, with Raithani as the tribal woman leader, he possessed 'an understanding of grassroots sanghatan(organising) and of tribal development'. With the final election of a Liaison Coordinator, the stage was now set for MVS to start functioning.

First a project proposal was formulated by MVS for tasar silk production by rural women, then the expertise of the Industrial Development Services (IDS) harnessed for pre-testing in the field, working out the economic viability as well as carrying out a feasibility study. IDS delegates the task to a young IIT graduate, the three relevant districts are visited, a final proposal developed with all the necessary components, scrutinized and passed by the Ford Foundation economist, Dr Dravid Seckler. A letter sent to the Government of India for clearance and the IDS is given another assignment by Ford Foundation - this time 'to unfold the pre-grant activities, to bring 'Tsaar' from a latent to an active state, to make the preparation more elaborate and systematic, and to bring it to maturity.'

To achieve all this, the relevant personnel began by approaching the manager of the Khadi Bhandar of Gram Nirman Mandal at Khadirganj to identify women functionaries, to be trained at the Central Tasar Research and Training Institute (CTRTI), Ranchi. And visit some of 'his' weaver families and the women in these families — living in dilapidated dwelings, in conditions of pitiful poverty.

The men weave and the women reel "Called thigh-reeling", the weavers' wives pull back their saris and rub with the left hand the boiled tasar cocoons on their bare left thighs...back and forth, back and forth very swiftly until in the friction the beautiful brown tasar silk filament detaches itself from its seemingly entangled cocoon; she winds the silk filament on the spindle in her right hand simultaneously.

Women also go with the NGO personnel to Sukhodeora Ashram, as they have heard that there may be jobs suitable for women in tasar silk production in the Sukhodeora Ashram, which was participating in a programme called Mahila Vikas Sangh. GNM sets up a spinning centre at Pratappur (near the tribal village Jhilar after a survey by the new extension workers). The Ford Foundation's fund arrived after a long delay and later, a disharmonious action of the member-agencies took place.

... An inglorious action which inevitably left a sour taste in the mouth ... two women from each member agency were supposed to go to Bhagalpur Zila Khadi Gramodyog Sangh for training in a new type of tasar reeling charkha (a cotton ambar charkha modified). "Whatever be the reason, the member-agencies had sent two men each."

Gram Nirman Mandal

The Gram Nirman Mandal was the member-agency most interested in the proposed project of the women's weaving centre and Desiree Koslin, of the Swallows Handicarfts, busy then in the USA teaching weaving skills, is written to and acquiesces to come to India, live in the Sukhodeora Ashram and teach the women how to weave with dexterity and finesse. Hira, one of the talented inmates of Sukhodeora, imbibes the weaving skills excellently and in record time and, spurred on by her unique achievement, set about to apply her diligence to developing a women's development centre; and at Warsaliganj, the Secretary of the Gram Nirman Mandal, makes an independent Mahila Vikas Samiti of GNM with Hira as the President. Pandeyji also got planted on several acres at Jhilar, *arjun* trees, the host plant of the tasar silk worm, tended to very lovingly and with infinite care by the earlier mentioned tribal woman leader, Rathini. 'This is the nearest (Mahila Vikas Samiti) any of MVS's member-agencies got to independence and women's control'.

Meanwhile MVS's Governing Body progressed in its affirmative action and it was decided that when MVS was formed there should be at least two women among the five representatives per member-agency on MVS's governing body. But later factionalism and problems set in, as they invariably do.

Vanvasi Seva Kendra

The Vanvasi Seva Kendra has begun its work in Nauhatta, the block adjacent to Adhaura, in Rohtas district of Bihar. The women spun busily at the tasar spinning centre with 'the continual whirr of the *charkhas*, the bits of fluff flying; the dark pupae, exposed to the cocoon melts and metamorphoses away into the yarn, are scattered everywhere ... the dank smell of boiled cocoons; the wonderful brown sheen of the tasar yarn ... the glorious feel of the tasar silk.

During next few years, an encouraging number of women and young girls joined the spinning centre and learnt their trade enthusiastically. Later, as the Nauhatta project looked for women to become carpenters, to learn carpentry from a traditional carpenter, Kaushalya of the chamar caste who used to work at leather tanning earlier, offered herself for this work. Along with seven other women, she became one of the first women carpenters in Bihar.

Around 1991, near Nauhatta, in a village of the Ghareris (sheep-rearer) with the musical sounding name of Banahi, where beautiful blankets were woven by the women on 'primitive' tin looms joined together, the Nauhatta project decided to take them under their wing and trained them on improved looms. Soon the women were weaving large and strong blankets - one every two days. In this manner, several hundred women got employment as wool spinners. Thus, the Nauhatta project developed several innovative and creative responses to the needs, concerns, aspirations and priorities of women of the area - and in such a remote block.

While in Adhaura the cocoon-rearing went on in full swing, other programmes as support service programmes such as education centres, child sponsorship are also developed.

By the years 1986-87 MVS had integrated women into all steps of tasar silk production. Now the MVS possessed every component needed for a succesful rural women's development programme. It had four member-agencies with infrastructure, with the same ideology, and world view; the four member-agencies had total legitimacy in the area in which they were working and had, as their ready-made constituency, several hundred rural and poor women spinners and weavers with necessary skills. By this time, they also possessed all the equipment they needed such as charkhas and looms and skilled instructors. They got either private land or land allotted from the Government to plant *arjun* trees - 500 acres all together. They obtained funds from STEP to develop these plantations and developed linkages with the Central Tasar Research and Training Institute (CTRTI), Ranchi. From the right bureaucratic representative (woman) at that point of time in charge of STEP, to technical assistance from CTRTI, to the all important aspect of having (then) a Governing Body of men and women who had been working together since 1981, to having in the KVIC structure, a market for the tasar, provided beforehand, within reach.

Problems not withstanding, perhaps the overall achievement of the MVS could be summed up best in the words of Dr Sachindra Narayan, an anthropologist and an evaluator, thus: "MVS has made a very positive impact on women spinners, weavers, etc. It has helped the women of rural Bihar in earning their bread. It is the only institution which provides cash employment to the rural women of Bihar at their door. MVS has also made them conscious of their social role and status in the family. Thus the MVS through this programme is contributing to the cause of eradication, of untouchability as well as developing a sense of community living. MVS through this programme is making the rural women of Bihar play a constructive role. For some it is for their bare needs and for some it is for their supplementary needs."

References

Srinivasan, Viji, 'The Housewifisation of the Lace-makers of Narasapur', *Women's Work Experiences*, New Delhi: Har Anand Publications, 1992.

Srinivasan, Viji, 'The Blue Waves of Desia Nagar', *Women's Work Experiences*, New Delhi: Har Anand Publications, 1992.

Srinivasan, Viji, 'The Dead Cry Out When We Dry Fish,' *Women's work Experiences*, New Delhi: Har Anand Publications, New Delhi, 1992.

Srinivasan, Viji, 'If Women Learn To Weave...', *Women's Work Experiences*, New Delhi: Har Anand Publications, 1992.

References

12
OUR NEIGHBOURS, NGOs AND ENTERPRISES

The true test of civilization is not the census nor the size of cities nor the crops-no, but the kind of man the country turns out.

Ralph Waldo Emerson

It is also most important, the kind of women the country turns out. By incorporating perceptive progress-oriented future plans for their growth, by evaluating value systems in their entirety. Thus paving the way for reform, rehabilitation and restoration of the woman to her rightful place in society and in the nation building activity of the country.

Donatus de Silva, Director, Panos Regional Programmes, maintains quite emphatically that, "for NGO-initiated credit schemes to succeed, some degree of infrastructure is an essential percursor. No economic activity can take place without adequate roads, transport, communications, power and water. Many of these factors are the responsibility of those in government. NGOs facilitate the creation of groups. Group effort has been the key to generating people's participation in all projects. For the poor, groups provide an opportunity for participation and also a sense of security. Some NGOs carry out effective training and marketing programmes in local languages."

Pakistan

The land of impressive Pathans, patriotic and political ferment; of beautiful burqa clad women, courageously emerging into the emancipated fora of women worldwide today; aided in their noble endeavours by NGO programmes which are properly designed and sensitively implemented and are proving to be the 'key in unlocking the creative and productive potential of the world's poor'.

The Northern Areas of Pakistan, where four of the world's most rugged mountain ranges viz. The Himalayas, Karakorum, Hindu Kush and Pamirs - crash head-on to explode into one of the biggest concentrations of towering peaks on the earth, is an extremely inhospitable terrain where over a million odd people live, through harsh winters and severely handicapped by lack of viable communication facilities, since no service roads exist here. The only vehicles to be seen are those of the major voluntary aid agencies working here, the rare private or government jeep, and sometimes bulldozers where army engineers are blasting the mountainside to widen or make new roads. People do not live in integrated villages but rather in groups of settlements close to one another. Only small hand-carts run over the uneven terrain and boulder-pocked roads. People seem to find it much easier to walk and carry loads on their shoulders. Other difficulties include coaxing the poor mountain soil to yield adequate produce and since rivers are often too far away or too difficult to reach because of the rocks, all water has to be channelled and clean drinking water has to be carried home.

This, then, is Giligit, a two-hour flight across 280 kilometres from Rawalpindi (the capital Islamabad's twin city) to the Northern Areas' largest and most central town which boasts of the region's only and tiny airport and a population of approximately 32,000 people (as per a 1989 estimate). "But life is not all hardship and deprivation in Gilgit, especially since various grassroots initiatives have begun to bloom." Whether they operate credit schemes on their own, in collaboration with national financial institutions or in conjunction with international financial institutions such as the IFAD, NGOs have proved to be agents for development.

Rugged looking, responsible Jahan, lines of care etched into her enigmatic face, stands testimony to the fact that the forces of progress have reached this remote town, landscaped against an awesome mountain mass. For Jahan is the president of the local women's organization, which owes its genesis to the Aga Khan Rural Support Programme (AKRSP). The Programme was created by the Aga Khan Foundation, a philanthropic organization. With a membership of about 45 women, ten of whom were widows and therefore, necessarily more dependent on the good auspices of their benefactors, the weekly meetings of the WO or women's organisation, were chaired by Jahan. The organisation also had pre-fixed bank deposit days when the relevant financial transactions were carried out, for all these poor illiterate women from the cluster of villages in this region. The poorest among the ten widows was young Nasima-widowed by her soldier - husband at the young age of 29 years and pregnant with her fifth child. Hardship imposed by an early widowhood, the dire needs of a rapidly growing family, the sparse produce of the land barely adequate for subsistence levels, created a perpetual and frustrating shortage of funds. The necessity of saving money for urgent financial need for a rainy day, was always understood, but proved to be increasingly difficult to implement. As far back as she could remember, as a child and later with her children, they gathered the first growth of alfalfa, that grew in wild abundance in the early spring to cook and eat as a leafy vegetable. They also collected a number of other shoots, grasses and fruit blossoms. But these were only edible in the first flush of March, after that they proved to be too bitter to eat. It was only after the first harvest that a little business could be done and chicken and eggs sold and certain needs fulfilled. In order to expand their small scale operations they required some credit and since they were considered a bad risk by banks, credit certainly wasn't forthcoming. The government had made huge amounts of money available specially for the poor, but it remained untouched because the banks demands for eligibility could not be fulfilled, and no one in the bureaucracy tried to devise a reasonable solution to the problem. Thereby creating an impasse which would have been much better avoided.

It was only after repeated visits by a caring and conscientious AKRSP volunteer who impressed upon Nasima (and other needy women like her) the imminent need to save, however meagre an amount that might be, to build up credit worthiness and to avoid the vicious clutches of the moneylender with his requirement for collateral, with his ever increasing rates of interest, that they realized the immensely beneficial aspects of such a proposition. Not only would they be able to avoid disastrous recurrent loans with never-ending debts accruing to the moneylender, which sometimes required them even to pledge away their land, thus leadiing to starvation and destitution, but with their joint savings they could qualify for a loan to operate a joint enterprise. The women's interest was aroused but they were troubled about their individual savings which, the social worker patiently explained to them, would not be affected. First they had to form an organization and open a bank account on behalf of the organization. Each member was to make regular deposits every week so that the pooled savings could grow into a sizeable amount and make them eligible for progressively larger loans. Records and registers of individual and pooled savings would be regularly maintained by the social organizer and 'the beauty of it was that once an enterprise was underway, equal labour would bring equal profits'. A business ideology which it took some time for these simple mountain folk to grasp and appreciate.

The well known Aga Khan Rural Support Programme has its roots, interestingly enough, in the famed Comilla Project in the former East Pakistan, now Bangladesh. It dates back several decades to an initiative by the distinguished Dr Akhtar Hameed Khan, a civil servant who sought to 'effect real upliftment among the impoverished Bengalis through grassroots approaches rather than by sterile bureaucratic edict'.

The Programme was initiated by the Aga Khan Foundation in the winter of 1982 and its development focus was, essentially, on income generation activities and its stated objectives — "a doubling of rural per capita income over a period of ten years".

The mechanism revolves around the creation of effective village organizations (VOs) and their female versions, women's organizations (WOs). Wherever possible, the organizations are encouraged to save and work together as one unit. Once established, each one enters into a formal partnership with AKRSP to receive technical and financial assistance.

Approximately 1030 villages in the Northern Areas, including Gilgit, accounting for three-quarters of a million people, were involved in the project of the AKRSP and over half of them had active VOs.

The Rural Support Programme did not, in fact could not, start with an exclusively female component as a part of its immensely worthy venture. For Gilgit is an area where women do not own land but only hold it in trust until male heirs come of age to take charge. May be the local men would not have been affronted if the women had been chosen earlier, for, except for the additional burdens of childbearing (and rearing) and carrying water and fuel from great distances, there is not such a wide disparity between the chores of the men and the women, but such a practicality was never put to the test. Also, as the then coordinator of the Women's Programme, Ameneh Azam Ali asserted, women were by nature and circumstance much better managers of money and more careful about savings, than the men. For men sometimes ventured 'abroad' to a near or distant urban area to try their fortunes whereas women were locked in their mountain prisons, never to escape except perhaps to another mountain home as a result of marriage. A saving of Rs 5 per month for Nasima (since May 1984) in global terms is hardly even worth considering (one rupee being worth 5 US cents) but viewed in the context of the local prices of home-grown and home-produce commodities, it was a useful sum. All other considerations apart, it inculcated in the women the all-important sense of self-worth, credit-worthiness and economic and social security. And so, slowly but steadily, Nasima's impressive entry in the passbook logged Rs 1377, an achievement she could justifiably be proud of.

Gradually, as more and more of the women were convinced of the viability and beneficial nature of the scheme, they cautiously came forward, soliciting membership. Consensus among existing members was indispensable to the admission of a new member though normally no one sounded a dissenting note for they understood the compulsions of their comrades, and entry was granted.

The common acreage of Nasima's WO included an orchard growing cherries, plums, peaches and newly planted saplings; vegetables were grown on seven out of ten kanals-cabbage, Chinese cabbage, peas, beans, and plenty of potatoes. AKRSP, as could be expected, provided seeds free for the first planting and the remaining less productive land, was left over for fodder. It is customary for AKRSP to contribute or take care of all WOs technical expertise such as contributing a set of appropriate tools, providing seeds for the first sowing, usually on an experimental plot where better agricultural techniques are simultaneously demonstrated. The rest, including any commercially acquired fertilizer or pesticide, has to be purchased with their own money or obtained on credit. It is interesting to note that in some of the far-flung villages, the women had never previously experimented with vegetable cultivation but with the newly gained knowledge of improved farming techniques, they were not only able to adequately meet the needs of the family but also sell substantial surpluses from the family kitchen garden.

Hardly three years after its formation, Nasima's WO sought and obtained the biggest loan asked for by any WO — Rs 74000 (US$3,700). Part of it was used to build a large poultry shed in the spring of 1988. Some 150 layers and 1000 broiler chicks at

Rs 6 (30 US cents) each were brought all the way from Rawalpindi, over 960 kilometres (596 miles) away by road. A huge quantity of these chicks perished at a later date due to neglect which arose as a direct, unpleasant consequence of vexatious disputes which broke out between the members, over differing opinions regarding management of the project. The tragedy, however, proved to be a sobering factor and they acquired 800 more chickens from nearby Gilgit, since they could no longer afford the expensive trucking charges for the better breed from across the mountains. But because they had not catered for 'the effects of the heat in the months of July and August in a closed shed without cooling' half of them died and the breeding venture received a major setback. However, the third time they took great care to provide suitable breeding conditions and fixed up the breeding room properly. The women bounced back from the setback with great resilience, purchased 900 more chickens and this time the flock survived and subsequently, the WO prospered. The chickens were sold from Rs 30 to Rs 32 per fowl during the winter months and from Rs 2 to Rs 7 less during the summer months. Simultaneously their personal flocks also flourished and they provided two to three times as much meat, so that there was that much more for the family to eat.

As they savoured the first heady feeling of success, their horizons widened, their ambitions increased and they were emboldened to seek an even bigger loan, purchase a pick-up truck and control marketing. For possessing their own pick-up vehicle would also make it possible to hire their own driver and salesman and send the produce to Gilgit for sale, or even further, perhaps, if the profits were good enough. Thereby, eliminating the crucial middleman's cut and a great reduction of profits. To make the return trip cost effective or at least useful, the pick-up could 'bring back everyone's groceries: rice, flour, spices and other goods much cheaper in the towns' not only serving their own WO but three others from adjoining clusters as well, thereby facilitating matters not only in terms of the time and effort factor but also indirectly leading to all these concerned families saving a lot of money over a protracted period of time.

The members of the WOs met once a week, not merely to make deposits but also to discuss the progress of their chickens or vegetables beds, to note queries about problems to be put to the social organizer or technical expert on their next visit or may be even to dream bigger dreams — dreams of acquiring land. For the women did not own any land and land was an essential component in all agricultural enterprises. To obtain an acreage large enough to be profitable, an appeal invariably had to be made to the generosity of someone with more land than he could till or with land he was willing to spare. And, invariably, there was a positive response to the appeal and land was obtained. The manure was provided, naturally enough, by their own animals. "But the earth was not always readily obliging simply because of ideal doses of fertiliser and water. The mountain soil was plagued by pestilential grubs that looked like jumbo shrimp. They made short work of seeds, shoots or fully grown vegetables." It was, thus, essential that they be removed and the process of removal before each sowing was an absolutely back-breaking job, not to mention a time consuming one. This brought out the necessity of obtaining pesticides for the job for which the WO's approached AKRSP, to help them obtain the necessary credit for the purchase.

Since WOs were being organized all over the area, it had seemed a good idea at one point to gather a representative or two from each village to meet for a conference and intensive training programme in Gilgit. There they would also be able to exchange notes and have immediate access to technical expertise which they would later be able to pass on to their fellow members. The response was enthusiastic, the women learned fast but getting them to travel such great distances over inhospitabel terrain, the hazards of such travel sometimes increased manifold by the omnipresent danger of landslides, the need to have a male family member escort them and thus neglect his own vital duties at home and other factors, made them suggest to Amenah Azam Ali, their co-ordinator, the far more practical practise of travelling training programmes imparting the requisite knowledge to them in the convenient environs of their own villages.

Various useful and lucrative sub-projects emerged as a result of Ameneh's get-togethers with the now mentally stimulated and thinking rural womenfolk, exchange of ideas, suggestions, etc. One of these where the women were trained to vaccinate chickens, to practically eliminate mortality among the fowl from disease, provided them with the much-needed extra income for rendering this service for neighbours and others. Within a period of seven years, the number of WOs grew from just a mere handful to an impressive 200 plus. Therefore, as is amply borne out by this and other innovative and successful NGO experiments in the field, "giving women access to income-earning opportunities certainly improves family living standards, nutrition, health and shelter, for example. But there are other consequences, not in the least, the boost in education availability for the women themselves and their children."

In Karimabad, there is a beautiful middle and high school and hostel built by Aga Khan to enable promising girls from distant villages to finish their matriculation and be able to continue their studies. For even in the village, the women are very education conscious and whenever enough money has been put by and a school is nearby, they enrol their children in it. Since it is not economically viable to build two separate schools for boys and girls for lack of separate students of each sex, they are not averse to constructing one school and allowing it to be co-educational. However, the priorities of the bureaucracy and the needs of the land (for more hands during harvesting season) do not always make it possible to realize advantageous educational goals. May be this gap could be bridged by introducing education such as is found suitable and relevant for those living in mountain villages.

With increasing economic independence, women are bound to question increasingly other issues which have been accepted on the basis of traditional practice so far. One of these perhaps might be the land question and sooner or later women may find out or bring to the fore of their consciousness the fact that, under Islamic law, they are entitled to inherit at least half of what men own. Or, breaking with tradition, they may just want to buy land, land which is now being reclaimed and being put to use for the establishment of VOs? The questions are many, the answers as yet somewhat nebulous, acquiring definite form through a haze of rapidly dawning realization of self-rights, etc. "In the meantime, hope and partial fulfillment occupy the visionary heads of the busy women in the Northern Areas."

Bangladesh

The burden of the Betias, the most disadvantaged people in Bangladesh who, until recently, made baskets from cane or *bet* (which is the Bengali word for cane) and thus acquired their quaint sounding Hindu caste name. Rural peasants all, they exist at barely subsistence levels in a village near the town of Tepra in the Manikganj district, 82 kilometres north-west of Dhaka, the capital.

Hardworking and intelligent, they live in small thatched huts, now eking out their meagre existence through the less profitable industry of making baskets from bamboo instead of cane, the skill of basket making handed down to them through the generations, over a period of time. Musing on the miserableness of their plight just about a decade ago brings to mind the sagacious words of Robert G. Ingersoll when he so rightly said. "There are in nature neither rewards nor punishments - there are consequences". And the consequences of the Betias not having the financial wherewithal to buy cane or bamboo to ply their trade and no money to sustain them during the months of flooding when there is no demand for their baskets, are indeed heartrending.They are miserable and hungry and their skills are rendered redundant by the calamitous vagaries of nature.

They needed just that little bit of support, just that catalyst to change their lives and show them a glimmer of hope for a more promising tomorrow. This came in the guise of a rural credit scheme by a local voluntary agency, the Christian Commission for Development in Bangladesh (CCDB) and provided the capital they needed to improve their basket trade while saving modest amounts of money.

One of the fortunate beneficiaries of the credit scheme was Minati of Betiapara, linked to the Dhaka-Aricha highway by a "kutcha" (unmetalled) road. She belonged to one of the 25 basket maker families living there. Amidst archaic and difficult conditions of transportation and communication, where only carts pulled by bullocks or buffaloes use the kutcha road to carry agricultural commodities to and from the village markets. Occassionally, cycle vans negotiate the uneven road, eroded here and there by last year's flood. A cycle van is a wooden platform fitted on rickshaw wheels; meant for transportation of goods, they often carry passengers also. During the rainy season travellers must wade through knee deep mud.

Enterprising Minati joined the Kandabashail Mahila Samiti (the Kandabashail Cottage Industry Women's Society) in April, 1987. Since then she has taken out short term loans on several occassions, the first in September 1987 being for Taka 800 (US$25) and the second for Taka 2000(US$61). But simultaneously she has regularly put away money in personal savings as well as having contributed to the society's collective savings fund. In addition, she, like the others, was required to pay a service charge at the rate of 12 per cent. Though she had no complaints about the interest rate, she like the other recipients of CCDB credit, felt that the repayment period of four months should have been extended. Nevertheless things have worked out for Minati who, along with her husband, Anukul, is capable of producing six baskets a day. The husband too is a loan recipient and a member of Kandabashail Sramjivi Samity (Kandabashail Working People's Society) which also works on the dual principles of personal and collective savings.

The credit scheme gradually spread to other adjoining villages and provided the much needed succour to other women, some of whom were not so fortunate as Minati to have the security of a stable home. One such person was Jahera, who has been the unfortunate sufferer of the common Muslim practice of bigamy and now lives with her parents. The mother of four sons and three daughters, out of which only one each are married, her's definitely is not an enviable position as her youngest child is only eighteen months old. In January 1989, almost exactly a decade ago, she took a loan of Taka 2500 (US $75) from CCDB and maintains herself by making pickles from a variety of ingredients like tamarind and other tropical fruits, with just the right dose of spices to give pickles flavours and taste. She has been a member of a women's welfare society called Baradia Bijaya Mahila Kalyan Samiti for five years.

In an arrangement which is not only unusual but speaks volumes for the wronged Indian women's tolerance of her male counterpart, Jahera entrusts her husband, now living with his second wife and away from her, with the sales and marketing of her pickles and is confident that she is not being done out ot her rightful dues.

A multi-work cottage industry, a many splendoured legacy of industry and cooperation and the many women who have benefitted from credit schemes in this geographically far flung and difficult terrain, further complements the efforts of those dedicated to the path of progress and upliftment.

Kalpana Ghosh, who lives along with her husband in Goswamipara, six kilometres north of Betiapara, is a Hindu and sells home-made curd in small glasses going from house to house in adjoining villages. She also buys butter and makes it into ghee (butter oil) which her husband, Haren, delivers to the better off families,mostly on credit. The clients, who are due to clear their dues on a monthly basis, don't always pay in time and overdue debts are a hazard of the business. She earns an equivalent of Taka 50 to 60 (US $1.50-1.80) a day from curd and may be another Taka 30-35 from ghee.

She has accummulated an impressive Taka 640 (US $19.40) in her personal savings fund, besides contributing to the collective savings fund of her samiti, the Madhurilata Mahila Kalyan Samity (Women's Welfare Society).

The village samities, which provided credit to Minati, Jahera and Kalpana, were created by the villagers with the assistance of CCDB, which is linked to the National Council of Churches of Bangladesh. It works with disadvantaged groups, irrespective of religion with special emphasis on involvement of women in development activities. A prime objective is to increase the satisfaction of basic credit needs of the target groups to a level that liberates them from exploitative burdens and encourages productive investments.

The provision of rural credit in Bangladesh has always been a problem as, despite government attempts to make credit available to the various disadvantaged groups, the major share has somehow always ended up with the rural elite. In order to provide a solution and also as a result of increased awareness that the poorest of the poor deserve credit, the involvement of NGOs has taken place on a large-scale.

CCDB's Shivalaya project, which believes in collective action, represents one of the programme's main development activities. In the Shivalaya Upazila (sub-district), the organization first encourages groups of disadvantaged people in the area to organize themselves into samities -—254 samities were ultimatley formed in 138 villages — to derive benefit from the activities of the project, known as the Shivalaya Rural Development Project. Out of these, 178 were exclusively women's groups with an impressive 5993 beneficiaries; 76 were exclusively men's with

1975 potential borowers. However, there were no mixed samities.

Among the people who were eligible to form samities were landless people, as well as small and marginal farmers who supplemented their income by working as hired labourers during part of the year, and producers and traders with small capital.

It was compulsory for the members of the samity to contribute Taka 5 each to the collective savings fund of the samity and Taka 10 to their personal savings fund. The cumulative savings of the societies (upto March, 1989) stood at Taka 1,837,000 (US$55,666). Two thirds of this comprised personal savings of the members; the remainder were collective savings. To obtain credit, a samity member was required to show personal savings to the value of 5 to 10 per cent of the total loan amount sought. The 12 per cent service charge which was levied on loans for such income generating activities as paddy-husking, making puffed rice and pickles, basket making, small trading and fattening calves was not, however, used for defraying administrative costs but re-invested in the credit programme. The rate of recovery was surprisingly good and CCDB's annual report for 1987-88 showed a 93 per cent recovery of current dues for the year, besides 33 per cent recovery of overdues. Service charges collected on dues during the year totalled Taka 191,388 (US$5800). During the then current financial year, CCDB's Shivalaya Project has extended (Upto March 1989) credits amounting to Taka 5,417,341(US$164,161).

Most of the loan recipients interviewed maintained that they took repeated loans, their usual practice being to pay back the current dues on their loans and then take out a fresh and higher loan. CCDB officials maintained that if they found a client maintaining good credit discipline and returning the borrowed amount in time, as well as making profitable use of the same, they readily advanced him a fresh loan. They found nothing wrong with the practice of repeated loans. And Susanta Adhikari, CCDB's dynamic director, was of the opinion that the savings and credit programme should be seen in the context of its total programme and viewed more as 'credit education'. The more clients take loans, use them sensibly, and then pay them back, the more they learn how to handle loans. They learn the rules and principles of using money. Meanwhile, their savings under the programme grow. CCDB intends to explore the possibility of an arrangement whereby they can use their savings to meet their credit needs. In such cases, according to Adhikari, people initially dependent on CCDB for loans, probably would not need them any more. It had made them economically free with grace.

However, in times of calamities or in cases of genuine hardship, CCDB has extended the repayment period of the loan beneficiary, who for various reasons enumerated above, has not been able to make a timely payment. One problem in providing credit in Bangladesh is the tendency of people to consider a loan as a mere paper debt - as a donation. They tend to confuse credit with relief.

Most Betias, however, are unable or not interested enough in maintaining accounts of their business transactions and possess a very lackadaisical attitude towards the education and improved literacy standards of their children. When questioned about why they had not taken their literacy classes seriously, Madhab Betia replied: "We need to be shocked into awakening." Although CCDB officials claim that their beneficiaries are becoming increasingly conscious through participation in development education classes.

It seems, therefore, that the Betias were becoming increasingly aware of their disadvantaged position and keen to build a better economic future by working hard. Not only through individual loans as in the case of Kalpana, Jahera and Minati as well as Mullya, who industriously worked at furniture making, but also through groups loans with longer repayment deadlines. A group of self-employed women set up a modest garment factory with the help of CCDB credit. The factory showed profit very rapidly; with another CCDB loan, another women's group was planning to open a chalk factory and so on and so forth. However, some observers are of the opinion that, despite repayment rates by borrowers being satisfactory, 'it might be a mistake if CCDB assumed that payments alone are necessarily an indicator of proper management of loans. Borrowers might clear their dues by borrowing money from some other source in order to remain creditworthy in the eyes of CCDB'.

Alfred Roy, senior project officer of CCDB's Shivalaya project, opined that the credit programme served the purpose of empowering the women, apart from providing financial support to disadvantaged people irrespective of sex and religion. He also found an increased awareness among them at a social awareness training conducted by CCDB and that they were responsive to what the trainer was telling them in this about development issues. Finally they seemed to be aware that loans did not constitute gifts and that saving could be a key to higher loans which you paid back promptly.

To sum up, "The first stony obstacles along the road to empowerment of rural women have been cleared away. With the help of consciousness-raising organizations such as CCDB, and the others which will hopefully follow, the next generation of Bangladeshi women may well find it easier to achieve full economic maturity and independence of action in disposing of their own assets and property, free to use at their will the resources they have themseslves earned through initiative and hard work."

References

Jazairy, Idriss in 'Preface', *Banking The Unbankable - Bringing Credit To The Poor*, Project Co-ordinators, Silva Donatus de and Denby Naella, Horizon India Books, 1992. In arrangement with the Panos Institute, London and The Ecological Foundation, New Delhi.

Rahman, Jawadur, 'Bangladesh: Empowering the disadvantaged,' *Banking The Unbankable - Bringing Credit To The Poor*, Project Co-ordinators, Silva Donatus de and Denby Naella, Horizon India Books, 1992.

Sadeque, Najma, 'Pakistan: When women earn, children learn', *Banking The Unbankable - Bringing Credit To The Poor*, Project Co-ordinators, Silva, Donatus de and Denby, Naella, Horizon India Books, 1992.

Silva, Donatus de in 'Introduction', *Banking The Unbankable - Bringing Credit To The Poor*, Project Co-ordinators, Silva Donatus de and Denby, Naella, Horizon India Books, 1992.

13

A RURAL MOSAIC FOR REFORM

Destiny is not a matter of change, it is a matter of choices; it is not a thing to be waited for, it is a thing to be achieved.

William Jennings Bryan

Progress, change, upliftment of the underprivileged and the unenlightened are a few essential elements of development. Or, if plagiarisation be permitted, development is the course of action taken by an individual or a group of individuals in order to achieve a greater realization of their aspirations, while rural development is one which promotes participation and involvement of rural masses in the process of economic, social, political and cultural development. This involves, 'humans' as distinct from materials. Among these humans, rural women have a major importance in the process of development, though deep-rooted age-old attitudes very often manifest themselves in a psychological aversion on their part to all happenings around them accept in their own limited family. This factor, coupled with the common tendency of menfolk to keep their womenfolk behind the scenes and away from light, creating a sort of imposed communication gap, is also responsible for the plight of women in our country. Dr Leela Dube observes that Asian women may have an egalitarian relationship with menfolk within a family and in kinship network and close social circles. Yet they may be considered as objects of exploitation in the outside world.

Rural Women

The unmistakable, vital importance of rural women in the scheme of things, as workers and in giving a fillip to the overall economy of the country, can perhaps be appreciated in its entirety if we stop for a moment and take stock of the facts; that out of 31 million women workers in India, as many as 28 million were in rural areas (1971 census). Table 13.1 provides more information about rural women workers.

Table 13.1

Women in Rural India (1980)

Particulars	*Statistics*
Population	249 million
SC Population	39.6 million
Percentage	16.0 per cent
ST Population	21.1 million
Percentage	8.5 per cent
No. of females per 1000 males	948
Literacy rate Overall	22.5 per cent
Scheduled Caste	6.1 per cent
Scheduled Tribe	5.2 per cent
Females among workers	18.9 per cent (1971)
Engaged in agriculture	
Among female workers	80.1 per cent
Unemployment rate	3.3 (1977-78)
No. of Mahila Mandals	
(Women's Club)	61.4 thousand
No. of members in Mahila Mandal	1722 thousand

While in rural areas the status of women is generally linked to 'her relationship with local flora and fauna and the deep attachment to their environment and soil', they can, however, be divided into the following occupational categories:

> Landholders-the families who hold large holdings, employ outside labour for farmwork and do not allow their womenfolk to work in the fields.
>
> Average farmers-these people work in the fields themselves, employ seasonal labour and take the

assistance of their family women to work on their own farm only;

Small/ marginal farmers - they seek outside employment in addition to farming their own piece of land, allow their womenfolk to work on other's farms; and

The landless agricultural labour-those who totally depend on labour work or others homes/ farms and their womenfolk and children are also forced to work for some body sometimes permanent or semi-permanent domestic/farm labour. Landless women labourers are, thus, estimated to constitute nearly 55 per cent of the total women workforce and the majority of them belong to Scheduled Castes and Scheduled Tribes. In addition, there are others who work according to family professions like 'nomads', shepherds, milk women, artisans, etc. And except for the really well-to-do families, the women and girls are compelled to work as self-employed labour or wage earning labour to supplement the family earnings and to struggle for making both ends meet. Therefore, rural women are, undoubtedly, important and practically indispensable organs of the large rural community by way of their labour contribution.

Underlining the fact as to how hard a rural woman labours every day, whether in domestic chores or outside work, is the following time distribution estimate *vis-à-vis* such work, on a typical day:

Finding and transporting water	3 hours
Cooking and food processing	5 hours
Farm work in season	8-10 hours
Collecting fuel	3-4 hours

It is thus, very obvious that all women, irrespective of the land status of the family, provide 14 to 18 hours of productive physical labour in a single day. When the above time/chore distribution is translated into woman days, it means that in a family of six, one day of a woman is spent in collecting and sorting fuel, another day in cooking and processing food, half a day in fetching and transporting water, one day in storing for the well-being of the family, half a day in craft, kitchen gardening, care of animals, cleaning and other activities every day. Different studies give somewhat varying pictures of rural women's Work-Time distribution as shown in Table 13.2.

Table 13.2

Work-Time Distribution of Rural Women in Hrs./Day

Work	*Landless Agricultural Labour*	*Small and Marginal Farmer*	*Average Farmer*	*Land holder*
Sweeping and cleaning	1	1.5	1.5	2
Drawing and fetching water	1.5	1.5	1.5	1
Washing clothes	1.5	1.5	1.5	1
Cooking and serving	2	2	3	4
Collecting fuel and making animal dung cakes	2.5	2	1	—
Work for cattle	—	1	2	—
Repair and maintenance of house(average of year)	0.5	1	2	1
Child care and looking after household chores	0.5	2	2	3
Marketing, food processing, storing etc.	—	3	2**	3**
Working in the field/farm	8	2	*	*

* stands for seasonally at sowing, transplanting, harvesting and threshing.

** cover cleaning, drying and storing foodgrains, making curd and butter, selling milk and milk products.

In the meantime, however, it has been observed that the pattern of labour utilization has not been as productive as it should have been, for energy inputs for performing more tasks than physically feasible for a barely subsistence-level, detract from maximum and desired productivity levels; the drudgery factor also contributes to lowering levels of productive work.

The womenfolk are subjected to a great amount of drudgery in performing the following tasks, day in and day out, irrespective of their health or other important considerations for their well-being—walking long distances to fetch water and drawing water from deep wells, collecting fuel for a major part of the day (partly to sell, partly to use for own cooking); cooking in a smoky environment.

To the above list, other never-ending tasks like taking care of the physical well-being of the husbands, giving birth to children (under the distressed environment) and nursing them without imbibing extra, essential nourishment; the continuous drudgery and back-breaking work sometimes causing abortions and premature births at advanced stages of pregnancy and so on so forth, can be added.

In many Scheduled Tribes and hill tribes, the lot of the women is, perhaps, even tougher. Not only is it the responsibility of the adult women to do the bulk of the work right from plantation, harvesting and processing, to employing their skills in marketing and bartering the produce and purchasing the necessities of life, but they have to perform the exhausting work of pounding the rice and maize; grinding the wheat and barley into flour and milling the pulses, besides collecting fuel, leaves and seeds in forest regions. While in their homes, it is the women who are responsible for maintaining the draught and milch cattle, piggery, poultry, sheep and goat. Some of them are even engaged in breaking stones required for road building or house construction, repair and maintenance work, in addition to coping with all the chores.

Development

Projects specifically tailored for rural women and aimed at involving them in their own development, were initiated as early as the Community Development Programme in India (1953). The projects which formed part of the then schemes of the Government and social voluntary agencies were:

(i) Adult education;

(ii). Recreational programmes including singing and playing of musical instruments;

(iii) Fruit and vegetable preservation;

(iv) Improvement in domestic *'chulha'* (cooking oven) and preservation of left-over food;

(v) Child-care, health and hygiene, nutrition, prevention from common ills and diseases;

(vi) Sericulture/apiculture;

(vii) Food grains and cereal storage;

(viii) Tailoring, embroidery, garment making and

(ix) Preparation of handicraft goods.

While some of these projects succeeded in meeting their objectives, they, nevertheless, failed 'in changing psychological barriers, traditionalism, taboos, superstition and defeatism. However, these schemes lacked in creating the requisite link between technological advances and such projects which generate a scientific temper. Therefore, what was required was appropriate technology for generating new and gainful employment and 'optimum utilization of women's energy, mitigating drudgery, providing improved skills, means and tools to achieve a better level of productivity and efficiency and permitting participation in production of value added manufacture in the village itself', by catering to the following areas of interests and ongoing activities of the rural women and girls:

(i) in what they are most interested;

(ii) the skills and knowledge that is most essential for them; and

(iii) the desired training to enable them to earn while they learn and learn to earn more.

While the Sixth Plan (1980-85), detailing the question of developmental activities related to women *vis-à-vis* science and technology, included:

(a) the contribution of women themselves to the development of science and technology and

(b) the contribution that science and technology can make to vastly improve the lifestyle and status of women which, in turn, "will depend on the development of home technologies, appropriate agricultural technologies, and technologies for improvement of productivity.

Forestry, sericulture, handloom and crafts like match box making, pottery, food processing, dairying and many other similar activities could be considered potential segments of women's work where application of simple technology can go a long way in improving their productivity and giving them enough time to participate in programmes for their educational and other development. The technology, therefore, should help in achieving the desired growth rate in agricultural and non-agricultural economic activities with some degree of stability in productivity, efficiency, quality and income.

A great need was envisaged to develop such appropriate technologies as would ensure qualitiative changes for those people working in tiny, small and unorganized sectors and the following approach outlined:

(i) Nonformal education to prepare them to appreciate change/development;
(ii) Training in skill and post-harvest technologies;
(iii) Provision of improved tools, equipment and related aids;
(iv) Provision of common facility and service centres and
(v) Provision of assured marketing and off take.

Apart from designing appropriate programmes, after exhaustively identifying needs, it was also found necessary to identify voluntary organizations and governmental agencies already operating and involving new forces showing interest, for the interaction of technology would be futile if it was not supported by local, scientific and research and development institutions. It is essential that when guidelines are being provided to scientists for generation of technologies for rural development, clear end objectives must be kept in view while not losing sight of certain existing constraints *in situ* and hence one would do well to work within the following broad parameters:

(i) technology should provide scope for utilization of local skills, talents and resources;
(ii) technology should meet some of the basic needs and provide social-benefit at a cost within the reach of people;
(iii) the technology should help in elimination of drudgery;
(iv) the technology should be more advantageous than the existing traditional method;
(v) the technology should have scope for replication and generation of maximum and more remunerative, employment and
(vi) technology should have scope for learning.

Pratical Implemention of Technologies for Development

Some efforts were made in India 'to translate the needs of women into a technological task, scope of its application, both for direct and indirect benefit'. Some of the areas where interaction of Science and Technology proved to be a success in India are given below:

Food

These included smokeless 'chulha' designs, fruit and vegetable preservation and utilization, techniques for extending the life of perishables like milk, eggs, fruits like bananas, oranges etc; solar cookers for conveniently cooking food on the farm while engaged in farm-work, provision of the biogas plant with its multi utility value, pelletization of coal dust (obviously where coal is available) and making it available at subsidized and affordable rates through the facility of rural depots for, among other things, keeping food warm during the winter months.

Water

Important measures in this area included not only the production of chlorine capsules /tablets for disinfection of well water but also the much needed production and use of ceramic filter candles for providing bacteria-free drinking water for infants, and other filtering techniques; improved well with light drawing wheel, parapet wall and improved outlet for waste water (leading to the kitchen garden), Solar water heaters for rural dispensaries, windmill for lifting water for meeting community needs, fortification of salt with iodine by the submersion process for the desired prevention and control of goitre disease, relevant techniques for the desalination of brackish water, etc.

Shelter

In the equally vital zone of shelter and habitation in the rural scenario, such laudable schemes came to fruition as those which provided the people with fire-proof thatched roofs, waterproof mud plaster for walls and stabilized earthern flooring; it brought to them the benefits of and provided them with scientific ventilation and layout of household needs; improved houses for low income groups, suitable and improved techniques for construction of simple, hygienic latrines with septic tanks and scientific disposal of waste and used water, were some of the other measures incorporated here. Not to mention improved kerosene lanterns and other innovations like smokeless lighting, construction of rural houses in seismic zones, the use of ferrocement for storage of water and foodgrains, the' use of agricultural wastes for making boards and corrugated sheets for partition walls and roofing and convenient bamboo/wooden furniture design to economize space'.

Mitigating Drudgery

To make life easier for the over-taxed rural women and lessen not only their burden of work but also method of implementing their numerous arduous tasks, various measures were undertaken such as: the production of improved and accident free chaff-cutter for cutting cattle fodder; improved techniques for the heat treatment of sickles used for harvesting; the provision of lighter and more efficient to use (by hand) grinding wheels—made on a ball-bearing basis-for making flour and for processing the grains of pulses; improved pulley with ball-bearing for rendering the water-drawing process less exhausting; improved hand tools for inter-culture like hand-hoe and other similar agricultural tools, etc. Cooking stoves requiring no pumping (kerosene based) and using less kerosene, more energy and no danger of bursting, improved designs for bullock-carts incorporating novel features like low friction bearing, adjustable draw-bars, pneumatic wheels, wooden wheels, lighter loading platform and breaking systems, were some of the other implemented benefits of technology which touched the life of the rural women labourers with an iota of brightness and hope.

Economic Projects

Some of the projects for the upliftment and improvement of the economic status of rural women undertaken, applying the use of science and technology with the projected aim of rural development were: improved cottage-scale, hand spinning and weaving machines for cotton, wool and other organic fibres; mushroom cultivation as well as cultivation and processing of spices; handicrafts design and development techniques as well as much improved techniques for processing of leather and preparation of leather goods; sericulture, epicultre and aquaculture as well as animal husbandry including milk, egg and meat production and primary preservation; tailoring and garment making and (homescale) soap manufacture; the preparation of breakfast ingredients for self-consumption and sale, organization and collection of non-edible oilseeds, its primary processing for possible value-adding and grading, collection of mango kernels, deseeding of tamarind, etc. (these are major raw materials for many industries), rearing of sheep, goat and pig; charcoal making; firing of pottery and the list goes on, firing one's imagination with the endless possiblities, the monumental potential for promoting change, ameliorating hardship and paving the way for economic emancipation.

Management Modes

An improvement in the content of the programme alone definitely would not be enough 'without evolving an appropriate organizational management and systems approach including monitoring and evaluation. The intensity and nature of problems differ from region to region and show variations for different socio-econimic strata and rural women. The approach should, therefore, have an inbuilt flexibility and diversity in tackling the needs in accordance with the local situation, the type of clientele and the environment in which their development must take place'. Meanwhile, project management covers aspects relating to:

(a) Project identification and survey techniques;

(b) Project development concepts;

(c) Project formulation;

(d) Resource mobilization;

(e) Project implementation-management of men, money, and material;

(f) Project monitoring, accounting and progress reporting and

(g) Project evaluation.

The Seventh Plan

"The long-term objective of the developmental programmes for women would be to raise their economic and social status in order to bring them into the mainstream of national development. In the Seventh Plan, the basic approach would be to inculcate confidence among women and bring about an awareness for their own potential for development. Integrated Rural Development Programme (IRDP), National Rural Employment Programme (NREP), Training of Rural Youth in Self-employment (TRYSEM) and other such programmes would have a component of functional literacy for women beneficiaries." So ran the impressive agenda for reform, renewal of long forgotten pledges and the revival of endeavours for according women their rightful place in Indian society and the economic ethos.

Employment

In the field of Agriculture and allied factors, special emphasis would be laid on improving the existing skills of women and imparting new and enhanced skills under the multidimensional programmes of farmers' training, exchange of development, fodder production, post-harvest technology, application of pesticides, budding and grafting, training in horticulture, fisheries, etc. "Horticultural research and development programmes would play a significant role in economic and nutritional progress, particularly with respect to the problem of under-nutrition of pregnant women and nursing mothers and their children."

Rural Development

The Integrated Rural Development Programme, meant for the very poorest in the rural areas, was formulated with a view to creating assets for increasing the productivity as well as the income generation ability of the beneficiaries, in a specified period of time and was extended to all the 5092 development blocks in the country during the Sixth Plan and an envisaged 20 million beneficiaries were to be covered by the Seventh Plan. Special efforts were made to identify and select households headed by women beneficiaries although the scheme covered landless labourers, small and marginal farmers, rural artisans and the like. "Households headed by women would account for at least 20 per cent of the coverage. The scheme of DWCRA would be strengthened and modified in order to ensure that the benefits reach the target groups." Similarly, great stress is purported to have been laid on proving employment to women beneficiaries under various other rural oriented schemes such as the National Rural Employment Programme (NREP) and Rural Landless Employment Guarantee Programme (RLEGP). Furthermore, under the TRYSEM Programme, one-third of the 40 youths in the age-group 18-35 years (per development block) identified for receiving suitable vocational training to help them set up self-employment ventures, would be women.

Land Reforms

The Central assistance for the scheme for providing financial assistance to the Assignees of Ceiling Surplus Land (ACSL) obtained from the implementation of land ceiling laws (effective from August 1975) and 'intended to enable allottees to buy inputs and other necessary wherewithals of cultivation' would be 'oriented to confer benefits on a larger number of households headed by women'.

Industry

Not only were strenuous efforts to be made to persuade 'public sector undertakings to sponsor ancillary industries in collaboration with State level agencies dealing with development programmes for women to provide increased employment opportunities around them, attempts would also be made to identify and target the women beneficiaries under Entrepreneurial Development Programme (EDP) and Industrial Estates.

Village and Small-Scale Industries

Not only would schemes for the introducation of new technologies and the induction of expertise through upgradation of training be further expanded, but the scope of the specific training programmes for women entrepreneurs would be widened in order to fully familiarize them with all the technical know-how needed for setting up enterprises. In addition, rural technology institutions and mobile technology and training units would be extensively expanded. And the training would be oriented, as far as possible, in consonance with schemes like IRDP, TRYSEM, etc. Care would be taken to ensure that such specialized training capsules would be conducted regularly and with maximum efficiency for the benefit of those wanting to enhance their skills. It was also visualized that a massive programme for the training of artisans, managers, supervisors and entrepreneurs, etc., would have to be implemented to expand and encourage efficient production and for the promotion of skilled employment.

Special infrastructural facilities like the availability of industrial sheds for enterprising women entrepreneurs, as well as plots on subsidized rates, would be encouraged; in addition the National Small Industries Corporation and other apex organizations would extend multipronged support for such necessary functions as marketing, product design and financial support for the procurement of raw material. Special attention and care would be taken to preserve the special status given to the handloom sector and expand the scope of its activities comprehensively.

Khadi and Village Industries

During the Seventh Plan it was envisaged to increase the employment coverage under khadi and village industries from 3.80 million persons to a whopping 5.86 million persons—an ambitious and impressive quantum jump. A considerable proportion of such increased employment opportunities were meant to directly benefit the women, attempting to increase the employment ratio from 46 to 48 per cent.

Other Measures

Other important and relevant measures which would have a direct bearing on the women in the rural areas and otherwise would be implementation of the Equal Remuneration Act in a more stringent manner to try and ensure that women workers are paid wages as prescribed in this vitally important Act from time to time. Studies were also proposed to be undertaken on the implementation of the Factories Act 1948, the Plantation Labour Act 1951 and the Mines Act of 1952 to further assess whether the interests of the women were being protected sufficiently and in commensuration with the important provisions laid down in the respecive Acts. An added beneficial proposal would be the consideration of relaxing the age limit for women for entry into government services and public sector undertakings.

Science and Technology

Commendably, the programme on Science and Technology for Women would be further strengthened to identify, formulate, sponsor and implement research and development, demonstration and extension programmes, with special emphasis on providing opportunities for gainful employment/self-employment to women, specially to those in rural areas.

The involvement of voluntary organizations on a more dynamic basis to provide relevant inputs regarding acceptance of programmes and transfer of technologies, would be encouraged, special training programmes would continue to be sponsored for women in Polytechnics and other institutions of technical education in areas previously considered to be tackled solely by men, such as repair and maintenance of radios, television and other electronic hardware or consumer durables, manufacture of PVC goods, lacquer work and fibre reinforced plastics, etc.

Social Welfare

It was proposed to establish and maintain extremely close linkages with such specialized agencies connected actively with women's development and welfare such as ICAR,ICMR, DST, Rural Development, Industry and Education, etc. The Central Social Welfare Board would definitely continue to extend grants-in-aid to voluntary organizations to set up a variety of income generating units under the 'Socio-Economic Programmes' for the benefit of needy women, "the scheme of assistance to pub'.c undertaking / corporations and autonomous organization or supporting projects aimed at income generation and employment among women from weaker sections, on a sustained basis with the help of Norwegian Agency for International Development (NORAD), would be further expanded."A new and commendable scheme such as the Women's Development Corporations for permitting employment generating activities and a Women's Development Planning and Monitoring Cell was also proposed to be taken up.

Monitoring

A proper monitoring mechanism was proposed to be developed, so as to ensure optimal utilization of all the facilities which were being provided for the benefit of women and to improve their economic status by providing them with the relevant related infrastructure. The 1991 consensus took elaborate ,pains to ensure that women's participation in work was not left out and that women-headed households were not under enumerated. The 1991 census reported 91. 397 million female workers (excluding J & K), of whom 66.189 million were reported to be main workers and 25.208 million as marginal workers. 'The percentage of female main workers to total main workers was 23.19 per cent. It was much lower in the urban areas. During the decade 1981-91, female workers in India increased by 42.26 per cent. The female workforce participation rate was 22.69 in 1991 as compared to 19.77 in 1981.' There is considerable inter-state variation in female work participation rate, as has been assessed over the years.

The Eighth Plan

The strategy of the Eighth Plan envisaged as being oriented towards ensuring that the benefits of development from different sectors do not bypass the women for whom they have been tailored and that special programmes are implemented to complement the general broad-based development programmes. Such problems reflect greater gender sensitivity both in scope and application of proposals and practical realities on ground. Not only should women be encouraged to function as 'equal partners and participants' in development and not remain mere beneficiaries of various schemes, but extending the reach of self-enhancing schemes to women, both quantitatively as well as qualitatively, is an important goal of the Eighth Plan.

Other important measures included taking a more holistic view of the women's role in the family and society, attempting to free her from erstwhile narrow and restricting perceptions and prejudices. The issues relating to women will be integrated in the overall and total development endeavours. This blueprint for women's development and subsequent emancipation also envisages the formation and strengthening of pivotal grass-root level women's groups which will then articulate the particular and specific needs of the local women and play an important role in decentralized planning and implementation of programmes.

Strenuous and sincere attempts would be made to expand women's employment in the household society by providing adequate support in the area of technology upgradation, training, credit, raw materials and marketing. In addition, the existing poverty alleviation programmes like IRDP, TRYSEM and Jawahar Rozgar Yojana would make sure that the target set for women beneficiaries, is reached and that there are no shortfalls.

The programmes of training women in soil conservation, dairy development, field, forestry and other occupations closely allied to agriculture like sericulture, dairying, horticulture and poultry, will be greatly expanded. In the programmes pertaining to the important area of agricultural production, strong emphasis would necessarily have to be laid on implementation of land reforms, restructuring of agrarian institutions and promotion of rural industries.

Welfare

Under the numerous measures to be incorporated in this sector, some important schemes which are given high priority include improvement of the income of women and their skill formation. The existing scheme of "Support-to-Training-cum-Employment-Programmes" (STEP) for implementation of projects seeking to provide training and employment in agriculture and allied activities, is proposed to be vastly strengthened. The Central Social Welfare Board's Scheme of assisting voluntary organizations to provide work and wage to poor women will be continued, beyond doubt. The scheme "Employment-cum-Income-Generating Training-cum-Producation Centres" with the assistance of the previously mentioned agency, NORAD, will also be consolidated.

So the saga of planning and implementing continues and hopefully we will witness an exceptionally high percentage rate in the fruition of farsighted developmental ideologies and practicalities and that the women of India, undoubtedly the backbone of its ethos in totality, will march onwards with confidence, with a staunch belief that their country and the people who attempt to govern it effecively, care for their welfare and well-being at all times.

References

Pujari, Premlata, and Kaushik, Vijay Kumari, 'Approaches to Plannng for Women's Development', *Women Power in India - Institutional systems for Women's Development*, Vol. 2, Delhi: Kanishka Publishers, 1994.

Srivastava, J.C., 'Technology for Development of Rural Women,' Women Power in India Institutional systems for women's Development, Vol. 2, (Eds.) Pujari, Premlata and Kaushik, Vijay Kumari, Delhi: Kanishka Publishers, 1994.

14
POLITICAL PERCEPTIONS

Man's capacity for justice makes democracy possible, but man's inclination to injustice makes democracy necessary.

Reinhold Niebuhr

In the glorious years when India's destiny was being shaped by stupendous acts of courage, selflessness and self-sacrifices and later, when as a result of her dogged persistence and equally unrelenting struggle for independence, she attained Independence, the colossus of Indian politics, Mahatma Gandhi very rightly maintained that "women are a great power in society, but if they misuse their power, it can shatter to bits the whole fabric of society." Nearly half a century later Susheela Kaushik an erudite Professor of Political Science and Director of Women's Studies and Development Centre, Delhi University, reiterated his views. But first they had to be suitably and unequivocally empowered in the political arena of life. Maintaining that "Politics is essentially an art of acquiring and exercising power — the power to effectively influence the decision making processes and policies, to reverse the existing situations wherever they are disadvantageous and to bring about the necessary social changes. A participation in this exercise of power is very much a necessity, particularly for the disadvantaged group, in this instance, the women. But then politics is also about power relations. Every social arrangement be it in the public, professional sphere or in the private space of domestic sphere, is an instance of power relationship. Thereby, whether it is the family, religion, caste or public institutions, they are all political institutions. Their mutual interaction thus becomes a political relationship and hence involves a modicum of power." Therefore, it follows that there exist a very close reasoning between the status of women and the social order and values. For, to create and maintain an ethos for the true political consciousness of women, in consonance with the spirit of modernization and her right to equality in all spheres of life, one would have to transcend, essentially, the barriers of bias posed by gender dichotomies and simple patriarchal institutions and proceed into the class nature of the state, maintains Manu Bhaskar emphatically.

Grant of Universal Adult Franchise to Women

Therefore one can rightfully assess the participation of women in the democratic process, under various relevant forces in the sociocultural, historical and politico-economic fields which shaped events and influenced her participation in the mainstream of life, `by citing one or two formal institutions in the Indian polity". The liberal and, undoubtedly, egalitarian legacy of the Indian National Movement had led to the Constitution of an independent India granting a position of equality to women, by way of political rights. Rightly or wrongly, it is customary to assess the status of women on the basis of their ability to exercise their franchise. Predictably enough, this electoral process went through a chequered history in accordance with various influencing processess in India's own history and culminated into women's full democratic participation as citizens, with the grant of Universal Adult Franchise in the Constitution of 1950. The provision of Fundamental Rights, with particular reference to the Right to Vote given to women, made one presuppose that now automatically all the various issues which had 'been bedevilling women' for years and years on end due to unfair restrictions, societal prejudices and customary practises rooted in history, would be justly redressed and women elevated to a more equitable position with their counterparts, the men.

Shortcomings

But whereas Indian women have judiciously exercised their right to vote through so many general elections and participated in the formal political processes of the country, there exist many studies and, naturally, as many informed opinions that articulate the following shortcomings in this vital area of women's participation:

(i) women are not independent voters;

(ii) that a majority of them are illiterate;

(iii) that a majority of them make their choice on the basis of suggestions from male members of the family, like their husbands and sons;

(iv) that women lack information and political awareness so crucial to making an informed and enlightened choice and

(v) women are not politically conscious. But events, mainly in the form of elections for over four decades where the women's participation has been infinitely greater 'than in many other countries developed or developing, except possibly in the countries that were going through radical revolutionary wars', belie such a presumptuous assumption and allegation.

Their active participation in India's freedom struggle and the very nature of this struggle when thousands of poor and illiterate women who had never ventured beyond the protective confines of their homes, now responded boldly to Gandhiji's clarion call for a concerted effort to throw out the foreign rulers and obtain Azadi, was, perhaps, a strong predisposing factor which led to their increasing participation in the voting process. Each time, thus, significantly narrowing down the wide gap that existed between the two segments of men and women voters. This increase in the turn out of women voters, particularly of the lower class and castes, may be attributed to a high degree of mobilization, rather than of one's own political consciousness. In India particularly, not only can one talk of the admirably high level of awareness of the value of the vote, 'which is possessed and cast eagerly by the poor and Scheduled Castes, at times very pragmatically and rationally', but one can also reiterate with firm conviction that they are politically sensitive, well aware of their interests and even the wider political issues. However, as Professor Kaushik so rightly states, "But this awareness, in order to be translated into a political exercise like voting, needs tremendous mobilization. This is all the more in the case of women, as poverty and daily work, household work and care, patriarchal and family norms act as great disincentives. Distance of booths, possibility of violence, health and other factors further discourage them. The linkage between the personal and the public is missing and people do not feel automatically impelled."

Indian women have amply proved in the past and continue to do so in the present as well, that given the right conditions, they are not only able to exercise their important right to vote in a responsible and mature manner, but given political power, they are equally capable of wielding it judiciously and with courage and conviction. Possessed of unique decision making capabilities in the home as well (like many of their Asian counterparts), Indian women have proved that they could seize all kinds of conceivable opportunities and long before women in countries like France, USA or England rose to high offices, there was a Chief Minister, Sucheta Kriplani in Uttar Pradesh, Lakshmi Menon and Violet Alva in Parliament and a Governor, Sarojini Naidu, apart from the famous Vijaya Lakshmi Pandit. It is history how the dedicated, compassionate and politically astute Sucheta Kriplani handled the highly contentious issues of as large and diverse a state as Uttar Pardesh, solving the problems of countless poor people, finding them jobs and healing the sick and suffering in a clinic she started in the slums and other poverty stricken areas. The height of her devotion to the people and the Party can be gauged by the fact that even after suffering from a severe heart attack, she campaigned for her party, the old Congress, dying in 1974 after a life of outstanding accomplishment.

The Indian National Congress, established in 1885, was in later years to become the major political party of India, and play a dominant and decisive role in her political destiny, for an impressive period in her chronological political evolution as a power to be reckoned with in world affairs. Even at its birth, its ranks were, surprisingly enough, open to women. An illustrious woman, namely Annie Besant, who presided over it at the Annual Congress session in 1917, established the precedent that was to continue for decades later i.e., that the President elected for a session would remain so for the whole year. "She also insisted that the same tests be applied to women as to men in regard to franchise and eligibility to all elective bodies concerned with local government and education." Further reinforcing such liberal and enlightened opinions, Tara Ali Baig, who later wrote an entire treatise on the power of women in her thought-provoking book entitled *India Woman Power*, emphatically maintained that 'discrimination on the basis of sex has never happened in all India's modern political life, nor did women ever demand special reservations or preferential treatment'.

However, it was not until the year 1926 that women gained the right to sit in Legislative Councils in the Provinces of the then British India. In Madras, in the South, Dr Muthulakshmi Reddy was the first woman to gain elective office. Not only did she have the distinction of being the first woman doctor to graduate from Madras University, she was also the first Vice-President of the Madras Legislature. The WIA or the Women's Indian Association, which had been extremely active during those early years, had also suggested the names of two other deserving candidates, namely, Kamaladevi Chattopadhyaya who became a veteran socialist leader in course of time and responsible too for the revival of India's ancient handicrafts, and Mrs Hannen Angelo. In 1921, 'since the battle for women's rights had been concentrated in certain States', the Madras Legislature had, ultimately, passed a resolution calling (very sagaciously) for the registration of women on the electoral rolls. Eminent English women like Annie Besant and Margaret Cousins, who identified themselves unconditionally and wholeheartedly with the cause of Indian women's emancipation, as well as other distinguished women like Dhanwanthi Rama Rao, the later champion and authority on Family Planning, Dr Muthulakshmi Reddy, T. Sadasiva Iyer, Dorothy Jinaraja Dasa, were actively behind these progress oriented and forward looking developments. The saga of Sarojini Naidu leading historic delegations to Mr Montagu and Lord Chelmsford, the Viceroy, to demand self-government, women's suffrage, education and medical colleges for girls, has already been dealt with in detail in another chapter and need not be repeated here. By the time Mahatma Gandhi returned to India from South Africa, having successfully experimented with the political process of 'satyagraha' there, and took up the leadership of the Indian National Congress and the struggle for freedom, 'women's leadership had been established all over the country and thousands of women rallied to the excitement of political events'. It is interesting to note that four eminent women have held the prestigious position of President of the Indian National Congress and by a strange irony, two of them were British. The first was Annie Besant who polled impressive 45 votes to Gandhi's 10. She was followed in 1925 by Sarojini Naidu at the Kanpur Session, in the '30s by the wife of the Bengali patriot Deshbandhu Gupta, Nellie Sen Gupta and, finally many decades later, by the charismatic Indira Gandhi whose illustrious family dominated Indian politics decisively for years.

The Montagu-Chelmsford Reforms, in which there was no mention of women despite the women's delegations, were embodied in the Government of India Act of December 1919 and established an Assembly and a Council of State in Delhi, the Capital, and Legislative Councils in each province. While it paved the way for political life to develop in India, the bitterness and violence that ensued in the wake of the stringent Rowlatt Bills which legitimized the Government's assumption of new powers to control political activity, initiated the powerful Civil Disobedience Movement. The powers which the 600 signatories who signed the famous Satyagraha pledge, signifying their violent opposition to such power as sanctioned by the "Black Bills" may be explained thus: The Rowlatt Bills had reinvested the hegemonistic British Government with powers which had lapsed with the Defence of India Act expiring automatically after the First World War. The unforgettable, epic proportions of the Civil Disobedience Movement too have been elaborated upon earlier and need not be discussed here in detail. Thousands of women went to jail, among them many women members of Jawaharlal Nehru's family; these included his wife and two sisters while the twelve-year-old Indira got her early training in political life by creating the "Monkey Army" of youngsters who could slip through cordons of police and deliver messages without being suspected. Other women included Rukmini Lakshmipathi, the first woman to be arrested in Madras and Durgabai, the well known revolutionary "dictator" of barely twenty, who was later to become the first woman in the Planning Commission in Independent India, and who built up the extraordinary army of voluntary social workers later in the Central Social Welfare Board.

However, courting arrest was only one significant aspect of women's work during these stirring times. Others continued to campaign relentlessly for the right to vote and participate in legislative affairs. The all-important Franchise Committee headed by Lord Lothian, had been counselled by the earlier Simon Commission to grant voting rights to not less than 10 per cent and not more than 25 per cent of the population. Such strictures notwithstanding, the bold Nallamuthu Ramamurthi, Taraben Premchand, Lakshmi Menon and Rajkumari Amrit Kaur pleaded for adult franchise for men and women and strongly opposed separate electorates where only Muslims would elect Muslims while other communities would be lumped together for purposes of election, thereby not constituting a very balanced or fair representation. Lord Lothian was forced to comment to the relevant authorities that the women representatives were very firm and would not budge from the stand that they had so determinedly taken in their demand for equality as the basis of the new Indian Constitution. All kinds of negotiations, therefore, went on during this period and a high-powered Round Table Conference in London took place, the end result of all these activities being the passing of the Government of India Act in 1935, enfranchising 35 million voters. The year 1935, therefore, assumed vital significance as this was the year that marked the specific period in India's chequered battle for political rights, when the principle of the right of vote for women, was granted. It did not cover either all men or all women.

Elections followed and in the 1936 elections which took place in the provinces of India, but not in the huge number of princely states, numberiing 603, Anusuyabai Kale was elected Deputy Speaker in the Central Provinces, Siphai Malani Deputy speaker in the Sind Assembly, Rukmini Lakshmipati became a Minister in the Madras Cabinet in 1937, Jyoti Venkatachalam in C.Rajagopalachari's Cabinet while the first woman to serve in any Cabinet was Vijaya Lakshmi Pandit in UP. In the Central Assembly, Renuka Ray, who was later to become the Minister of Rehabilitation in Bengal, Radhabai Subbarayon, an elite member of one of the Round Table Conferences and Ammu Swaminathan who, along with many of her other colleagues was elected to Parliament in the 1952 First General Elections after Independence, played an active role.

The Constituent Assembly, set up in the year prior to India's independence, i.e., 1946 October, and a body elected by the existing Legislatures, had among its members Sarojini Naidu, Durgabai, Renuka Ray and Hansa Mehta, among others, to frame the Constitution of India on Independence. It was definitely and without doubt, that this period of India's history with the four previous decades of the heroic struggle for freedom, in which women participated as courageouly and unflinchingly as their male counterparts, that established woman's right of equality with man. Embodied in India's Constitution, its Fundamental Rights and Directive Principles of State Policy are clear indications of a just, equal and humane society. Article 325 of the Constitution also makes clear that no special electoral rolls on grounds of religion, race, caste or sex could be entertained, and Article 326 emphasizes that election to the House of the People and to the legislative Assemblies of States were to be on the basis of adult suffrage thereby vindicating the noble work done by Margaret Cousins, Kamaladevi Chattopadhyaya and the other farsighted women several decades ago.

In the First General Elections three women came into prominence as parliamentarians—the intrepid Rajkumari Amrit Kaur was the first cabinet minister with the all-important health portfolio, the Deputy Minister was Margatham Chandrasekhar, Not many women over the years played a role in the Lok Sabha and Rajya Sabha Secretariats or as Speakers and Deputy Speakers, though they featured as alternates in the lists of the latter. Lakshmi Menon, however, was made a Parliamentary Secretary for the first five years of Parliament's life and subsequently remained as Deputy Minister for External Affairs under Jawaharlal Nehru who was also Foreign Minister, till 1967.

In various General Elections, despite the monetary requirements to campaign successfully and fight other canditates in order to be elected, despite the objections of husbands and other reservations that both the spouse and his family may have against the woman standing for elections, 'a field of action which may be marked by crudity and violence', despite problems of party nominations, despite the extraordinary demands made upon the health and the strength of the women in coping with inevitably strenuous schedules, despite all these potent and potential deterrents, women have managed to maintain a fairly even position year after year. The year 1962 was one of the most promising with six women members in the Centre as Ministers of State or Deputy Ministers; twenty-one Ministers or Deputy Ministers in State Governments, 34 elected to the Lok Sabha and 12 were returned through the voting process in the State Legislative Assemblies by the normal process of returning members to the Upper House in Delhi. The earlier experience of the First Genral elections however demonstrated amply the need to impart training in more sophisticated Parliamentary techniques. The late Prime Minister, Indira Gandhi, who then led the women's section of the Indian National Congress, sought to address this imminent need and initiated useful and educative legislative seminars. She was assisted greatly in her laudable ventures by Lakshmi Menon, already a highly experienced person in procedures and one who had often represented India at the prestigious United Nations commission on the Satus of Women, and Sucheta Kriplani, who also displayed great political acumen and organizational capability.

It is evident from the statistical analysis of the Fourth General Elections of June, 1967-a publication brought out by the Indian National Congress-that as many as 230 Congress women candidates were put up for the 1962 elections; out of these well over 50 per cent viz., 152 to be exact; were elected to the State Legislative Assemblies. The figure reduced somewhat by the time 1967 elections came around, out of the total 175 there were 85 elected.

One of the stars on the political firmament of India as well as one of the most celebrated Indian women, Vijayalakshmi Pandit had the distinction of being the first woman to serve as a Minister in a Provincial Government. But she was destined for even greater events in her life and after Independence, her career reached its pinnacle when she represented in the world forum where she became the first woman to be elected President of the U.N. General Assembly. Later on she was appointed Ambassador to the USSR, the United States and High

Commissioner in London. No woman diplomat has matched her performance or her impressive achievements in these fields.

In fact, women in top offices in India can be compared favourably with most other countries, most certainly outstripping such supposedly advanced countries such as England , USA and France during the entire period. In spite of the world's history of ruling queens, India's record of 'women in high places' has been remarkable. Indira Gandhi came to office in 1966, making a triumphant entry after defeating a well matched and tense contest, with senior statesman Morarji Desai. Desai had virtually been functioning as deputy Prime Minister when Lal Bahadur Shastri died suddenly, under suspicious circumstances in Tashkent. In the years which followed, she demonstrated in indisputable and ample measure, 'a flawless sense of timing, a fine-tuned courage, political insight of a singularly well-developed nature and the power that comes from waiting, learning and seldom speaking'. She made short shrift of the political party bosses of 1967 who mistakenly thought she could be used as 'a compromise candidate' behind whom they could successfully continue to indulge in powerful party politics and power games. In a series of brilliantly conceived and executed manoeuvres, she soon turned the tables on those wily political constituents, beginning by isolating the old bosses by splitting the Congress, and carrying the new Congress forward from one victory to another.

At the top level, India also led the world in its illustrious women Governors from Sarojini Naidu, who queened it over the Raj Bhavan in the vast state of Uttar Pradesh, from August 1947 to 20th February, 1949 when she died. Her daughter, Padmaja Naidu who shared with her the unique qualities of head and heart, a ready wit and an unusually compassionate nature, was to remain Governor of Bengal for nine long years. Padmaja, ensconced in the vast palace of the former Raj, modelled by Lord Wellesley on the stately home of the Curzon family at Keddleston, exercised her powers as Governor of West

Bengal, judiciously. In Bombay, Vijayalakshmi Pandit remained Governor for a full five years.

While the work of a Governor is concerned with many ceremonial activities, that of a Chief Minister runs the gamut of every conceivable and even inconceivable administrative problem, in additon to the complex interactions of party politics. Sucheta Kriplani, as has been mentioned earlier, handled with commendable political aplomb the tangled, tortuous and complex political problems of Uttar Pradesh. Nandini Satpathy, one time Minister of State for Information and Broadcasting in the Union Government, successfully completed a tenure of over two years as the Chief Minister of the backward state of Orissa while in the picturesque state of Goa, Shashikala Kakokkar assumed the office of Chief Minister on the demise of her father. It is of course a coincidence, but with two cases of daughters succeeding to the office previously held by their capable fathers, there has, however, been no instance in India of such succession on the death of a husband. As with Madame Aung Sang in Burma, Prime Minister Sirimavo Bandaranaike in Sri Lanka and President Isobel Peron in the distant country of Argentina. In fact it was single women like Rajkumari Amrit Kaur and Sushila Nayar, who were both Ministers of Health in the Central Government and widows like Indira Gandhi and her illustrious aunt, Vijayalakshmi Pandit, who came to their positions of tremendous power entirely on their own merit and not through the relatively easier means of succession.

In the chequered political history of Indian political life, we come across many other wellknown and well remembered names such as Tarakeshwari Sinha who, with her good looks and fiery temperament , also earned the epitaph of "glamour girl" of Parliament, Violet Alva, Dr Sushila Nayar, Dr Soundaram Rama Chandran who also did outstanding work in Gandhigram, South India, Sushma Swaraj, Girija Vyas, Jayalalitha, Rabri Devi, Maneka Gandhi and so on and so forth.

Some of these women rose to power before 1967, by when Mrs Indira Gandhi had firmly ensconced herself as Prime Minister and some came later, long after her death. However, when she - Indira Gandhi - firmly established herself in the seat of power (1967), she then swept the polls. While she retained the additional portfolios of Minister of Atomic Energy and Planning and External Affairs, she made Dr Phul Renu Guha, Minister of State for Social Welfare, Jehanara Jaipal Singh, Deputy Minister of Tourism and Civil Aviation, Dr Sarojini Mahishi without portfolio and Nandini Satpathy, Deputy Minister, Information and Broadcasting.

However, for the political process to be successful to its optimum level and in consonance with the rapid pace of modernization, it is essential to create an all pervasive ambience of political efficiency. Political efficency refers to the person's belief that political and social change can be effected or retarded and that his efforts alone, or in concert with others can produce desired behaviour on the part of political authorities. It is a psychological disposition of an individual towards the political system that manifests itself in a feeling of "personal competency or personal effectiveness." An efficacious person feels herself/himself confident, views his political self with respect and assumes that the political people are concerned about her/his vote and definitely need her/his demands. He is of the firm opinion that the relevant political authorities of the concerned country care for its citizens (in a democracy) and is confident that "leadership circles, can be influenced and penetrated." Campbell, a noted authority on the subject, defines the all important virtue of political efficacy as the "feeling that individual political action does or can have an impact upon the political process, that is, that it is worthwhile to perform one's civic duties." The views given above, thus unequivocally substantiate the contention that political efficacy and political participation are closely related. Such a close link between the two i.e., efficacy and participation has been confirmed and amply brought out by such authors of standing as, Almond and Verba, Berelson, Campbell, and Dahl. Political efficacy being, essentially, a feeling that a sufficient mastery in the political sphere, the 'locus of casaulty' may be fixed on the self and not on the environment. De Charms has very sensibly categorized people's 'origin' and 'pawn' on the basis of their perceptions to social casuality. Following a system of deductive logic, according to him, a person who perceives his behaviour to be the outcome of his own choice, is termed as 'origin' and a person who believes that his behaviour is determined by external forces beyond his control (an unmistakably fatalistic approach), is definitly a 'pawn'. According to Rotter the internal controls of an individual are the rewards which are the necessary outcome of an individual's own behaviour and naturally follow from such behaviour. Whereas the various external controls are equally the result of luck, chance, fate, as under the control of powerful other, or as unpredictable because of the great complexity of forces surrounding him. Rotter goes on to say that, a reinforcer on the other hand, is that which changes behaviour in some way by either decreasing or increasing the potentiality of its occurrence. And these, necessarily, include both internal as well as external reinforcements. Whereas the internal reinforcement, in his opinion, refers to an individual's perception about an event having had some value for him, external reinforcements, obviously, refer to those acts or events which hold predictable reinforcement value for the group or culture to which the individual belongs. Since Politics in the present day society is 'mainly a skill controlled area' and 'persons skilled enough to control the environment are definitely active in politics, political efficacy and personal control necessarily perceive the political system to have great influence on the socio-economic and other personal pursuits. If the political system functions in a sagacious manner, with the correct degree of checks and balances and keeping the differing needs and aims of his various segments of society at all times, the benefits to the people will be of great value and will monitor and ensure their steady growth and progress. Therefore for them the political system, which they perceive as being the only source from which they can get certain benefits, is of vast significance; and hence, they have an obligation to be concerned with the political process. The political process must ensure not only the availability of relevant political data and information for the people to judge and make informed choices regarding not only the issues affecting their destiny, the variable economics of their situation and other influencing factors, but also dissemination of relevant political information, procedures, amendments and other technicalities of the complex and complicated political machinery, must be made available to them at regular intervals. To keep them fully in the picture as much as possible, to keep them in the true picture of political events and happenings, to enable them not only to make discerning choices themselves, but influence and guide others as well, who may not at all times have access to vital information. So that the fabric of our society can be competently and cohesively knitted into one integrated, progressive whole. Ensuring better and improved standards of living, and increased social and political awareness and a lessening of the evil and debilitating forces of ignorance and misinformation, negating in time what V. Rajlaxmi perceived: 'An enormous disparity exists between women's formal political equality and their meaningful exercise of political power'. So that they are brought into the mainstream of life once and for all, their energies and acumen suitably channelized to make vital contributions to the on-going process of modernization and progress.

References

Ali Baig, Tara, 'Politics and Legislation,' *India's Women Power*, New Delhi: S. Chand & Co. Pvt. Ltd.

Angus Campbell, Gerald Gusin and Warren Miller, The *Voter Decides*, Evanston III, Row Peterson, 1954.

Bernard Berelson et al., *Voting*, Chicago: Chicago Press, 1954.

Gabriel Almond and Sidney Verba, *The Civic Culture*, Princeton: Princeton University Press, 1963.

Kaushik, Sheela , ed., 'Introduction' of *Women's Participation In Politics*, New Delhi: Vikas Publishing House Pvt. Ltd., Copyright Indian Association For Women's Studies, 1993.

Panda, Snehlata, *'Political Efficacy And Political Participation: A Study of Women's Involvement In Politics In India'* (Paper Presesnted aat the Third National Conference, Chandigarh, in 1986), In Kaushik, Sheela *(ed.), Women's Participation In Politics*, Vikas Publishing House Pvt. Ltd., New Delhi.

Rober Dahl, *Who Governs?*, New Haven: Vale University Press, 1961.

Rotter, J.B., *Generalised Expectancies for Internal Vs.*

External Control of Reinforcement, Psychological Monographs, General and Applied.

Rotter, *Social Learning and Clinical Psychology*, Englewood Cliffs: N.J.Prentice Hall, 1954.

15

GENDER BIAS OR GENDER FARCE

It's always been classier, and a lot more dignified, to be a woman than a female. Thanks to 30 years of feminist striving, the category "woman" has expanded to include anchorpersons, soccermoms, astronauts, firefighters, even the occasional Senator or Secretary of State. But "female" still tends to connote the oozing, bleeding, swelling, hot-flashing, swamp-creature side of the species, its tiny brain marinating in the primal hormonal broth. From Aristotle to Freud, the thinking on gender has been that only one sex had fully evolved out of the total pool, and it wasn't the sex that wears panty hose.

Barbara Ehrenreich

"Gender issues are of great importance in contemporary society and culture" emphatically maintains Ursula King. Elaborating that while such issues encompass both men and women, at present "gender studies are still mainly focused on women because women have been voiceless for so long. Throughout most of human history there has existed an asymmetry in the relations of power, representation, knowledge and scholarship between men and women. Thus, there exists a large agenda to be addressed in order to overcome women's invisibility, marginalization and subordination in history and society." Thus the idea of "genderedness" is now viewed as an important new insight of feminism taken out of the dimensions of conventional construct and imbued with more dynamic interpretations. It is not derived from earlier philosophical positions, 'it represents a new breakthrough in the history of human consciousness'; the analysis of gender identity and gender relations are seen as central for the understanding of the social order of any society'.

It is imperative to acknowledge that gender ideologies are 'frequently hierarchically organized and sexual inequality is embedded in thought, language and social institutions'. According to anthropological folklore, in traditional societies one's identity was fixed, solid and stable. Identity *per se* being a function of predefined social roles and a traditional system of myths which provided orientation and religious sanctions to one's place in the world, while rigorously circumscribing the realm of thought and behaviour. One was born and died a member of one's clan, a member of a fixed kinship system with one's life trajectory fixed in advance. Even in pre-modern societies, with their relatively uncomplicated lifestyles and pace of life, the issue of identity continued to be unproblematical and not subject to undue reflection, discussion and debate. 'Individuals did not undergo identity crises, or radically modify their identity'. However, in modernity, identity becomes 'more mobile, multiple, personal, self-reflexive, and subject to change and innovation'. Here there is 'still a structure of interaction with socially defined and available roles, norms, customs, and expectations, among which one must choose, appropriate, and reproduce in order to gain identity in a complex process of mutual recogintion'. Theorists of identity in modernity, from Hegel through G.H. Mead, have broadly subscribed to such an ideology.

However, viewed from the postmodern perspective, as predictably 'the pace, extension and complexity of modern socities accelerate, identity becomes more and more unstable, more and more fragile'. As changing norms of acceptablity, expectations, aims and ambitions coalesce in the crucible of such a complex and complicated sociological and psychological scenario, recent discourses of postmodernity problematize the very notion of identity, claiming that it is a myth and an illusion. One reads in the Frankfurt School, in Baudrillard, and in other postmodern theorists that the autonomous, self-constituting subject that was the achievement of modern individuals, of a culture of individualism, is fragmenting and disappearing, owing to the social processes and the levelling of individuality in a rationalized, bureaucratized, mediatized and consumerized mass society. And so, male and female roles, relations and interaction are influenced by so many cultural variables that now, when the complexity and contradictions of local gender practices are better known, it is becoming increasingly more difficult to state gender insights in terms of universals.

Alice Schlegel, who has succinctly summed up 'gender' as 'the way members of the two sexes are perceived, evaluated and expected to behave', states simply that gender is a cultural construct. True in its essence perhaps, but feminist theorists tend to draw stricter delineations between the terms 'sex' and 'gender'. Dividing sex from gender, here sex refers to the biologically given differences between women and men, whereas gender refers to the broader social and cultural meaning assigned to these differences. However, both the historical and cultural constriction of these interpretations are sometimes perceived as too separate from the biological angle. Kari E. Borreson addresses the problem admirably and attempts to correct this one-sidedness when she considers gender as a socio-biological category and not simply as the result of history and culture. Emphasizing thus the interaction between biologically determined sex and culturally expressed gender, her attempt at achieving greater theoretical clarity and balance (ground in her historical work on women in the Christian tradition) is paralleled by several significant developments in contemporary gender studies.

To maintain the delicate delienative balance so essential to the objective study and dissemination of the gender issues, is, in itself, a Herculean task. Proceeding from the premise that human genderedness is a primary source of individual and social identity, when used as an analytical category it also becomes an important perspective for organizing knowledge. It is imperative to pause here and take cognizance of the fact that gender has two centres, not one. Douglas Kellner strongly advises that 'a holistic anthropology must pay attention to both female and male gender construction and overcome the polarization created by some representatives of women's studies and critical feminist thought'. Whereas earlier sociological studies of specific sex roles took sexual differences for granted by accepting and examining them from an overwhelmingly androcentric perspective, whereby (and wherein) male experience and male roles alone were valued as exemplary and normatively human, later women's studies deemed otherwise. Partly as a reaction, partly due to greater research and enlightenment on the subject and partly due to the demolition of man made barriers by the onslaught of feminism, 'women's studies critiqued such androcentric universalism by establishing the importance, specificity and inherent value of women's own experience'. During the 1970s especially, women's studies developed into a rich body of theory, ideas and facts and the undeniable impact of feminism on traditional academic disciplines was aptly described by Dale Spender in 1981 as Men's Studies Modified. During the 1980s, the influence of this critique as well as of feminist theories on gender differentiation, led to the emergence of a startlingly new field of quite different, critical and self-reflective 'men's studies'. Such studies not only highlighted the diversity of men's lives and the subjectivity of men's personal and private experience in contrast to male public roles, they also critically analysed the construction of masculinity by examining (and exploding?) its myths and heroes, and considering male-female relations from classical times to the present.

While Harry Brod has argued that men's studies is 'essential to fulfilling the feminist project, for it reconceptualizes the field by focusing on broader issues of gender rather than simply on women's studies', Lillian S. Robinson-based on her survey of contemporary men's studies-is of the firm opinion that 'even when it makes use of the insights and results of feminist scholarship, men's studies lack the urgency of women's studies'. Men's studies, women's studies, how do we mere mortals attempt to compartmentalize and classify this exhaustive genre of material relating to the two components-male and female-that constitute it, with such impunity. Thankfully, there now exists a rapidly increasing volume of critical gender studies which produce 'more fine-grained analyses of gender ideology', appropriately highlighting the variability and contradictory views on femaleness and maleness in different cultures. Kellner forcefully maintains, "the ever expanding literature on women, sexuality and gender produces a more nuanced understanding of sexual differentiation which appreciates the important contribution of new insights without denying their complexity, ambivalence and contradiction."

The notable contribution made by Sandra Lipsitz Bem towards a more broad-based, sensitive and comprehensive understanding of the gender issue, perhaps sums up, in essence, the concept of an ideal approach and treatment of the subject. A professor of psychology and women's studies at the prestigious Cornell University and widely known for her studies on sex roles, androgyny and psychosexual identity Bem, in her remarkable study *The Lenses of Gender*, moves away from her earlier emphasis on androgyny and concentrates on transforming the debate on sexual inequality by looking at the lenses through which our culture views male and female gender. Quaintly termed as 'the lenses of gender', she identifies three different beliefs or 'lenses' which affect construction of femininity and masculinity; Bem defines these as gender polarization , androcentrism and biological essentialism.

Gender polarization provides mutually exclusive scripts for being male and female, and, predictably, defines any person or behaviour deviating from this script as problematic. The effect of these two processes is obviously then 'to construct and to naturalize a gender-polarizing link between the sex of one's body and the character of one's psyche and one's sexuality'.

Androcentrism has already been touched upon, so we move on to the third of Bem's lenses i.e., biological essentialism, which maintains that male-female difference and male dominance are natural. To acknowledge the pervasiveness of these three 'lenses of gender' which are deeply ingrained not only in our cultural discourses and the psyche of individuals but are also an inseparable constitutent of our social institutions, is vital if we are to move towards change and progress. We no longer need to look through these lenses of gender but should instead view them critically for what they are and what they can do to humanity."Sexual inequalities are an illegitimate form of discrimination which was first religiously defended as God-given and natural and then, with the rise of secularized science, these inequalities have been argued for on scientific grounds in the biological and social sciences."

The intrepid Bem has courageously taken it upon herself to crusade for an ideological shift in the debate about sexual inequality; to take it away from its focus on male-female difference to how a predominantly androcentric approach-via discourses and institutions - transform male-female difference into decided female disadvantage. "Her goal of eradicating gender polarization is described under the title 'Toward Utopia', a recognition perhaps of how difficult it is to create a society wherein the biology of sex might be considered as one of minimal presence in human social life, important only in the narrowly biological context of reproduction."

Bem's approach is essentially grounded in a broad and broad-minded, all-encompassing humanistic concern when she deals with the way gender polarization prevents both men and women alike from developing their full potential as human beings. Unfortunately, we have polarized or compartmentalized, (call it what you will), human values and experiences into the masculine and the feminine, yet our culture has failed to develop a comparable concept of a 'real' human being. Traditional religious thought and teachings are replete with noble ideals of what it means to be truly human, but these ideals have been predominantly interpreted and propounded by men, to the detriment and exclusion of women. And of course with no attention or importance given to gender specificities.

It is, therefore, eminently desirable, that we evolve a new critical gender awareness. This, in turn, would mean seeking a new, more differentiated and at the same time more inclusive definition of what it means to be human. Including essentially, both the religious and spiritual dimension, but in a manner more in consonance with modern needs and aspirations. To develop and embody 'such a comprehensive and humanly empowering vision' demands a profound social transformation which definitely cannot be wrought without the psychological revolution of which Sandra Lipsitz Bem speaks thus:

> a psychological revolution in our most personal sense of who and what we are as males and females, a profound alteration in our feelings about the meaning of our biological sex and its relation to our psyche and sexuality. Simply put, this psychological revolution would have us all begin to view the biological fact of being male and female in much the same way that we now view the biological fact of being human. Rather than seeing our sex as so authentically as who we are that it needs to be elaborated, or so tenuous that it needs to be bolstered, or so limiting that it needs to be traded in for another model, we would instead view our sex as so completely given by nature, so capable of exerting its influence to those domains where it really does matter biologically, that it could be safely tucked away in the backs of our minds and left to its own devices. In other words, biological sex would no longer be at the core of individual identity and sexuality.

Barbara Ehrenreich, who has rather uninhibitedly exploded age old myths that society has doggedly (and dogmatically) clung to with a desperation matched only by its clawing need to believe in the inferiority and weakness that the female is usually typecast in, reiterates Bem's views. Startling a passive, slumbering social order out of its conventional smugness; shattering illusory concepts of male superiority and male strength as opposed to the weak, languishing female, with a force and faith that brook no prevarication. Of purpose or intent. The purpose here is to disdainfully discard what Ehrenreich forcefully terms as the 'prostitution theory of human evolution' touted unashamedly by the sociobiologists of the '60s and '70s, followed by the evolutionary psychologists of the '90s. "..a new attitude is bubbling out of that female hormonal swamp, powered by new research and, at least in preliminary form, fresh perspectives on the gender-bifurcated human conditon." A new genre of emboldened feminists, resolutely discarding the protective chrysalis that has cocooned women for far too long, are emerging as a reckonable force to establish an authentic gender picture; devoid of sentimental disapproval. Signalling the imminent revolution embodying conceptual and attitudinal changes, are a plethora of thought provoking publications. Heading the list of the manifesto for positive change is Natalie Angier's ebullient new publication, *Woman: An Intimate Geography*. Other 'female-positive' books hitting the stores include Diane Hales' thoughtful and eloquent, *Just Like a Woman: How Gender Science Is Redefining What Makes Us Female* and anthropologist Helen Fisher's *The First Sex: The Natural Talents of Women and How They Will Change The World*. While *Just Like a Woman* pans a sensitive exploration based on biological and physiological research of the multifaceted ways in which women are turning out to be special: stronger than men in some ways, vulnerable in others; *The First Sex* is a bit lazy about challenging conventional evolutionary wisdom: however Helen Fisher the anthropologist here predicts that women are psychologically primed to be the leaders of the 21st century. But as Barbara Ehrenreich bluntly states 'it's Angier, a Pulitzer Prize winner, who decisively lifts the concept of the human female out of its traditional oxymoronic status'. Quaintly terming her a "female chauvinist sow" who writes like Walt Whitman crossed with Erma Bombeck, *Woman: An Intimate Geography* is "a delicious cocktail of estrogen and amphetamine designed to pump up the ovaries as well as the cerebral cortex."

Perhaps the more delicately nuanced term "feminist" could be replaced by the more full blooded, realistic sounding "femaleist" while referring to the new consciousness. Subsequently, this femaleist premise could be summarized thus in Ehrenreich's words: "Uptil now, feminists have usually been leery of acknowledging gender differences, arguing that all but the most obvious of them are the products of culture, not genes, and could be erased by the appropriate legislation and child bearing practices. But the differences are real, various and not easy to parse in terms of the Framer's intentions, if any" Facts, figures and exhaustive research have robbed the facetious claim of male superiority of any authenticity and put it on the shelf. Men and women are increasingly being considered equal and, in certain spheres, 'the fairer sex' as they are somewhat euphemistically known, have even proved themselves to be more resilient, and, therefore, the stronger sex. While the female brain, in consonance with the smaller body size of women, is smaller, it is more densely packed with neurons than that of a male. Women have more immunoglobins in their blood, though men have more haemoglobin. While it cannot be denied that men definitely are the physically more imposing sex, being on an average, '10% taller, 20% heavier and 30% stronger, especially in their upper bodies', it is women who are more resistant to fatigue. The longer the race, the more likely they are to win it, it seems. "Furthermore, as millions of women prove daily by the sweat of their brow, the muscle gap is not carved in stone." *In Just Like a Woman*, author Diane Hales reports on a 1995 US Army test of female physical potential, in which 41 out-of-shape women-students, lawyers, bartenders and new mothers — achieved the fitness level of male army recruits in just six months of working out, getting to where they could jog

3 km with a 34-kg back-pack and do dozens of squats with a 45-kg weight on their shoulders. In the field of competitive sports too, women 'have been playing a stunning game of catch-up. Today's women stars can run, swim and skate faster than any man of a few decades ago, and the gap may eventually close.

In the last three and a half decades, precisely 1964 onwards the athelete women's record running times have dropped an impressive 32 per cent, compared with only 4.2 of men. If such an amazing trend continues, it would not be surprising at all if female marathon runners leave their sweating, panting male counterparts 'in the dust' sometime in the 21st century. Obviously being the more exsanguinous of the two sexes, they have continued to remain undeterred in the pursuit of excellence, in the conquest of hitherto predominantly male preserves of achievement of excellence. In 1975 Junko Tabei of Japan became the first woman to reach the summit of Mount Everest, thus squashing the sceptical (and negative) musings regarding a woman's innate physical strength and determination in the face of all odds. Since then other women have followed suit. Women have dared to undergo and successfully, the rigorous regimen considered mandatory prior to undertaking space missions, and have proudly stood by their male counterparts in their endeavours to map the mysteries of the unknown. Kiran Chawla, originally of Karnal, is another exemplary model of the fact that one's sex need not be a debilitating and limiting factor in the achievement of one's aims and aspirations, no matter how gruelling the goal.

True, some metaphysically meaty differences exist between the sexes, differences which can neither be denied nor swept under the carpet. However, it would be pedantic to let these differences dictate which of the two sexes should rule. While biology has endowed men and women differently, specifically nominating the latter for their noble reproductive roles and its essentially interrelated physical overtones and undertones, such differences, according to Hales, should be viewed in more pragmatic fashion. As she bluntly puts it "the differences between men and women, we can now see, are exactly differences and not signs of defects, damage or disease. Women are not the second, but a separate sex."

For with the numerous advances made in biology over the decades, it has been proved that testosterone and estrogen (formerly believed to be exclusively male and female hormones respectively) are, in actuality, present in both sexes. Though obviously the ratios differ. Nor does the absence of estrogen in a man imbue him with any extra manly attributes, it merely makes him more prone to such debilitating diseases such as osteoporosis. Women also produce testosterone and may even need it for sexual arousal. But whatever the molecular motives of estrogen and testosterone, men's testosterone is actually reported to fall before undertaking such physical challenges as parachuting etc., scientists have been unable to establish a clear cut relationship between testosterone levels and aggressiveness. What's more, researchers have found that PMS or premenstrual syndrome - which has assumed the proportions of a handy three letter slur directed at the aggressive, or merely irritated—woman', is experienced by many as a state of heightened activity, intellectual clarity, feelings of well-being, according to Angier. No longer is the customary 'time of the month' treated as an impeding or inhibiting factor, preventing women from leading as active an existence as during the rest of the month. Taboos pertaining to this cleansing cycle every month, observed in certain orthodox societies, are fast disappearing with the relative demystification of the process and parallel evolution of a greater participatory need of women, for women and by women, in the complex societal milieu of today.

The popularity of evolutionary theories, featuring as Ehrenreich so quaintly phrases it, 'man-the-hunter from Mars and his Venusian sidekick, woman' has led many feminist scholars to scornfully assert that biology is a sexiest ideology, and not a science and Darwin just another dead white male with an axe to grind. But, if man and woman evolved so very differently, then in the field of sexual dimorphism or matter of size, there should, logically, have been a much greater disparity in physical body sizes between the two, as there seem to have existed between the two sexes of our primordial ape cousins. Thus suggesting, though not proving in any way, that early men and women sometimes had overlapping job descriptions, like having to drive off the leopards. Be that as it may, after centuries of a stoic acceptance of the role bequeathed to them by destiny, something snapped and broke in the female psyche, propelling the genesis of a rebellious revolution, challenging arbitrarily defined roles. The movement, which galvanized a remarkable number of women into action, gradually acquired the dimensions of a formidable force. Beginning in the '70s, women began to elbow their way into the field and develop serious alternatives to the old, male centred theory of human evolution. It shouldn't matter, of course, what sex the scientist is, but women had their own reasons for being suspicious of the dominant paradigm. The first revisionist blow, so to say, came about a quarter of a century ago when enterprising anthropologists Adrienne Zihlmen and Nancy Tanner made some relevant findings. They pointed out that among surviving "hunting" peoples, most of the communities calories - upto 70% - came from plant food patiently and painstakingly gathered by women, not merely carnivorous fare heroically captured and prepared by the menfolk. Needless to say, evidence for Stone Age consumption of plant foods has mounted steadily since then. Five years ago, in 1994, paleobotanist Sarah Mason concluded that a variety of plant material discovered at the ancient Paleolithic site of Dolni Vestonice in the Czech Republic, was in fact edible roots and seeds. At the very least, it seems, the Paleolithic dinner was potluck, and it was probably the women who provided most of the starches, salad and raspberry-mousse desserts. The mother-of-us-all was beginning to look a little peppier and more self-reliant.

But, obviously, even the most efficient gatherer who was also busy being full time mother and performing all the other numerous strenuous tasks that it entails, including lactating her infant, needed help. Therefore, the grandma hypothesis : that maybe the evolutionary purpose of the postmenopausal woman was to keep her grandchildren provided with such foods as berries, tubers and nuts while the young mother was preoccupied with a new baby, came into being. For if grandma herself were still bearing and nursing her own babies, she would be too busy to baby sit. Hence nature may have selected for a prolonged healthy and mature, but infertile, stage of the female life cycle, for this purpose.

To authenticate and test such a possibility, anthropologist Kristen Hawkes carried out an intensive study among the hunting-gathering Hadza people of Tanzania, meticulously charting the hour-by-hour activities of 90 individuals, male and female, and weighing the children at regular intervals. The findings of her study, formally published in 1997, firmly established that children fared better if grandmother or a similar grand-mother figure like a grandaunt was on the scene. While this in no way proves the grandma hypothesis for all times and all people, it does strongly suggest that in the Stone Age family, Dad-the-Hunter was not the sole provider, and as Hawkes and her workers concluded about the Hadza," it is women's foraging, not men's hunting, that differently affects their own families' nutritional welfare." And if, in the course of time, the grandma hypothesis gathers greater credibility and continues to hold up, one may be compelled to conclude that the male-female pair bond was not quite so central to human survival as the evolutionary psychologists assume. The British anthropologist Chris Knight, a male, also suggests that alliances among females may have been more important in shaping the political economy of the ancient Paleolithic peoples.

The line of thinking that led to man-the-hunter (and provider) theory was largely inferential : that if a posse of women and squealing brats were to accompany the man, it would surely scare off the game. But such an inference was based on a particular, more formal, more male oriented style of hunting; the alternative of "communal hunting" in which the entire group of people, men, women and children, drive the animals over a cliff into a net or *cul-de-sac*, had only indirect evidence available in support of this practice. Not only did the Blackfoot and other Indians employ this modus operandi of hunting bisons before they acquired the horse but net-hunting is the most productive hunting method employed by the Mbuti people of the Congo today. When driving animals into a place where they can be effectively cornered and subsequently slaughtered, noise is a positive asset, whether it's the clashing of men's spears or the squeals of massed toddlers.

It took the discerning eye of a woman-Olga Soffer-as gender traditionalists might say, to spot more conclusive evidence of the practice of communal hunting during Paleolithic times. While sifting through clay fragments from the ancient Paleolithic site of Pavlov, now in the Czech Republic, the existence of a series of parallel lines impressed on some of the clay surfaces - evidence of woven fibres dating back some 2500 years, at once alerted this female archaeologist, possessed of an unusual visual and mental acuity. Intrigued to find signs of weaving from this early date, Soffer and her colleagues examined 8400 more clay fragments from the same and nearby sites, eventually coming across the traces of a likely tool of the communal hunt-a mesh net. As the erudite archaeologist explained, the entire theory of man-the-hunter had been based upon 'durable media', meaning items like the sharpened stones that can serve as spearheads, rather than softer, bio-degradable goods like baskets, fabrics and nets. But in archaeologically well-preserved pre-historic sites, such as those found under water or in dry caves, the soft goods predominate over the durable by a ratio of approximately 20 to 1. Lending credence to the theory of communal hunting where whole families participated in this exciting and useful sport. As Soffer so succinctly sums up that if the hard stuff was the work of men, then "we've been missing the children, the women and old people". Thanks largely to Soffer's findings, Paleolithic net hunting is no longer invisible and in net hunting, maintains Soffer, everybody participates.

Increasing evidence points out that there is no reason to believe that women were precluded from rigorous hunting activities. In fact Mary Zeiss Stange goes a step further and mentions in her recently published book *Women the Hunter* (1997), that there is no reason to rule out women's hunting with hard edge weapons too, perhaps even of their own making. Most of us are probably not aware that among the Tiwi Aborigines of Australia, hunting is considered women's work and until the introduction of steel implements, was done with relatively crude handmade stone axes which the women fashioned for themselves. Thus by putting women's work share on record, the new female evolutionary scientists may have helped re-write the biography of the human race.

There are many other reasons to doubt the veracity, the eternal equation of masculinity with aggression and violence, femininity with gentleness. From sources the world over, we have some compelling examples of the innate strength and power of female goddesses, whether associated with primarily outdoor hunting activities or in other important spheres of life. In ancient Greece and Sumer the deities of the hunt, Artemis and Ninhursag, were essentially female for they were also the goddesses who presided over childbirth. Even more striking is the association of ancient goddesses with nature's original hunters, the predatory animals. In Anatolia, the predator goddess was Kybele, known as the commander of lions. In Egypt, she was Sekhmet, portrayed as a lioness whose "mane smoked with fire (and whose) countenance glowed like the sun." All pointing towards an attitudinal propensity that 'about 3000 years ago, at the dawn of civilization, the idea of the fearsome huntress, the woman predator, generated no snickers among the pious.'

Coming from different disciplines and experiences, Wadley, a female American anthropologist, and Nandy, a male Indian social psychologist, both locate sources for the configurations they note in the same characteristics of Indian culture and cosmology. All animating power is female in Hindu cosmology. The word for power is *Shakti* and it can be used to refer to energy or strength. It is also a name of the goddess. Womanliness, to use Nandy's term, is associated with energy, animation not weakness. As he so concisely sums it up, 'the ultimate authority in the Indian mind has always been feminine', while the Indian male he identifies with 'what he sees as the passive, weak and masculine principle in the cosmos'. And corroborating Nandy and Wadley's configurations, Heinrich Zimmer, while defining *Shakti*, which comes from the Sanskrit root *sak*, and means 'to be able', 'to be possible' emphatically maintains that, "It is 'power, ability, capacity, faculty, strength, energy, prowess, regal power, the power of composition, poetic power, genius, the power or significance of a word or term, the power inherent in cause to produce its necessary effect, an iron spear, lance, pike, dart, a sword". The legend that recounts the genesis of Shakti is related in the *Markandeya Purana,* edited between the fourth and sixth century BC.

When the potent demon king Mahishasura, shaped like a colossal water buffalo bull, alongwith his legions managed to defeat the gods and force the whole pantheon out of heaven, the deposed gods prayed to the higher deities, Vishnu and Shiva. These great divinities then swelled with wrath and from their rage there emanated a great radiance. "The other gods then proceeded to emit a hot and lustrous anger as well. A flaming cloud was formed, which condensed into the shape of an eighteen-armed goddess." Zimmer (190-191) then recounts :

Upon beholding this most auspicious personification of the supreme energy of the universe, this miraculous amalgamation of all their powers, the gods rejoiced and they paid her worship as their general hope. In her, the perennial primal female, all the particularized and limited forces of their various personalities were powerfully integrated. Such an overwhelming totalization signified omnipotence. By a gesture of perfect surrender and fully willed self-abduction they had returned their energies to the primeval shakti, the 'One Force', the fountainhead, whence originally all had stemmed.

It would appear, therefore, that in South Asia it is perfectly natural or cosmologically appropriate for women to attain and exercise supreme power. Ann Grodzins Gold, in her essay *Gender, Violence and Power : Rajasthani Stories of Shakti* reiterates that during her travels and research in Rajasthan in 1979-80, she often heard the local people casually refer to Indira Gandhi (the Prime Minister then) as Shakti and explicitly identify the male assistance serving her interests with the lesser male deities who accompany and serve the goddess.

"The angry, weapon-wielding female divinities who people India's rich mythology, present compelling images. Such larger-than-life figures emerge from and interact with real peoples' minds, hearts and gender politics; the realities of sword wielding, skull garlanded goddesses somehow interpenetrate the realities of their worshippers." While there certainly is no dearth of scholarly attempts to explain these figures' existence and meanings, whether in psychoanalytic, religio-historical, or sociological terms, the explanations forwarded are as diverse as they are fascinating. Intrinsically Hindu images of divine female fury may be viewed as emerging from the projected terrors of docile, obedient boys overawed by their sexually frustrated mothers all-consuming love; or, alternatively, as manifestations of destructive and creative harmonies that sustain the universe; or even as projections of a patriarchal kinship system that fears and suppresses female sexuality while exalting motherhood. "In one culturally sensitive exploration of females in the realms of oral traditions, A.K.Ramanujan describes the way that an ordinary woman literally swells into a goddess in righteous anger, and suggests that Hindu culture understands all women to have such capacity." However, when social scientists attempt to generalize about gender differences and the position of women in India—particularly in contrast to the West—they very often highlight certain evidently paradoxical aspects of the Indian case. Susan Wadley's classic essay on *Women in the Hindu Tradition* is a case in point. The following passage states rather unequivocally that:

> Clearly Indian women present a paradoxical situation for the interpreter of South Asian society. The view of the Hindu woman as downtrodden represents one behavioural reality; her participation in the highest political and social arenas is another undeniable reality.

However, if we do acknowledge existing links and identifications among goddesses, women, and Shakti as power, the paradox brought out by the duo of Wadley and Nandy still remains partially unexplained. For example, why are women subordinated in household hierarchies, kept in seclusion, subjected to discrimination on the job market? Why are sons so obviously preferred to daughters and the health of male children of much greater concern to its parents, than of female children? Most important, why, since the introduction of aminocentesis (ostensibly to rule out deformities and abnormalities), has the problem of aborting female babies become a major ethical issue?

Perhaps a 'negative' manifestation of surplus female energy needs to be contained. If women have an excess of power, a corresponding excess of sexuality, and the potential to swell into angry goddesses, men have a strong interest in restraining them. Hence the infamous advice from the classical Hindu book of moral law, the *Law of Manu*, that a woman must be subjected to lifelong control by male kin. Hence the urgency to marry daughters before they attain puberty, the inauspiciousness of widows, the pervasive male fear of women draining their vital fluids and life force.

The fear of women as the agents or possessors of Shakti does not, however, account 'for other factors in the complex of Indian women's apparent subordination'. For instance, there are a host of socially and religiously salient reasons for the strong preference for sons that have to do with the nature of patrilineal descent and inheritance, patrilocal marriage and ancestor worship; with village exogamy and dowry; with women being considered unfit to study Sanskrit or offer sacrifices—to name just a few elements. None of these are based apparently on an understanding of power as female, nor as uncontrolled female power as dangerous; rather a scenario of male biological, political and economic dominance emerges as one much closer to the partiarchal orientation of the Western world.

It must be mentioned here that male dominance in Hindu South Asia does definitely not imply 'sharply differentiated male and female gender identities'. This, in essence, is Nandy's chief point about 'woman versus womanliness'. Men may be motivated to cultivate womanly traits for positive reasons, as did Mahatma Gandhi when he consciously or subconsciously emulated certain noteworthy qualities of his mother. Moreover, sources of female power are sometimes located in just that self-restraint and suffering imposed on women by their subordinate roles, but analogous to the self-restraint and suffering embraced by male ascetics to increase spiritual power.

Summing up the salient points of the gender issue as pertaining to the South Asian sociological scenario, Nita Kumar maintains that:

(i) Power is cosmologically associated with the female gender.

(ii) Goddesses are female powers both alien and intimate, not separate and unreachable from the human world, and sometimes incorporated into mortal female identities.

(iii) Women are socially, politically, economically and ritually disadvantaged.

(iv) Suffering is understood to be a source of power, and women are better at it than men.

(v) Gender identities are relatively fluid.

This erudite researcher, passionately committed to finding a balance for the cohesive construction of an identifiable South Asian feminine identity, muses that her discussion on the subject is 'grounded in the problematizations of a Western based feminist theory, and a Eurocentric postmodernism'. This, she maintains, is not because she tends to be 'unreflexively derivative' but because she thinks that is the direction that South Asian women's studies should take: "not to reject feminist and critical theory in the fear that they threaten to model our data in their own images, but to question, modify and adapt the theory to make sense of specific South Asian Discourses'. Asserting that such an approach would surely serve the dual purpose of more incisive analysis as well as of building a bridge to both non-South Asian feminist work and non-feminist South Asian work, she posits the eternal enquiry familiar to both history and anthropology: 'How do we conceptualize women and write about them?' Reflecting the methodology and thought processes articulated by such experts on the subject as Krishnamurti (1989), Forbes (1988), Chatterjee (1989), and Oldenburg (1991), she advances some thought-provoking theories:

"One way is to make women further the object of our gaze, by enlarging the scope of each particular discipline and including them in topics, further objectifying them. Another is to see them as actors and subjects, with the will, rationality and meaning to re-make the world, in short, to give them the prerogative of males. A third is to focus on the structures within which they exist and which seemingly control them without a chance for them to exercise agency, especially patriarchical, ideological, discursive structures. Yet a fourth is to look at the hidden, subversive ways in which women exercise their agency even while outwardly part of a repressive normative order."

Exploring various models and ideologies in juxtaposition with the crucial gender issue in South Asia, she advocates the adoption of a modified postmodernist, particularly Foucauldian approach. Foucault's approach consists of dispensing with the subject in favour of genealogy, a form of history that can account for the constitution of knowledges, discourses, domains of objects etc., without having to make a reference to a subject which is neither transcendental in relation to the field of events or runs in its empty sameness throughout the course of history'. Therefore, a modified Foucauldian approach would approximate the following: "since history consists of practices that fuse knowledge and power, individuals and groups can comprehend their 'subjection' to be at the hands of not an absolute, but one of a plurality of discourses, one that is deploying-typically in the case of women - one of several knowledges to define statue."

Even while we are keen to act for the liberation of women, we must acknowledge that women, as such, have neither been liberated nor repressed. Rather, there have been a succession of lofty discourses about femininity, purity, virtue, honour and womanhood that have 'displayed knowledge and power differently at different periods' though the pattern of these discourses has been predictably, essentially, androcentric and patriarchal. The constitution of man as subject has been a power ploy. So must the constitution of woman as subject be seen to be.

For the comparatively new approach of a feminist social science (and for the relatively new politics of feminism) where the postmodernist questioning of subjecthood appears to be luxury we cannot afford at all times, O 'Hanlon's comments on the political use of a subaltern identity, are comprehensively self-explanatory. He says:

> We must also bear in mind the siren attractions of the idea of the self-constituting human subject, in a political culture in which the free and autonomous individual represents the highest value. To lay claim to this highest value for our subaltern peoples represents an overwhelmingly attractive and apparently effective move, creating possibilities for retributive polemic along the lines of primordial being and distinctive identity, which outstrips any in a nuanced focus upon practice alone. We can be sure, moreover, that none of the genres of dominant historiography, with their own much more towering subject agents are about to perform any act of deconstruction upon themselves, thus giving us very little incentive at all to remain from taking up the same metaphysical weapons in our own cause.

References

Ehrenreich, Barbara, 'The Real Truth about the Female', *Time*, March 8, 1999.

Gold, Ann Grodzins, 'Gender, Violence and Power: Rajasthani Stories of Shakti', *Women as Subjects*, Kumar Nita, ed. Stree.

Kellner, Douglas, 'Popular Culture and Construction of Postmodern Identities', *Modernity and Identity*, Lash, Scott and Friedman, Jonathan, Ed. Oxford, UK: Blackwell Publishers, 1992.

King, Ursula, ' Introduction : Gender and the Study of Religion', *Religion and Gender*, King, Ursula, ed. Oxford, UK: Blackwell Publishers, 1995.

Kumar, Nita, 'Introduction', *Women as Subjects*, Kumar, Nita, ed. Stree

Mitter, Sara S., 'Female Prowess : Shakti', *Dharma's Daughters*, Penguin Books, 1992.

16
HOLISTIC HEALTH

Look to your health; and if you have it, praise God, and value it next to a good conscience; for health is the second blessing that we mortals are capable of; a blessing that money cannot buy.

Izaak Walton

A vital state of being, both physically and mentally, without which all else stands at naught. Achievements, progress, acquisitions, power, position or any other permutation/combination of similarly descriptive terms which we are wont to use with the utmost impunity. Lulling ourselves into a false state of complacency regarding the existence of a particular scenario amplified or qualified by one or more of these carefully pre-selected terms. Unless based on a viable, enduring foundation of good health and well-being, the balance is at best precarious, the temporary sense of well-being and economic prosperity just that—temporary and transient. Not one on which one can build a future that promises success and advancement, not to mention peace and contentment—two exceedingly rare `commodities of the human mind' in the context of the modern ethos. Where the basis of priority to matters is governed more by material considerations, where the emphasis is, increasingly, on the acquisition of economic wealth and a spirit of competition directly related to it. Not merely relating to performance gradings where the satisfaction of a job well done is the basic motivating factor underlying a healthy competitive attitude.

Woman not only nurtures life from its inception within the womb, through birth and the entire complex gamut of human existence, she nourishes and protects the child she has brought into the world. It is mandatory, therefore, that suitable provisions exist at the national planning and execution level to ensure that women's health, more so, those residing in rural and backward areas at barely subsistence levels, be taken care of in sufficient measure. As S.K. Sapru (Reader, Department of Public Administration, Panjab University) so rightly said : "An investment in health is an investment on human resources development on which depends the national development. Development of health in terms of quality of woman's life, is therefore imperative."

The World Plan of Action issued from the World Conference of International Women's Year (1975) 'is the most significant and far-reaching document about the human role of women ever to be conceived.' This all-encompassing document, which focuses on the need to place the situation of women separately in the center of the United Nations commitment to social progress for the human community, states emphatically that if women remain peripheral in the eyes of the policy-makers and decision takers, the human race cannot progress. Here we will only consider those excerpts as given below from the World Plan which directly or indirectly have a significant bearing on the health and overall well-being of women.

1. "In subscribing to the charter, the peoples of the United Nations undertook specific commitments : to save succeeding generations from the scourge of war... to reaffirm faith in fundamental human rights, in the dignity and worth of the human person, in the equal rights of men and women and of nations large and small, and ... to promote social progress and better standards of life in larger freedom.

2. As a result of the uneven development which prevails in international economic relations, three quarters of humanity is faced with urgent and pressing social and

economic problems. The women among them are even more affected by such problems and improvements in their situation, must by an integral part of the global project for the establishment of a new economic order.

3. The achievement of equality between men and women implies that they should have equal rights, opportunities and responsibilities to enable them to develop their talents and capabilities for their own personal fulfilment and the benefit of society. To that end, a reassessment of the functions and roles traditionally allotted to each sex within the family and community at large is essential. The necessity of a change in the traditional role of men as well as of women must be recognized. In order to allow for women equal participation in all societal activities, men must accept shared responsibility for home and children... "

The determinative factors implicit in the highly laudable principles or action-plan outline above, all in the long term have a vital bearing upon the physical well-being and good health of women. In fact the introduction to the Plan was followed by a series of highly useful guidelines for national action for the decade 1975 to 1985 which included some very specific recommendations for : a) more equitably distributing health care and nutrition services to take account of the responsibilities of women everywhere for the maintenance of health and provision of food for their families. b) reordering priorities with regard to social support systems for the family. Of course there were many other guidelines provided for the useful translation of principles into practice but we need not deal with them here.

Reiterating India's increasing awareness of the health factor, especially with regard to its womenfolk, and the imminent need to effect qualitative improvement on a priority basis, is the fact that it is a signatory of the Alma Ata Declaration recommending "Health For All by AD 2000". The 20-point programme provides a special thrust to the issue of improving women's health and pinpoints various measures for doing so.

The primary aim of the health policy in India is the promotion of health care services leading to improvement in the health status of her people; practically what seems to have happened, is embodied poignantly in the following words taken from the Book of Common Prayer:

> We have left undone those things which we ought to have done; we have done those things which we ought not to have done; And there is no health in us.

In spite of impressive progress in certain areas, the vital sphere of women's health "has largely been neglected. A large proportion of rural women have no access to health care and for many of the rest what they receive does not alleviate their problems." Estimates till about a decade ago indicated trends that approximately 80 per cent of rural women and 80 per cent of the poor urban women in India receive little medical care. Obviously the situation would only have improved since then bringing an increasing percentage of similarly affected women, within the ambit of greater health care facilities. But how much, remains to be analysed and assessed accurately. However, it cannot be denied that the health status of women has shown great improvement in the four decades immediately succeeding India's independence, particularly in the attainment of the basic health indicators, namely reduction in the maternal mortality rate 'from 4.8 (1976) to 3.5 (1986), and increase in life expectancy from 51.6 (1980) to 56.5 (1986), reduction in the female infant mortality rate from 148 (1972) to 100 (1985) and production of women power and so on.'

Possession of sound health by women is important for a host of other reasons, other than the well-being of the women themselves. It considerably reduces the financial burden of the family because she can then contribute to the income of the family whenever the opportunity comes. It promotes more hygienic living conditions within the home and (hopefully) more sustaining victuals for the entire family, because if the woman is in good health she will be able to devote sufficient time and attention to these important duties within the home. Furthermore, the greater exposure of women to health care and access to such facilities has led to 'women's assumptions of a range of social roles ' and created an awareness of higher and better living standards in general. This, in turn, has proved to be an important determinant for reducing the family size as raising the standard of living is certainly not compatible with maintaining a large family efficiently and in good health. It has thus led to lower fertility patterns and also a more positive participation in life outside the home, be it social, political or in the sphere of economics and holding on to jobs continuously for a greater length of time. Further good health is an essential determinant for understanding social problems and coping with social changes. Therefore, extension of health care facilities to women enhances the prospect for relative equality within the home. To this effect a fair number of conferences have been held from time to time, one such was by the International Union for Health Education (IUHE) and the South East Asia Regional Bureau (SEARB)—the Second Regional Conference on Promotion of Women's Health and Welfare for Better Child Survival, held in Bangalore some years back.

Inextricably and irrevocably linked to the task of effectively facing the challenge of promoting women's health and welfare for the family's future, is the imminent need to strengthen professional education and training.

To evolve a perceptive and result oriented strategy, it is imperative — maintain Premalata Pujari and Vijay Kumari Kaushik, authors of several viable works on women's development— to consider the two facets of the role of women, in production and reproduction, in tandem with each other. In order to release women's potential for fuller participation in the productive and decision making processes, there is a need not only for sharing of parental responsibilities but also for institutional provisions which would benefit children and families. Women should have the right, the requisite knowledge and the resources to regulate their reproductive capacity. Many governments have launched subsidized family planning programmes and even offered incentives to encourage people to reduce and limit the size of their families. Experience has shown that a predominantly clinical approach which threatens social values, beliefs and customs does not succeed and is, paradoxically, even a disincentive. How then does one break through the vicious circle of poverty, high fertility and mortality rates among the affected population? Obviously through recourse to a more carefully planned and more humane public policy with a judicious balance between individual choice and dignity and promotion of a sense of responsibility among parents to ensure a better future for their children. This could be further stimulated and promoted through various forms of technical assistance at various levels, as well as enriched through mutual exchange of information and experience among developing countries. Such information, techniques and the dissemination of useful practical knowledge then imparted to relatively large groups of women at the grassroots level through government-sponsored or voluntary agencies competitively equipped for the purpose. For the mode and level of communication is of vital importance here, appropriate degrees of sensitivity and compassion while dealing with much a delicate issue, are essential to ensure positive results. The pressure target groups here should preferably constitute women from lower income groups with a low level of literacy, low and insecure income and low health and nutritional levels, which are more prone to be quite disastrous for they are bound to affect adversely the efforts of countries to achieve food security and to reduce pressure on the natural resources; also their effect on urbanization and on land and capital will exacerbate inequalities. While insufficient food supplies will drastically degrade nutrition and health levels, extreme urbanization will bring its own set of health hazards in its wake.

Rapid urbanization in developing countries has caused serious problems since a large proportion of urban migrant workers are living in temporary hutments and settlements, in sub-standard conditions and without adequate basic amenities. The growth of cities and the steep rise in rural-urban migration, is a manifestation of imbalances in the location and expansion of productive activity. Women are most severely affected as many of their activities are connected directly with their homes, and bad housing and deplorable conditions of hygiene and sanitation are infinitely detrimental to both themselves and their families health. The rapid growth and expansion of cities has also created severe ecological imbalances and resultant problems. Obviously, the growing demands of expanding cities have exercised undue pressure on natural resources, effectively destroying the harmony between man and nature, and has led to a degradation of productive resources like water, land and forests. With increasing pressure on the land, overgrazing and deforestation, severe environmental damage has resulted.

The expansion of agriculture and subsequent deforestation of substantial tracts of land, has led to severe soil erosion and paved the way for undesirable, desert like conditions, an extremely serious problem which exists already in Sub-Saharan Africa, North-Western Asia and the Middle East. Forests are crucial to the ecological life of many developing countries, like India; therefore deforestation has created major problems, as the consumption of forest resources has exceeded replacement possibilities through natural growth. This has not only affected millions of rural households and the vital role of women in these households, it has also affected in a positively detrimental fashion the nutritional level in these families. The unbelievably high human costs of malnutrition, famine and disruption in the lives of people such as these are disastrous and prone to promoting further ill health, disease and harmfully retrogressive economic trends.

Environmental issues 'conceiving the environment in its broadest social context' are most relevant to women. The increasing marginalization of certain sections of the population, growing poverty and deprivation of the masses, decreasing food production, the energy crisis and human environmental degradation in numerous developing countries are all 'symptoms of a pattern of growth and resource utilization which is geared to existing power structures and prevents a large section of the population from satisfying its basic needs.'

The section on health in the Draft National Perspective Plan for Women suffers from the inherent flaw of a failure to perceive that, fundamental to any review of the health status of women in India, has to be an analysis of the socio-economic factors accounting for the pitiful condition of overall health in the country. It states, rather erroneously, that 'any serious attempt to improve the health of women must deal firstly with the biased social customs and cultural traditions' as well as that 'the enormous wastage of female life and well-being occurring at present has been demonstrated to be well within human capacity and existing resources to contain'. Whereas it is obvious to any discerning reader that social customs and cultural traditions, whatever they may be, cannot prove to be insurmountable obstacles in the face of a decisive and imaginatively planned policy/strategy for improving the health of women in our country. As for 'containing' the 'enormous wastage of female life and well-being' well, surely, such an ambitious goal cannot be realized unless there is a radical restructuring of priority in our socio-economic framework. As well as a broad-based, multipronged highly efficient and technologically advanced health care system with practical conduit facilities to provide appropriate care and medication as and when needed. Establishment of such a system would necessarily require vast allocation of funds on a regular basis.

While the draft plan does point towards the need for radical restructuring of the highly inadequate health care delivery system in regard to women, it is astonishingly silent about the meagre allocation of funds by the Government to Health. A brief glance at the Table 16.1 below shows the progressive reduction in budgetary allocation for health in successive Five Year Plans (not inclusive of allocation for Family Planning) :

Table 16.1
Plan Allocation for Health

Plan Period	*Per cent Share of Healt Budget*
1st Five Year Plan	3.30
2nd Five Year Plan	3.00
3rd Five Year Plan	2.60
4th Five Year Plan	2.10
5th Five Year Plan	1.90
6th Five Year Plan	1.86

Source : India 1986, Ministry of Information and Broadcasting, Government of India.

The result of such low priority given to health, judged from data available approximately a decade ago, is :

(a) only 20 per cent of our people have access to modern medicine;

(b) 84 per cent of health care costs are paid for privately;

c) only 33 per cent of deliveries are attended by trained people;

(d) Maternal mortality is 400 - 500 per 1,00,000 live births and figures from some rural areas are as high as 1000 - 1200. It is estimated that Indian women run a life-time risk of one in 18 of dying from pregnancy related causes. And the draft itself admits that 70 per cent of these deaths can be prevented;

(e) 50 per cent of children and 65 per cent of women suffer from iron deficiency—anaemia;

(f) only 25 per cent of children are covered by the immunization programme. 13 million (3000 a day) children die of diseases which could have been prevented by immunization;

(g) 1/3 of the total population of India is exposed to Malaria, Filaria and Kalazar every year;

(h) 5,50,000 people die of T.B. every year. About 9,00,000 people get infected by tuberculosis every year;

(i) about half a million people are affected with leprosy which is 1/3 of the total number of leprosy patients in the world;

(j) 1.5 million children die due to diarrhoea every year;

(k) a comparison of Infant Mortality Rates (IMR i.e., number of deaths under the age of one months per thousand live births) of some countries in 1960 and 1985 shows that many countries with a poorer or comparable record 20 years back are today much ahead of India. (Table 16.2)

Table 16.2

Comparative Study of IMR in some Countries

Country	*IMR in 1960*	*IMR in 1985*
Turkey	190	84
Egypt	179	93
Algeria	168	81
India	165	105
Vietnam	160	72
China	150	36
UAE	145	35
El Salvador	142	65
Jordan	135	49

Source : The State of the World's Children 1987— UNICEF.

In addition, if one makes a comparative study of the percentage allocation on health in some other countries as compared to India, the callousness of the situation is further highlighted. Table 16.3 illustrates this point :

Table 16.3

Percentage Allocation on Health in some Countries

Country	*Percentage of Central Government Expenditure Allocated to Health(1983)*
Bolivia	3.1
India	2.4
Egypt	2.8
Zaire	3.2
Iran	5.7
Zimbabwe	6.1
Kenya	7.0
Brazil	7.3
Switzerland	13.4
FRG	18.6

Source : the State of the World's Children — 1987, UNICEF.

Meagre as they are, even these resources are not equitably distributed and judiciously used, in a ratio proportionate to need. A major portion of these resources, about 80 per cent, are spent on big hospitals and research institutions which are situated in metropolitan cities and large, flourishing urban centres. They cater to approximately 20 per cent of the people. On the other hand, just a meagre 20 per cent of the resources are utilized for primary health care which caters to a staggering 80 per cent of the population. It is a universally recognized fact that the Primary Health Care System has to be drastically overhauled and then strengthened if the devastating figures, particularly those pertaining to maternal mortality rates, are to be brought down. Notwithstanding the semantics of the draft plan where it categorically states, "recognising that the renewal of the human race is the unique contribution that women make at considerable personal cost to the nation's existence and productivity, it must be taken as a national obligation to ensure that the fulfilment of this role occurs with minimum personal risk to women's lives and health" the national infrastructure for translating this noble precept into a practical reality, does not exist. The annual report of the Ministry of Health and Family Welfare (1987-88) very candidly states, "because of the resource constraints, only 50 per cent of the Community Health Centres would be established by 1990." Which, translated into practical, brutal reality means that the lives of lakhs of women who today die needlessly, are expendable.

Apart from the resource crunch and other relevant issues, one of the major problems for the PHC system has been the monumental burden imposed on it by the FPP or Family Planning Programme with its terrible fetish for targets. At the cost of health, particularly that of women, the Government has pushed such programmes through. Expenditure in this area is increasing by leaps and bounds. From a mere 0.14 crores in the First Plan to 409 in the 5th Plan, 1426 crores in the 6th Plan and a proposed whopping 3256 crores in the 7th Plan (equalling the outlay on health of 3392 crores).

While the draft plan seeks to present the family planning programme as a progressive measure, opening the choice of control of their lives and health to women, in actual fact it has virtually become an assault on women. This is evidenced by the fact that accompanying the increase in expenditure, female sterilizations have increased, amounting to almost 90 per cent of all sterilizations. Many of these operations, the draft plan itself admits, are being performed without proper care and follow-up, leading to severe complications.

The draft plan has cursorily touched upon the need to emphasize the preventive and promotive aspects of health. It has failed in the all important task of pinpointing both the responsibilities as well as the methodology of bringing this about. India has the dubious distinction of being among those countries who have the lowest life expectancies in the world. About 75 per cent of all diseases in India are caused due to malnutrition, contaminated water and non-immunization. The majority of diseases can, thus, be prevented or at least reduced drastically to begin with, by the supply of clean drinking water, by providing adequate nutrition to all, by timely immunization of children against prevalent diseases, as well as by ensuring a reasonably clean and hygienic environment and educating women about common ailments with useful information of how to contain them and prevent them from further degenerating into something more serious. It is indeed pathetic and a cause for serious concern that out of the 23 million children born every year 2.5 million die within the first two years ; of the rest, one of nine roughly dies before the age of four, or five out of ten suffer from malnutrition. The Plan bluntly states 'women from infancy to adulthood are the worst victims of this assault of malnutrition' their agony further compounded as victims of social discrimination as well. So, even though the food grain production in India increased from 82 million tonnes in 1961 to 124 million tonnes in 1983, the per capita intake decreased from 400 gms of cereals and 69 gms of pulses to 392 gms and 38 gms respectively. Due to the rapidly increasing economic burden on a majority of the people and women being a substantial proportion of such an underprivileged section of our society, the food supplies that were theoretically available could not be purchased. Due to the blatant and sharp unequal distribution of the wealth and resources of the nation, such people lacked basic purchasing power. Resultantly the health of the vast majority of women, already adversely affected by increasing poverty and exploitation, deteriorated even further, making them increasingly vulnerable to debilitating malnutrition and deficiency related illnesses.

On the basis of the Medium-Term Programme for Technical Cooperation among Developing Countries for Health for All (1984-89) and in view of the urgent calls for an acceleration of the development of national health care capabilities and the establishment of local points for TCDC in the area of health, the highly committed duo of Premlata Pujari and Vijay Kumari Kaushik—authors of *Women Power In India,* have identified certain priority activities below :

(i) introduction of an effective health surveillance system at the national level, of health indicators for target setting and formulation of national priorities and plans of action, and of appropriate systems for assessing strengths and weaknesses of national health programmes;

(ii) linking of health policies and programmes with economic development and those facilities which can directly reduce women's drudgery and work burden and directly improve their health situation, i.e., provision of adequate housing, water supply, sanitation, health regulations at the work-place, and health protection of women, particularly those working in the informal sector of the economy who are not covered by social protection policies;

(iii) integration of maternal and child health care with family planning services and accelerated development of national capacities through development of health institutions and infrastructures and increase of the number of health experts and particularly health workers;

(iv) involvement of women's organization in primary health care activities and their representation on national and local health councils;

(v) promotion of health education and indigenous system of health care;

(vi) involvement of women's organizations in primary health care activities and their representation on national and local health councils;

(vii) promotion of health education and indigenous systems of health care;

(viii) introduction of ECDC/TCTC programmes for the promotion of industries which are important for the development of health care systems. The developing countries could evolve suitable mechanisms for cooperation in training and development of human resources, collaborative research, joint programming, exchange of information and references, and exploring the application of low-cost technologies for water supply and waste disposal.

Certain milestones have been achieved in the Sixth, Seventh and Eighth Five Year Plans to address some of the glaring shortfalls in the area of women's health and the scenario is not quite so dismal now. We furnish below and evaluate the salient features and achievements of each Five Year Plan mentioned above, in a systematic and dispassionate manner.

Sixth Plan

This plan aimed to expand the minimum health care facilities and link them in such a manner which is integral to family welfare and nutrition. Improving women's health and nutritional status acquired paramount importance, for the nutritional status of a child at birth is directly proportional to the nutritional status of its mother during the entire term of her pregnancy and at the time of birth. It is a well established fact that a majority of pregnant and nursing mothers, especially those belonging to the low socio-economic strata of society, consume diets which are highly inadequate and lacking in requisite vitamins, iron, calcium intakes, etc., which leads to a high incidence of premature, underweight babies as well as to neo-natal mortality. Under the Integrated Child Development Services (ICDS), special nutrition was provided both to pregnant women as well as to lactating mothers, and by the end of the Sixth Plan it was indeed gratifying to know that 1.2 million such women had benefited substantially from the programme. Prophylactic programmes to prevent and reduce the incidence of nutritional anaemia among pregnant and nursing mothers were implemented on a fairly large-scale. In addition, iron and folic acid tablets were distributed to over 72.5 million would-be and nursing mothers and Tetanus Toxoid administered to about 36 million expectant mothers.

Adequate provision was made for expanding maternal and child health (MCH) programmes including antenatal, natal and postnatal services and proper training of popular *dais* who are already practising in the villages, so as to reduce maternal and neonatal deaths and complications. In order to meet the increasing requirement of sub-centres and to overcome field problems, training capacity for ANMs or auxiliary nurse midwives was further augmented and the minimum requisite educational qualifications relaxed. The latter was done in order to induct local women as ANMs and girls who had cleared the seventh grade were accepted for training if those with higher educational qualifications could not be found. To facilitate enrolment, the upper age limit of ANMs was also raised.

The long term approach of the Sixth Plan in attempting to eradicate malnutrition among women, included generating employment among them, thus equipping them with greater purchasing power and the sure ability to raise the nutritional levels of the entire family. To facilitate opportunities for employment and subsequently for holding on to such jobs, so that they could benefit substantially economically, the creation of creche-cum-*balwadis* was also planned for the comfort and convenience of such working mothers.

Seventh Plan

Despite the various measures incorporated in the Sixth Plan for considerably improving the health and nutritional status of women, especially from the weaker sections of our society, the Seventh Plan Perspective recorded certain observations and major areas of concern which needed to be tackled on an urgent basis. Reproduced below are some important excerpts :

> The health problems of women in society at large is another crucial area which is substantially ignored. Due to the predominantly patriarchal order, women are confined within an oppressive environment.
>
> Nutritional surveys have indicated high rates of inadequacies among females as compared to males. Female infants and children are subject to neglect in respect of nutrition and health care. Statistics from primary health centres show that adult women do not generally take treatment from them. Maternal mortality continues to be very high. Anaemia among rural women is estimated to be as high as 60-80 per cent which leads to low birth weight among babies.

In view of the above problems, under the health sector, the major thrust envisaged by the architects of the Seventh Five Year Plan for the next ten years, was the reduction of the high rate of mortality then prevailing among mothers and infants. With this aim in mind, they planned to increase MCH care with special emphasis on preventative, promotive and educational services. They also aimed at making health and family welfare services available to all women in the vital reproductive age group, increasing the bed strength in the various district hospitals and allocating a sizeable proportion of these for women and children. To ensure better treatment and care, the health sub-centres coverage for providing health services would be progressively reduced to below 5000 persons per centre. Apart from stepping up of schemes to hand out nutritional supplements and iron and folic acid tablets to mothers to counter the calorie-vitamin and mineral deficiency and fight anaemia, it was thought to expand significantly the training services for birth attendants and ANMs. Mass media, voluntary agencies, village health committees, women's organization's and *dais* were all sought to be utilized for the spread of useful information and knowledge regarding simple remedies for common disorders; women cautioned against misleading advertisements regarding the use of tonics, health drinks, etc. Published information regarding the demographic and socio-cultural implications of the then existing sex ratio and early age of marriage would be widely publicized; important information about the nutritional status of girls and its impact on the health and weight of babies born in times to come, has been included here.

The Eighth Plan

The planners of the Eighth Five Year Plan, who applied a more holistic approach towards women's role in the family and society as diametrically opposed to the hitherto restricted view of her as mother and homemaker alone, presented a budget more sensitive to the needs and problems of women, than before. Thus conceived that a major thrust in the strategy for women's development would be on the formation and strengthening of grassroot level women's groups....... "Services for women under various programmes of employment, education, health care, family welfare, drinking water and nutrition would be made available at the grass root level in the form of a package through convergence and integration."

One of the constructive features of this broad-based programme for women now included a hitherto neglected category viz. adolescent girls who had not so far benefited, or even been a target of various social service programmes. Prime importance would now be given to their developmental needs in order to prepare them suitably for their adult roles. Special programmes would be developed for young and adolescent girls, as females in this segment of society have generally suffered on account of food nutrition as well as restrictive social customs and health care.

In the ongoing battle against nutrition, special efforts would be made to bring about a change in the discriminatory attitude of society with regard to the food intake of females within the family and in the traditional beliefs and practices, wherever prevalent, with regard to the essential nutritional needs of women. Nutrition programmes, fashioned with particular care, would lay emphasis on nutrition education, particularly increasing the awareness about the specific nutritional needs of women especially during infancy, adolescence, pregnancy and breast-feeding of the newborn.

Mass media, as an important agent of change, information and knowledge, would play a major role in propagating vital news, views and information concerning women's nutrition. Powerful audio-visual aids like documentary files, video tapes and audio-cassettes would be produced and transmitted widely through radio, cinema, television and other communication channels. Not only would booklets and pamphlets containing relevant data, be produced on a large-scale for the community but exhibitions on the theme 'Women's Nutrition and Health' would be organized as well in rural, urban and slum areas. Further strengthening this multipronged approach, camps and short-term nutrition training programmes would be arranged for women, adolescent girls, women's organizations and school girls by trained ICDS workers, ANMs, teachers, members of Mahila Mandals and through informal channels. Furthermore, for effective implementation of training programmes, educational material would be produced in local languages.

While local women's organizations as well as the female adolescent population would be encouraged to promote the active participation of women in the monitoring of nutrition care and social support measures provided for them, certain other important link-ups were also provided. The nutrition education programme would be linked with other programmes like family planning, environmental sanitation, potable water supply, ecological balance, horticulture, education and training for income generation, etc. Thus imbuing this underprivileged and relatively ignorant and uninformed segment of our society, with confidence based on knowledge and awareness based on information. To make them both individually and collectively, into citizens that the country would be proud of.

References

Pujari, Premlata and Kaushik, Vijay Kumari, 'Women and the Development Process, *Women Power in India — Institutional Systems for Women's Development*, Vol. 2, Delhi : Kanishka Publishers, Distributors, 1994.

Pujari, Premlata and Kaushik, Vijay Kumari, 'Approaches to Planning for Women's Development', *Women Power in India — Institutional Systems for Women's Development*, Vol. 2, Delhi: Kanishka Publishers, Distributors, 1994.

Pujari, Premlata and Kaushik, Vijay Kumari, *'Health Systems for Women's Development'*, *Women Power in India — Institutional Systems for Women's Development*, Vol. 2, Delhi: Kanishka Publishers, Distributors, 1994.

Sapru, R.K., 'Some Determinants for Women's Development', *Women and Development*, New Delhi: Ashish Publishing House, 1989.

17
THE DOWNTRODDEN DALITS

"DALIT DYNAMITE" boldly screamed the evocative caption over the picturized political cameos of Kanshi Ram and Mayawati, jubilant at the downfall of the Vajpayee government on 17th April, 1999. The blurb under the caption, expanding gleefully on its theme, read thus: "The most unreliable pair in Indian politics will demand a price. They'll want to unseat the BJP regime in Uttar Pradesh and injure Mulayam. With them Congress can't rebuild Dalit base."

'Beginning of a Nightmare',
Cover story in *India Today*, April 26, 1999

This is now as India stands poised on the threshold of its entry into a new millennium. And a new, more lasting political order? That is a vitally crucial query, the answer to which is still crystallizing in the crucible of a complex political phenomena. What emerges, and, more important, which dominant or disparate political party/coalition comes to power, will have far-reaching consequences not only on the destiny of the Dalits but on the fate of other downtrodden and backward classes of people in our vast subcontinent as well. However, that particular political prognosis will prove the political maturity of its citizens at a later date, stand testimony to India's fate at a distant point in the future. Needless to mention that the multipronged policies for the progress of Indian womanhood will also depend on the broad spectrum of activities undertaken by such a government, its perceptions of women's imminent needs and whether or not it considers it imperative to right the balance. So, before we discuss the position and problems of the Dalit women, it is necessary to first recapitulate how the Dalit movement originated and who were its progenitures.

The present usage of the term *dalit* goes back to the nineteenth century when a Marathi social reformer and revolutionary, Mahatma Jotirao Phule, used it to describe the outcastes and untouchables as the oppressed and broken victims of the Indian caste-ridden society, maintains James Massey in *Dalits in India*. At the same time it is believed that this usage was first coined by B.R. Ambedkar. But it was during the 1970s that followers of the Dalit Panther Movement of Maharashtra gave currency to the term *Dalit* as a constant reminder of their age-old oppression, denoting both their state of deprivation and people who are oppressed.

Today, however, this term is used frequently and has become popular among the Dalit people of various protest movements in India and even Christian circles. Besides its widespread common usage, the term *dalit* in the present day modern context, is specially used for those people who, on the basis of caste distinction, have been considered "outcaste". Such a socially derogatory and humanly degrading distinction was made 'because they were not according to the architects of the system fit to be included in the fourfold graded caste structure of Indian society'. On the basis of such a low delineative status they were 'made to bear extreme kinds of disabilities in the form of oppression for centuries, which made them almost lose their humanness'.

It is not within the purview of this chapter to discuss in great detail the historical roots of the Dalits but suffice to say that such a derivative academic exploration can take place broadly under the four following heads :

1. The Rigveda
2. The Archaeologists
3. The Rigveda and the Archaeologists
4. Development of the Dalit problem

The most important task is to identify the time or period when the Dalits of today started losing their identity. `For at that particular time, the history of the Dalits began. Before they were not in a Dalit State; they were normal human beings enjoying their full self-identity'. Hence the attempt to establish, albeit in brief, the historical roots of the Dalits.

The Rigveda

Chronologically, the Rigveda is the earliest (and the most important) written literary source of the ancient history of India. A significant portion of the text which is addressed to Lord Indra, narrates a fierce war-encounter having taken place among different groups. Two opposing forces may be seen in the *Rigveda* — *first*, on whose behalf the hymns of the *Rigveda* are addressed to different gods and, *second*, against whom they are addressed. The learned Ramprasad Chanda, making this important observation, maintains that "These hymns reveal two hostile peoples in the land of the Seven Rivers now called the Punjab—the deva worshipping Arya and deva-less and the riteless Dasyu or Dasa." This conflict between the two major groups of people took place around the middle of the second millennium (1500 BC). Very likely this is the point or moment in history from which the history of the people known as Dalits began. Let us examine a few of the relevant verses from the *Rigveda* which throw light on these two opposing groups of ancient times :

I (a) *vi janihayaran ye ch dasyvo....*
You (Indra) know well Aryas and Dasyus...

(b) *...hatavi dusyun prarya vaarnamavata.*
...he (Indra) killed the Dasyus and protected the Aryan race (colour)

II. (a) *Indra panch Kachhatinama.*
Indra is the ruler of the five (races)

(b) *Tadindragni Yadus Turvasesu yad*
Druhyus Pavanusu Purusus sath.

O Indra-Agni, you live among (the people of)
the Yadus, Turvasas, Druhyus, Anus and Purus.

(c) *par yat samudramati sur parshi*
paraya Turvasa Yadu svasita.
O hero (Indra)! When you came over the seas,
you brought over it Turvasa and Yadu.

III (a) *vadhihi dasyu dhanini...*
You (Indra) killed rich Dasyu...

(b) *akarma dasyurabhi no amanturanya -varto*
amanus.
All around us ritualless Dasyu, inhuman, who are
following alien laws.

(c) *anaso dasyu...*
Noseless dasyu...

IV (a) *sa jatubharma chhadadadhana ojo.*
puro vimindannacharada vi dasi.
vidana vajirna dasyuve hetimasnarya
saho vadhrya sumamindar...
dasyu hatyaya
Armed with his thunderbolt, Indra went about
destroying the forts of Dasas.
O Indra, throw your thunderbolt at the Dasyus,
increase the power and glory of Aryas.

(b) *yo hatavahimarinata sapat sindhuna*
yo go udajadapadha valasaya
yo asamanorantargina jajana
savivak sa janam Indra.
One who killed the Dragon and freed the Seven
Rivers (Saptasindhu):
he who drove the cows from the Vala,
One who created fire between stones,
and had beaten the warriors in battle,
He, O people, is Indra.

(c) *sa vartrahendra Karsunayoni*
purandaro dasiraraiyada vi...

hatavi dasyuna pura ayasinin tarita.
Indra the Vartra-killer, fort-destroyer,
scattered the dasa,
who dwelt in darkness...

he killed the Dasyus and broke the forts made of iron.

V (a) *dasa cha vartra hatamayrani cha*
Sudasmindravrunavasavatama.
Indra and Varuna killed the Dasa and Arya who were Sudas enemies and helped him with favour.

(b) *yo no dasa ayro vapurustutadeva*
Indra yudve chiketati
O Most respected Indra, the godless people, whether Dasas or Arya, who want war with us.

VI (a) *yatha deva asureshu sadramugaresu chakirre.*
Even the gods kept faith in the mighty Asuras.

(b) *hatyaya deva asurana...*
When the gods killed Asuras...

VII (a) *apasedhana raksaso yatudhanansthada deva...*
Driving off raksasas and Yatudhanas, the god is present...

(b) *jahi nyatrina pani varko hisa*
You (Soma) kill Pani. He is like a wolf.

It is not at all surprising to infer from a serious Rigvedic hymnology, therefore, about the numerous contemptuous allusions to the obviously inferior Dasyus, who were believed to be 'ritualless, inhuman, following alien laws'. References were made to their colour as 'dark and dusky skin', they were rather insultingly described as "noseless" which meant that 'the appearance of their faces differed from that of the Aryas'. As did their racial and cultural salient features from this obviously superior race.

The Archaeologists

While archaeological sources are, undoubtedly, a great help in reaching the historical roots of the Dalits, such archaeological literature, it must be remembered, has not been written keeping the Dalits in mind; however, the fact that it sheds abundant light on various significant aspects of the life of the ancient peoples of India, helps us to restructure the social system then prevailing and come to our own conclusions about caste denominations and differential treatment of peoples, among other things. In this connection the stupendous work of reference *Ancient Cities of the Indus*, edited by Gregory L. Possehl and containing the main research papers written between 1924 and 1979 by such 'famous pioneer archaeologists' such as John Marshall, Ernest Mackay, Mortimer Wheeler, and well-known Indian archaeologists S.R. Rao, Gurdip Singh, C. Ramasamy, Iravathan Mahadevan, A. Ghosh, B.M. Pandey, B.B.Lal is invaluable. As are the individual tomes authored by Ernest Mackay and Mortimer Wheeler titled *Early Indus Civilization* and *The Indus Civilization* respectively.

The Rigveda and the Archaeologists

Research and diligent dissemination of relevant historical data has proved that :

(a) the groups of people mentioned in the *Rigveda* are the same as those established by the archaeological findings at ancient sites such as Mohenjodaro and Harappa. Basically they belonged to two groups, one already settled at these places and the other invaders.

(b) Both the *Rigveda* and archaeological findings testify to the fact that calamity struck the people and their cities in the form of floods, climatic changes, and in a major way invasions.

(c) The time of conflict between the two major groups of people took place around the middle of the second millennium. This is possibly the point in history from which the history of the people known as Dalit begins.

Historical Development of the Dalit Problem

It is reasonable to assert from the data established above, that the history of the Dalits began almost 3500 years ago. The prolific writer H.G. Wells tells us how at that point of history, one group (the nomad folk) vanquished the other groups (the settled folk) and how, subsequently, the history of both the groups was completely changed. He wrote :

> Down pour the united nomads on the unwarlike unarmed plains; there ensues a war of conquest. Instead of carrying off the booty, the conquerors settle down on the conquered land which becomes all booty for them; the villagers and townsmen are reduced to servitude and tribute-paying, they become hewers of wood and drawers of water, and the leaders of the nomads become kings and princes, masters and aristocrats.

Other writers like Ramprasad Chanda, Prabhati Mukherjee, Romila Thapar in *From Lineage to State*, have reiterated similar views. Whereas J. Waskom Picket states that Dalits have been reduced to their present state "by centuries of exploitation and servility."

Therefore, it is relevant to record here and substantiate the Dalit phenomena — its evolution and existence — as rooted in historicity, relevant religious texts and early societies and not as some modern mania juxtaposed upon the map of time in a haphazard or quixotic manner. As such, the Upanishads, composed between 800 BC and the end of the sixth century BC, contain references that by the time these texts came into existence, 'the problem of the Dalits was getting entrenched.... the *Chandogya Upanishad*, not only refers to the three upper castes, but also compares Chandala (outcaste) with a dog or a swine. In the tenth *Khanda*, verse seven reads as follows :

> Accordingly, those who are of pleasant conduct here—the prospect is, indeed, that they will enter a pleasant womb, either the womb of a Brahman, or the womb of a Ksatriya, or the womb of a Vaisya.

> But those who are of stinking conduct here—the prospect is, indeed, that they will enter a stinking womb—either the womb of a dog, or the womb of a swine or the womb of an outcaste (*chandala*).

This verse, therefore, not only conclusively testifies to the existence of caste but by referring to the womb of an outcaste as "a stinking" one, it clearly establishes the further degradation of the Dalits.

The two great Indian epics, the *Ramayana* and the *Mahabharata* explicitly tell us how far the condition of the Dalits had deteriorated by the time these were composed. In the former, which was composed around the 5th century BC, the point is illustrated through an apt anecdote related by sage Valmiki, the author of *Ramayana*. In the latter (*Mahabharata*), in which the different stages of composition have been fixed by scholars differently i.e. the period of the Pandu stage being between 600 BC and 200 BC and the Krishna stage between 200 BC and 500 AD, unjust caste distinction is brought out through the sensitively rendered incident of Ekalavaya, a low caste indigenous boy who had to lose his right thumb because he had learnt archery and was in no way inferior to Arjun in his skill; low castes or the Dalits did not have the right to education in those times, hence Ekalavya apparently committed the ultimate blasphemy.

The *Srimad Bhagavad Gita* not only affirms faith in the four castes but also maintains that these had been created by Lord Krishna himself. The only difference here being that `by taking refuge in Lord Krishna, the outcaste, women, Vaisyas and also Sudras can attain the highest goal'.

Among the literary sources which throw abundant light on the pathetic, degraded state of the Dalits is the *Manusmriti* which is believed to have come into existence between the years 1-700 AD. It is the authors of *Manusmriti*, who now onward even removed the human identity of the Dalits, who till then were considered outside the pale of the *chaturvaryam* or four accepted castes, but their existence at least was recognized. According to the *Manusmriti*, however, the most hated groups were *Chandala* and *Sapaka'*, who were the offspring of a Sudra male from a Brahmin woman, and *Chandala* male and a *Pukkasa* female respectively'. Narrating the degraded non-human state of these groups, the *Manusmriti* 10.51.52, says disparagingly :

> The dwelling of Chandals and Cavpacas (sapaka) (should be) outside the village; they should be deprived of dishes (apapatra); their property (consists of) dogs and asses. Their clothes (should be the garments of the dead, and their ornaments (should be) of iron, and their food (should be) in broken dishes; and they must constantly wander about.

Thus by the time the *Manusmriti's* composition was complete — around 700 AD - the negative development of the Dalits had not only reached its climax but even the followers of the non-controversial Gautam Buddha were considered untouchables. In course of time, 'Buddhism also got influenced by the caste system'. In post-Independence India, hundreds of thousands of Mahar Dalits of Maharashtra became Buddhists, in 1956 and later and their progeny are known as *Bauddh*, which in Marathi has become a synonym for Mahar (untouchable). Thus, it came about that the protest of Jainism and Buddhism, against Brahmanism or the Hindu caste system, in course of time got diluted.

The Muslim Period

One would have thought that with the Arabs' first conquest of Sind in 712 AD and the long period of Muslim domination in India from the time the Slave Dynasty established its rule in India in 1206 AD, through successive Muslim rulers and dynasties like the Khiljis, Sayyids, Suris and Moghuls, till the death of the last Mughal King Bahadur Shah in 1862, there would have been 'some changes in the lot of the Dalits as Islam upholds the principle of equality of all human beings'. But after going through the social and religious conditions of the Muslim period and the written testimony of well-known travellers and scholars like Al-Biruni (1030 AD) and J.S. Grewal (among others), one is forced to admit, albeit extremely reluctantly, that the dismal state of the Dalits continued as before, without any reprieve. Al-Biruni states :

> The people called Hadi, Doma (Domba), Chandala, and Badhatau (sic) are not reckoned amongst any caste or guild. They are occupied with dirty work, like the cleaning of the villages and other services... they are considered like illegitimate children; for according to general opinion they descend from a Sudra father and a Brahmani mother as the children of fornication; therefore they are degraded outcastes.

In fact, a number of well-known research works have corroborated that Muslim society was divided into a number of different grades/classes, though not exactly like the Hindu caste system. The highest grade, which was and is comparable to the Hindu "twice-born" upper castes were Ashrafs (meaning honourable), Shaikhs (chiefs) and Mughals and Pathans (corresponding to the Hindu Kshatriyas). The middle group was made up of those who have clean occupations. The last group included the converts from the untouchables, who do scavenging, sweeping and other menial tasks. Grewal has also observed that the differences on the basis of religion or race or occupation were reflected in the morphology of cities and towns. Urban centres were divided into separate quarters for the various social groups. On the outskirts of the towns generally lived the scavengers, the leather dressers and the poor beggars... The respectable social groups among Muslims lived apart from the common populace...

"Acculturative influences of Hinduism" was very likely one of the reasons why the caste system continued to flourish even during the Muslim period with no change even in the case of the Dalits who embraced Islam. For more detailed dissemination on the subject, it would be advisable to refer to the introduction by Imtiaz Ahmad in his edited work *Caste and Social Stratification Among the Muslims*.

Other religions which were practiced during the Muslim period and more often than not, had their own peculiar caste or class distinctions, were many. The religions which came from outside India included Christianity, Judaism, Zoroastrianism and the Bahai faith. While the inscribed copper plates given to the Jewish leader Joseph Rabban by a Hindu King, conferred 72 privileges upon the Jews settled in Cochin (Kerala) and in and around Bombay (Maharashtra), similar privileges granted to the Syrian Christians by the Hindu King, gave both the communities the status of caste Hindus. The Jewish scholar, Shalva Weil, says about this phenomenon:

> In terms of the larger order of ranking, both these groups individually have had to internalize caste perceptions in order to provide legitimation for their ascribed status. As intermediaries in a ranked order of things between the local king and inferior castes, they have both, individually, shared what Fuller (1976) has termed a common "orthopraxy" with Hindus, while at the same time retaining theoretical adherence to the egalitarianism of the Judeo Christian tradition.

Both the ancient Jewish communities of Cochin and Bombay were divided into two main castes or *jatis* (groups) known simply as the *Gora* (White) Jews and *Kala* or (black) Jews. Mandelbaum maintains that these two groups of Jews, "did not interdine or intermarry, though they did worship in the same synagogues. Those of the higher *jati* claimed poorer Jewish ancestry. The lower, they alleged, were of mixed origins."

Surprisingly enough, even the Parsees, the followers of Zoroastrianism, were divided into four castes on the pattern of the Hindu caste system, before they came to India from Persia in the seventh century AD. These were :

(i) Clergy (*Athravans* = Guardians of the fire) corresponding to the Brahmins among the Hindus.
(ii) Warriors (*Rathaeshtars* = he who is standing on a war chariot) corresponding to the Kshatriyas.
(iii) Peasants (*Vactrya* = He who cultivates the land) corresponding to the Vaisyas and
(iv) Artisans (*Huiti* = Someone who produces objects corresponding to the Sudras.

But since the Parsees did not believe in conversion, so neither they nor the followers of Lingayatism or Veerasaivism, as the followers of Shiva are known in the pocket of northern Mysore in the state of Karnataka, could influence constructively the social order in India based on the caste system and thereby have some bearing on the plight of the Dalits. The Lingayats constituted too small a community to have an impact and despite their profession of egalitarianism and treating women as equals, "despite the explicit rejection of caste-ordering in Lingayat scripture, Lingayats group themselves into ranked jatis. The highest are the Jangamas, hereditary priests and teachers."

The second indigenous faith, apart from Lingayatism, which came into existence during the Muslim period was Sikhism 'which also upholds the concept of egalitarianism.' And while the founder of the Sikh religion, Guru Nanak, very sagaciously did away altogether with caste distinctions and ceremonials, there are any "number of testimonies available which show that by the time of the first half of the nineteenth century, the caste hierarchy among the Sikhs was well established." The erudite Ethne K. Marenco, while summing up the discussion on caste hierarchy among the Sikhs, gives us this broad overview on the subject :

> "... therefore from the evidence of the Sikh Empire period, the many sources show that the Sikh maintained

caste practices, despite the fact that their religious dogma was against caste... The original conversion to Sikhism was striving for upward mobility, particularly when the lower Hindu caste converted. This type of corporate caste mobility, where whole groups convert to a religion that promises them an escape from their lower caste position, has occurred more than once in India..."

Mark Juergensmeyer maintains in his thought provoking book *Religion as Social Vision* that "opportunities for ambitious social change come to the oppressed classes only in rare moments in history, moments in which change seems feasible and support for some sort of change seems available." A number of reform movements, including those by Christian missionaries, were at work for the betterment of the Dalits, which ultimately also influenced the British Government to do something in this regard.

Earlier Bhakti saints, who were mainly non-Brahmins or Dalits themselves, helped the cause of the Dalits in the spiritual sphere through their Bhakti Movement, later 'the momentum of other Untouchable activities across India encouraged the Adi Dharmis to organize, and the stalemate of communal politics in the Punjab made that organization opportune.' Untouchables began to form political and social organizations early in the twentieth century and the first independent Scheduled Caste political movements in India appeared to have been launched in 1910 when the All-India Depressed Classes Association and All-India Depressed Classes Federation were established under the active encouragement of the Bombay Presidency Social Reform Association. Their initial purpose was to pressurize the Indian National Congress to include the removal of untouchability as one of its main planks and they succeeded in the 1917 meeting of the Congress at Calcutta. Soon thereafter, the political climate changed substantially and the Government of India Act, which took effect in 1919, 'provided explicitly for communal representation in Indian parliaments. This stimulated the formation of new Scheduled Caste political organizations, which aimed not only to secure benefits for untouchables but also to organize them into coherent political blocks.'

Complex and diverse reform movements and political developments notwithstanding, the unforgettable contribution of some outstanding personalities, who were involved directly in the struggle either for change or reform, deserve to be mentioned here for they certainly left their impact on the present Dalit movements. They include Jotiba Phule, Ambedkar and Gandhi. While both Phule and Ambedkar were for the total uplift of the Dalits, Gandhi's work was limited to certain reforms, more within the Hindu society.

To Jotiba Phule (1826-90), the nineteenth century social revolutionary and main founder of the anti-caste movement in India, "the national unification of the masses of the people in India required an attack on Brahmin domination and Hinduism itself." This attack he carried on at all levels, elaborating a theory of history along with a reinterpretation of Indian mythology, and communicating to the masses with polemic tracts, songs, plays and organization-building. Perhaps the noble spirit behind his pioneering work can be assessed in the magnificient tribute that Ambedkar paid to him. Dedicating his work *Who were the Sudras* to Mahatma Jotiba Phule, as he respectfully called him, Ambedkar elaborates that he was :

> The greatest Sudra of modern India who made the lower classes among Hindus conscious of their slavery to the higher classes, and who preached the gospel that for India social democracy was more vital than independence from foreign rule.

Indeed, Phule's commitment to the cause and passionate zeal for the upliftment of his less fortunate brethren — he himself was of the Mali caste and possessed very little education — could best be summed up in the following words :

There cannot be a 'nation' worth the name until and unless all the people of the land of King Bali, such as the Shudras and Ati-Shudras, Bhils and fishermen, etc., become truly educated and are able to think independently for themselves and are uniformly unified and emotionally integrated.

By reversing the 'Aryan theory of race' and interpreting it 'in terms of a broader historical framework of a stress on force and violence in history, gave emphasis to a theory of exploitation that stressed the peasants as primary producers looted by the state'. And thus these low caste people whom Phule sometimes called 'Shudras and Ati-Shudras' and sometimes simply referred to as 'Kumbis, Malis, Dhangars... Bhils, Kolis, Mahars and Mangs', were the original inhabitants of the country, enslaved and exploited by conquering Aryans who had formulated a caste-based Hinduism as a means of deceiving the masses and legitimizing their own power. "The state exploited the peasants through direct extraction in the form of taxes, cesses and 'funds' of various kinds, and indirectly through takeover of their lands; as a result 'the peasants are so looted that they have neither bread to fill their stomachs nor clothes to cover their bodies." Phule's major work, *Shetkaryaca Asud*, expands further on the subject and sheds valuable light on practice and prejudice in this context.

Phule's descriptions of exploitation and his subsequent suggestions for economic development, centre around the peasantry and agriculture rather than subscribing to the elite's fascination for industrial development. His was a strong, two-pronged ideology, namely, that first he sought to build up the community of the exploited by emphasizing the attack on Brahminism and exploitation through religion; and second, by stressing the necessity of modern education and the acquisition of scientific knowledge, described as *vidya* as in contrast to the Brahminic and ritual bound *shastra*. He made it abundantly clear that education was a weapon to change 'eastern morals' and to bring about a kind of cultural education as well as a technological one. While in the cultural and educational field, he staunchly defended the enlightened Pandita Ramabai against the orthodox Brahmins who attacked her, arguing that while she had been a primary force in encouraging education among girls, the Brahmins had stopped sending their daughters and daughters-in-laws to schools since (they were 'throwing away the scriptures' and revolting against family authority), he also took other measures to improve the ambiently restrictive milieu. He not only wrote new marriage ceremonies, incorporating many significant peasant traditions but without the use of Brahmin priests, and stressing equality between men and women. He also took the courageous and rather radical step of proclaiming a new, theistic religion, the *'sarvajanik satya dharma'* with a strong, moralistic emphasis. His commendable initiation of a Buddhist conversion movement that ultimately attracted more than 3 million untouchable adherents, deserves special mention. As does his initiation of a program which led to the development of a system of colleges organized by the People's Education Society, for the advancement of untouchables. What is so commendable though, is that throughout, his emphasis on rationality and independent thinking remained.

Phule's concept of strengthening the position of the peasantry and promoting economic development, was an immensely modern one also. His focus here was on biotechnologies and watershed developments. He recommends the building of canals, bandhs, small and big dams to direct water to the fields, with soldiers and policemen providing the labour; returning to village control of all lands appropriated from them by the forest department; inter breeding with sheep and goats from other countries to increase production of organic manures as well as wool; sponsoring agricultural exhibits and holding training programmes and examinations, with awards for model farmers, to upgrade traditional skills; and reducing the pay of 'both white and black' government officials except for those in manual labour.

Another colossus in the field of the Dalit movement - infact, perhaps its most charismatic leader came-to the fore from the Marathi-speaking areas of the Bombay Presidency comprising three districts in the Konkan (Thana, Kolaba and Ratnagiri), five in western Maharashtra (Poona, Satara, Ahmednager, Sholapur and Nasik) and East and West Khandesh (present day Jalgoan and Dhule), in the first quarter of the present century. This was none other than Dr Ambedkar and as a result of various tumultuous and catalytic events in those early years, he made a conscious political choice in the context of Maharashtrian politics namely, the rejection of the existing nationalist politics and an alliance with the non-Brahmin movement. In Maharashtra, therefore, the Dalit movement was transformed from its genesis in 1920, to a liberation struggle with the famous Mahad satyagraha in 1927. Linked with the untouchables' rights to live as full human beings and a sustained agitation (in the 1920s) for the opening of public places, particularly wells and tanks, to untouchables. Connected to the highly casteist, horrifying reaction to A.V. Chitre, a Kayasth's injunction to the crowds to drink *en masse* from the Chawdar tank at the conclusion of the Kolaba Zilla Bahishkrut Parishad (Kolaba district conference of the boycotted) of which he was an activist. Ambedkar established the *Bahishkrut Bharat* to rally mass sympathy and support. Thus for the December 'satyagraha conference' to re-establish the right to drink water, "this brought a vastly increased mass of Dalits — between 10,000 and 15,000 — and featured the famous burning of the *Manusmriti*, a dramatic symbolic act that took away the sting from the fact that Ambedkar honoured the injunction of the district magistrate not to take water from the tank by calling off the 'satyagraha'. Later both events were known as the 'Mahad satyagraha', but it was the first day, 20th March, that was celebrated for a long time as Asprushya Swatantra Din or 'Untouchable Independence Day', the day of the mass struggle of Dalits to assert their human rights.

Apart from his valuable general support for peasant movements, Ambedkar, whose attitude was pro-peasant and anti-landlord, took up the special problems of the Dalits on two very significant fronts. One was fighting the specific caste-exploitation that was known in many areas as *vethbegar* or *vethi*. Initiating his campaign against the 'Mahar *watan*', which he perceived as 'a major aspect of Dalit exploitation, and the false security it provided as a major socio-psychological barrier keeping the Mahars integrated into an exploitative village community' he was responsible for initiating a struggle which would go on throughout the 1930s and 1940s. It was actually the concrete form of the fight against 'feudalism' which Marxists in many parts of India have struggled against with the general term *vethbegar*.

The other important question with which he was concerned was the 'problem of entry' or more appropriately from the point of view of the Dalit agricultural labourers, it could be termed as a 'problem of exit'. What *is* remarkable is that throughout his career Ambedkar adopted almost no programme or campaign for agricultural labourers as such; his main concern was that the Dalits should cease to be agricultural workers, that they should escape from their landlessness either by securing industrial or white collar employment, or by obtaining land for cultivation. The chief type of land that interested him was government 'forest land' or 'wasteland' much of which had belonged to the village communities anyway.

Dr Ambedkar, a dynamic personality, also drew back from a decisive rejection of Hinduism and of the Gandhian trend within the Congress. This was consistent with the position he was to take at the 1930s Depressed Classes Political Conference in Nagpur. It was only later that he made a decision to take a fully anti-Congress stand to build an independent political party in the context of an anti Gandhism that was to remain with him throughout his life.

The crucial years between 1930 and 1936 proved to be a 'turning point' in the history of the Dalit movement in India because they not only witnessed the important All-India Depressed Classes Conference in Nagpur in 1930, but also Bhimrao Ramji Ambedkar's attendance at the First Round Table Conference and his subsequent clash with Mahatma Gandhi before and at the Second Round Table Conference, culminating in the Poona Pact of 1932. As well as the famous conversion announcement in 1935, 'I have been born a Hindu but I will not die a Hindu'. The events of 1930-32 led to Ambedkar's final disillusionment with Hinduism with even the best and most 'reformist' of the Congress leadership while at the same time proving him to be the 'unparalleled leader of the Dalits, forcing the Congress leadership to deal with his demands.'

Representing, the untouchables at the First Round Table conference, along with M.N. Srinivasan of Madras, Ambedkar campaigned furiously for their cause. Stating unequivocally that these untouchables needed political power which could be gained only within the framework of an independent India; he spoke for a unitary state and adult suffrage with reserved seats and safeguards for untouchables. The Congress was absent here.

The first conference was followed by calling off the Civil Disobedience Movement and the famous Gandhi-Irwin Pact leading to the appearance of Mohandas Karamchand Gandhi at the Second Round Table Conference, with all the prestige of the national movement behind him and a claim to be the sole real representative of the Indian people. After Gandhi and Ambedkar's turbulent meeting in London in August 1931, failure of consensus on the Minorities Committee, the significant Rajah-Moonje Pact and Gandhi's threat of an imminent fast, a large conference of 'Hindu and Untouchable leaders' was held in Bombay that included Ambedkar, M.C. Rajah, P. Baloo, Madan Mohan Malviya, Sir Tej Bahadur Sapru, M.R. Jayakar, Sir Chimanlal Setalvad, C. Rajgopalchari, B.S.Moonje and A.V. Thakkar (in other words, primarily Hindu nationalists and

Gandhians). It was at this meeting that 'the final agreement was hammered out by Sapru and Ambedkar' in which a two-tier system of voting would allow untouchables first to select a panel of four Dalit candidates and then the general constituency (including caste Hindus) would decide among them.

In the battle of wills that seemed to flare up intermittently between Gandhi and Ambedkar and did come to the surface again after Gandhi's formation of his League against untouchability and certain important principles which would constitute its main line of action, the momentous events of 1930-32 finally proved that

(a) Gandhi, who represented the best of Hinduism, would not budge from paternalism and acceptance of *chaturvarnya*;
(b) in spite of the moralistic atmosphere that surrounded the fast and Pact it was hard bargaining and power (mobilizing strength) that counted;
(c) large sections of the caste Hindus did not support Gandhi in giving even limited rights and representation to the untouchables, as illustrated by the storm of opposition to the Poona Pact; and
(d) other Dalit leaders could be used by the upper castes as long as they identified with Hinduism.

There was a striking absence of any section of left Congressmen in the negotiating process and no visible involvement of any kind by Indian Marxists in the events of the Poona Pact and the Gandhi-Ambedkar confrontation. The Marxists did not take part because they did not perceive the issue of caste and untouchability as an important issue. Over half a century later, E.M.S. Namboodiripad's comment in his *History of the Indian Freedom Struggle*, makes this abundantly clear :

> However, this was a great blow to the freedom movement. For this led to the diversion of the people's

attention from the objective of full independence to the mundane cause of the upliftment of Harijans.

Concerning the Scheduled Caste people of India's vast subcontinent, the Constitution has followed the very same basis that the British Government laid down in 1936. This applies not only to the list but also to the criterion, which the British Government used to define "Scheduled Caste", because the same is followed for the Order of 1950. However, first let us examine the Order, which because of 'the use of its flexibility... has proved bad'. It is because of this truth that the condition of the Dalits, even after Independence, has not improved.

The Constitution (Scheduled Castes) Order, 1950

The Indian Constitution as per Article 341 (1) empowers the President of India "...by public notification, (to) specify the castes, races or tribes or parts or of groups within castes, races or tribes which shall, for the purpose of this Constitution be deemed to be Scheduled Castes..." Again the Constitution, without defining in Article 366 (24) only refers back to the power given to the President of India in Article 341. But once the President has given such an order, this list prepared on the basis of Article 342 (2) or Scheduled Castes can be changed only through an Act of Parliament. In the list of the Scheduled Castes, the Constitution (Scheduled Castes) Order, 1950, 'almost re-enacted the list of the Government of India Scheduled Castes Order, 1936'. As regards criterion, the third paragraph of this Order reads as follows : "Notwithstanding anything contained in paragraph 2, no person who professes a religion different from Hindu, shall be deemed to be a member of a Scheduled Caste." This highly significant paragraph was changed in 1956 by Parliament to "Hindu or Sikh" and again 34 years later, in May 1990 to "Hindu or Sikh or Buddhist."

Therefore, the positions of the President and Parliament are the same as that of the imperialist British Government in 1932-36, because it has used "religion" as the criterion to define the Scheduled Castes. However, utterances by senior leaders of political parties, in this instance that of Mr. L.K. Advani of the BJP on 12th June, 1990, at Thiruvananthapuram in South India, displayed a much more orthodox and biased ideology as regards criterion pertaining to the Scheduled Castes or Dalits. This stand, which represented the BJP viewpoint, was reported by the *Indian Express* as follows :

> The BJP leader, however, said that his party was stoutly opposed to any move by the V.P. Singh government to extend reservation to converts to Islam and Christianity from Scheduled Castes and Scheduled Tribes. It had supported the extension of reservation to SC/ST converts to Buddhism because under the Constitution Buddhists and Sikhs and Jains were classified as Hindus. Reservation to converts to other religions would violate the recommendation of the Constituent Assembly, he added.

Unfortunately this is the basic contradiction that India has, 'which the Constitution of the country and those responsible for its implementation are faced with, because the views expressed above, and decisions based on such views, not only violate the fundamental rights (Article 15.1), they also raise the question of human rights based on the principle of equality...'

Shrikant as the first Commissioner (Special Officer) on 18th November, 1950 , took an extensive tour to acquaint himself thoroughly with the state of the Dalits or *dalitness* which these unfortunate people had reached as a result of the ongoing oppression of the caste and the flawed social system which Indian society continued to maintain. Commenting on this condition, L.M. Shrikant, covering the period up to 31st December, 1951, says forcefully :

> Caste in Hindu society is still the most powerful factor in determining men's dignity, calling or profession. Such a rigid caste system is not found anywhere else outside India. All such professions involve handling of the so-

called dirty jobs like tanning and skinning of hides, manufacture of leather goods, sweeping of streets, scavenging, etc. allotted to some castes, also known as Harijans, who are about 5 crores according to the latest figures available.

In another part of his statement, illustrating vividly how the power of the abhorrent caste system has the ability to reduce or transform a person into such a pitiable state of self captivity and slavery from which it seems almost impossible for him to be liberated, Shrikant eloquently states that "... the Harijan (Dalit) has lost his self-respect to such an extent that he regards his work to which his caste is condemned not as a curse from which he should extricate himself but as a privilege or preserve which he must protect." Commenting that their laziness of mind, which is responsible also for many of their ills, cannot be cured by mere legislation but must be dealt with at a more basic level such as providing education for his progeny. To prevent this callous attitudinal malaise of not caring to provide education for their children, from spreading further and affecting subsequent generations of Dalits, Shrikant advocates that the non-willingness of the Dalit psyche needs to be addressed first. And that providing them with any amount of economic facilities will not be of much use until this deep-rooted problem is eradicated first.

Commenting upon the implementation of the Social Disabilities Removal Act adopted by various states, he opined that the incidence of crimes committed against the Dalits, hardly ever came to light. Ascribing that the main reason for such a deplorable state of affairs was inherent in the attitudes of the Dalits themselves. For the Harijans (Dalits) "have no courage to come forward" to either visit the public restaurants, shops, hotels, etc., or even to draw water from the common wells as they are "generally economically dependent on non Harijans in one way or the other. At places where offences committed under these Acts have not been made cognizable, it is very difficult for the Scheduled Caste people to take any action against culprits because the police are incapable of taking any action if a report is made to them."

Thirty-five years later, Shrikant's views were corroborated by the Report of the Commissioner for Scheduled Castes and Scheduled Tribes of April 1985-86. Even the later Commissioners have observed that while 15% of the posts were reserved for the Scheduled Castes, only about a mere 2.2% were filled.

The all-important Mandal Commission's discussion on the "Social Dynamics of Caste" abundantly illustrated "that despite the resolve of our Constitution-makers to establish a casteless society, the importance of caste has increased in some of the most important spheres of our national life." A statement which obviously speaks volumes about how the evils of the seemingly ineradicable and evil caste system have been allowed to assume such disproportionate importance so as to effect the progress of society and the betterment of its people in keeping with the times and the needs of the modern era. Stating with a pragmatism which far belies the hope for a just implementation of some of the sentiments voiced below, the Commission is of the opinion that: ...What caste has lost on the ritual front, it has more than gained on the political front. This has led to some adjustments in the power equation between the high and low castes and thereby accentuated social tensions. Whether these tensions rent the social fabric or the country is able to resolve them by internal adjustments, will depend on how understandingly the ruling high castes handle the legitimate aspirations and demands of the historically suppressed and backward classes.

Therein lies the problem as well as the solution to the problem, crying out to be sorted out by those with courageous idealistic convictions and the strength to implement them.

References

Al-Biruni, *India* (abridged edition of Dr. Edward C. Sachau's English translation Ahmed, Qeyamuddin (ed.) New Delhi, 1988 (revised).

Basu, Amrita, 'Decentering Democracy: Adivasi Women and the Shramik Sangathana', *Two Faces of Protest*, Delhi: Oxford University Press, 1993.

Basu Amrita, 'Societal Dimensions of Seclusion and Solidarity', *Two Faces of Protest*, Delhi: Oxford University Press, 1993.

Basu, Amrita, 'Political Mobilization and Immobilism in Midnapur District', *Two Faces of Protest*, Delhi: Oxford University Press, 1993.

Burnell, Arthur Coke (tr.), *The Ordinances of Manu*, New Delhi, 1971.

Chanda, Ramaprasad, *The Indo-Aryan Races, A study of the Origin of Indo-Aryan People and Institutions*, Calcutta, 1969.

Consult for detailed discussion :

Dumont, Louis, *Homo Hierarchicus, The Caste System and its Implications*, Chicago, 1970.

Mandelbaum, David G., *Society in India*, Bombay, 1990 (reprinted).

Chanda, Ramaprasad, *The Indo-Aryan Races, A Study of the Origin of Indo-Aryan People and Institutions*, Calcutta, 1969.

Chowdhry, Prem, 'Customs in a Peasant Economy : Women in Colonial Haryana', in Sangari, Kumkum and Vaid, Sudesh, (eds.), *Recasting Women*, Kali for Women, 1989.

Dasgupta, Swapan, 'Beginning of A Nightmare, Cover Story, *India Today*, April 26, 1999.

Galauter, Marc, *Competing Equalities in Law and the Backward Classes in Media*, Delhi, 1984.

Grewal, J.S., *Guru Nanak in History*, Chandigarh, 1979 (reprinted).

Hume, Robert Ernest (tr.), *The Thirteen Principal Upanishads*, London, 1951 (Reprinted).

Indian Express, New Delhi, June 13, 1990.

In Joshi Barbara R. (ed.)

Juergensmeyer, Mark, *Religion as Social Vision*, Berkeley: University of California Press, 1982.

Kapil Kumar, *Peasants in Revolt : Tenants, Landlords Congress and the Raj in Oudh, 1886-1922*, Delhi: Manohar, 1984.

Kumar, Kapil, *The Baba Ram Chandra Papers* (BRP), collected by Kumar during his field work and preserved in the Nehru Memorial Museum and Library (NMML).

Kumar, Kapil, 'Rural Women in Oudh 1917-47 : Baba Ramchandra and the Women's Question'. InSangari, Kumkum and Vaid, Sudesh, (ed.), *Recasting Women*, Kali for Women, 1989.

Kumar, Kapil, 'Peasants' Perception of Gandhi and his Programme, Oudh 1920-22', *Social Scientist* 11, No. 2 (February, 1983).

Kumar, Kapil,'Using the Ramcharitmanas as a Radical Text: Baba Ram Chandra in Oudh, 1920-50'. In Chandra, Sudhir (ed.) *Social Transformation and Creative Imagination*, Delhi: Allied Publishers, 1984.

Kulke, Eckehard, *The Parsees in India*, New Delhi, 1993 (reprint)

Kumar Ravinder, 'Gandhi, Ambedkar and the Poona Pact, 1932', in Masselos, Jim ed., *Struggling and Ruling : The Indian National Congress, 1885-1985*, New Delhi: Sterling Publishers Pvt. Ltd., 1987.

Majumdar, R.C., *Struggle for Freedom*, Bombay, 1969.

Majumdar, R.C., 'Evaluation of Religio-Philosophic Culture in India'. In Bhattacharya, Haridas,(ed.), *The Cultural Heritage of India, Volume IV, The Religious*, Calcutta, 1983.

Marenco, Ethne K., *The Transformation* of Sikh Society, New Delhi, 1976.

Massey, James, *Dalits in India*, New Delhi: Manohar Publishers and Distributors, 1995.

Mittal, S.K. and Kumar, Kapil, Baba Ram 'Chandra and Peasant Upsurge in Oudh 1920-21', *Social Scientist*, 6, No. 11 (June, 1978).

Murugkar, Lata, *Dalit Panther Movement in Maharashtra*, Bombay, 1991.

Namboodiripad, E.M.S., *A History of The Indian Freedom*

Movement, Social Scientist Press, Sd 1986, Trivandrum.

Narasu, P. Lakshmi, *The Essence of Buddhism*, Bombay, 1948.

Omvedt, Gail, in *Economic Review* - paper for Delhi seminar on 'The State, Social Movements and Democracy', New Delhi, 5-8, Ocitober 1992.

Omvedt, Gail, *Dalits and the Democratic Revolution*, New Delhi: Sage Publication,1994.

Phule, Jotirao, *Samagra Waagmay*, Bombay : Government of Maharashtra, 1991.

Picket, J. Waskom, *Christian Mass Movements in India*, New York, 1933.

Porter to Hailey, 19 January, 1921, F.No. 50/3/1921, Gen. UPSA.

Rigveda — All the *Rigveda's* Sanskrit verses text is taken from *Rigveda* in Devanagri script edited by Shriram Sharma Acharya, published in four volumes by Sanskrit Sansthan, Bareilly (U.P.), 1985.

Savara, Mira and Gothoskar, Sujata, 'An Assertion of Womanpower', In Kishwar, Madhu and Vanita, Ruth (eds.) *In Search of Answers* (Indian Women's Voices from Manushi), London: Zed Books Ltd., 1984.

Sen, Amartya, *Poverty and Famines : An Essay on Entitlement and Deprivation*, Oxford : Clarendon Press, 1981.

Shrikant, L.M., *Report of the Commissioner for Scheduled Castes and Scheduled Tribes for the period ending 31st December, 1951*.New Delhi: Inter-India Publications,1991.

Singh, Prabhash P., *Women in India : A Statistical Panorama*, New Delhi: Inter–India Publication, 1991.

Singh, K.S., *The Scheduled Castes Volume* II, Oxford University Press, New Delhi, 1993.

Singh, Ram, 'The Incredible Community', in *The Sugar in the Milk*, op. cit. p.3.

Swami Vireswaranands (tr.), *Srimad Bhagvad Gita*, Madras, 1987.

Wallestein, Immanuel, 'Development : Lodestar or Illusion', *Economic and Political weekly*, 24 September, 1988.

Weil, Shalva, 'Symmetry between Christians and Jews in India : The Cananite Christians and the Cochin Jews of Keralas, *Indian Sociology*, 16/2, Paris, 1992.

Zelliot, Eleanor, *From Untouchable to Dalit*, New Delhi: Manohar Publications, 1992

Zellit, Eleanor, 'The Psychological Dimension of the Buddhist Movement in India'. In Oddie, G.A.,(ed.) *Religion in South Asia — Religious Conversion and Revival Movements in South Asia in Medieval and Modern Times*, New Delhi, 1991.

Census of India 1921, United Provinces, Vol. 16, pt.2.

C.I.D. Report on Guhuana Sabha, F. No. 50/1921, Gen. UPSA.

F. Nos. 195-216A/February, 1921-B, Home Pol., NAI.

For studies of forest policy and indigenous resistance to it, see Ramchandra Guha, 'Forestry in British and Post-British India', *Economic and Political Weekly*, 29 October and 5 November, 1983, and *The Unquiet Woods : Ecological Change and Peasant Resistance in the Himalayas*, Delhi : Oxford University Press, 1989; also J.F. Richards, 'Cotton Cultivation and Land Clearing in the Bombay Deccan and Karnataka, 1818-1920 (Mss. May 1981).

Leader, 24 June, 1921.

The most authoritative account of the Mahad Satyagraha and of some of the varying interpretations of it (with a strong attack on some caste Hindu distortions) is given by Ratnakar Ganvir, *Mahad Samta Sangar* (Jalgoan : Ratnamitra Prakshan,1981) pp. 1-65. See also the newspaper and Bombay police account cited in *Source Material on Dr Babasahib Ambedkar and the Movement of Untouchables*, Volume I (Bombay: Government of Maharashtra, 1982) pp. 13-33, which give a sense of the degree to which the campaign became a major event. (As appears in *Dalits and the Democratic Revolution*)

Report of the Backward Classes Commission, Government of India, First part, Volumes I and II, 1980.

18

DALIT AWAKENING

Social structures provide crucibles in which collective identities are forged and interests developed. However, social patterns are not monolithic or static; by selectively highlighting certain elements within given cultures, political organizations may reinforce or reshape dominant patterns. A key instance is provided by the way that political organizations interpret the place of women : upholding women's traditional roles often places inherent limits on the potential for radical change. Conversely, an organization that appropriates emancipatory themes from subaltern traditions stretches the limits of the possible in ways that go beyond conventional leftist agendas.

Amrita Basu

The discrimination against the Dalits is legendary. It follows, therefore, that in an era when women in general are still not accepted at par with their male counterparts, that the fate of the Dalit women would necessarily be even more trying and abysmally vexatious. But let us review the position about a few decades ago and attempt to recreate or recapture the ambience of rural India at the beginning of the twentieth century.

It was the legendary land of the Nawabs-Oudh-or present day central Uttar Pradesh, that witnessed a massive peasant uprising during the early 1920's which was an outcome of the oppression and exploitation faced by the peasants at the hands of the British Raj and its allies, the *taluqdars* (landlord of a *taluqa* or group of villages).

Amongst the peasants was a doubly exploited section — women. On the one hand, women faced all the miseries of the tenants and agricultural labourers and, on the other, they also suffered as women due to the rigid traditional structure of rural society. The peasant movement, organized under the leadership of Baba Ram Chandra, not only highlighted the pitiable, oppressed conditions of the peasantry as a whole but also, more specifically, the question of the position of women. This violent upsurge of rebellion and reaction left its mark in the annals of history. Thus official documents and private papers provide some evidence of the various issues that formed part of the movement in rural Oudh. Despite various advances made in the field of historical investigation, the role of women from the oppressed social strata particularly peasant women in transforming economic, social and political life in the countryside stands neglected in historical analysis, here an attempt has been made to remedy this error. All the women of those times may not be dumped together as the 'oppressed' for there were women taluqdars as well as women moneylenders who imbibed the role of extortioners. Due to their control over the means of production, such women had a dominant position in society with greater privileges. However, the prevalent problems of these women and those women from landlord families who had no direct control over the means of production, were largely related to social customs and patriarchy while those faced by women cultivators and agricultural labourers were economic as well as patriarchal in nature and content.

By the important contextual Taluqdari Settlement of 1858, the British government established a social base in the Oudh countryside and officially recognized taluqdars as the natural leaders of the masses, simultaneously endowing them with "absolute ownership" rights of the land. Thus, the peasantry, which had made common cause with the princes and taluqdars in opposing the British, were converted into tenantry and agricultural labourers. The ultimate outcome of the struggle was that "the princes and taluqdars not only compromised with the British but threw in their lot with the colonial power."

Thenceforth, the unfortunate peasantry faced double oppression both at the hands of the feudal lords and imperial government.

We shall specifically focus here on "the issue of exploitation of women". While the ratio of men and women in the rural areas of Oudh in 1921 did not exhibit much disparity, the number of men being 5,851,754 and that of women 5,497,147, other significant disparities did make a difference to the situation. Amongst ordinary cultivators, there were 1,635,036 female and 2,895,552 male actual workers, with 3,711,437 dependents. There were only 2.1 per cent secure tenants, while 97.9 per cent cultivators were tenants at will, mostly with a seven year lease of land. Amongst these, 85.8 per cent could be termed as poor peasants, 11.3 per cent as middle peasants and only 2.9 as rich peasants. Amongst agricultural labourers, 3,48,600 were women, 3,79,910 men along with 3,78,885 dependents. In the 7 out of the 12 districts of Oudh, namely, Rai Bareily, Fyzabad, Gonda, Baharaich, Unnao, Sultanpur and Pratapgarh, women outnumbered men as agricultural labourers. Moreover, the agricultural labourers were a socially degraded class not merely on account of their occupation which kept them at the lowest economic stratum, but also because of the caste structure. The bulk of the rural proletariat was drawn from 'low castes' who for many generations had been prevented by the feudal aristocracy from owning land for cultivation in order to facilitate the supply of labour. They were not only paupers and serfs but 'untouchables' as well. The extreme economic and social pressure was responsible to a fairly great extent, for drawing large numbers of women amongst the labourers coming out to work. In addition, the 'low castes' as compared to the 'high castes' peopled these districts of Oudh in greater numbers. The number of actual workers whose income was from agricultural land was 20,588 women and 57,279 men. There were 2283 women money lenders as compared to 7953 men in the trade.

Predominant among the oppressive practices was the extraction of *nazrana* (extra premium on rent) by landlords. This evil was so deeprooted and had penetrated to such an extent that some tenants were ultimately forced to go through the traumatic procedures of selling their daughters (*Kanya Vikray*) in order to raise this mandatory *nazrana*. Many such cases have come to light from Pratapgarh for the years 1919-20, during an inquiry conducted by the Deputy Commissioner (D.C.) to investigate the causes of agrarian disturbances in the district. The vicious practice of *kanya vikray* was intensified by the fact that "there was enormous disparity in years between the ages of wife and husband" and the nubile young maiden's marriage was more often than not "consecrated before the funeral pyre of her husband."

Yet another evil practice, that of *Murdafaroshi* or selling of holdings after the death of the lease holder, was another potent weapon of the *taluqdari* (conferment of proprietorial rights in land) system and the worst victims again were the women. Although legally, the heirs of a lease-holder could not be evicted till the end of the seven year lease, in actuality immediately after the death of the lease holder, the holding was let out to the highest bidder at enhanced rates by the landlord. Many a time even the payment of *nazrana* by the heir did not save the property from arbitrary appropriation, by the concerned individual.

It was left to Shridhar Balwant Jodhpurkar or Baba Ram Chandra as he was more widely known, to implement changes after his own broad-based experiences with women, especially in Fiji. He went to Fiji as indentured labour and had his marriage arranged to a beautiful *Chamarin,* whom he ultimately had to divorce as he had to flee Fiji due to his own political activities. During 1918-20, Ram Chandra was not only making efforts to mobilize the peasants against the British and the landlords, symbolic of a much wider all-India movement practically that was manifesting itself as an 'awakening' Dalit revolt, but also attempting to articulate issues related to women and break caste barriers. Some time late in the 1920s, he married Jagi, a woman from the Kurmi caste and broke the caste barriers yet again. This marriage, solemnized on the sage advice of Mr. V.N. Jaggi — a pro-peasant senior government official—brought in its wake an ugly trail of vulgar propaganda against Chandra by the landlords and his other opponents. A constant charge against Ram Chandra, levied by the landlords, was that he was an outsider, instigating peasants to rebellion in Pratapgarh. Whatever the criticism and whatever the underlying reason for this daring inter-caste marriage in those turbulent times, a modicum of political expediency in the matter cannot be ruled out. However, the calculated gamble paid rich dividends for, under Ram Chandra's influence, Jaggi became an activist on the Kisan front, on women's issues and in the freedom struggle. It would be appropriate to mention here that while Ram Chandra passed away in 1950, the intrepid Jaggi continued to work as a Kisan Sabha activist in Pratapgarh till 1983, trudging 10 to 15 kilometres at the ripe old age of ninety plus, for such work.

Ram Chandra, was a broad minded person and he not only advocated strongly against incompatible and unhealthy child marriages with a vast age difference between the two partners whose nuptials were prearranged, but was also a staunch votary of intercaste weddings. He believed that arranged marriages should be based on considerations of compatibility, such as intelligence. This would not only be considerably healthier and more long-lasting but also ameliorate the incidence of adultery.

Intercaste marriages were virtually non-existent due to rigid caste norms. Predictably enough, the landlords upheld these norms and as part of their attempt to control social mobility, they would impose fines on peasants for breaking caste customs. Therefore, it was no surprise that Ram Chandra worked for reforms through caste panchayats. Though the various caste panchayats with which he was associated were the Kurmi Sangh, Harijan Sangh, Satnami Sabha and Tamoli Sabha, etc., it was at an all male conference attended by 271 Kurmi representatives, that the Kurmi Sangh resolved, among other measures, that :

(a) Marriage customs of the *biradari* (caste brotherhood) should be changed.

(b) Marriage or *gauna* (post-puberty ceremonial bringing of the girl bride to her husband's home) should be regularized,and should take place with the signature/ sanction of the head of the panchayat with registration of the marriage in the village records. Failure by the parents to follow this procedure, would rob the marriage of its legal sanction.

(c) Reforms for women are necessary.

(d) Women should not be sent to work in another person's house. Men should go upon payment of full wages only. This Resolution, however, should not be interpreted to construe a rejection of women's right to work ,but should be seen in the context of exploitative working conditions for women in the existing feudal culture. Women were the worst victims of the reprehensible practice of *begar* (forced labour) as well as a target of sexual exploitation by the *karindas* (landlord's agents) and *sipahis* (soldiers) of landlords. The irony of the situation was such, however, that if women were to be saved from sexual harassment, they stood to loose their right to free movement and to certain forms of wage earning.

But it was at another Kisan Council meeting at Rure, the headquarters of the Kisan Sabha that certain resolutions were brought forward by the women, led by the indomitable Jaggi at the behest of her husband. They advocated social sanction for relationships otherwise considered illegal and maintained that one man and one woman could stay together without being considered as illegal. Furthermore, such women (who stay with a man without formal marriage) should not be treated as belonging to any particular caste. Nor should they be dismissed as merely being there for the purpose of begetting children. Though those women who begot sons through such a union ought to be revered as *devis*, those who were unable to produce a coveted male heir, were still to be respected as *kanyas*. The underlying aim here being that women of such liaisons should enjoy a modicum of security at all times.

From time to time, a number of exploited women addressed petitions for redressal to the dauntless Ram Chandra. All these problems were related not only to individual women but were, obviously, manifestations of a much wider malaise-the exploitative character of the agrarian structure as a whole. Ram Chandra was considered as the undisputed leader of the peasants by these women, and continued to campaign vociferously for upward mobility for lower caste women. Therefore, when the Sarda Committee was seeking evidence, he strongly advised the village panchayat heads to demand a similar status for the women of lower castes as was enjoyed by high caste women. However, as regards elevating the status of peasant women, he was firmly of the opinion that such women "must earn their right to a higher status by changing themselves into highly austere, pious and moral persons." What he visualized was a new model of woman who would also enjoy a greater measure of equality with her husband. It was this model of the new peasant woman that made him propose certain measures which in fact restricted the free movement of women. In his commendable write up entitled *"Oudh ki Nariyon per Mere Vichar"* (My Views on the Women of Oudh), he began by quoting Maithli Saran Gupta Thus :

Nari ninda na karo nari nar ki khan,
Nari se nar hota hai Dhruv Prahalad saman.

Literally translated, this read as :

(Do not talk ill of woman, she is the origin of man. From her are born men like Dhruv and Prahalad.)

Interestingly enough, we find the first active political participation by women in the peasant struggles here in August-

September, 1920. When Ram Chandra was arrested for the first time, an impressive 40,000 peasants surrounded Pratapgarh jail and the Government was forced to accede to their pressure and release him. Women had, undoubtedly, taken an active part in this agitation, the first of many in which they continue to play progressively bolder and more decisive roles.

In the Thakur Din Singh revolt against the Raja of Parhat in October 1920 - a movement directed against landlords, moneylenders and traders, women were again to suffer miserably. The police and taluqdari agents crushed the uprising with great difficulty, whole villages plundered mercilessly and women molested shamelessly in eight villages during the hunt for Thakur Din.

The Ajodhya Kisan Conference of December 1920 was a unique spectacle in the history of peasant struggles in India. About 50,000 to one lakh peasant men and women reached the town in spite of the cold weather. So determined were they all to attend that ultimately some of the very old, very exhausted women who had undertaken arduous journeys to reach the venue, had to be transported the final lap by the quaint *ekka*. Thus, for the first time, women's presence was asserted separately from men in this historic meeting. Satya Devi spoke from the stage on behalf of women and assured their participation in the movement.

Thereafter, the peasant movement in Oudh rapidly gathered momentum and soon assumed the dimensions of a class war as the desperate peasantry resorted to militant action on a large-scale in Rai Bareily district. The year 1921 began with the *jacqueries* of Oudh peasants. The peasants, in their thousands, moved from one state to another destroying the crops of the taluqdars. On one pretext or the other, there were outbreaks of violence and pitched battles between the two opposing sides. On the 13th and 14th of January specifically, in Fyzabad district, huge crowds composed mainly of landless labourers moved about the Baskhari and Jehangirganj police circles, mercilessly looting the zamindars, moneylenders, merchants and goldsmiths. The main targets of attack were the grain stores of the zamindars and mahajans. Fuelled by the fires of injustice, tyranny and want and driven by the forces of revenge, among other reasons, hordes of men — numbering between 1000 to 5000 — descended upon these predetermined targets; they were followed swiftly by similarly charged crowds of women who carried off the "booty" of their "pillage." In numerous instances, women belonging to upper classes were subjected to humiliation, maltreated and abused by groups of oppressed women. This demonstrates the awareness on the part of women of the class contradictions of rural society. The active participation of the large numbers of women here and in other instances of rebellion where they pelted stones on the police party, exhibited in no uncertain manner the immense revolutionary potential of the women in the countryside. In fact, it is quite creditworthy that the peasant movement in Oudh assumed such significant dimensions that there was considerable interaction between it and the Non-Cooperation movement. Mahatma Gandhi's name cropped up several times in varying contexts during the peasant movement, one fakir Faruq Ahmed going so far as to say that "Gandhi would ascend the throne of Delhi on 15th February" and "three lakhs of English ladies" would be "distributed at the Guhana Sabha." While the talk of Gandhi ascending the throne is understandable, that of the English ladies is either a sexually motivated statement to attract the menfolk or else vengeful anticipation of a punishing action to be meted out to the original perpetrators or those who gave tacit approval to the excesses committed by the landlords against the peasant women. Any derogatory action or insult traded against the imperial British women would at least temporarily tend to vindicate the endless miseries of the halpess peasant women. However, the great Mahatma was projected in a totally different manner at the actual Guhana Sabha on the

27th of January. Ram Devi compared Gandhi's agitation with the Mahabharata ...war: just as in the Mahabharata, Draupadi's honour was at stake, Gandhi's agitation was seen to maintain the honour of Bharatmata (Mother India). Infact, the peasants had their own perception of Gandhi and of his programme and were anxious about their economic emancipation.

Progress of the women's cause was concretized in the 1930s with the formulation of key peasant women's organizations and among the activists who took the initiative were the wives of the Kisan Sabha leaders. A Kisanin Panchyat was formed with Jaggi as its leader. This organization functioned as a branch of the Praja Sangh organized by Ram Chandra. Both the nature and aims as well as the pledge of the Kisanin were such that they amounted to an overt expression of the oppression faced by women in the countryside. They amply demonstrated the awareness and determination on the part of women to fight tooth and nail against the unwanted suppression and oppression of the female peasant force. Not only did Baba Ram Chandra take recourse to traditional 'customs and ceremonies to mobilize peasants against taluqdars and the British' but the Kisanin Panchayat also adopted such methods to create awareness amongst women. It organized exhibitions and meetings to educate and inform the kisanin about relevant issues and such meets were financed by the Praja Sangh. Separate intimation and invitations were sent to the women who attended eagerly, journeying to the venue from the various *tehsils* of Pratapgarth and thereby exhibiting their boldness in acquainting themselves with issues serious enough to affect their future destiny.

Around the mid/late 1930s an evocative petition titled *Anath Ablaon ki Pukar* (The Helpless Woman's Appeal) was sent to Prof. Braj Gopal Bhatnagar. The brainchild of Ram Chandra, this was indeed a significant move to attract the attention of intellectuals towards the miserable plight of the oppressed rural woman with the petitioner aptly signing herself as a *dukhit praja ki abla* (A helpless woman of the oppressed masses). The following five grievances were candidly listed in the petition :

a) We are beaten with *lathis*.

b) Being forced to stand on a mudpot in the glaring sun, we are watched with lustful eyes (obviously by landlords or their agents).

c) During *begar* they make us grind. If we refuse, we are beaten with *lathis*. They break our heads.

d) After the death of our husbands we are evicted from our holding, houses, orchards, etc.

e) Thus, we cannot repay loans nor manage our family.

While the late 1930s witnessed a sharp ideological struggle within the Indian National Congress and the right wing leadership was particularly hostile towards the Kisan Sabha, not permitting the peasant members of the Congress to vote in the organizational elections at many places, the women peasantry continued their efforts for more equitable conditions undaunted.

Cutting determinedly across rigid caste barriers in the winter of 1940, December to be more precise, ten women under the leadership of the indomitable Jaggi offered satyagraha fearlessly and courted arrest. A handwritten leaflet which was issued under her signature, contained among other statements, the following two highly important appeals:

a) Break all caste norms in crisis.

b) Be with the poor and not with the rich as they are all one and at many places the taluqdars, small zamindars and capitalists, with the help of high classes and arms want to create disturbances.

The struggle to free the peasants, and even more especially the women of these classes, from opression somehow meshed with the larger, nationalist cause and acquired even more significant dimensions. Therefore the inter-caste satyagraha's class composition *vis-à-vis* the names of its members is of importance. They were :

	Names of Women	*Caste Delienations*
1.	Mussamat Putta	Harijan (Chamar)
2.	Sampati	Kurmi
3.	Razi	Kurmi
4.	Sukhi	Teli
5.	Sukhmani	Pasi
6.	Bubai	Kurmi
7.	Putra	Kurmi
8.	Abilakhi	Kurmi
9.	Basanti	Brahmin
10.	Sundra Devi	Ravidas

Through their solidarity and staunch adherence to noble principles, these women from poor peasant families "demonstrated ...that satyagraha could be a combined effort of the oppressed." But the high caste lawyer leaders in the DCC were, however, most displeased about this development as they were strongly opposed to the peasants organizing in one class. Displaying blatant casteist prejudices Munishwar Dutt Upadhyaya, an important Congress leader commented thus: "Had the women from high families offered satyagraha it would have brought fame to the Congress. What could the women from Shudra (low caste) families bring?" History stands mute testimony to the inevitable fall out of such narrow-minded, casteist views. It also records, albeit informally, the heroic endeavours of Baba Ram Chandra as he struggled for transformation in the condition and status of women which he sought by using traditional and cultural idioms to mobilize them not only as peasants but also as a separate group — women. The organization of the Kisanin Sabha was an effort of this kind.

Southward Bound—Maharashtra, Andhra Pradesh and Karnataka

A specific look at the occupational pattern among women workers in the three linguistically contiguous States of Maharashtra, Andhra Pradesh and Karnataka and even comparing it briefly with Madras State (of an earlier time) indicates, from data available, the following interesting observations :

"...low work participation of women among the Brahamin castes in all regions; contrastingly, among the 'peasant' jatis it is quite high (except for the Vokkaliga in Mysore state), while it is highest of all among the Dalits. Everywhere the incidence of female participation in agriculture is much higher than that of male workers and more so as 'field labourers' than 'cultivators'. It is clear that women were substantial 'economic producers' along with men and that they tended to be more proletarianized; though this meant, primarily, that their wage labour was mainly as agricultural labourers and as unskilled casual labourers, they also participated substantially as toiling peasant cultivators (their labour on family farms being undoubtedly underestimated, in 1921 as in 1971-81)." Tables 18.1 and 18.2 indicate caste and agrarian occupations as follows :-

TABLE 18.1

Caste and Agrarian Occupation, 1921 (Male Workers)

		Recorded Principle Occupation (%)		
	Actual Workers (Numbers)	*Income from Rent of Land*	*Cultivators*	*Field Labourer*
Mysore State (1921)				
Brahamin	51,221	17.13	21.79	0.35
Lingayat	142,366	3.15	79.43	2.62
Vokkaliga	246,329	0.44	89.83	2.08

Contd....

Holeya	157,289	0.97	35.95	37.72
Madiga	63,363	1.58	45.13	26.17
Hyderabad State (1921)				
Brahaman	79,345	7.37	17.52	0.32
Maratha	500,638	6.99	60.90	16.33
Lingayat(Shopkeeper)	170,508	3.50	9.01	1.30
Kapu	291,130	1.60	51.56	26.15
Telaga	146,230	1.01	61.22	15.68
Mahar/Mala	130,008	3.79	8.40	8.25
(menial service)				(65.33)*
Madiga	203,492	0.65	10.28	10.16
(menial service)				(83.54)*
Chambhar	37,991	1.07	4.21	7.69
Madras State (1911)				
Brahman, Telugu	27,029	34.53	32.37	0.29
Brahaman, Canarese	10,647	13.96	71.89	0.08
Holeya	29,696	—	3.29	75.46
Mala	196,259	0.18	14.78	71.89
Madiga	79,924	1.17	10.71	54.71
Central Province and Berar (1921)				
Brahaman	149,193	3.22	36.67	6.22
Maratha	65,520	4.29	46.00	27.78
Kunbi	385,368		55.00	34.08
Mahar/Mehra	280,101	2.09	22.37	41.02
(Cotton Weavers)				(11.33)*
Mang	26,007	1.25	3.42	47.73
(native musician)				(21.97)*
Bombay Presidency (1911)				
Brahman, Chitpavan	10,407	17.00	2.47	0.13
Brahman, Deshastha	14,494	18.68	64.55	2.69
Lingayat	205,813	3.24	83.54	22.39
Maratha	426,649	1.58	47.63	14.93
Kunbi	319,813	1.59	66.88	20.67
Mahar, Holeya, Dhed	69,542	0.75	48.79	22.63
Mang, Madiga	22,672	0.52	16.60	41.71

* Refers to traditional caste occupation.

TABLE 18.2
Caste and Agrarian Occupation, 1921 (Female Workers)

	Percentage of Female to Male Workers	*Income from Rent of Land*	*Cultivators*	*Field Labourers*
Mysore State (1921)				
Brahman	10.58	37.38	25.61	2.62
Lingayat	20.34	13.25	49.47	17.80
Vokkaliga	18.71	2.09	72.13	7.57
Holeya	35.22	1.26	11.35	61.63
Madiga	31.51	1.96	13.12	56.36
Hyderabad State (1921)				
Brahman	18.12	15.68	33.97	—
Maratha	63.03	3.06	54.60	31.71
Lingayat	52.49	6.44	16.73	1.92
Kapu	50.95	1.21	70.07	19.75
Telaga	75.22	1.08	57.26	20.87
Mahar/Mala	98.83	2.66	13.90	39.50
(menial service)				(37.24)*
Chambhar	59.70	0.76	10.37	2.98
Madras State (1911)				
Brahman, Telugu	26.69	54.60	34.74	0.11
Brahman,Canarese	28.10	14.74	69.25	0.40
Hoyela	37.73	—	2.45	84.43
Mala	85.53	0.16	8.48	87.55
Madiga	70.69	3.98	2.89	82.31
Central Provinces and Berar (1921)				
Brahman	34.58	2.71	45.61	15.40
Maratha	51.23	2.55	21.97	58.00
Kunbi	70.79	—	32.65	62.16
Mahar/Mehra	91.28	0.40	16.56	60.25
(cotton weavers)				(9.76)*
Mang	99.42	0.20	1.29	66.04
(native musicians)				(2.41)*

Contd...

Bombay Presidency (1921)				
Brahman, Chitpavan	15.00	30.17	3.14	1.54
Brahman, Deshastha	11.09	40.08	22.77	2.43
Lingayat	56.45	3.49	25.41	46.24
Maratha	68.53	1.57	47.67	30.84
Kunbi	71.63	1.07	54.23	41.33
Mahar, Hoyela,Dhed	76.63	0.34	43.50	41.52
Mang, Madiga	79.13	0.55	6.33	66.79

Sources : Censuses of India, 1911, 1921

* Refers to traditional caste occupation

(Table 18.1 Caste titled and Agrarian Occupation, 1921 (Male Workers) and Table 18.2 titled Caste and Agrarian Occupation (Female Workers) have been taken from the book *Dalits and the Democratic Revolution* by Gail Omvedt, Sage Publications, New Delhi, 1994)

Let us now attempt, briefly, to establish a fundamental base of the situation as it existed earlier, shaped by the many highly complicated and inextricably interlinked forces of nature. Such as varying socio-economic, socio-historic, socio-political and cultural factors which had an important bearing on caste perceptions and class consciousness and determined the personal, professional and political destinies of the people concerned, for decades to come.

Apart from sharing a 'southern' type of kinship system with preferential cross-cousin marriage among the main castes, as Iravati Karve has so succinctly put it, in addition the 'three way' caste division (Brahman, non-Brahman, Untouchable) seems particularly prominent here. While there are no 'Kshatriya' *jatis* anywhere in the south i.e. the three states of Maharashtra, Andhra Pradesh and Karnataka in stark contrast to the definitely more inequalitarain hierarchies of Tamil Nadu and Kerala, are characterized by the dominance of large peasant *jatis* with landlord rights "who historically supplied many of the zamindars and rulers but remained classed as 'Shudra' in the accepted *varna* scheme." Significantly enough in addition all the three states enumerated have large, vigorous Dalit *jatis*. It is important to mention here that this Shudra-cultivator status was also linked with a relatively more liberal treatment of women. While the aristocrats and overlords among them observed the stricter social customs of *purdah* and *gosha*-thus secluding their women. The majority of villagers had 'vigorous, independent women who worked in the field and who played important economic, even managerial roles.'

While the major peasant jatis, the Kunbi-Marathas of Maharashtra, the Vokkaligas in Karnataka and the Kapus, Kammas, Velamas and Telaga of Andhra Pradesh (their names all derived from vernacular terms having to do with agriculture or simply denoting 'peasant' : *kunbi, kapu, vokkaliga*) — made up 25-30 per cent of the population of their respective states, the two major Dalit jatis made up approximately 15 per cent. And it is striking that the region has almost everywhere two such relatively large Dalit castes, firmly marked off from one another and traditional rivals. These were the Mahars, Malas and Holeyas on one hand (about 10 per cent of the total population) and the Madigas and Mangs (about 5 per cent) on the other. It is not within the ambit of our discussion here to study the discrete sub-castes, lineage and other factors which must have influenced the distribution of duties and labour among the peasant and Dalit jatis. However, it is pertinent to state that it was the Mahars, Malas and Holeyas who made up the main social base for the Dalit movements of the twentieth century, whereas the Mangs and Madigas provided the bulk of lower caste converts to Christianity. In spite of differences, the main Dalit castes shared some important religious customs which highlight some significant aspects of the 'sexual dynamics' of the relations among castes. Embodying in its most fundamental aspects, overpoweringly strong connections with the mother goddesses and manifested also in the practice of popular cults and sacrifices.

However, it was an event of major world importance- the perpetuation of British colonial rule in India and the latter's integration into the system of world capitalism along with most of the rest of Asia and Africa, during the period 1750-1850, that had ramifications of great importance upon the caste-class issue in our country. Perhaps, like Dr. B.R. Ambedkar, it would be wisest to follow the broad Marxist critique of colonialism, taking off from Marx's brief comments on 'primitive accumulation' and the role of force and violence in history, we argue that non wage forms of accumulation, including women's domestic labour, the extraction of cheap natural resources, the extraction of surplus (primarily from Third World peasants) through slave and serf relations and petty commodity production, have been equally crucial, as more standard interpretations advanced for explaining the processes of caste-class development in India during British rule. It focuses too much on the wage labour/ capital relation as the driving force, and perceives the main dynamic in the expansion of capital from the centre. Within contemporary interpretations of Marxism and certainly less inherently 'Orientalist' in its assumptions 'about the stagnation of non-European relations and systems of production' has been the 'world capitalist systems' theory represented by Immanuel Wallerstein and others. Briefly but, it treats the dynamics of the system as "not simply deriving from the impetus of capital formation and the surplus value relation at the 'centre' but also from the dialectic between 'centre' and 'periphery',with dynamic also coming from the movements of the exploited in the Third World". Wallerstein explains that while at the beginning of the historical process, there seemed little difference in the economic wealth of the different geographical areas, a mere one century's flow of surplus was enough to create a visible distinction between core and periphery in terms of three criteria: the accumulation of capital, the social organization of local production processes, the political organization of the state structures.

The toiling castes such as the Shudra peasants and artisans, Dalit village labourers, Adivasi forest dwelling peasants et al., were hardest hit by the new devolution of power, by the commodification process of incorporation into a (world) capitalist economy. They were subjected to new forms of exploitation by colonial rule as the restructuring of 'local production processes' led to the destruction of many traditional crafts and artisan industries through competition with cheap European manufactures and forced specialization in many raw materials. Embodying an increased 'peasantization', they were forced to cultivate crops such as indigo, raw silk, opium and cotton not only for their own subsistence or local consumption but for the needs of Europe; rather cruelly, their traditional 'caste duties' were used for these new forms of surplus production which aided centralized accumulation in nations far away from their homes. Demand of a heavy land revenue which was 'both a primary mode of extraction of the surplus and the financial basis of the colonial state until the 1930s when peasant struggles very nearly brought it to an end', moneylenders, those crucial intermediaries who advanced credit on the crop-lien system and took control of the marketing of the crop in ryotwari areas, all had a devastating effect. They not only resulted in the subordination of the entire peasantry (rich, poor, wage labourer, *balutedar* and all) to production for the needs of a European market but 'the increased cash-crop production took place in the context of local environmental destruction. Forests were degraded and occasionally devasted as trees were cut down to build railways, cultivation was extended into previously forested areas. As a result, forest areas and commons could no longer provide, to the same degree, 'inputs' for agriculture and various subsistence needs for villagers'. The squalid living conditions of the peasantry denoted a state of the most abysmal destitution with the people pitifully struggling against poverty and debt.

The heavy incidence of famines during British rule, cited so forcefully by that staunch champion of the Dalits — Ambedkar in his 1930 speech, acted as a catalyst in an already rapidly deteriorating situation and very likely forced the entire peasantry to the margin of existence. As he pointed out, the heaviest burden of all this continued to fall on the lowest castes and on women and children, those who lacked entitlements to the land and other sources of sustenance.

The area of merciless exploitation by the colonial British masters included wage labour as well. Factory production increased only very gradually. Data cited by Anupam Sen indicates that there were 815 factories with an average daily workforce of 3,50,000 in 1894; 3400 factories with 1,171,000 workers in 1919, and 10,466 factories with 1,751,000 workers by 1939; not a very large number for the subcontinent. However, labour was also used in other significant spheres such as the railways and docks and for all the construction and irrigation projects. The most important factor is that the use of such labour was not confined to India only but spread throughout the empire as, providing the most exploited producers of surplus, bonded and overworked to exhaustion and death, were huge numbers of Dalits and Adivasis who migrated to work in plantation economies spanning a vast area from the West Indies to South Africa to South-East Asia and Fiji. However, this worldwide movement of Indians and colonialism had only a very complex effect on the functioning of the caste system. New groups like a factory working class and plantation proletariat came into existence, and new professionals developed from high caste Brahmins and Banias. Peasantry also acquired an accentuated existence...while at one level formally non-scriptive openings (such as education and entry into factory occupations) could mean that a very few from the lower castes could win their way into non-traditional occupations, by and large, caste channelized workers to segmented labour markers. Brahmins, with their near-monopoly over administrative positions and professions, retained their position at the top of the caste hierarchy and maximum mobility; merchant castes (Banias, Jains, Chettiars) became moneylenders, merchants and businessmen;

middle Shudra castes dominated factory occupations while miners and plantation workers were drawn from the lowest groups. The middle 'peasant' classes, impoverished, yet more attached to villages than they had been before, retained a modicum of mobility with the depressed and downtrodden Dalits, so miserably oppressed, impoverished and exploited as to render such so-called mobility practically useless.

Resistance to colonial repression came from the poor, severely persecuted Dalit peasants, other peasants and exploited people drawn from the lowest classes. The major form of resistance was through peasant revolts and movements ranging from seemingly traditional 'restorative' tribal uprisings to agitations against local exploiters (landlords and moneylenders) to both sporadic agitations and sustained campaigns against the British bureaucracy on forest issues and land revenue issues. A case in point being the famous Bardoli anti-revenue struggle of 1928. An example of the broad process of exploitation through commercialization leading to a broad unity of resistance, it was also an illustration of the complex hierarchies of caste and community linked to the struggle. In fact the extremely complex population of Bardoli, ranging from the Dalit-tribal Raniparaj ('forest-dwellers', originally somewhat crudely termed 'Kaliparaj' or 'black people') to the Vanias, Anavil Brahmans, Parsees and peasant Kanbi-Patidars, had in common 'exploitation through commercialization' in which low prices and high revenue demands 'combined to squeeze the entire rural sector'. The ground for mobilization in Bardoli was prepared by Gandhian 'constructive work' centering among the Patidars and Kaliparaj tribals, and the struggle itself saw a wide mobilization of peasants, labourers and more elite commercial classes. Emboldened and inspired, even the largely uneducated and unsophisticated rural women participated in the struggle with amazing aplomb and commitment to common cause. Not only did the Bardoli Dalits actively participate in the struggle but they had Ambedkar's full support and sanction as well. Though in the ultimate analysis it was the Gandhian-led Congress and not the left aspirants to working class leadership, that succeeded in creating a broad united front and in addressing the diverse economic and cultural issues which had arisen. It goes without saying that 'the very unevenness and variabilities of the colonial exploitation processes imposed on a hierarchical traditional society' had created a highly differential impact of exploitation, though not polarization. It was essentially, by linking the varying economic demands of the variously exploited groups and by articulating these with culture and community, that the resemblance of a solution could be arrived at.

Addressing The Adivasi Problem in Maharashtra

The praiseworthy efforts of the Shramik Sangathana, an organization formed at the insistence of Ambersingh Maharaj in Dhulia district of Maharastra in January 1972, deserves kudos for the constructive changes it wrought in the pitiable plight of the Adivasis, most especially its women. And activists in the Shramik Sangathana, as in other grass-roots movements in India, readily acknowledge, "the influence of new social movements in the West upon their own struggles". Having made that tacit admission, let us proceed to trace the genesis of the organization. The Shramik Sangathana, as such, must essentially be viewed against the backdrop of the Maharashtrian Bhils' indigenous tradition of protest against abominable abuse by Hindu cultivators. The shocking sexual exploitation of *adivasi* women being an especially potent catalyst here.

The most eminent Bhil social reformer was definitely Ambersingh Suratvanti (1940-74) or Ambersingh Maharaj as he was more commonly, yet respectfully called. Although he joined a Gandhian organization, the Sarvodaya Sangh, established in Dhulia district in the mid-fifties, for a period of six years, he ultimately left in 1968 as he felt that the Sarvodaya Sangh's constructive activities were not effective in curtailing exploitation. The Gandhian traditions in this organization complemented adivasi attempts to combine social reform and political struggle. He now began organizing independently among the oppressed adivasis and this rejection of his formal organization was to have a great bearing on the Shramik Sangathana itself.

In the beginning, the tribals and the oppressed bore their oppression with an admirable restraint and fortitude, with only occasional outbursts. However, around 1970, a horrific incidence took place, rousing Ambersingh out of his calm demeanour and galvanizing him into some action. Some rich Hindu peasants had brazenly raped a group of women, including a pregnant woman, in his native village of Padalda. He was approached for assistance and reproached, as the most educated villager, for his silence. Thoroughly ashamed of his inaction, Ambersingh speedily contacted the superintendent of police, who found eight Gujars guilty of committing atrocities against *adivasi* women. The verdict was, subsequently, overturned in court. Although it is noteworthy that Ambersingh was politicized by the exploitation of *adivasi* women, he characteristically sought to preserve women's honour rather than encouraging women's own activism. He remained in close contact with the agricultural workers and spoke to them about their oppression.

Such oppression often took cruel and rather tortuous forms. The landless women labourers, who share certain problems with their menfolk such as abysmally low wages, irregular work, and long working hours and, in addition, are deprived of vital health care facilities like maternity leave, medical care or even the burden relieving facility of creches, are mercilessly beaten by the landlords and rich peasants on minor pretexts. Requests for grain or more money were grave enough offences for thrashings in villages where organization was completely weak. Atrocities by police as well as by forest employees and forest guards such as beating, corruption and rape of women were common. At Kudawad, for instance, especially during the Emergency, special arrangements used to be made by the callous and rich peasants to harass the landless labourers, particularly women. Sadistic manifestations of such cruel treatment meted out to the hapless women labourers included the installation of live wires spread around the sugarcane fields in such a manner that the women received near fatal shocks while on their way to or from work.

Another form of harassment of women was perpetrated by the watchmen of crop protection societies which are registered co-operative societies of the peasants. They are dominated by the rich peasants. They not only had licenses for guns to protect the crops, from the British period right upto 1974 but the same year a sugar tycoon devised an ingenious scheme for a private para-military force, the professed aim of which was to protect crops. This was the beginning of armed attacks on the labourers, extracting fines from them, confining, beating, and torturing them. The watchmen searched the clothes of the labourers to see if they had stolen grain. This searching of women by watchmen is very insulting and is disapproved of by the women. As if all this were not demeaning enough, in addition, insulting, inhuman treatment and abusive language were commonly used by the oppressors to establish their dominance over the oppressed, especially women. Harangued by outsiders and those from a more economically privileged class of society, suppressed by men of their own class who carelessly drank away a significant portion of the small amount of family earnings and regularly beat up their wives, the lives of such women had become a miserable, endless saga of deprivation and exhausting physical labour. They had to tackle all the tiring, time consuming household chores themselves.

Ambersingh subsequently dedicated himself to eradicating *adivasi* oppression and formed the Bhil Adivasi Seva Mandal around 1970-71. But his efforts at improving the pitiable prevailing conditions for this largely victimized segment of society through peaceful, legal means were fruitless and came to naught. It was the gross mishandling of what could even be termed as 'a human rights issue' that acted as the much needed catalyst and ultimately led to the final formulation of the Shramik Sangathana. It was the brutal assault on *adivasis* by Hindu cultivators which persuaded him to intensify the struggle. On May2, 1971, several hundred starving *adivasis* visited Vishram Hari Patil, the biggest landlord in Patilwadi village, Shahada *taluka*, to request a loan of twelve kilos of grain each, for this was a severe drought year." While Patil pretended to comply, he, in fact, called the police and a several hundred strong petitioning crowd was accosted by an armed mob of landlords and rich peasants, accompanied by the police. Though the police found the Bhil crowd peaceful and refused to open fire, they, nevertheless, arrested them. But not before some physical damage had been done and the landlords had themselves opened fire, killing one Bhil needlessly and injuring many more.

Recorded for posterity as "the Patilwadi incident" this bizarre incident focussed attention on the area and attracted the attention of some Sarvodaya volunteers to work with Ambersingh. It threw up three committed men from diverse disciplines into the fray, who however, had one thing in common i.e. all three had been working with the social reformer Baba Amte in Chandrapur district. They were Vijay Kanhare, Kumar Shiralkar and Dinanath Manohar. They came to Dhulia in November 1971 and two months later founded the 'Sangathana.' Their arrival marked a turning point in the movement for until then the *adivasis* had 'largely organized independently in a dispersed and isolated fashion.' Moreover, the enthusiasm the movement now generated among middle-class supporters in Bombay, some of whom had excellent contacts with the press, provided the movement much needed visibility, valuable material support and protection from suppression. However, it must be mentioned here that the stepping stone to the formation of the 'Sangathana was, briefly, the Gram Swarajaya Samiti (GSS), a Sarvodaya-sponsored village improvement association, with whom the volunteers worked.' Whereas the GSS was influenced by Gandhian precepts and completely committed to nonviolent, accommodative politics, Shramik Sangathana activists were Marxists.

The period between 1972 to 1975 undoubtedly represented the high watermark of the early Shramik Sangathana movement. Motivated by the urgent need to eradicate or at least ameliorate the severely oppressive milieu in which the *adivasis* existed, they framed their objectives and modus operandi accordingly. Accordingly, it challenged Hindu cultivators' appropriation of *adivasi* land, labourers' receipt of subminimum wages, and state restrictions on *adivasis,* cultivation of forest land. Addressing the question of agricultural wages, the SS organized an Ekta Parishad which ten thousand people attended and which paved the way for further negotiations in the matter, albeit not without resistance from the concerned quarters. The SS also organized numerous demonstrations demanding increased public employment and improved working conditions. Mainly through its ceaseless efforts, the government finally allotted more relief employment to Dhulia than to any other district in Maharashtra when severe drought and famine struck in the years 1972-73. After the government had introduced the Employment Guarantee Scheme (EGS), granting lean season work to the unemployed in 1972, the Shramik Sangathana relentlessly kept up pressure for the implementation of EGS and liberalization of its provisions. It organized struggles around the *adivasis*' right to cultivate forest land — in Dhulia district approximately 4000 *adivasis* earned their livelihood principally from cultivating forest wasteland and thousands more relied on the forests for food, firewood, and fodder and collaborated with important leftist leaders like Sharad Patil in this connection.

The Emergence of Women's Resistance

Participatory action by the women in the early struggles of the Shramik Sangathana on issues concerned with land, wages and employment, though not of great political significance, did percolate downwards and fuel a need for these women to explore their grievances and demands specifically and independently of the men. For this purpose, the activists convened a three-day meeting in April 1973, attended by 151 women from 31 villages. They not only efficiently articulated the multipronged difficulties that they had faced in their villages-sexual harassment by landlords, watchmen, and the police, inordinately long hours of work within and outside their homes, and their husbands' alcoholism and abusive behavior, they took immediate action on these major irritants.

Galvanizing the women into action when one of the (women) speakers appealed for help in stopping liquor production in her village. Despite the activists' opposition, the crowd or women responded almost instantaneously and marched off to the village *en masse* and proceeded to smash the liquor vessels without further ado. Subsequently, they *gheraoed* the house of the panchayat chairman, who had encouraged drinking and cordoned off the entire village to prevent bootleggers from escaping. This dramatic incident provided a precedent for women's repeated struggles against alcoholism. For the adivasi women, who were always careful to move in groups for this somewhat daring exercise, felt that alcoholism was encouraged by traders for commercial reasons and by the affluent peasants because it effectively blunted *adivasi* militance.

Women's opposition to men's excessive drinking foreshadowed their subsequent forms of protest. Women did not create a structured organization, hold regular meetings or appoint leaders. But through their informal network, they could quickly assemble large groups. Women's militancy now assumed unique, distinctive forms. Rather than the brutish use of force, they believed in humiliating their opponents so that the latter would understand more comprehensively their own experience of degradation. Singing being a powerful vehicle for expressing hope, resistance, and collective spirit for the *adivasi* women, they often articulate their experiences of oppression through the composition and singing of songs.

Thus the Shramik Sangathana's emphasis on change at the level of cultural relations had significant implications for women. One of them being an attempt at the abolition of rigid, tradition-bound, sexist practices during the customary Adivasi weddings. The SS decided to celebrate May Day in 1979 by organizing a group wedding ceremony. The salient features of the subsequent SS bulletin issued, are as under :

Initiating Changes in Traditional Marriage Customs

From the beginning to the end, adivasis' marriages involve great expenditure and a lot of trouble...men say, "we have bought this girl", so she is not considered a human being ....According to the old customs, the girl is not asked whether or not she likes the boy.

Adivasis have come to realize that this form of marriage is unnecessary. They lose their land to moneylenders and rich farmers and their poverty increases.

The Shramik Sangathana has taken the initiative to end these traditional customs which oppress *adivasis*. Girls and boys who belong to this organization will freely choose their marriage partners. There will be no bride price, no presents, no liquor, no ceremonial lunches. The principle should be to keep expenses to a minimum. If some cannot afford even these, all the labourers should help them meet the expenses.

The Shramik Stri Mukti Sangathana

It was the crass brutalization of a Muslim woman by her employer in Shahada town in 1979, that proved to be the catalyst for the genesis of the Shramik Stri Mukti Sangathana which is a more decentralized and democratic version of the Shramik Sangathana. In a spontaneous reaction to the incident, an impressive number of women (seven hundred to be exact) organized a protest rally. 'As the incident that led to its creation signified, the SSMS was committed to organizing women across caste and class lines to challenge the varied manifestations of sexual inequality'.

While the SSMS encouraged all the women who attended the meetings, to actively participate in its deliberations and many important leaders emerged from among the *adivasi* women viz. Hirkana, Tagibai, Saraswati, Bhuribai, Surtanbai, Sukmabai, Vimlabai, and Pitabi, none of these women exercised any formal authority and the SSMS rejected fixed membership, office holders, and subcommittees.

In 1982 the SSMS invited Nirmala Sathe, a feminist from Bombay, with a view to broadening the focus of its activities and range of issues to be tackled. This enterprising lady patiently organized week-long workshops in Dhulia, addressing the various disturbing issues that plagued adivasi women. Such issues ranged from rape and sexual harassment to the patriarchal character of Bhil ritual and superstition, women's lack of control over their own bodies, and the unequal division of labour within the home. These meetings also provided much needed opportunities for regular contact between the *adivasi* women and urban feminists.

One of the major issues that the SSMS addressed over two protracted camps in March 1983, dealt with the benefits and disadvantages of adivasi customary law when compared with Hindu law, and of the judicial system compared with the *adivasi panchs*. While they agreed unanimously that *adivasi* law was in most respects superior to Hindu law, they felt that this needs revision to prohibit polygamy, give mothers custody of the children upon divorce, eliminate the bride price, and provide for women's representation in the *panchs*. They were also in favour of raising the age of marriage and of the couple choosing their own partners. They were of the opinion that *advisi* law must, necessarily, encompass *adivasis* women's inheritance rights.

The Shramik Stri Mukti Sangathana worked in close collaboration with the women's wing of the Satya Shodak Communist party, which strongly advocated bringing *adivasi* women under the purview of the Hindu Code Bill on the grounds that Hindu law was preferable for women to *adivasi* customary law. But the SSMS was not particularly favourably inclined towards such a proposition for it felt that their inclusion would result in the further assimilation of Bhils into caste Hindu society. Instead they pressurized the Satya Shodhak Communist party to demand in the writ petition that they filed in the Supreme Court, for the formulation of a new *adivasi* personal law immediately and the ultimate formulation of a uniform civil code that would apply to all women.

Predictably, as the SSMS gained in strength and experience, it began to chafe at its ties with the mother organization, the Shramik Sangathana and incidents of rape of *adivasi* women, subsequent arbitration by the SS and involvement in political activities for it to survive, all exerted unpleasant pulls and pressures. The expulsion of the SS's three important activists viz. Dinanath, Tagibai and Chander greatly weakened the Shramik Sangathana. The first was expelled on account of rape of an adivasi female political candidate (Bhuribai) and the latter on account of illicit sexual liaison. The erosion of the Shramik Sangathana's democratic character was further manifested by the attempts of middle-class activists to impose sexually puritanical attitudes upon *adivasis*. To some extent this was a result of the tension between achieving a democratic structure on the one hand and a relatively egalitarian, non-exploitative relationship between *adivasis* and urban, middle class activists, on the other. The SS was basically very disapproving of sexual liaisons between middle-class male activists and *adivasi* women for fear of further magnifying inequalities between them. Ironically enough, the activists' puritanism also strongly represented a form of cultural domination in which potentially restrictive attitudes toward sexuality were imposed upon the more emancipated *adivasis*.

Repression against the Shramik Sangathana, which had hitherto been contained in the wake of the movement's widespread popularity and the subsequent wariness of the dominant classes to lie low, erupted as the strength and affiliations of the SS were threatened by break-ups. Three major riots occurred in the month of December 1983 alone. Horrifying incidents all, in each case hordes of aggressive armed young men ransacked *adivasi* homes, ravaged *adivasi* shops, and attacked *adivasi* men and women. In the third riot, they even went as far as attacking Muslims who had sheltered *adivasis* in the past. It was three months later, however, that the most serious massacre of the *adivasis* that Dhulia had ever experienced, took place in Shahada district. Armed landlords descended on Shelti village one night and cruelly murdered five *adivasis*, some of whom they alleged, had stolen a bundle of dried cotton sticks with which to light a fire for a Holi festival.

The character of repression in Dhulia district, as in other parts of the country, was markedly different in the 1980s than it had previously been, acquiring sinister political overtones and fuelled further by deadly political affiliations. The dominant classes now broke out of their self-limiting isolation and formed linkages with state-wide political organizations; for instance, P.K. Patil, who had masterminded the "Purshottam Sena", became President of the Maharashtrian Janata Party. In addition, Dhulia's dominant classes also forged linkages with the Patil Pawan Sangathana, "a Hindu revivalist organization that had linkages with the Shiv Sena and the Bharatiya Janata Party at the state level. The PPS attracted support across caste and party lines among such diverse groups as wealthy landowners, *panchayat* members, shopkeepers, small merchants, and unemployed youth in the towns." Despite solid evidence to implicate the Janata Party as well as the PPs in the violence of the Shelti massacre, the superintendent and deputy superintendent of police vehemently denied, in subsequent interviews, the involvement of these guilty parties. In fact they went so far as to express utter disdain and indifference towards the hapless *adivasis* and demonstrated solidarity instead with the wealthy cultivators. Not an encouraging portent for alleviating serious problems, let alone eradicating them.

The demise of the Shramik Sangathana and SSMS embodying a political movement that appeared to provide an ideal leftist alternative to the CPI (M)— was both unfortunate and inevitable. Why did it take place and what were the implications implicit therein with reference to the lot of the *adivasis*? The SS's attitude toward the state oscillated 'between two poles' so to speak. On the one hand, it flatly refused to accord centrality to the state, in order to politicize arenas of social life outside the purview of state power and fervently hoped that rejecting parliamentary participation would provide some protection against co-optation and reformism. On the other hand, recognizing the dangers of marginalizing itself completely from the formal political arena, it tried to de-legitimate the state and ultimately placed itself in a position of continual disadvantage. For it certainly couldn't afford to be as audacious as the Congress.

Congress rose to the occasion and addressed one of the most urgent needs of the *adivasis* and provided them with invaluable protection against repression by the dominant classes. Over the years the government had made a number of concessions to *adivasi* demands on a number of issues such as drought relief, restoration of agricultural wages, and regularizing encroachment on forest land. The Shramik Sangathana, like other grass-roots organizations however, rather unwisely dismissed these on the grounds that they were reformist measures, without recognizing their extreme significance for impoverished groups. As SS's commitment to an independent stance waned, so, too, did it lose the support it had at one time enjoyed amongst the urban middle-class.

However, while on the one hand an extremely democratic approach seems to have signalled the end of the SS, on the other hand, from a different perspective, it was the lack of adherence to such democratic functioning that contributed to its untimely demise. The Shramik Sangathana's decision to ally itself with the CITU suggests that personalities played a more crucial role than ideas in determining organizational strategy and the secretive manner in which some members like Kumar (who professed egalitarianism) and other activists decided to join the CPI(M), contradicted their professed commitment to openness.

To a far greater extent than the SS, the SSMS had to face and cope with a vast array of issues. Nor could the nemesis of this organization be explained merely by "the personality conflicts or the sense of enervation that crippled the Shramik Sangathana. Whereas the SS suffered from the excess of middle-class leadership, the later organization, the SSMS suffered most definitely from a dearth of middle-class activists. In contrast, grass-roots organizations in which women have been substantially represented in addressing the all-important issue of gender inequality, have met with a fair degree of success. The Chhatra Yuva Sangharsh Vahini, a Gandhian Socialist organization that became active in the famous Bodh Gaya district of Bihar, in 1977 was one such organization. Since nearly 50 per cent of its urban activists were women i.e. out of a total of ten such members, four were women, the Vahini was able to address a range of women's issues from the start. Women activists subjected the Vahini's internal workings to close scrutiny, drawing attention to interpersonal dynamics, meeting times, and domestic responsibilities among the activists. The most 'path-breaking' move and very likely attempted for the first time in India, was the women's bold demand that the land that the Vahini had appropriated from a vast Hindu *math* (temple, monastery complex) should be distributed to female labourers rather than to their husbands. Although Chetna, one of the women activists, conceded that in fact the Vahini had distributed land to women in only a few villages and elsewhere jointly to men and women, she believed that the presence of women activists provided the crucial impetus for addressing the issue.

A number of questions come to mind, and for them to be answered dispassionately, yet after an indepth analysis which considers various facets of the query, so that fruitful lessons may be drawn for posterity, one needs to view a broad sweep of events in their collective as well as individual context. Keeping in view the peculiar complexities that govern them, and the emotional and economic compulsions that propel the players of each specific drama to move towards its own unique conclusion.

One of the questions which needs explanation in the present context is one which had been the subject of much debate and discussion, namely, whether peasant movements can sustain themselves in the absence of outside support. "On the one hand, *adivasi* seem to have been much more active than the peasantry as a whole in autonomous political organization; the tradition of *adivasi* protest in Dhulia district in the nineteenth and early twentieth centuries provides eloquent testimony." On the other end of the scale, however, it was only in the formation of the Shramik Sangathana that the *adivasis* gained 'a significant sense of efficacy' to shift their attention from social reform to opposition directed at the state and the dominant classes. Even more specifically, in the case of the women's struggles among the *adivasis,* urban feminist support seemed quite unnecessary initially because adivasi women in Dhulia district had such a comprehensive understanding of their own situation and the oppression inherent in it. However, its importance increased perceptibly as *adivasi* women sought determinedly to broaden their own agenda from questions of violence against women to the more subtle sources and manifestations of sexual inequality. Urban feminist support was also critical to reducing SSMS dependence on the Shramik Sangathana and providing it with the kind of resources that the

Shramik Sangathana acquired through its linkages with the Shramik Mukti Dal and the CPI(M).

References

The most authoritative account of the Mahad Satyagraha and of some of the varying interpretations of it (with a strong attack on some caste Hindu distortions) is given by Ratnakar Ganvir, *Mahad Samta Sangar* (Jalgoan : Ratnamitra Prakshan,1981) pp. 1-65. See also the newspaper and Bombay police account cited in *Source Material on Dr Babasahib Ambedkar and the Movement of Untouchables*, Volume I (Bombay: Government of Maharashtra, 1982) pp. 13-33, which give a sense of the degree to which the campaign became a major event. (As appears in *Dalits and the Democratic Revolution*)

19

HISTORY OF WARFARE: THE INTRODUCTION OF WOMEN IN THE FORCES

The art of warfare is as old as life itself. As Thomas Jefferson, the third President of the United States of America and the architect of its famous Declaration of Independence, so succinctly summed up :

> The tree of liberty must be refreshed from time to time with the blood of patriots and tyrants. It is its natural manure.

Different battlegrounds across the globe have witnessed bloodshed through the ages, for a complex plethora of reasons, conducted with varying degrees of efficiency and battle preparedness. Religious sanction has been implicit in some of the most ancient historic battles as the *Bhagvad Gita* (II,37) so optimistically states, exhorting Arjuna to battle :

> Either slain thou shalt go to heaven;
> or victorious thou shalt enjoy the earth;
> therefore arise, O son of Kunti (Arjuna),
> resolved on battle.

Be that as it may, "the beginnings of organized warfare, the deployment of the column and the line, the invention of strategy and tactics, the use of massive defence fortifications, and the development of a military weapons technology with its long, intermediate and short-range weapons can all be traced back into prehistoric times. Warfare, except for its various modern refinements, cannot be credited to civilized man, although ancient civilizations of the Near East and Greece added powerful new ingredients to the war machine they inherited from Neolithic times."

While historians, philosophers, military strategists, statesmen, writers *et al* have advanced numerous viewpoints on the methodology, motivation and psychology of warfare, each convincing from his own perspective, surprisingly enough modern archaeologists and anthropologists have generally ignored the development of warfare in prehistory. As one observer has so astutely maintained about modern studies of primitive war, "Anthropologists, sociologists and other social scientists have largely confined their writings to deprecating war rather than attempting to understand this behaviour pattern which has played such a tremendous role in human affairs." Such an attitude is given further weightage by Robert Ardrey's unequivocal denunciation of Man and his nature thus:

"Man is a predator whose natural instinct is to kill with a weapon." Within the last quarter of a century or so, marvellous new discoveries of the traces of early man-like creatures (sometimes called 'premen') have occurred in Africa. By 1975 both archaeologists and physical anthropologists had turned up about forty Australopithecine skulls proving the existence of at least two if not three hominid species at the dawn of man's evolutionary development, in a timeframe that extends roughly from 1,00,000 to 5,00,000 years ago. These discoveries, predictably enough, generated a tremendous amount of controversy, and one that raged the most among them concerned the apparent aggressive nature of man's early biological ancestors. Has man from the beginning been biologically programmed for war then? The answers to the posited query are infinitely more complicated than one would initially assume while attempting to shed some light on the subject. While it is not within the ambit of this study to verify exhaustively or even in great detail such a viewpoint, an attempt is certainly being made here to shed some light on the subject and present the thought processes of noted authorities from different disciplines. Actually, the controversy predates the discovery of Australopithecine remains by over two hundred years. Jean Jacques Rousseau, the French philosopher, painted a charming picture of the life of the Noble Savage uncontaminated by the evils of civilization, in response to the English philosopher, Thomas Hobbes' often-quoted description of primitive life as 'nasty, brutish and short'. Therefore, while Hobbes in his famous work *Leviathan* (1651), essentially projected man as being selfish, Rousseau held that mankind is essentially good but corrupted by society, and his novel *The New Heloise* (1761) proposed spiritual refreshment through a return to nature. In the early years of the present century, William James argued in an essentially pacifist essay that 'History is a bath of blood', and that there was an element of inheritance in man's warlike drives:

> The prehistoric men were hunting men, and to hunt a neighbouring tribe, kill the males, loot the village, and possess the females was the most profitable, as well as the most exciting way of living. Thus were the more martial tribes selected, and in chiefs and peoples a pure pugnacity and love of glory came to mingle with the more fundamental appetite for plunder. Modern man inherits all the innate pugnacity and all the love of glory of his ancestors.

Sigmund Freud, the renowned Austrian psychiatrist, in *Civilization and its Discontents* (1930) and in a famous letter to Albert Einstein, observed that Man's 'desire for aggression has to be reckoned as a part of his instinctual endowment...' Amplifying on his theory in the said letter to the German born U.S. Nobel Laureate, thus :

> You are amazed that it is so easy to infect men with the war fever, and you surmise that man has in him an active instinct for hatred and destruction, amenable to such stimulations. I entirely agree with you. I believe in the existence of this instinct and have been recently at pains to study its manifestations. The upshot of these observations, as bearing on the subject in hand, is that

> there is no likelihood of our being able to suppress humanity's aggressive tendencies.

Although these views were deeply disturbing to pacifists, a major escalation of the controversy only came with the historic discovery of the *Australopithecus* (literally, 'Southern Ape') by Raymond Dart in 1924, its subsequent interpretation by him and the rather blunt polemical discussion in an article entitled *The Predatory Transition from Ape to Man* published 45 years ago, in 1954. Attacking their cannibalistic and warring propensities quite abrasively in his article, Dart says that the small brain of the Australopithecine (c. 400-500 cubic centimeters) was :

> demonstrably more than adequate for the crude, omnivorous cannibalistic, bone-club wielding, jaw-bone cleaving Samsonian phase of human emergence. The loathsome cruelty of man forms one of his inescapable, characteristic and differentiative features; and it is explicable only in terms of his carnivorous and cannibalistic origin.

In all likelihood, 'the issues raised by Dart about man's genetic drive to kill' might well have remained in the relative obscurity of academic books had it not been for the enthusiastic efforts of his ardent disciple, Rober Ardrey, who with the publication of *African Genesis* (1961) and a host of equally popular books on the subject in the next 25 years, brought the subject right out in the open. Neither should the importance of Konrad Lorenz's *On Aggression* (1966) be undervalued; a Noble Prize winner for his earlier work on animal behaviour, Lorenz's views on the animal nature of aggression in man, 'carried respected authority'. Inevitably, however, they provoked a counter attack in the form of Ashley Montagu's *The Nature of Human Aggression* (1976) and Richard E. Leakey's *Origins* (1979), both of which challenged the authenticity of Dart's rather outspoken views and went on to argue the opposite view-that early man was generally peaceful and cooperative.

However, it was during the Epipalaeolithic and Proto-Neolithic period—collectively known as the Mesolithic Age—from 12,000 to 8,000 BC that there was a remarkable revolution in weapons technology that has very few modern parallels—the invention of gunpowder, the locomotive, airplanes, tanks and the atomic bomb. Four fantastically powerful new weapons, namely the bow, the sling, the dagger (or the short, short sword) and the mace made their first appearance. Weapons which, along with the Paleolithic spear, would dominate warfare down to the present millennium. This new, revolutionary weapons technology was 'combined with the invention of military tactics and, by historical standards, produced true warfare'.

The appearance of the column and the line, which imply command and organization, is synonymous with the invention of tactics and it is generally assumed that both strategy and tactics emerged out of the rather complex hunting patterns of Paleolithic man. In fact there is considerable evidence that organized groups of men, 'almost certainly under the command of a leader, helped to stampede large animals over cliffs or to draw them into bogs'. Available information regarding the hunting habits of primitive societies surviving into modern times, further confirms such an assumption.

The Neolithic Age provides ample authentic evidence of the deployment of the column and the line. Not only do evocative Neolithic paintings from the Spanish Levant depict adherence to this , one of the most significant features of early, organized warfare, in numerous hunting and warring scenes, but an authoritative view is expressed as under :

> Those people who do not avail themselves of these two sociologic devices are below the military horizon without argument. Their fighting can be nothing but a scuffle, regardless of the amount of bloodshed, and cannot be called a war... The line is the simplest tactical formation, and a sociologic trait without which there can be no true war.

It cannot be denied that with the birth of civilization we have records of the use of large national armies on a scale definitely far greater than we could have envisaged for prehistoric times. The famous civilizations of Egypt and Mesopotamia being illustrative of this point for ample evidence exists to prove the early militarization of the peoples of both these kingdoms. "Partly this development was due to the tremendous population explosion brought about by the irrigation and cultivation of the great river valleys. Partly it may be attributed to the political power and authority of the new rulers who were a major by-product of that complex phenomenon, the origins of the state."

The ancient Near Eastern kingdoms of Egypt, Assyria and Persia also stand out like towering giants with their relatively more complex systems of military organization when compared to the simple systems of military organization that prevailed in the Greek world in the age of the hoplite phalanx or heavy infantry, developed sometime between 700 and 650 BC probably. Organization being the *sine quo non* of warfare, so organization in its broadest sense including logistics, conscription, armament, command structure, tactical formation, and military engineering , shapes grand strategy, strategy and tactics. There is obviously much more to cavalry and chariot warfare than the mere romance and glory of the charge at the gallop and judicious selection of horses for effective performance thus assumes vital significance. An exhaustive study of the vast collection of over 2000 surviving letters, sent by the kings' agents in the provinces to the kings themselves, 'illustrates sometimes in microscopic detail the active attention of Assyrias's rulers to matters of horse recruitment'. Not only was Assyrian horse supply supervised by high-ranking governmental officers called *musarkisus*, usually two to a province, appointed by the central government and reporting directly to the king rather than to the provincial governors, but the *musarkisu* was assisted by scribes and other helpers. Sometimes he worked only for a single branch of the horse army, i.e. for the 'palace chariotry', or 'the cavalry bodyguard'.

The problems of horse supply have, however, plagued many modern nations and have not, by any means, been associated with earlier armies alone. For instance, at Waterloo, 2,500 years after the fall of Assyria, Napoleon is considered to have performed a near miraculous feat in procuring enough horses to have mount a cavalry of 20,000. The following excerpts taken from *Cavalry in the Waterloo Campaign* by General Sir Evelyn Wood, throws valuable light on the subject:

> That Napoleon could in two months collect 20,000 horsemen for his invasion of Belgium, after providing for the Army Corps guarding the other frontiers of France, and having had a nucleus of 8000 horses only on which to start the mobilization, is one of the many proofs of his marvelous genius; but the inevitable hurry, and consequent want of training, accounts in a great measure for the want of success attained by the French Cavalry.

Therefore Marshal Ney 'the bravest of the brave', who went through all of five mounts during the course of the battle (of Waterloo), rather ill-advisedly charged the British line without French infantry support, and all the valour in the world could not make up for the error. For the most effective use of cavalry is in pursuit, after the enemy ranks have been broken and are in flight. Usually the heaviest casualties are effected at this highly vulnerable juncture.

But hundreds of years before this historical battle was recorded permanently in the annals of history, a tremendous military revolution in the Greek world changed the nature of ancient warfare dramatically and produced one of the finest armies 'in the military history of the western world'. The Greeks and Macedonians, effectively created a finely integrated army

— heavy and light infantry, skirmishers, and heavy and light cavalry and mastered the art of supporting such a force logistically. Therefore the legendary Alexander the Great, in the last half of the fourth century BC, 'stormed into Asia with a superb army that defeated every Persian force in its path and eventually marched into India, where it rolled over the great army and elephants of king Porus at the battle of the Hydaspes (326 BC)'.

It is of vital importance to note that Greek mercenary troops played an immensely decisive role in the fusion of ancient Near Eastern and Greek military institutions, for one of the most deadly low intensity conflicts which saps India's massive military might today, is the incipient induction of this deadly element across India's borders from Pakistan. 'Deadly element' constituting mercenaries who, as foreigners, have, since those early times, been less susceptible to the blandishments of dynastic, political change. Motivated to perform well for purely mercenary considerations, such 'troops' on the whole, 'served with a sense of professionalism and faced the dangers of battle with a calmer and more deadly sense of purpose than armies of raw, citizen conscripts'. With their multi-skills they were particularly useful in the specialized skirmishers arms of archers and slingers and the Persians found it useful to hire them in both small and large numbers for different utility roles. While in small numbers they were used as bodyguards where their expertise in hand-to-hand fighting was important, in large numbers they fought in formation as shock troops in assault, a role they played more easily on Asian soil, where their opponents were not well armed, than in Greece.

Mercenaries in modern warfare are generally regarded as contemptible for after the successful burst of nationalistic, patriotic fervour associated with the American and French Revolutions, 'it has been fashionable to regard foreign troops who fight for pay rather than for love of country as potentially disloyal, and in any event unlikely to display the fierce tenacity of citizens fighting for the fatherland'. Moreover, the scale of warfare has since increased so dramatically in the nineteenth and twentieth centuries and has acquired much more complex and deadly dimensions because mercenaries are not so easy to recruit in large numbers.

The vicissitudes of war, the rise and fall of empires and the transient fate of nations have, perhaps, been summed up best in Rudyard Kipling's sagacious verse thus :

Nations have passed away and left no traces,
And History gives the naked cause of it.
One single, simple reason in all cases,
They fell because their people were not fit.

The subcontinent of India, comprising India, Pakistan, Nepal, Bhutan, Bangladesh and Sri Lanka, has been invaded several times in the past. Even after 15 August, 1947, when India gained Independence and was freed from the yoke of imperialist British power, this great and glorious country faced major aggressions many times. Yet it acquitted itself admirably and in keeping with its glorious military traditions by and large.

India was known in the Puranas as Bharata Varsha and believed to be a part of a larger island known as *Jambu Dvipa* and subsequently termed as Hindustan in the medieval period. India is really a peninsula. The portion of the subcontinent under the British had an area of approximately 4,095,000 square kilometres, while India as it is today has an area of about 3,276,141 square kilometres. Since it will not be possible to describe each distinct geographical region of the country in detail, mentioned here is a broad topographical division of India. It can be divided into three major parts. These physical delienations will not only make it easier for the reader to readily recall the vast and varied terrain that comprises our country, but also make it easier for him to understand that to effectively man and protect so many borders with other countries, is a Herculean task. The three divisions are as under :

(a) The mountainous terrain in the North-West, North and North-East. This includes the Baluchistan and North-West frontier Provinces of Pakistan, Jammu and Kashmir, Himachal Pradesh, the hill areas of Uttar Pradesh, Arunachal Pradesh, Nagaland, Manipur, Mizoram, Meghalaya and Tripura States of India; Nepal and Bhutan.

(b) The Indo-Gangetic plain including the valleys of Indus, Ganges and Brahmaputra rivers and their tributaries; and the Thar desert. This includes the Sind and Punjab Provinces of Pakistan; Gujarat, Rajasthan, Punjab, Haryana, Uttar Pradesh, Bihar, Bengal and Assam States of India; and Bangladesh.

(c) The Central Indian and Deccan Plateau with the Western Ghats in the West, Vindhya mountains in the North and Eastern Ghats in the East; and the narrow coastal plains around the Plateau. This includes Maharashtra, Madhya Pradesh, Orissa and the Southern States.

(The above geographical divisions have been taken from *Prepare or Perish : A Study of National Security*—by General K.V. Krishna Rao, PVSM (Retd.).

India has a common border with Pakistan, Bangladesh, Nepal, Bhutan, Burma and China. Its boundary with the 'Red' giant, China is, perhaps the most complicated of all. Hence it is being described here in great detail. "India's boundary with China extends over 3440 kms from North-West Kashmir to the Tri-Junction of India, Burma and China near the Talu Pass. The entire frontier is traditional, well-known and in some sectors has been demarcated. In the Western Sector, it runs along the watershed formed by the Mustagh, the Karakoram and the Kuen Lun mountain ranges to a point East of longitude 80°. Thereafter, it turns south and runs along the watershed through the Lank La (Pass) and along the Chang-Chenmo range. Cutting across the

Pangong Tso (Lake) and the Spanggur Tso, it continues through the Chang La and along the Kailash range. It then turns to South-West through Demchok and skirting the Hanle mountains cuts across Para Chu river South of Chumar. Then in the Central sector, it follows the watershed between the Ganges and the Sutlej rivers to the Tri-junction of India, Nepal and China. Continuing along the Sino-Nepalese boundary, the boundary between Sikkim and Tibet also runs along a watershed. The boundary between Bhutan and Tibet is along the crest of the Himalayas too. Then in the North-Eastern sector, the boundary which is about 1136 kms. long, continues from the Eastern limits of Bhutan to a point near the Talu Pass, along the Northern Watershed of the Brahmaputra, excepting where the Lohit, Dihang, Subansiri and Namjang rivers cut through." It would be pertinent to mention here that the Northern Frontier, not merely based on geographical features but also sanctioned by specific international agreements, historic rights, custom and tradition, actual exercise of sovereign powers and international law, has been universally recognized as the frontier of India for well over 3000 years. It (the Northern Frontier) is mostly based on the crest line of the Himalayan Ranges.

Such a painstaking effort to delineate in detail physical geographical features of our multifaceted terrain, is an attempt to understand in reasonably comprehensive measure, its lengthy and somewhat complicated boundary with one of its most formidable adversaries . Simply because the well-knit Indian Army, over nine lakh strong today, and men and women who comprise this formidable force, must be fully conversant with the daunting task they face in guarding their nation's honour. Yes, WOMEN! for women now form an integral part of this military might of the country and have begun to be regularly recruited in the non-fighting arms of both the Army and Air Force. It is not surprising, in a country which has had numerous deeds of valour performed by women, to accord this resilient segment of society a permanent role in the defence of our country. The indomitable Rani of Jhansi, the beautiful and brave

Rani Padmini of Chittor, the courageous women of the Nehru family, Aruna Asaf Ali and the millions of stoic, heroic and undaunted Indian womenfolk, many of them uneducated but inspired and held together by a glorious common commitment to throw off alien domination and restore the nation to its erstwhile independent status, who braved lathi charges, imprisonment and even sacrificed their lives unflinchingly, have gone down in the annals of Indian history permanently. In fighting against the British through conventional warfare and by participating in satyagrahas, non-cooperation movements, etc. Then what brought about the revolution of formally incorporating women in the army? Perhaps it would be difficult to pinpoint a singular specific reason for this broadminded and progressive step in this age of emancipation of women. The Indian Army Chief's wife, Dr (Mrs.) Ranjana Malik, herself a liberated army wife and an Army doctor who has very successfully combined the professional duties of her career with the demanding needs of maintaining a happy, cohesive family unit, says "Women of today need to shed their inhibitions, break their shackles, overcome illiteracy, shed outdated religious beliefs and need to step out of their homes. Education of women will lead to increased self confidence and economic independence. They will be able to fight against domestic violence and the agony of humiliation, being taken for granted, patronized and discriminated against. Until they are educated and they develop a sense of purpose and determination, they will never have their rightful place in society and will not be treated with respect. They must be taught to be self-reliant. It is time for us to realize that girls of today must be brought up as equal from day one. Their education should be purposeful. Each girl has tremendous potential if she is permitted to blossom, unhindered by social prejudices. She must be given equal opportunities inside and outside the home." She herself played a pivotal role in ensuring that two very special women viz. Ravinder Jit Randhawa and Sabina Singh, the widows of the late Major SJS Randhawa and Captain Gurmeet Singh respectively, were given such equal opportunities. To rise like the proverbial phoenix from the ashes of their dreams and dare to dream again, to imbue their splintered existence with a modicum of meaning again, a quiet purpose which tragedy could not/would not be allowed to subdue. In fact it was in the crucible of grief that such purpose was distilled. When Major Randhawa of the 832 Light Regiment of the Regiment of Artillery, on deputation to the Rashtriya Rifles, was fatally wounded and killed while fighting militants in the valley and Captain Gurmeet Singh of 12 Reconnaissance and Observation Flight, Army Aviation Corps, became a victim of the deadly counter-insurgency operations in the North-East. Lesser women would definitely have opted to stay away from the Force which claimed two of their precious menfolk. But not these two, who displayed an exemplary courage of the mind in wanting to join professions which had already entailed the supreme sacrifice in both their families. They were determined to become officers. Thus began the long and arduous struggle for the realization of their dreams, which certainly would not have been possible without AWWA. The organization left no stone unturned. In a move without precedents the President, AWWA, pushed for the age waiver, bent the 'single' clause and laboured with them through each phase till all the hurdles were cleared. It was a moment of great pride for AWWA to see them enter the portals of OTS, Chennai.

Predictably, the greatest adjustment has been 'in becoming an officer from an officer's wife'. The respect they received earlier was on account of their husbands and the position that they enjoyed in the units. As self-made officers now, however, they will be judged on the basis of their own deeds as young officers. Though here again their husbands' reputations will help. However, neither of these courageous aspirants found it a problem to cope with the various aspects of training and, presumably, other women officers before and after them, would have approximately similar views. Commenting on the rigours of training, says a justifiably proud Ravinder, "I may be older than most but I am not in the last few to reach my destination." Maintains Sabina, "The training is so designed that I was able to catch up in 15 days and today I am so much stronger, not just physically but also mentally."

Boldly entitled *Women Special Entry Scheme*, the brief yet comprehensively worded Army Press Note dealing with the entry of women into the Indian Army and inviting "bright, young, unmarried" girls and issuless widows to join its Non-Technical, Technical and Specialist Branches as officers, further elucidates that it is looking for :

"Women with intellect, idealism and courage. Women who can lead and inspire others.

Women who believe that when it comes to any challenge, they are second to none."

Herein lies a tacit acceptance of women as equals, in a hitherto predominantly male domain. Herein do the guardians of the nation's honour, the honour and safety of all its women, children and civilian population, openly acknowledge their faith in their female compatriots. Contrary to conventional concepts of courage being synonymous predominantly with the male species of the population, this attribute exists in abundant measure in the female psyche. Coupled with an inner resilience inherent in women partly as a result of the role models they embody and partly as a subconscious build-up to cope with vicissitudes peculiar to them alone. In the modern era, with strict delienations of 'male' and 'female' areas of responsibility fast disappearing and re-emerging in more coalescent forms, it is only fitting that women be accorded the opportunities to express their individuality — Unconditionally.

Although it will probably take some time before women officers are accepted as integral to the Forces, as complete equals in every sense of the term and not treated as "different", muses Major Sonal Gupta, a computer expert from the Signals Corps, calm, competent and obviously fulfilled in the profession of her choice, she maintains that no concessions are made for the women aspirants in training, except that they are exempted

BPET or Battle Physical Efficiency Tests and join three months after the male cadets, and do not participate in the first Camp. The training period for women is, therefore, six months as compared to the men, who undergo a total training period of approximately nine months.

The Officers Training Academy or OTA threw open its doors to women candidates in the early nineties and courses commence in March and September every year. The number of vacancies for each course being about 50, candidates are required to be not less than 19 years of age and not more than 25 years of age at the time of joining the course.

It is indeed interesting to note that among those women considered eligible for applying, are subjects of Bhutan and Tibetan refugees who came to India before 1962 with the intention of settling down in the country, as well as persons (in this instance women) of Indian origin from African and South East Asian countries but they would need an eligibility certificate from the Indian Government prior to applying.

After screening and selection by the various SSBs or Service Selection Boards, candidates found medically fit are inducted into OTA strictly on the basis of merit. And upon the successful completion of the prescribed training at the prestigious Officers Training Academy, they are granted Short Service Commission in the rank of Lieutenant for a period of five years initially, subsequently extendable to ten. The extension is dependent upon a number of factors. First and foremost whether the (lady) officer desires to even apply for an extension, then depending on whether or not she gets a recommendation from her commanding officer to that effect and finally, based on the nature of the said recommendation and her various ACRs or Annual Confidential Reports during the short tenure of her service, the relevant Board decides whether extension of service is to be granted or not.

Unlike the male aspirants, who cite their preferences for arms after joining and list their choices at some point, the women follow a procedure of 'reverse selection' so to say. Based on their qualifications prior to gaining entry into the OTA, their selection of arms is, in a way, pre-decided or at least their choices are narrowed down depending upon what technical, non-technical or specialist qualifications they possess. For example, the minimum qualifications required for joining the technical arms like the Corps of Engineers, EME and Signals is BE or B.Tech. or equivalent or higher qualifications in Civil/Electrical/ Mechanical Electronics/Computer Science and Tele-communications Engineering.

For joining the non-technical arms like the ASC, ACC, Signals, Engineers, EME, the minimum qualifications required are B.A, B.Com, B.Sc, BCA or equivalent or higher qualification with a minimum aggregate of 60% and above. The cut-off percentage of minimum aggregate marks for candidates possessing an NCC 'C' Certificate with 'B' or a higher grade is 50 per cent.

The women aspirants at the OTA are not permitted to opt for any of the three active fighting arms like Infantry, Armoured Corps and the Artillery.

However Specialist arms like the ASC, AEC, and Intelligence Corps are open to them. For this a PG Degree or PG Diploma or Graduate with diploma in specified subjects is essential.

In keeping with the spirit of emancipation, understanding and even compassion in comprehending even the most exceptional professional needs of women, it is important to take cognizance of the Special rules or would it be more appropriate to say 'relaxation of rules', regarding the Commission of widows into the Army.

Relaxation for Widow Officer for Grant of Commission

Approval of the Government is being accorded on a case to case basis for relaxation in eligibility for induction into the army through WSES (O) of widows of army officers who have died in action and have been declared battle casualties. The relaxation is granted in the following spheres :

(a) Relaxation in age upto 30 years (intake to postgraduate entry is upto 27 years).

(b) Relaxation to widows with issues are also available.

(c) Waiver to apply after last date of receipt of applications.

The widows are, however, inducted to WSES(O) entry, only if they qualify in SSB. Thus making them an integral part of the glorious army traditions and in keeping with the highest principles of democracy and equality granted to the citizens of India.

References

Ferril, Arther, *The Origins of War*, London: Thames and Hudson Ltd, 1985.

Freud Sigmund, *Civilization and Its Discontents*, London, 1930, and 'Why War' (the letter to Einstein) in Bramson and Goethals, (eds.), *War.*

James William, 'The Moral Equivalent of War'. In Bramson and Gorthals, (eds.), *War.*

Krishna Rao, General K.V., *Prepare or Perish*, New Delhi: Lancer Publications Pvt Ltd., 1991.

Malik, Dr. Ranjana, *'Emancipation of Women'*, *The AWWA Journal*, New Delhi, 1998.

Shankar, Rekha, 'Profiles in Courage', *The AWWA Journal*, New Delhi, 1989.

For a brief, reasonably recent survey see Rensberger, Boyce, 'Ancestors, A Family Album', *Science Digest*, 89, No. 3, April 1981; and *The First Men*, Time-Life Series, 'The Emergence of Man', New York, 1973.

In addition to Turney-High, 1971, see Wright, Quincy, *A Study of War*, Chicago, 1942; Schneider, Joseph, 'Primitive Warfare: A Methodological Note.' In Bramson, Leon and

Goethals, George.W.,(eds.), *War: Studies from Psychology, Sociology, Anthropology.* Carniero, Robert, '*A Theory of the Origin of the State*', *Science*,169 (1970), Webster, David, 'Warfare and the Evolution of the State-A Reconsideration', *American Antiquity*, 4 (1975); Wenke, 1980.

See Stanford, Dennis, 'Bison Kill by Ice Age Hunters', *National Geographic*, 155, No. 1, (Jan.1979), which contains a section on the use of the spear-thrower.

Women Special Entry Scheme, Army Press Note, Army Headquarters, New Delhi—110001.

ANNEXURE 1

Summary of SEWA Actions in the Informal Sector

Trade	*Issue*	*Direct Action*	*Legal/Govt. Action*	*Policy Action*
Vendors	Police beating, bribes	1. Morcha 2. Delegation to the police 3. Confrontation with individual policemen 4. Involviing consumers	1. Complaints to the Police Commissioner	1. Attempts to legalise vendors 2. Attempts to find places for the vendors
Vendors	Confiscation by the Municipality (no licences),removal from place of vending	1. Morcha 2. Application for licences 3. Demonstration at the Municipality 4. Satyagraha (sit-in)	1. Complaints to Municipal Commissioner 2. Cases in The Supreme Court for licences	1. Attempts to influence Town Planning of the Municipality 2. Attempt to get Municipality to allot space for vendors 3. Alternative plan for market places 4. Involviing the School of Planning
Beedi Workers	Minimum wages bonus, and	1. Morcha 2. Strikes	1. Complaint to Labour Officer	1. Attempt to include sale-purchase workers

Contd..

Trade	Issue	Direct Action	Legal/Govt. Action	Policy Action
	dismissal	3. Confrontations/ meetings with employers 4. Demonstration at the Labour Office 5. Sammelans 6. Negotiation	2. Over 100 cases in Labour Courts 3. Complaint to the Legal Aid Committee 4. Complaiants to Welfare and Labour Commissioners	in law 2. Attempt to change Labour Department attitude to home workers 3. Studies on socio-legal,and economic condition of women workers
Beedi Workers	Non-availability of medical aid and welfare fund Respiratory problems	7. Meetings 8. Study by National Institute of Occupational Health	5. Medical Centre opened in Ahmedabad	4. Attempt to include beedi workers under Contract Labour Act. 5. Agitation with International trade union Federation (IUF) 6. ID card to be issued by Government and not by employer
Garment Workers	Minimum wages and other benefits Commercial rates charged by the electricity company	1. Sammelan 2. Direct negotiations 3. Letters to electricity company	1. Complaint to Labour Commissioner 2. Agreement with employers through the Labour Office	1. Attempt to include garment workers under Wages Act 2. Setting up of tripartite board to handle problems

Contd..

Trade	Issue	Direct Action	Legal/Govt. Action	Policy Action
			3. Delegation to Labour Minister	
Head Loaders	Minimum wages and other benefits	1. Sammelan 2. Strike call 3. Direct negotiations 4. Agreement	1. Complaints to Labour Commissioner	1. Setting up of tripartite board to handle problems
Cotton pod openers	Minimum wages and other benefits	1. Sammelan 2. Strike call 3. Direct negotiations	1. Complaints to Labour Commissioner 2. Negotiation through Labour Office	
Papad rollers	Minimum wages and other benefits	1. Strike 2. Direct negotiations		1. Attempt to bring them under Contract Labour Act
Contract workers	Minimum wages and other benefits	1. Strike 2. Direct negotiations 3. Dismissals	1. Complaint to Labour Commissioner 2. Cases in Labour Court	
Paper pickers	Work takes away by traders	1. Satyagraha	1. Complaints to the Industries Ministry	1. Paper pickers should get waste paper from the Government offices

SEWA UNION MEMBERSHIP, 1989

Vendors	
Vegetable/fruit	3040
Used-garments dealers	300
Fish, kerosene, others	180
Tobacco Workers and Food Processors	
Bidi workers	7695
Milk producers	3158
Tobacco, agricultural workers and processors	3180
Papad workers	60
Agricultural and Allied Workers	
Agricultural labourers	4590
Textile and Garment Workers	
Quilt-makers	680
Garment stitchers	1480
Weavers	140
Block printers	100
Handicrafts	1140
Others	20
Other Labour and Service Providers	
Paper pickers	1400
Headloaders	200
Contract labourers	400
Others	240
Other Home-based Workers	
Carpenters	20
Household workers	260
Child care workers	40
Agarbatti workers	180
Others	630
Total	29,133

ANNEXURE 2
COOPERATIVES : KIND, MEMBERSHIP, PRODUCTION

Cooperative	*Members*	*Active Members*	*Total Annual Income (Rs.)*	*Average Monthly Income/ Member (Rs.)*
Crafts and Artisan				
Sabina patchwork	181	51	1,19,352	196
Block printing	77	44	85,219	194
Cane and bamboo	165	12*	30,263	222
Vijay Handloom weavers	44	4	64,718	84
Utsah Handloom weavers	51	17	2,97,015	318
Baldana weavers	17	17	44,709	219
Banascrafts				
Embroidery		274	3,00,725	91
Leatherwork		26	3,05,025	998
Beadwork		40	62,125	129
Applique work		45	20,000	37
Mirror work		30	24,000	67
Ornamental Work		85	38,000	37
Kachcchi embroidery		22	14,680	55
Metal beadwork		16	12,023	83
File Making		16	6,760	123
Stitching		12	13,035	26
Khadi work		21	13,126	52
Ahmedabad weaving		6	5,169	99
Electornics assembly		4	11,894	248
Trading and Vending Cooperatives				
Haryali vegetable vendors	51	45	1,13,573	355
Matsyagandha fish vendors	61	15	43,050	400
Service Cooperatives				
Saundarya industrial cleaning	200	135	2,09,147	1271
Paper pickers group collecting		232	36,455	—

Contd..

Dairy Cooperatives

Cooperative	*Members*	*Year Registered*	*Total Annual Income (Rs.)*	*Average Monthly Income/ Member (Rs.)*
Ahmedabad District				
Devdholera	100	1979	4,44,579	335
Baldana	165	1979	5,19,854	288
Lagdand	35	1988	1,36,355	260
Dumali	72	1984	1,78,220	176
Ranesar	70	1988	77,599	202
Rupal	140	1986	2,79,933	249
Chikada	25	1989	24,418	183
Katwada	72	1987	1,26,584	294
Pasunj	100	1987	4,61,986	223
Vanch	48	1989	64,881	179
Bilasiya	85	1988	1,61,092	285
Miroli	25	1989	43,873	241
Bahiyal	65	1987	45,455	107
Amarajinamuvade	26	1989	30,189	148
Nanimorali	25	1989	53,128	165
Waghpura	26	1989	38,884	262
Navapura	20	1989	7,398	155
Banaskantha District				
Gulabpura	52	1989		151
Latia	47	1989		144
Sherganj	59	1989		190
Najupura	60	1989		168
Kalyanpura	62	1989		290
Gadh	48	1989		234

Land-based Cooperatives

Kind of Cooperative	*Members*	*Land Developed*	*Water Resources*	*Sapling Raised/ Planted*	*Income/ Month*
Ahmedabad District					
Baldana Wasteland Rehabilitation Agro-Forestry Cooperative	20	35 acres	3 ponds 1 check	10,800	282
Kind of Cooperative	Members	Land Developed	dam Water Resources	Sapling Raised/ Planted	Income/ Month
Metaal Wasteland Rehabilitation Cooperative	20	10 acres		4,000	282
Dumali Wasteland Rehabilitation Cooperative	20	10 acres	boundary trenches	4,000	162
Mehsana District					
Sri Ganeshpura Wasteland Tree growers	44	10 acres	nursery tankpond, tubewell	27,000	143
Junagadh District					
Girnar Nursery	20		Nursery tank	1,25,000	400
Banaskantha District					
Sheragadh	5			20,000	240
Satun	4			20,000	300
Nanipipli	5			20,000	240
Cokhankar	5			20,000	240
Gadhakar	4			20,000	300
Kaliwada	5		tank	200,000	240

* Only 12 women sell their products actively through SEWA's shops and exhibitions. The majority of other members purchase bulk bamboo through the cooperative, but market on their own, and are therefore not counted as 'active' members.

Members work only 2-4 hours per day.

ANNEXURE 3

OVERVIEW OF SEWA BANK 1974-1989

The Growth of SEWA Bank

Years	*Number of Share-holders*	*Share Capital (Rs.)*	*Number of Depositors*	*Deposits (Rs.)*	*Working Capital (Rs.)*	*Profits (Rs.)*
1974-75	6287	71320	6188	243010	332231	-11802
1975-76	6634	74990	10459	936388	1060431	33016
1976-77	6945	78970	11038	1053480	1198872	21623
1977-78	7044	81100	11656	1448586	1267452	13729
1978-79	7131	81800	12366	2523722	2743564	35244
1979-80	7321	84080	13060	3024230	3324844	36953
1980-81	7507	88690	14022	2728876	3194930	54152
1981-82	7943	131350	16164	3503986	4119379	77632
1982-83	8398	195830	19057	5060240	5815669	116284
1983-84	8938	302610	20122	6830768	7981869	200085
1984-85	9457	427970	21656	6093587	7897007	161752
1985-86	9825	538130	22208	11278880	13537252	222767
1986-87	10339	707000	23834	10790000	13928000	334000
1987-88	10972	883730	23156	11232537	14930963	370054
1988-89	11742	1074000	23582	13890000	18301000	480000
*1989-	12089	1150000	25311	15600000	20000000	375000

Source : SEWA Bank.
* Provisional data for July through December 1989.

Table 2
SEWA Bank Loans

Years	***Number of loans Extended*	*Total Funds Advanced*
1974-75	0	0
1975-76	5	680
1976-77	70	37253
1977-78	73	39295
1978-79	113	79875
1979-80	145	150985

Contd..

Year	**Number of loans Extended	Total Funds Advanced
1980-81	163	248375
1981-82	301	618220
1982-83	413	1085750
1983-84	1297	2421315
1984-85	2801	3839234
1985-86	3366	4312237
1986-87	4030	6215000
1987-88	5058	7251000
1988-89	6354	8552000
*1989-	7017	9293228

Source : SEWA Bank.
* Provisional data for July through December 1989.
** These numbers represent cumulative number of loans dispersed.

Table 3
Comparision of Public Sector Banks and SEWA Bank

Particulars	Public Sector Banks		SEWA Bank	
	Dec 86 Crores Rs.	Dec 87 Crores Rs.	June 86-87 Lakhs. Rs	June 87-88 Lakhs Rs
Deposits	111581	128389	108	112
Loans	64321	73114	62	72
Profit	192	261	3	4
Reserves and Reserve Fund	1095	1503	8	11
Ratios				
Profits/Deposits	0.17	0.20	2.77	3.57
Profits/Loans	0.29	0.35	4.83	5.55
Reserve/Deposits	0.98	0.35	4.83	5.55
Reserve/Loans	1.70	2.05	12.90	15.27

Source: SEWA Bank. Figures for 28 Public Sector Banks from *Indian Express*, 20th July 1988.

ANNEXURE 4

PARLIAMENT

Year	Cabinet Ministers	Minister of State	Deputy Ministers	Women Elected	Total Elected
1952	Rajkumari Amrit Kaur (Health)	Lakshmi Menon (Parliamentary Secretary)	M. Chandra Sekhar (Health)	Lok Sabha 23	489 (4.7)
				Rajya Sabha	
				1952-14	214 (6.5)
				1955-12	219 (5.9)
1957	Rajkumari Amrit Kaur (Health)		Lakshmi Menon (External Affairs)	Lok Sabha 27	494 (5.5)
			Violet Alva (Home)	Rajya Sabha	
				1957-8	232 (3.5)
			Tarakeshwari Sinha (Economic Affairs)	1958-17	232 (7.3)
				1960-14	236 (5.9)
1962	Dy. Chairman, Rajya Sabha Violet Alva	Dr. Sushila Nayer (Health)	Dr. S. Ramachandran (Education)	Lok Sabha 34	494 (6.9)
		Lakshmi Menon (External Affairs)	M. Chandrasekhar (Home)	Rajya Sabha	
				1962-12	236 (5.1)
		Indira Gandhi (Information & Broadcasting)	Tarakeshwari Sinha (Finance)	1964-17	238 (7.1)
				1966-20	238 (8.4)

Contd...

Year	Cabinet Ministers	Minister of State	Deputy Ministers	Women Elected	Total Elected
1967	Indira Gandhi, PM, Minister of Atomic Energy & External Affairs	Dr. Phulrenu Guha (Social Welfare)	Jehanara Jaipal Singh (Tourism & Civil Aviation) Dr. Sarojini Mahishi Nandini Satpathy (Information & Broadcasting)	Lok Sabha 31 Rajya Sabha 1967-17 1970-9	520 (6.0) 240 (7.8) 240 (3.5)
1971	Indira Gandhi, PM, Minister of Atomic Energy and Planning	Dr. S. Mahishi (Tourism & Civil Aviation) Later : Law, Justice & Company Affairs	Nandini Satpathy (Information & Broadcasting) Dr. S. Rohatgi (Finance)	Lok Sabha 22 Rajya Sabha 1972-19 1974-14	519 (4.2) 243 (7.8) 243 (5.8)

STATE ASSEMBLIES

Year	Cabinet Ministers and Chief Ministers	Minister of State	Deputy Ministers (Place & Portfolios in Bracket)	Place	Total Elected	Women Elected
1952	Renuka Ray (Bengal, Rehabilitation) Dr. Sushila Nayer (Delhi - Health & Transport)		Indumati Chamanlal Basant Manjri Devi Poorbi Mukherji	Bombay(ED) Orissa (Health) Bengal (Women's Edu.)	3641	98 (2.74)
1957	Basant Manjari Devi (Orissa, Health)	Gauri Thomas (Kerala, Revenue) Lourdhammal Simone (Madras Local Admn.) Poorbi Mukherji (Bengal)	Usha Khatkur Naima K. Ayder Joytimoyee Devi N. Raje Bhonsle Rani Padmavati Prakash Kaur Prakashvati Sood Maya Banerjee	A.P Bihar(Jail,Relief) Bihar(Soc. Wel.) Bombay (ED.) M.P.(Pub. Health) Punjab(Health) U.P.(Soc. Wel) Bengal (Refugees)	3,284	196 (5.9)
1962	Dr. Sada Lakshmi (A.P.-Minister of State) Sucheta Kripalani (CM, UP, from Oct. 1964)	Sucheta Kripalani (C. Dev. U.P) M. Raje Bhonsle (Mah. Soc. Wel.)	K. Barua Urmila Ben Bhatt Grace Tucker Chandrakala Sahai Saraswati Pradhan Om Prabha Jain	Assam Haryana (1966) Kerala (Ed.) M.P.(Ed.) Orissa Punjab (Planning)	3,287	173 (5.1)

Contd...

Year	Cabinet Ministers and Chief Ministers	Minister of State	Deputy Ministers (Place & Portfolios in Bracket)	Place	Total Elected	Women Elected
	Indumati Ben (Guj.)		Kamla Beniwal	Raj. (Home)		
	Yasodara Dasappa		Prabha Misra	Raj. (Health)		
	(Karnataka - Soc. Wel.)		Prakasavati Sood	W. Ben. (Harijan)		
	Dr. P. Kaur (Punjab)		Usha Maiti	Bihar (Reh.)		
	Jothi Venkatachalan		Maya Banerjee	(Bengal (Ed.)		
	(Tamil Nadu)		Radha Rani Mahtab	Pondicherry (Home)		
	Poorbi Mukherjee		Sakila Khaton	Delhi (Rehab.)		
	(Bengal)					
1967	Om Prabha Jain	Roda Mistri	P. K. Gohain	Assam		
	(Haryana)	(A.P., S. Wel)	Urmila Bhat	Gujrat		
	Sucheta Kripalani	Sumitra (U.P.)	Gauri Thomas	Kerala		
	(C.M., U.P.)		Satyavanimuthu	Madras	3,709	134
			Pratibha Patil	Maharashtra		(3.9)
			Basara Rajeshwari	Karnataka		
			Prabha Misra	Rajasthan		
1971	Shashikala Kokadkar	Sathiavani Mutthu	B. Jayaprade	A.P.		
	(C.M., Goa)	(Tamil Nadu)	Manorama Pande	Bihar		
	Nandini Satpathy	S. Mahanta (Assam)	Ayesha Sheikh	Gujarat (Ed.)		
	(C.M., Orissa)	Beula Doza, Bihar	Sharda Rani	Haryana		

Contd...

Year	Cabinet Ministers and Chief Ministers	Minister of State	Deputy Ministers (Place & Portfolios in Bracket)	Place	Total Elected	Women Elected
	Ram Dulari Sinha	Vimla Verma, M.P.	Sarla Sharma	H.P.		
	(Bihar)	R.K. Bajpai, U.P.	Prabha Rao	Maharashtra(Ed.)		
		Begum Habibulla	Pratibha Patil	Maharashtra(Ed.)		
		U.P. (Social Welfare)		(Social Welfare)		
		Kamla Beniwal	Sarla Pareshwar	Punjab	3,697	164
		(Rajasthan, Tourism)	S. Basana	Tripura		(4.4)
			Chakraborty Animala			
			Soren	West Bengal (Edn.)		

Sources : Who's Who, Lok Sabha and Rajya Sabha, Chandidas, India Votes.
Times of India Directory and Year Book Including Who's Who: 1952, Vol. XXVIII, 1957, 1962, 1968, 1972.

Also Consulted : Fourth General Election — Statistical analysis, Indian National Congress; India Annual *Reference; Election Commission Publications, 1952, 1957, 1962, 1967 & 1972.*

Note : Excludes information in respect of nominated members and also those elected other than in general elections. Figures in brackets : O/o.

ANNEXURE 5

Action Plan for Removal of Sexist Bias Operating against the Girl Child

Intervention Strategies and Inputs	Implementing Agencies	Outcome
1. Household Activities	1. Policy-makers	1. Better Enrolment
2. Classroom Activities and Intervention	2. Educational Planners and Administrators	2. Increased Retention Rate of Girls in Schools
3. Co-curriculuar Activities	3. Curriculum Framers	3. Fall in Drop-out Rates
4. Textual material	4. Textbook Writers	4. Better Self-perception in Girls
5. Socially Useful Productive Work	5. Departments/Boards of Education	5. Development of Self-Confidence and Self-reliance
6. Work Experience	6. Textbook Bureaus/ Corporations	6. Dignity of Labour
7. Guidance and Counselling Services	7. Teachers	7. Sharing of Responsibilities and Duties
8. Instructional Facilities	8. Mass Media	8. Economic Growth and Independence
9. Support Services	9. Community	9. Equal wages / pay

Contd...

Action Plan for Removal of Sexist Bias Operating against the Girl Child

Intervention Strategies and Inputs	Implementing Agencies	Outcome
10. Play Activities	10. Society	10. Equal Status
11. Infrastructural Facilities		
12. Special Orientation Programmes		
13. Implementation of Rights		

Source : Department of Women's Studies, NCERT, 1989.

ANNEXURE 6

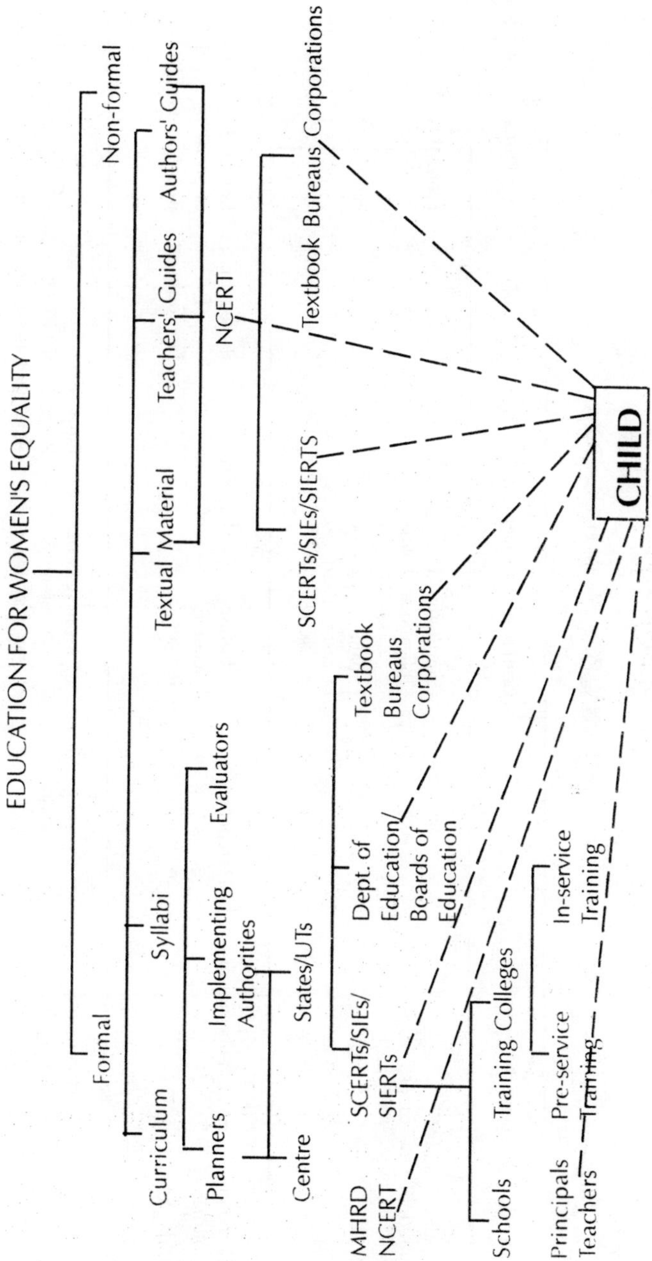
EDUCATION FOR WOMEN'S EQUALITY
Formal
Non-formal
Curriculum
Syllabi
Textual Material
Teachers' Guides
Authors' Guides
Planners
Implementing Authorities
Evaluators
NCERT
Textbook Bureaus Corporations
SCERTs/SIEs/SIERTS
Centre
States/UTs
MHRD NCERT
SCERTs/SIEs/ SIERTs
Dept. of Education/ Boards of Education
Textbook Bureaus Corporations
Schools
Training Colleges
Principals Teachers
Pre-service Training
In-service Training
CHILD

ANNEXURE 7

NATIONAL POLICY ON EDUCATION

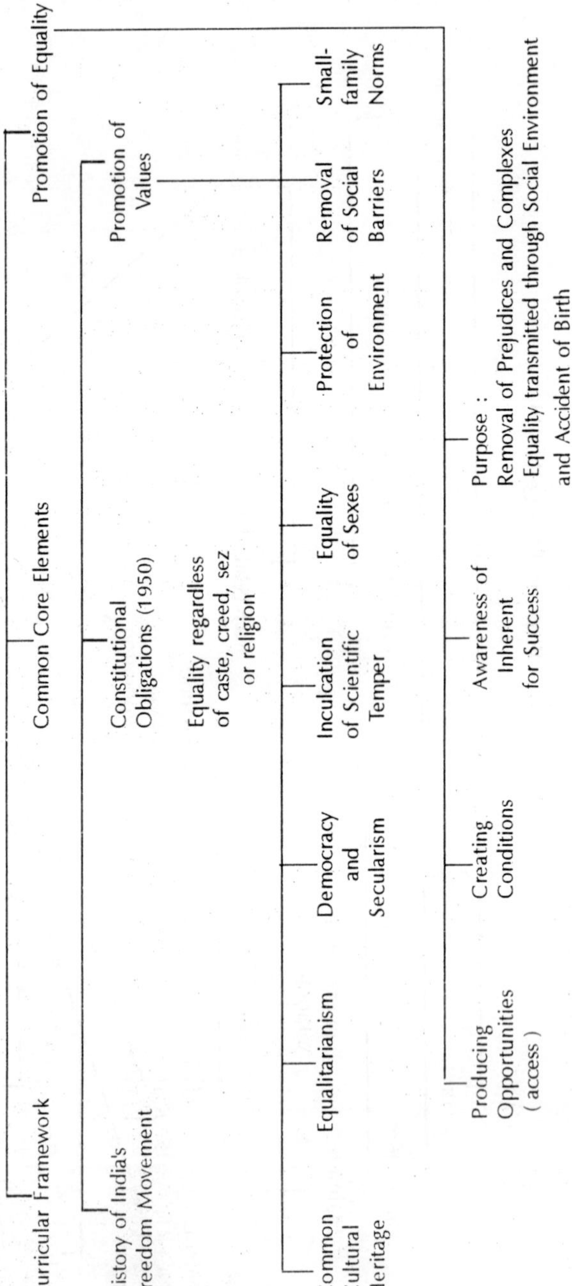

ANNEXURE 8

Population of Scheduled Castes by Sex and States, India, 1981

Scheduled Castes

State/ Union Territory	Male	Female	Persons	Rural	Urban	Percent to Population of State / Union Territory
India (1) (2)	5,42,10,594	5,05,44,029	10,47,54,623	8,79,96,992	1,67,57,631	15.75
State :						
Andhra Pradesh	40,39,242	39,22,488	79,61,730	67,52,368	12,09,362	14.87
Arunachal Pradesh	1,833	1,086	2,919	1,940	970	.046
Bihar	51,58,486	49,83,882	1,01,42,368	92,82,243	8,60,125	7.15
Delhi	6,18,550	5,03,093	11,21,643	1,04,012	10,17,631	18.03
Gujarat	12,55,512	11,82,785	24,38,297	16,41,070	7,97,227	7.15
Haryana	13,22,088	11,41,924	24,64,012	20,92,920	3,71,092	19.07
Himachal Pradesh	5,37,989	5,15,969	10,53,958	9,97,427	56,331	24.62
Jammu & Kashmir (2)	2,58,789	2,38,574	4,97,363	4,40,017	57,346	8.31
Karnataka	28,43,413	27,51,940	55,95,353	43,68,731	12,26,622	15.07
Kerala	12,60,874	12,88,508	25,49,382	22,40,011	3,09,371	10.02
Madhya Pradesh	38,08,259	35,50,274	73,58,533	60,40,141	13,18,392	14.10
Maharashtra	22,99,098	21,80,665	44,79,763	30,65,938	14,13,825	7.14

Contd...

State/ Union Territory	Male	Female	Persons	Rural	Urban	Percent to Population of State / Union Territory
Manipur	9,075	8,678	17,753	14,795	2,958	1.25
Mizoram	120	15	135	97	38	0.03
Meghalaya	3,068	2,424	5,492	2,950	2,542	0.41
Nagaland	—	—	—	—	—	—
Orissa	19,44,071	19,21,472	38,65,543	35,02,195	3,63,348	14.66
Punjab	24,15,903	20,95,800	45,11,703	36,66,372	8,45,331	26.87
Rajasthan	30,52,375	27,84,504	58,38,879	47,90,504	10,48,375	17.04
Sikkim	9,558	8,723	18,281	14,365	3,916	15.12
Tamil Nadu	44,85,332	43,95,963	88,81,295	70,90,664	17,90,631	18.35
Tripura	1,59,796	1,50,558	3,10,384	2,90,832	19,552	15.12
Uttar Pradesh	1,23,97,321	1,10,56,018	2,34,53,339	2,10,00,331	20,53,008	21.16
West Bengal	62,31,795	57,68,973	1,20,00,768	1,05,11,836	14,88,932	21.99

Contd...

State/ Union Territory	Male	Female	Persons	Rural	Urban	Percent to Population of State / Union Territory
Union Territory :						
Aand N. Islands	—	—	—	—	—	—
Chandigarh	36,093	27,528	63,621	6,813	56,808	14.09
D and N Haveli	957	1,084	2,041	1,818	223	1.97
Goa, Daman and Diu	11,787	11,645	23,432	14,076	9,356	2.16
Lakshadweep	—	—	—	—	—	—
Pondicherry	49,210	47,426	96,636	62,526	34,110	15.99

Source : (1) Registrar General, India, Ministry of Home Affairs.

(2) India, Ministry of Planning, Central Statistical Organization : Statistical Abstract of India, 1985., New Delhi, Manager, Government of India Press, 1987, p. 34.

Note : Population of Scheduled Castes by Sex and Status, India, 1981 has been taken from the publication *Women In India : A STATISTICAL PANORAMA* by Prabhash P. Singh, Inter - India Publications, New Delhi, 1991.

INDEX

Absolute ownership, 412
Acculturative influences of Hinduism, 392
Adivasi Problem in Maharashtra, 432
Adoption, 246
Advani, L.K., 404
Aga Khan Rural Support Programme, (AKRSP), 289
Agrarian Occupation, 423-26
Ahmad, Nazir, 88
Aims and Objectives of the Society, 262
Ajodhya Kisan Conference of Dec., 1920, 418
Aksar Dipika, 98
Ali, Syed Ameer, 88
All-India Depressed Class Association, 395
All-India Depressed Classes Federation, 395
All India Women's Conference (AIWC), 23, 29, 34
Alternative Trading Organization, 258, 266
Alva, Violet, 336
Ambedkar, B.R., 384
Amrit Kaur, Rajkumari, 41
Anath Ablaou Ki Pukar, 420
Andhra Pradesh Education Programme, 121
Apollo, 13
Archaeologists, 387-90
Ardhanarishwara, 15
Area of merciless exploitation, 430
Arjuna, 447
Arthashastra, 234
Arya Samaj, 83
Asaf Ali, Aruna, 41
Assignees of Ceiling Surplus Land, (ACSL), 317
Azad, Chandra Shekhar, 75
Azad, Maulana, 46
Azad, Maulana Abul Kalam, 86

Badran, Margot, 37
Bahishkru Bharat, 399
Bain, F.W., 13
Bajaj, Jamnalal, 76
Balodvan Sangeet, 98
Bandaranaike, Sirimavo, 336
Bandavarkar, G.R., 19
Banerjee, S.N., 48
Bangladesh, 296-302
Baradia Bijaya 2Mahila Kalyan Samiti, 298
Bardoli Satyagraha, 63
Basic Education Committee, 96
Basu, Amrita, 411
Batik Women of Desia Nagar, 263
Bem, Sandra Lipsitz, 347
Beginning of a Nightmare, 383
Bem's Sex Role Inventory, 197
Besant, Annie, 41, 42, 45, 49
Bhagalpur Zila Khadi Gramodyog Sangh, 280
Bhagvad Gita, 11
Bhandarkar, R.G., 31
Bharata Mahila Parishad, 20

Bhatt, Ela, 201
Bhikaji, Dadaji. 21
Bihar Education Project, 121
Bombay Presidency Social Reform Association, 395
Book of Common Prayer, 366
Borsad Satyagraha, 63
Bose, Subhas Chandra, 75
Brahmaputra, 457
Brahmo Samaj, 85
British Sex Discrimination Act-1975, 191
Buddha, Gautam, 391
Burke, Edmund, 185
Byron. Lord, 233

Central Tasar Research & Training Institute, Ranchi, (CTRTI), 281, 284
Chanda, Ramprasad, 389
Chandogya Upanishad, 389
Chhatra Yuva Sangharsh Vahini, 443
Chhatri Sangha, 74
Chattopadhyay, Kamladevi, 41, 68
Chaudhurani, Sarladevi, 22
Chawla. Kiran, 350
Child Marriage Restraint Act, 33, 235
Chittaranjan Das, Deshbandhu, 62
Christian Commission for Dev. in Bangladesh (CCDB), 297-302
Civil Disobedience Movement, 78
Clergy, warriors, peasants and artisans, 394
Cochin Christian Succession Act-1921, 245
Colette, 233
Committee on Status of Women in India-1975, 108
Community Service Guild in Cuddalore, 267
—Wosem, 271
affirmative action in, 272
affirmative action statement, 273
Comparative study of IMR in some countries, 372
Congress League Scheme, 42
Congress Radio, 73
Constitution Scheduled Castes Order 1950, 403
Co-operative Cottage Industrial Society, 262
Cormack, Margaret, 95
Crime and Punishment, 125-62
—ironical dichotomies, 125
philosophical dictum, 125
by Manu, 126
sexist approach, 127
dowry deaths, 128
wife-murderers, 128
domestic discord, 129
causative factors, 131
violent marriages, 131
lack of support structures, 131
burden of childcare, 131
IPC Section 319-26, 132, 143
grievous hurt,132
Domestic Violence Act, 133
social support network, 135
most vital factors, 136
crisis intervention,136
unhappy marriages, 137
Dowry Prohibition Act-1961, 138
rape reasons, 139, 150
socio-psychological reasons for rape, 140
rape on minor girls, 142
custodial rape, 143
honour killing, 146
economics of female infanticide, 157
murder, crime, abduction, desertion, cruelty and adultery, 159
culture of crime, 160
Cursetjee, Serenmai M., 20
Czech Republic, 354

Dalhousie Square, 76
Dalit Dynamite, 383
Dalit Panther Movement of

Maharashtra, 384
Dangerous operations, 251
Daughters of India, 44
Degraded Condition of Women, 101
Depressed Classes Political Conference in Nagpur, 400
Desh Sevika Sangh, 68
Devi, Basanti, 62
Dharasana Salt Works, 65
Directive Principles of State Policy, 176
Dissolution of Muslim Marriages Act-1939, 238
District Primary Education Programme, 121
Doosri Pathwali, 98
Dube, Dr. Leela, 305

Education Commission 1964-66, 106
Education For All, 121
Education for Women's equality, 481
Education Guarantee Scheme, 121
Ehrenreich, Barbara, 341, 347
Eighth Five Year Plan, 169
Eight Plan, 380
Ekalavaya, 390
Emergence of Women's Resistance, 436
Emerson, Ralph Waldo, 287
Employees State Insurance Act-1948, 251
Employment and Education, 249
Enrolment in Educational System, 113
Entrepreneurship and enterprise, 179
Enterpreneurship Development Institute, 182
Equal Pay Act of 1970, 190
Equal Pay for Equal Work, 189
—Randhir Singh Vs. Union of India 1982, 192
Equal Remuneration Act-1976, 186

Factories Act 1948, 250
Fallen Women, 92
Feminist Nationalism, 37
FICCI Ladies Organization, 195
Fight for Freedom, 59
—non-cooperation resolution, 60
women's role in, 64
Free trade zones for women, 178

Gandhi, Indira, 11, 233, 330, 334, 337, 357
Gandhi, Kasturba, 62
Gandhi, Mahatma, 14, 26, 30, 35, 48, 59, 64, 71, 325, 359
Gandhi, menka, 336
Gandhi, Sonia, 148
Genuine Occupational Qualification, 191
Ghosh, Kalpana, 298
Giele, Janet Zollinger, 166
Godavari Delta Cooperative and Working Women's Forum, 259
Gokhale, Gopal Krishna, 48
Gora Jews, 393
Government of India Act, 1935, 332
Gram Nirman Mandal, 280, 282
Gram Swarajaya Samiti (GSS), 435
Grant of Universal Adult Franchise to Women, 326
—shortcomings, 326
Grievances of SCs and STs, 421
Gujarat Provincial Conference, 62
Gupta, Maithli Saran, 417

Harassment of Women, 434
Harnessing Human Resourcing, 170
Hartog Committee, 96
Health for All by AD 2000, 365
Herodotus, 257
Hindu Adoptions and Maintenance Act-1956, 240, 246
Hindu and untouchable leaders, 401
Hindu Child Marriage Bill, 32
Hindu Minority and Guardianship Act-1956, 248
Hindu Marriage Act-1955, 235
Historical Dev. of Dalit problems, 389

History, Growth and Dev. of Society, 261
Home Rule Agitation, 42, 49
Home Rule League, 42
Holyrood, W.M., 91
Hossein, Rokeya Sakhawat, 100
Hume, A.O., 60
Husain, Zakir, 87
Imam, Hasan, 69
Indian Economic roles, 167
Indian National Army, 76
Indian National Congress, 18, 20, 42, 60, 328, 334
Indian Succession Act, 244
Indra and Varuna, 387
Industrial Development Services (IDS), 281
Ingersoll, Robert G., 296
Initiating Changes in Traditional Marriage Customs, 438
Inquilab Zindabad, 66
Integrated Child Development Services (ICDS), 377
Integrated Rural Development Programmes, (IRDP), 230
International Congress of Orientalists in Delhi in 1964, 246
International Labour Organization, 185
International Union for Health Education, 367
Irwin, Lord, 70
Islam, Kazi Nazrul, 99

Jaggi, Mr. V.N., 415
Jahan Ara Shah Nawaj, Begum, 20
Jayalalitha, 336
Jefferson, Thomas, 447
Jenkins Activity Survey, 197
Jodhpurkar, Shridhar Balwant, 414
Joshi Committee, 33
Joyful Learning Programme, 121

Kala Jews, 393
Kalekar, Kaka, 64
Kandabashail Mahila Samiti, 297
Kanuga, Nandubehn, 71
Kara, Maniben, 28
Karve, Maharishi, 17
Katha Vidhi, 98
Khan, Dr. Akhtar Hameed, 290
Kisan Sabha, 416
Kolaba Zilla Bahishkrut Parishad, 399
Kothari Commission 1964-66, 107
Kriplani, Sucheta, 72, 76, 78, 328, 336
Kurmi Sangh, 416

Lace Makers of Naraspur, 257
Lakshminarayana, 15
Lal, Munshi Chatar Bihari, 94
Law of Manu, 358
League of Nations, 31
Literacy Rates in 1981 by Residence, 112
Literate population, distribution of, 113
Lohia, Rammanohar, 77
Lord Hardinge, British Viceroy, 48
Low castes and High castes, 413

Macdonell, A.A., 12
Mackay, Ernest, 388
Madras Children's Act, 24
Mahabharata, 390
Mahar Dalits of Maharashtra, 391
Mahar Watan, 400
Mahila Samakhya, 121
Mahila Vikas Sangh and Tasar Silk, 279
Mahishasura, King, 356
Mahmud, Shamsunnahar, 99
Maita, Hari Mohan, 31
Malviya, Madan Mohan, 401
Mandal Commission, 406
Manusmriti, 234, 391
Marriage and Divorce, 234
Marriage customs of biradari, 416
Marshal, John, 388
Masala-i-Niyog, 94
Maternity Benefits Act 1961, 251

Mayo, Katherine, 32
Medical Termination of
Pregnancy Act 1971, 253
Medium-Term Programme for
Technical Cooperation, 375
Mehta, Sir Pherozeshah, 48
Menon, Dr. R.V.G., 117
Mexico City Conference-1975, 202
Mexico Klan of Action, 186
Minto-Morley Reforms and Muslim
Separatism, 45
Monkey Army, 331
Montagu-Chelmsford Reforms, 330
Montagu-Chelmsford Report, 55
Montagu-Chelmsford Scheme, 55
Montagu, E.S., 52
Muhammadan Educational
Conference, 88
Mukherjee, Prabhati, 389
Murdafaroshi, 414
Muslim period, 391

Naidu, Sarojini, 41-56. 65-66, 68,
330, 332, 335
Naini Jail, 72
Namboodiripad E.M.S., 402
Nanda, B.R., 14
Naoroji, Dadabhai, 64
Naoroji, Khurshedbehn, 71
Nari Satyagraha Committee, 69
Napoleon, 453
National Adult Education
Programme of 1978, 110
National Alliance of Young
Entrepreneurial, 195
National Association of Women
Entrepreneurs and Executives
(NAWEE), 195
National Commission on Self-
Employed Women, 186
National Council for Churches of
Bangladesh, 299
National Council for Women's
Education-1961, 107
National Council of Women inIndia
(NCWI), 23
National Dairy Development Board
(NDDB),
222
National Institute of Desigh, 215
National Intitute of Entrepreneurship
and small Business Develop
ment (NIESBUD), 195
National Institute of Forensic Medi
cine, 145
National Literacy Mission, 121National Perspective Plan for Women,
168
NationalPlanning Committee, 55
National Policy on Education-1986,
108, 482
National Programme for Nutritional
Project, 121
National Resource Centre for
Women, 169
National Sample Survey Organization, 118
National Science and Technology
Entrepreneurship Board, 182
National Small Industries Corporation, 318
—Khadi and Village Industries,
319
Science and Technology, 319
monitoring, 320
National Social Conference, 18, 20,
22
National Women's Organization, 23
Nawabs of Oudh, 411
Nayar, Sushila, 61
Nehru, Jawaharlal, 11, 17, 26, 59,
77, 81, 331
Nehru, Uma, 52
New Age Woman, 19
New India Spirit, 54
Niebuhr, Reinhold, 325
Nikhil Jatiya Nari, 69
Non-Formal Education, 109
Norwegian Agency for International
Development (NORAD), 320

Notions of patriarchy, 102
Operation Blackboard, 104, 121
Order of the Rising Star, 44
Orphanages and other Charitable Homes (Supervision and Control) Act-1960, 252
Oxfan Trading, Licester, United Kingdom, 263

Pahli Pathawali, 98
Pakistan, 287-96
Palace Chariotry, 453
Panchal Pandita, 97
Pandit, Vijaya Lakshmi, 41
Panos Regional Programmes, 287
Parsi Marriage and Divorce Act,1936, 240
Parvati Devi, 70
Patel, Vallabh Bhai, 77
Patnaik, J.B., 147
Patra Kaumudi, 98
People's of Civil Liberties, 146
Percentage of Institutions Exclusively for Women, 114
Percentage allocation on health in some countries, 373
Peron, Isobel, 336
Personality assessment, 195
Phule, Jotiba, 396
Phule, Mahatma Jotirao, 384
Plan allocation for health, 371
Political pulls and pressures, 45
Population of SCs and STs, 483-85
Prabhat-pheries, 70
Practical utility, 96
Pradhan, Debendra, 148
Pragjoytika Mahila Sangha, 146
Praja Sangh, 420
Prarthana Samaj, 19
Primary Health Care System, 373
Punjab Education Report-1869-70, 91
Putrikaputra, 234

Queen Marry College in Lahore, 88
Quit India Movement, 99
Rabri Devi, 336
Rahim, Abdur, 88
Rai, Lala Lajpat, 70
Rajagopalachari, c., 332
Rajah-Moonje Pact, 401
Rakshasi-Sarkar, 60
Ramamurthi, Nallamuthu, 331
Ramanujan, A. K., 357
Ramayana, 390
Ram Chandra,Baba, 414
Rao, R. Raghunath, 31
Rao, Sir T. Madhwa, 31
Rashid, Capt. Abdul, 76
Rashtriya Mahila Sangh, 69
Ray, Renuka, 61
Reddy, Dr. Muthulakshmi, 24
Remuneration and reconstruction of policies, 173
Rigveda, 12, 384-87,
Risk taking behaviour, 197
Round Table Conferences for Dalits, 401
Round Table Conference in London, 332
Royal Indian Navy, 76
Roy, Raja Rammohun, 17, 46
Roy, Rammohun, 82
Rukhmabai, 21
Rural Women, 305
—Work-Time Distribution of, 308
Development of, 310, 317
Technologies for, 312
Food, Water and Shelter, 313
Mitigating Drudgery, 314
Economic Projects, 314
Management modes, 315
Employment, 316
Land Reforms, 317
Industry, 317
Small Scale Industries, 318
Social Welfare, 320, 322
Eighth Plan, 321
Sabramati Ashram, 71

Sadharan Brahm Samaj, 19
Salt Satyagraha Movement, 69
Sanatan Dharma Paliani Sabha, 43
Sapru, S. K., 364
Sarabhai, Mridula, 41
Saraswati, Dayanand, 83, 85
Saraswati, Pandita Ramabai, 19
Saraswati, Swami Dayanand, 18
Sarda Act, 30
Sarda Committee, 417
Satpathy, Nandini, 337
Second Regional Conference on Promotion of Women's Health and Welfare. 367
Sen, Keshub Chandra, 28
Serve Self-Help Handicrafts, Windsor, USA, 263
Seventh Five Year Plan, 168
Seventh Plan, 378
SEWA, beginning of, 201
—Self-employed, 203
Woman of tiol, 204
Organizing women, 205
intrepid women, 207
bank of 2001-10, 472-80
organization, 211
Holistic Health Reforms, 212
Maternity benefits, 213
Family Planning, 213
Health Workers, 215
Pharmacy, 217
Cooperative Ventures, 218-21 469-71
Intervention in NDDB for Women, 222
Operation Flood, 222
Women's Dairy Cooperatives, 223-25
Sex appropriate, 109
Sex Determination Act of 1975, 190
Sex Role Orientation, 197
Shikshak Samakhya, 121
Shivalaya Rural Dev. Project, 299
Shradhanand, Swami, 70
Shramik Stri Mukti Sangathan, 438
Shudras and Anti-Shudras, 397
Silva, Donatus de, 287
Simon Commission, 331
Sinha, Kamala, 173
Sinha, Tarakeshwari, 336
Sixth Plan, 377
Slave Dynasty, 391
Social Disabilities Removal Act, 405
Social dynamics of caste, 406
Sons of India, 44
Sorabji Cornelia, 28
South East Asia Regional Bureau (SEARB), 367
Southward bound, 423
Spirit of renaissance, 86
Srimad Bhagavad Gita, 390
Srinivasan, M.N., 401
State Social Welfare Advisory Board, 280
Stanton, Elizabeth Cady, 163
Stri Zarthosti Mandal, 20
Sucharu Devi, Maharani, 28
Sugrihini, 101
Swallows Handicrafts Industrial Cooperative Society Ltd., 266
Swaminathan, Ammu, 24
Swaraj, Sushma, 336
Syed, Abdul Mannan, 99
Syrian christians, 393

Taluqdars, 411
Tanner, Nancy, 352
Tarjuman-al-Quran, 247
Tata, Herabai, 52
Tata, Mehribai, 26
Tigress of Nationalism, 73
Tilak, Bal Gangadhar, 48
Tilak Swaraj Fund, 61
Trade Aid Importers, Christ Church, New Zealand, 263
Trading Partners, Australia, 263
Travencore Christian Succession Regulation, 1916, 245
Tripathy, Amiya Bhushan, 148

Thapar, Romila, 389
Theosophical Society in Adyar, 23
Umamaheshwara, 15
UN Decade for Women, 187
United Nations General Assembly, 164
United Nations International Women's Year, 202
University Education Commission, 107
University of Delhi, 194
Valmiki, Sage, 390
Vanvasi Seva Kendra, 283
Verna Scheme, 427
Victoria, Queen, 21
Vidhwa Ashram, 97
Vyas, Girija, 336

Walton, Izaak, 363
Wellesley, Lord, 335
Wheeler, Mortimer, 388
Whitman, Walt, 201
Women and Girls Act-1956, 252
Women in Hindu Tradition, 358
Women in the Forces, 447-6
—neolithic age, 451
herculean task, 456
special entry scheme, 460
intellect, idealism and courage, 460
in Officers Training Academy, 461
relaxation for, 462
Women's Decade (1976-85), 186
Women's Indian Association, (WIA), 23
Women Self-Employment Scheme, 275
Women Work Force and Technological Advances, 171
Working Women's Forum, 259
World Conference of International Women's Year 1975, 364

Yama, 13
Yousuf's Choice Dilemma Qiestionnaire, 197

Zamindars, 419
Zihlmen, Adrienne, 352
Zutshi, Lado Rani, 70